Disappointment

Disappointment

Its Modern Roots from Spinoza to Contemporary Literature

Michael Mack

BLOOMSBURY ACADEMIC
NEW YORK • LONDON • OXFORD • NEW DELHI • SYDNEY

BLOOMSBURY ACADEMIC
Bloomsbury Publishing Inc
1385 Broadway, New York, NY 10018, USA
50 Bedford Square, London, WC1B 3DP, UK

BLOOMSBURY, BLOOMSBURY ACADEMIC and the Diana logo are trademarks of Bloomsbury Publishing Plc

First published in the United States of America 2021

Copyright © Michael Mack, 2021

Cover image © Getty Images

All rights reserved. No part of this publication may be reproduced or transmitted in any form or by any means, electronic or mechanical, including photocopying, recording, or any information storage or retrieval system, without prior permission in writing from the publishers.

Bloomsbury Publishing Inc does not have any control over, or responsibility for, any third-party websites referred to or in this book. All internet addresses given in this book were correct at the time of going to press. The author and publisher regret any inconvenience caused if addresses have changed or sites have ceased to exist, but can accept no responsibility for any such changes.

Library of Congress Cataloging-in-Publication Data
Names: Mack, Michael, 1969–2020 author.
Title: Disappointment: its modern roots from Spinoza to contemporary literature / Michael Mack.
Description: New York City: Bloomsbury Academic, 2021. | Includes bibliographical references. | Summary: "A literary and intellectual history of the trope of disappointment and its political implications from the 17th century through today"–Provided by publisher.
Identifiers: LCCN 2020033590 | ISBN 9781501366864 (hardback) | ISBN 9781501366888 (epub) | ISBN 9781501366895 (pdf)
Subjects: LCSH: Literature, Modern–History and criticism. | Disappointment in literature. | Self in literature. | Philosophy and literature. | Politics and literature. | Disappointment. | Postmodernism.
Classification: LCC PN56.D554 M33 2021 | DDC 809/.93353–dc23
LC record available at https://lccn.loc.gov/2020033590

ISBN: HB: 978-1-5013-6686-4
PB: 978-1-5013-6687-1
ePDF: 978-1-5013-6689-5
eBook: 978-1-5013-6688-8

Typeset by Deanta Global Publishing Services, Chennai, India

To find out more about our authors and books visit www.bloomsbury.com and sign up for our newsletters.

Contents

Acknowledgments — vi

Introduction: Spinoza and the Simultaneity of Promise and Disappointment — 1

1 Spinoza and F. H. Jacobi's Idealist Disavowal of Disappointment or How Romanticism Questions Idealizations of the Anthropocene — 13

2 Rendering Dialectics Disappointing: Spinoza's Specter Haunting the Anthropocene from Romanticism to Postmodernism in Literature and Science — 33

3 The Destructive Element: Keats and Conrad or How Romanticism Avows Idealism's Disavowed Disappointment — 63

4 Modernity's Promise and Its Disavowed Disappointment: Hannah Arendt's Analysis of Totalitarianism Out of the Sources of Conrad's *Heart of Darkness* — 89

5 The Trajectory of Conrad's Novel of Disavowed Disappointment: Hegel's Dialectics, F. Scott Fitzgerald's *The Great Gatsby*, and Saul Bellow's *Ravelstein* — 123

6 Political Promises and History's Disappointments: Leo Strauss as the Esoteric Center of Bellow's *Ravelstein* and the Critique of Grand Political Promises — 143

7 Disappointment in the Age of the Anthropocene: How D. H. Lawrence and Kafka Render Dialectics Inoperative — 173

8 Disappointing Expectations of Redemption: Modern Jewish Writing and Thought — 209

9 Conclusion: Expecting Disappointment, or, from Pynchon's, Roth's, Strauss's, and Vonnegut's Postmodernism to Anna Burns's *Milkman* and D. F. Wallace's *The Pale King* — 239

Bibliography — 269
Index — 281

Acknowledgments

There are many debts to acknowledge but the greatest debt I owe is to the Leverhulme Trust, perhaps the world's most impressive charity for research and education.

Preparations for this book go back to 2007 when a Leverhulme Early Career Fellowship brought me back to the UK academia with a project which Bloomsbury published as *Spinoza and the Specters of Modernity*. Thanks to the award of a Leverhulme Research Fellowship to 2012/2013, I had time to conceive of a project about Hegel and the end of history, which informs large parts of this book. The award of a Leverhulme Research Fellowship on the theme of disappointment for 2019/2020 made it possible to complete this book. Part of the funding was a research stay at the D. F. Wallace archive in the Harry Ransom Center in Austin. The travel restrictions that accompany the current pandemic crisis thwarted this undertaking. By then the book was over the 115,000-word limit, and I hope to follow up this aspect of the Leverhulme project with a future monograph on sincerity and irony in modern and contemporary literature.

I am most grateful to Elizabeth Millan and Paul Mendes-Flohr for their great help and advice and encouragement. In different and related ways, they have encouraged me to analyse the modern roots of disappointment. As Bertrand Russell has shown in his *History of Western Philosophy*, after the collapse of Greek and Roman antiquity, Western writing and thought was preoccupied with a sense of unhappiness regarding worldly affairs. This mood prevailed until the Renaissance. As this study shows, Spinoza first most cogently articulated expectations for happiness in terms of an inclusive modernity of diversity. Historical events rendered these hopes disappointing. After the turn of the French Revolution into a reign of terror, various expectations for happiness proved to be disappointing from the collapse of real-existing communism to disillusionment with free markets after the financial crisis in 2008/2009 to our contemporary 2020 pandemic health crisis.

Michael O'Neill was another strong supporter of this book. Up to a few months before his death in late 2018 he kept offering most helpful advice and encouragement. This is very much his book. I am also grateful to my Durham colleagues Sarah Wooton, Fiona Robertson, Mark Sandy, James Smith, Stephan Reagan, John Nash, and Marco Bernini.

I am most grateful to Joyce and George Schlesinger for their great help in most difficult times. George's expert knowledge of Keats's poetry has been invaluable. Many thanks to Andrew Kent, Kate Peters and Louise Huscroft.

Acknowledgments

Gillian Beer has been most supportive and encouraging of this project and so have been the following colleagues throughout the world: Hasana Sharp, Richard Velkley, Sander L. Gilman, David Clark, Patrick Hayes, Margery Vibe Skagen, Norelle Lickiss, David Jasper, Anna Grundy, Jeff Malpass and M. Vatter.

I am most grateful to Dan Meyer and the Saul Bellow archive at the University of Chicago for allowing me to quote from Bellow's unpublished eulogy speech at A. Bloom's funeral.

As always it has been a great honor and delight to work with Haaris Naqvi and his great team at Bloomsbury. I am grateful to Rachel Moore for all her great support during this most uncertain and difficult time.

I am grateful to Victoria J. Penn for her excellent index to this book and for her most helpful proof reading.

I am most grateful to Rachel Walker and Joseph Gautham for their excellent and generous help in the printing stages of this book.

Introduction

Spinoza and the Simultaneity of Promise and Disappointment

A Brief Word about the Title of This Book

Let me first explain the provocative title of this book *Disappointment: Its Modern Roots from Spinoza to Contemporary Literature*. The wide-ranging time scale of the subtitle is not to deny historical differences and the validity of periodization as such. Rather the title of this book takes issue with too rigid boundaries in historicist approaches to our world. This is not yet another proclamation of the end of history. Rather this book is going to show how promises of such an end to historical injustices and inequalities have shaped the itinerary of modernity from Spinoza onward. This, however, with the important caveat that Spinoza's modernity is simultaneously a postmodernity, which has endured the disappointment of what the former has held out in hope.

The first two chapters of this study will analyze how Spinoza's political promise of modern liberal democracy informed the thought of Rousseau and Diderot and the authors of the *Encyclopédie*, thus shaping the foundations of the French Revolution (Israel 2001: 157–320). The crucial point of this book is that Spinoza already thought the promise of modernity side by side with its *post festum* (its postmodernity) and disappointment. This disappointing moment of Spinoza's thought resides in his investigations into the limits of the human mind: our minds are not created in the image of an omniscient deity but partake of the limitation of embodied and mortal existence. According to Spinoza, the mind is the idea of the body, and hence there is an inseparable identity or contamination between the two.

To think modernity with Spinoza is to countenance promises with their disappointment. This Spinozist revenant of modernity's hopes in the form of disappointments of precisely such promises has shaped romantic, modernist, postmodern, and contemporary writing and thought, as will be explored throughout this book. One of the reasons why there has been an unwillingness to recognize the simultaneity of hope and disappointment in previous discussions of modernity and postmodernity has been the long history of

Spinoza's marginalization despite the evidence of having laid the foundation of our modern and, at the same time, postmodern world. As regards the historical evidence, Jonathan Israel has recently made clear Spinoza's leading role not only in the early but also in the radical enlightenment of the French Revolution:

> The question of Spinozism is indeed central and indispensable to any proper understanding of the Early Enlightenment European thought. Its prominence in European intellectual debates of the late seventeenth century is generally far greater than anyone would suppose from the existing literature; one of the chief aims of this present study is to demonstrate that there has been a persistent and unfortunate tendency in historiography to misconstrue and underestimate its significance. [. . .] The pattern is the same in the later French *Encyclopédie* edited by Diderot and d'Alembert: for all the lavish praise heaped on Locke by d'Alembert in his preliminary discourse to the *Encyclopédie*—praise which, as we shall see, may have had a diversionary purpose—in the body of the *Encyclopédie* itself the coverage given to Locke is far less, scarcely one fifth, of the coverage extended on Spinoza. (Israel 2001: 12–13)

In Israel's careful historical investigation, Spinoza emerges as the thinker of the early and then radical enlightenment promise of equality and diversity. These hopes were first attempted to be fulfilled in the French Revolution. However, the revolution turned into a reign of terror, ending in the disappointment of Napoleon Bonaparte being crowned as emperor.

To be sure, Spinoza did not foresee the contours of these historical developments. However, we may see Spinoza's motto to be cautious (*caute*) not only as a maxim for an individual's way of life but also as a wary awareness of the limitations that accompany our existence in its entirety. Indeed, in his posthumously published *Ethics* he investigates how the mind is exposed to misleading information that partakes of its embodiment (as brain). Only recent neuroscientific research has discovered Spinoza as the investigator of the mind's identity with the body (Damasio 2003: 211–12).

As a political philosopher Spinoza's modernity is one of promise and hope. As a scientific investigator of the mind, he simultaneously thinks both the promissory and disappointing, being aware that our embodied minds are prone to the potential violence that results from buying into fictions of the real rather than being endowed with a clear sighted or omniscient perspective. Thinking through the simultaneity of modernity and postmodernity, this study develops a new approach to the analysis of how disappointment in the certainties of human knowledge has shaped our modern and contemporary understanding of culture and communities. This book thus proposes an innovative methodology through which Spinoza emerges less as a single isolated figure and more as a sign for an intellectual constellation of thinkers and writers who, from the romantics to contemporary theory and literature, have introduced various shifts in the way we see humanity, not as a quasi-divine representative on earth, but as being limited and prone to disappointment.

The topic of disappointment is a timely one in our contemporary context of various populist promises. These promises differ from Spinoza's radical enlightenment, because they are not inclusive but exclusive: various anti-immigration and xenophobic forms of economic and populist nationalisms—from Donald Trump to Brexit—hold out the hope of making Britain or America "great again" precisely through the condition of excluding those who are perceived to be foreign or different. After the financial crisis of 2008 (Mack 2014b), which has turned first into austerity and then into a political crisis, we live in a time of disavowed disappointment. What various populist movements disavow is precisely the disappointment of the great recession and its repercussions (i.e., austerity and a further destruction of the post–Second World War welfare state). Rather than facing the causes of such economic misery, attention shifts to those who are at the margins of society, who are a minority within a given country. This shift of focus to those who are on the margins of society (the non-natives or immigrants) partakes of a disavowal of disappointment, and at a contemporary moment when what is disappointing has actually become what we can societally expect (from the bleak future of climate change to the changing demographics of an increasingly unequal society).

Contemporary Expectations of Disappointment

In the following quotation from Anna Burns's 2018 novel *Milkman*,

> [. . .] that Milkman's name really was Milkman. This was shocking. (Burns 2018: 304)

the recognition of the literal meaning of a name is shocking as well as disappointing. Rather than being a mysterious code, Milkman turns out to be the surname of a top-ranking paramilitary who stalks the adolescent female narrator of the book. Here the literal meaning of the sign (Milkman as mere surname) disappoints expectations of the postmodernist mark which always shifts in its meaning and could thus be a code for a larger, more exciting set of meanings. The reduction of the mark to the sign makes Burns's novel reverse hopes for an infinitely open horizon of meaning that has shaped postmodern critiques of authorship:

> And it is this fact—the fact that the same mark of the same sound can be used to mean many things—that requires Derrida to insist that no one can control the meaning of the text and produces the characteristic deconstructive pathos of the author who strives but necessarily fails to achieve such control. If (and only if) we think of signs as marks and therefore of texts as made up of marks, we must necessarily think of writers as producing texts that mean more or less than what they mean by them. Writing in deconstruction becomes "abandon[ing]" the text to "its essential drift" because writing in deconstruction is essentially the production of marks (which in different contexts will come to mean different things) rather than signs (which will always mean whatever they were made to mean). (Michaels 2004: 125)

Milkman traces the reversal of expectations of the promissory meaning of the mark (the name "Milkman" as a code for some significant project) to the fixed meaning of the ordinary sign of a surname, Mr. Milkman.

Burns's novel introduces us to the ordinariness of the sign without promising the redemption of everyday life. As Toril Moi has argued, Michaels's critique of deconstructive marks has given rise to "the recent obsession with the physical object, the thing, pure materiality" (Moi 2017: 130). Moi accuses Michaels of subscribing to what he takes issue with: "Michaels's incisive critique nevertheless relies on the concept it wishes to undo. For all his hatred of the idea of the mark, the very idea that signs can be 'marks' remains the starting point for his own alternative vision of meaning" (Moi 2017: 130). Moi attacks deconstruction, new historicism, and what she takes to be the recent move countering Saussure's and Derrida's linguistic turn in affect theory and the new materialism by questioning what she assumes to be literary theory's general demotion of the singular, the particular or exemplary: "By now it should be clear that Wittgenstein's understanding of theory, concepts and examples in *Philosophical Investigations* is at odds with traditional philosophy, and with the prevailing understanding of theory in literary studies today" (Moi 2017: 88). According to Moi, literary theory from Derrida and de Man to Michaels fulfills a pseudo-scientific longing for generality. The way out of this generalizing distortion of the particularizing capacity which the discipline of the humanities offer is "Wittgenstein" who, so Moi says, "teaches us anything he teaches us" in "*how to think through examples*" (Moi 2017: 88 [italics in original]).

However, the ordinariness of meaning implies yet another form of generality: that of sanity and stability. Rather than threatening us with the uncertainty and instability of the shifting, deconstructive mark, Moi's example of the ordinary sign promises another form of redemption, one that "goes as deep as our life" (Moi 2017: 87): "It is not about uncertainty but about sanity, not about epistemology but about our life in language" (Moi 2017: 87). However, our life in language can be as uncertain and troubling as it can be reassuring and calming. Words can disappoint us as much as they can raise our expectations only to deflate our hopes. This deflation is precisely what takes place in Burns's *Milkman* with its reduction of the promissory range of meaning characteristic of the mark to the disappointing denotation signifying an ordinary surname. Rather than uplift or reassure the ordinary here teaches us to expect the deflation of promises.

Burns's novel depicts a contemporary social setting wherein we have become accustomed to disappointment. In Kafkaesque manner it leaves out references to historical coordinates except the "border" and the two sides of paramilitary community that it divides, both being replicas of each other, both "totalitarian enclaves" where the self has come to reject itself and where violence and love have become shockingly and disappointingly linguistic forms of equivalence—a sectarian world where minorities are no longer protected. Although *Milkman* takes place in a past (resembling the Northern Ireland of the Troubles), it appears eerily contemporary and familiar. The current return of identity politics (Brexit in the UK and various anti-immigrant movements in continental Europe and America) relates to the claustrophobic sense of sectarianism and oppression which Burns's novel so powerfully narrates.

Disappointment of Promising the Telos or End of History

While being historical—moving from Spinoza's seventeenth century via idealism, romanticism, modernism, and postmodernism to the twenty-first century—this study also analyzes our contemporary situation in which past issues such as nationhood, homogeneity, and identity return to haunt the present with a vengeance: "It is disappointing, though not wholly surprising, that Russia has reverted to authoritarian traditions. What was far more unexpected was that threats to democracy should arise from within established democracies themselves" (Fukuyama 2018: xi). Diverging from the critical consensus on the reasons for the contemporary resurgence of economic and populist nationalism, this study does not lay the blame on fear alone.

Fukuyama has kept faith with his hope in various promises, which, in the age of populism, have by now shifted from the free market and liberalism to what he takes to be our identity-based humanity, premised on Hegel's concept of the struggle for social recognition. The same Hegelianism that shaped his book *The End of History and the Last Man* (1992) informs his *Identity: Contemporary Identity Politics and the Struggle for Recognition* (2018). Fukuyama makes clear that his previous neoconservative proclamation, that after the collapse of the Soviet Union we have finally arrived with liberal free market economics at the golden age where history coincides with its telos or end, shares the same promissory note with his more recent return to the Hegelian topic of the struggle of recognition which coincides with the contemporary rise of identity politics.

Indeed, by referring to the presumed progress-driven rationalism of Hegel, Fukuyama attempts to silence the "simple misunderstanding" (Fukuyama 2018: xii) of those of his critics who have pointed out that history has not found a harmonious end point with the collapse of the Soviet Union. The misunderstanding seems to reside in Fukuyama's critics' inability to appreciate the idealism of Hegel's grand end point of history which should presumably make one ignore any empirical, historical event that might disappoint such promise:

> I have regularly been asked whether event X didn't invalidate my thesis. X could be a coup in Peru, war in the Balkans, the September 11 attacks, the global financial crisis, or, more recently Donald Trump's election and the wave of populist nationalism described above. Most of these criticisms were based on a simple misunderstanding of the thesis. I was using the word *history* in the Hegelian-Marxist sense—that is, the long-term evolutionary story of human institutions that could alternatively be labelled *development or modernization*. The word *end* was meant not in the sense of "termination," but "target" or "objective." Karl Marx had suggested that the end of history would be a communist utopia, and I was simply suggesting that Hegel's version, where development resulted in a liberal state linked to a market economy, was the more plausible outcome. (Fukuyama 2018: xii)

Spinoza's critique of the anthropocentric and Anthropocene delusions accompanying idealist or theological or rationalist conceptions of humanity's grand telos—in the sense of "target" or "objective" or "aim"—makes him one of the first thinkers of disappointment who is cautiously wary of misleading deceptions and expectations generated by what seems to be innocuous, that is, hope. The allure of human history's telos (conceived as dialectically unfolding throughout history's development leading to greater modernizations) still holds sway in our contemporary moment, when humanity's ever progressive domination of nature has confronted us with its rather dark, polluting, and regressively disappointing aspect in the form of climate change and other industrialist-technological developments whereby we as species have profoundly cast into imbalance the geological and meteorological ecosystem of our planet.

Neoconservatives like Fukuyama still trust the Hegelian progressive narrative of market modernization while addressing the remaining economic injustices of such a capitalist system by precisely furthering an identity fueled struggle for recognition which will be discussed in Chapters 5, 6, and 7 in various analyses of Hegel's master-slave dialectics and its left (Kojève) and right wing (Allan Bloom/Saul Bellow's Ravelstein and F. Scott Fitzgerald's Jay Gatsby) repercussion in D. H. Lawrence's *Women in Love* and Kafka's *Das Schloss*. As will be discussed in Chapter 7, Kafka's last novel sets into relief our contemporary moment wherein identity politics turns into a scapegoating mechanism by which a majority population can blame those at the margins of society—those who, like Kafka's Joseph K., are perceived to be non-natives, strangers, or immigrants—for the economic resentment that accompanies the triumph of unfettered free market economics.

As Fukuyama has recently acknowledged, the telos of "the liberal world did not, however, benefit everyone" (Fukuyama 2018: 4) and "inequality increased dramatically, such that the benefits of growth flowed primarily to an elite defined primarily by education" (Fukuyama 2018: 4). So the discourse seemingly has recently shifted from an economist preoccupation with numbers and other forms of objectification (as discussed in my Mack 2014b analysis of the repercussions of the great recession and how the ensuing politics of austerity was employed to put, as the title of my book announced, *Philosophy and Literature in Times of Crisis*) to a return to cultural identity politics—to, as Fukuyama highlights, Hegel's struggle for recognition. Identity as the struggle for recognition should make us forget about economic and other materialist injustices. Rather than bemoan our real-existing financial plight, we should take pride in our identity.

In this fight for social recognition, those who are perceived as strangers or immigrants emerge as the new enemy on whom the identity conscious majority can vent their resentment. According to Fukuyama, the economic benefits of immigration are ambiguous. While there is doubt, so Fukuyama, about the economics, it is clear to him that immigrants are detrimental to what he calls "cultural identity":

> This is why immigration has become such a neuralgic issue in many countries around the world. Immigration may or may not be helpful to a national economy: like trade, it is often of benefit in aggregate, but does not benefit all groups within a society. However, it is almost always seen as a threat to cultural identity, especially when cross-border flows of people are massive as they have been in recent decades. (Fukuyama 2018: 89)

Here, in Fukuyama's linguistic register, there arises the point where the economist paradigm (grounded in numbers and quantities) coincides with the seemingly opposite concern with culture and identity. The expression "massive" pinpoints how the shift from economics to identity clings to an objectifying way of thinking where individuals turn into numbers, into masses, into "cross-border flows of people" that are "massive."

Thus, while the financial has turned into a political or cultural crisis of identity, the parameters of discourse are still objectifying, grounded in masses and numbers (as will be discussed in Chapter 9, the concluding chapter to this book). Left-wing intellectuals like Walter Benn Michaels have endorsed this apparent shift from ideology to identity while not analyzing that both share the same objectifying way of disavowing what appears to be disappointing—thereby projecting the abject onto the object of scorn, be it the ideological enemy or the Other of identity. Endorsing Fukuyama's 1992 proclamation of the end of history, Michaels maintains that "the real effect of the end of history had not been to get rid of difference but to transform it, to replace the differences between what people own (class) with the differences between what people are (identity)" (Michaels 2004: 24). In 2004, Michaels anticipates Fukuyama's recent (i.e., 2018) move from celebrating liberal, free market economics as the end or "aim" of history to identity politics that opposes natives and strangers (or immigrants) in a struggle for recognition: "Only at the end of history could all politics become identity politics" (Michaels 2004: 24).

Having thus endorsed Fukuyama's thesis of the end of history as well as Huntington's about the clash of civilizations, Michaels reconceives the ideological left and right opposition in politics along the lines of either a mobile (that is to say left or deconstructive) identity or a fixed (i.e., nativist, grounded in one country or place) right-wing identity:

> The function of the opposition, in other words, is to assert that what matters is the question of whether your position can be changed. And

this is just as true for all those on the cultural Left—insisting on mobility and the performative—as it is for those, like Huntington, on the cultural Right. Indeed one way of describing the difference between the cultural Left and the cultural Right is precisely in terms of this difference over the nature of subject positions, over whether they are fixed and stable or mobile and unstable. (Michaels 2004: 41)

Being on the cultural left, Michaels subscribes to the deconstructive, mobile mark rather than the fixed sign. Substance here transmutes into the solipsism of different subject positions about interpretation. This is a world that has become the word, wherein "anything" may become a text, while, on the other hand, nothing is a text—since the effects of the mark—the effects it makes us think of—are not its meaning (Michaels 2004: 128). The crucial point here is that the shift from ideology to identity is that of a phantom.

This shift from ideology to identity is caught up in a theater of mirrors. This is so because both apparently opposed terms belong to Hegel's idealist disavowal of matter, of what Hegel identifies with Spinoza's substance and a Spinozist, from idealism's vantage point, rather disappointing identity of body and mind. For Fukuyama, Huntington, and Michaels, the collapse of the Soviet Union has ushered in a cessation of meaning and an end to all political causes: "History ended (in 1989) because the Soviet Union, as a distinctive ideological entity, collapsed, and, insofar as the Cold War was imagined by Fukuyama and Huntington as a war between beliefs—between liberalism and socialism—its end made ideological disagreement and political argument obsolete" (Michaels 2004: 78). As if the disappointment and collapse of the Soviet Revolution had no historical precedent! What about the French Revolution and its descent into a reign of terror, followed by a disappointing return to monarchical forms of oppression? Rather than acknowledge political and economic disappointments and their historical precedent, the whole of history becomes disavowed either as failure writ large or as being "right on target" fulfilling liberalism's or identity politics' hidden idea or aim or telos. Having abdicated all quest for meaningful causes, we have arrived at a world of boredom which is the theme of David Foster Wallace's posthumously published *The Pale King*. By investigating boredom Wallace refrains from disavowing disappointment. However, this is the subject matter of a book of its own which I hope to write after the completion of the current one.

The crucial point here is that our current wave of identity politics partakes of an illusory embrace of various misleading hopes and promises and a concomitant disavowal of boredom and disappointment. Those who argue that disappointed voters voted for Brexit in the UK and for Donald Trump's "America first" policies merely out of fear, neglect the hope and the promises which go with these renewed forms of nationalism. Indeed, leading proponents of Brexit label those who are critical of it "promoters of project fear." In the United States, President Trump promises his supporters to "make America great again."

Addressing the so far neglected issue of hope and promise within contemporary populist nationalism, this book establishes a new approach to modernity and postmodernity as a long history of various disappointments that are either avowed and thus worked through or disavowed and thereby repressed and projected upon the other, the stranger, the immigrant. The main aim and subject of this analysis is to discover how our current sense of disappointment with our ecological, economic, and political state of affairs partakes of a history of failed promises that goes back to the inception of modernity, namely, to Spinoza's radical enlightenment of diversity and equality.

For many writers and thinkers the Spinoza-inspired quest for equality and diversity was rendered paradoxical when the French Revolution, having done away with old, feudal structures, reintroduced new hierarchies and inequalities and destroyed diversity in the course of Robespierre's reign of terror. Here we see emerging, perhaps for the first time, what I call the trope of disappointment in the wake of Spinoza's radical enlightenment. The trope of disappointment would, after the destruction of diversity and equality in the aftermath of the French Revolution's reign of terror, give rise to Hegel's formulation of dialectics wherein what is perceived or symbolized as negative becomes included only to be excluded or transmuted into the idealized notion of the positive. This means that disappointment does not dare to show its face. It becomes obfuscated and displaced onto whatever appears to be negative: "the Other," "the Jew," "the immigrant," "the Muslim."

The socioeconomic instance of disappointment thus transmutes into nonexistence: instead of a sense of disappointment we encounter the exhilaration of liberation; once we are freed from the negative—say, the immigrants, in current populist discourse—then we will be purely positive. This posited positivity—as the expulsion of the included negative—renders references to real economic issues (such as taxes) irrelevant and undesirable. References to the socioeconomic would spoil the show: they would only remind one of real-existing disappointments which the transmutation of the negative into the positive imaginatively achieves to overcome.

The significance of the trope of disappointment resides in its insistence on the factuality of failed hopes as manifested in perversions or distortions of promises through socioeconomic and political events such as the reign of terror that actually degraded Spinoza's and the French Revolution's ideals of equality and diversity.

Combining the methodology of intellectual history with that of literary and scientific theory, this book traces this collapse of traditional values and orders from Spinoza to Nietzsche and then to the literary modernism of Joseph Conrad and postmodernism of Philip Roth and Thomas Pynchon. In the course of such analysis, Leo Strauss will emerge as perhaps the most profound modern thinker of disappointment.

Leo Strauss—the modern Jewish thinker who rendered mutually suspicious both faith and reason—started his philosophical life by composing his doctoral thesis on Friedrich Heinrich Jacobi. Jacobi caused the Spinoza scandal at the end of the eighteenth century that then informed the specter of communism in the nineteenth century. Spinoza disappoints traditional claims to knowledge and power either via revelation (theology) or via science or philosophy (the autonomy of human reason in Kant or humanly made "rational" history in Hegel). Strauss is relevant here, not least, because from his doctoral work on Jacobi onward; he renders mutually disappointing two binary opposed poles that separate reason from revelation, philosophy from theology, modernity from pre-modernity. This state of aporetic or, in other words, paradoxical reason characterizes our sense of modernity and postmodernity, which I would call our post-Spinozist age of disappointment (either avowed or disavowed).

The literary and theoretical methodology of this study connects Conrad's "The way is to the destructive element submit yourself, and with the exertion of your hands and feet in the water make the deep, deep sea keep you up" (Conrad 1986: 200) with the significance of such reevaluation of the negative or destructive for community concerns that partake of new scientific discoveries and conceptions of human knowledge.

1

Spinoza and F. H. Jacobi's Idealist Disavowal of Disappointment or How Romanticism Questions Idealizations of the Anthropocene

Introduction: Spinoza, the French Revolution, F. H. Jacobi, Leo Strauss, and the Disenchanting Disappointment of Modernity

> May I say this in passing that I have leaned very heavily in my analysis of these things on Spinoza. One can learn much from Spinoza, who is the most extreme, certainly of the modern critics of revelation, not necessarily in his thought but certainly in the expression of his thought. (Strauss 1989: 397)

In this quotation Strauss singles out Spinoza as the thinker from whom he learned most for his conceptualization of the modern impasse between progress and return, between philosophy and revelation, and between fact and value. Spinoza promises a modernity of equality and diversity (Mack 2010), freed from the dogmatic restrictions and hierarchies, which revelation has traditionally sanctioned and sanctified. However, at the same time, Spinoza disappoints any hope to reach a clear account of how the human mind could provide insights into its own condition and that of the universe as a whole.

There are two sets of disappointments that partake of Spinoza's legacy. Strauss names the first, which is Spinoza's clear critique of the claims of theology or revelation. After such a humiliating disappointment of theological claims to truth, it might seem that the road has been prepared for the confident progress of philosophical reason. Whereas for Strauss Spinoza is clear to the point of being extreme when it comes to the philosophical critique of revelation, he is as obfuscating and obscure when it comes to delineating what human or secular reason can achieve to illuminate its own condition and that of its environment: "But is Spinoza's account of the whole clear and distinct? Those of you who have ever tried their hands, for example, at his analysis of the emotions, would not be so certain of that" (Strauss 1989: 308). Spinoza sits in between the modern (having gone through the study of Descartes and Hobbes and Machiavelli) and the premodern (his debt to the medieval Jewish philosopher Maimonides whose *Guide for the Perplexed* sets out to render compatible rationalism with *Talmud Torah*). By rendering disappointing both revelation and reason, he may be called postmodern in that he conditions what Derrida would later call un-decidability and what will be discussed in this study as Strauss's aporetic thought. How does Spinoza reach this impasse of both reason and revelation? By disappointing both the truth claims of revelation and that of the autonomous human mind. While Spinoza's critique of theology is clear and well known, only recently neuroscientists (most prominently Antonio Damasio) have rediscovered the validity and accuracy of his analysis of the human mind.

Strauss voices his consternation with the lack of clarity, he encounters while reading Spinoza's *Ethics* (which tries, in part at least, to analyze the emotions and how they, as passions or appetites, are contaminated with what has traditionally gone under the name of virtues and how the mind is identical with the lowly sphere of the body). As Judith Butler has recently put it, "for Spinoza, the body establishes a singularity that cannot be relinquished in the name of a greater totality, whether it be a conception of a common life or a political understanding of *civitas*, or, indeed, of the multitude (*multitudo*), a term that becomes important, very briefly, in Spinoza's *A Theological-Political Treatise*, a work that remained incomplete at his death" (Butler 2015: 67). In a way similar to which the singular body disappoints grand societal political aspiration, Spinoza's famous conception of self-preservation (*conatus*) relies on an inextricable bind between the individual and society. Spinoza disappoints both grand schemes of collectivism and individualism.

The self has to look out for the well-being of others, if it does not turn self-destructive. Spinoza's seemingly bright and optimistic thought indeed includes the potential for a destructive element that disappoints single-minded approaches to our world. In this way, the "self that endeavours to persevere in its own being is not always a singular self for Spinoza, and neither does it necessarily succeed in augmenting or enhancing its life, if it does not at once enhance the lives of others" (Butler 2015: 63). Butler clearly shows that the room for disappointment is spacious in Spinoza's thought and includes the prospect of destruction. Butler establishes "within Spinoza not only a critical perspective on individualism, but also an acknowledgement of the possibility for self-destruction" (Butler 2015: 63). What disappoints Strauss, who might well have expected the clarity he singles out as Spinoza's characteristic while engaging in the philosophical critique of revelation, is the obscurity of the emotions and the human mind as presented in *Ethics*. However, it is not so much the way in which Spinoza presents what he says than what he actually says about the mind that is disconcerting to the point of disappointment. Spinoza literally renders the autonomy of human reason obscure and thus disappointing. The human mind here depends on and indeed partakes of—because it is contaminated or identical with—the body. Bodily input, however, often obscures rather than illuminates attempts to understand our universe. Spinoza inherits to the centuries that follow his dismantling of both traditional philosophical reason and traditional theological revelation a paradoxical position that Strauss describes as the paradox of the fact and value distinction in America in the latter half of the last century, because facts are themselves the product of values:

> But what then does the choice of philosophy mean under these [i.e., post-Spinoza] conditions? In this case, the choice of philosophy is based on faith. In other words, the quest for knowledge rests itself on an unevident premise. And it seems to me that this difficulty underlies all present-day philosophizing and that it is this difficulty which is at the bottom of what in the social sciences is called the value problem: that philosophy or science, however you might call it, is incapable of giving an evident account of its own necessity. I do not think I have to prove that showing the practical usefulness of science, natural and social science, does not of course prove its necessity at all. I mean I shall not speak of the great successes of the social sciences, because they are not so impressive; but as for the great successes of the natural sciences, we in the age of the hydrogen bomb have the question completely open again and whether this effort is clearly reasonable with a view to its practical usefulness. (Strauss 1989: 310)

The romantics did not have to face the prospect of life with the hydrogen bomb. Their sense of disappointment ensued from the failed promises of what Strauss identifies with Spinoza's notion of liberal democracy. What Strauss calls Spinoza's original conception of a modern liberal democracy, the historian Jonathan Israel has recently explored as Spinoza's radical enlightenment promise of equality that does away with traditional hierarchies of monarchical rule premised as they were on biblical notions of revelation (the divine right of kings and so forth):

> Spinoza himself, assuredly, abhors popular tumult and fears political revolution. But, at the same time, while acknowledging that vast benefits

accrue from the transition from the "state of nature" to civil society under the State, he also demonstrates that monarchy and aristocracy, in other words, the institutionalized inequality which dominated European society in his time are nothing else than forms of corruption and degeneration from the equality and democratic republicanism which represent the normative condition most "natural" to man. The inequality and hierarchy dominant in European society and culture in his day is thus devoid of all legitimacy. (Israel 2001: 272)

This account clearly turns Spinoza into a predecessor of Rousseau. The romantics associate Rousseau, in turn, with the social hopes and promises of the French Revolution. Much of this chapter explores the way in which Spinoza's notion of nature diverges from Enlightenment contrasts with civilized society. Indeed, Spinoza is an early critic of what we now call the Anthropocene, and this becomes amply clear in his questioning of anthropomorphic and anthropocentric misunderstandings and distortions of the nonhuman universe (*deus sive natura*).

However, the centrality of nature in Spinoza's thought must certainly have been attractive to Leo Strauss and his concern with natural right over against the modern claims of history as the product of the human autonomous mind. As Steven B. Smith has put it: "In the final analysis Strauss's difference with Spinoza is not with what he said, but with how he said it" (Smith 2006: 83). According to Strauss, Spinoza denied the incomprehensibility of god. This statement is true in a theoretical way, but Spinoza indeed doubts that the human mind would in practice be capable of understanding god, which he interprets as the universe in its entirety. As will be explored in greater detail in Chapter 2, Spinoza's is not a pantheistic conception but one that denotes the universe as a whole, without deifying either nature or humanity as in pantheism. Such insight into the world in its entirety is theoretically possible but for the embodied and flawed human mind, such comprehension nevertheless remains subject to all kinds of disappointing fictions (*figmenta*) and distortions.

Spinoza's legacy, as discussed in this and the following chapters, is that of an Enlightenment that promises, theoretically at least, the absence of envy and inequality. A disappearing validity of traditional notions of God that had been grounded in hierarchies, as sanctioned by revealed religion would give rise to a rational, egalitarian, and liberal democracy.

As Strauss argues in his early work *Spinoza's Critique of Religion*: "Before philosophizing can even be begun, belief in revelation, which calls trust in human reason into question, must itself be questioned. In this sense the critique of revealed religion is not the achievement, but the very basis of science" (Strauss 1997a: 113). Writing long before the neuroscientific rediscovery of Spinoza in our twenty-first-century context, Strauss could not understand that his own critique of reason's insufficiency is already part of the seventeenth-century philosopher's notion of the mind as the idea of the body. Strauss's impasse (or aporia) of reason and revelation—or, in other words, of Athens or Jerusalem—is already that of Spinoza's when one combines his critique of the autonomy of the mind (as not autonomous but embodied and subject to misleading, corporeal input) with his radical questioning of religion that Strauss holds to be insufficient: "His [i.e., Spinoza's] criticism of the knowability of miracles as miracle is then defective. This defect is remedied by the following consideration: If the natural causes known to us do not suffice as explanation of an occurrence which is asserted to be a miracle, nothing can be inferred from this. It is rather a case for the suspension of judgment" (Strauss 1997a: 133). It is this impasse or suspension of judgment what Derrida would later call un-decidability that is modernity's postmodern element that already lies at the heart of the first radically modern thinker.

In other words, while radically critiquing revelation of a supernatural kind, Spinoza at the same time disappoints any hopes that could endow the human mind with promises of an inner-worldly revelation. Kant and Hegel would later propound the validity of immanent, cerebral revelations either by autonomous reason (Kant) or by a quasi-miraculous, inner-worldly equation of historical (i.e., humanly created) reality and that of rational perfection (as in Hegel's world spirit or Kojève's Hegelian end of history).

In contrast to idealism, romanticism differs from such an immanent reevaluation of revelation. Here, hopeful expectations were attached to social promises of a Spinoza-inspired radical enlightenment of equality and diversity. However, hope for such a new rational age wherein enmity and inequality cease to exist came to a crushing end first with the reign of terror and then with the crowning of Napoleon as new emperor. Rather than turning a page in the history of rivalry that accompanies embittering hierarchies between those at the top and those at the bottom of society, the repercussions of the French Revolution brought about the bourgeois and capitalist age of economic injustice.

This historical disappointment with inspiring Spinozist ideas (as further developed by Rousseau and Diderot) of a modernity that does not replicate the injustices that characterize a society grounded in the hierarchies of revealed religion (with a divinely sanctioned monarch at the top) meet in Spinoza's thought, an otherwise rather sober or disappointing account of the limitations of the human mind. This is so, because Spinoza identifies the mind with the frailty of the body. Spinoza here disappoints rational or philosophical accounts of the mind's accuracy in formulating adequate notions of the universe and its purported teleology.

Spinoza indeed inherited to romanticism a sense of disappointment with one single, teleological line of thought. Rather than being isolated or alone, the romantic vision fuses or contaminates what traditional conceptions have separated as mutually exclusive opposites. This contamination of what is purportedly noncompatible diminishes the force implicit in one-dimensional, aprioristic conceptions of the universe as being teleological. Romantic poetry renders fictive and diminutive such grand schemes of teleology (which have traditionally been revelation based and theological). Byron's Childe Harold is "by pensive Sadness, not by Fiction led" (Byron 1975: 25). Spinoza renders fictitious traditional anthropocentric and anthropomorphic conceptions of nature, god, and the universe. No wonder that his diminutive and, at the same time, contaminating rationalism gives rise to a sense of sadness in romanticism and later on in modernism as well as postmodernism.

This and the following chapters analyze Spinoza's legacy in romanticism as one of disappointment. This may be surprising, because Spinoza is commonly associated with the social promise of equality and democracy. Leo Strauss rightly argues that Spinoza was "a political philosopher" (Strauss 1989: 7) who first introduced the promise of equal, democratic rights, freed from any religious and theological statutes into the intellectual, social, and historical arena:

> That society, as described by him, can be characterized as a liberal democracy. Incidentally, Spinoza may be said to be the first philosopher, who advocated liberal democracy. Spinoza still regarded it as necessary to underwrite liberal democracy with a public religion or a state religion. Now it is very remarkable that that religion, that state religion, which is emphatically not a religion of reason, is neither Christian or Jewish. It is neutral in regard to the differences between Judaism and Christianity. (Strauss 1989: 254)

Despite tracing the relationship between conceptions of nature and history throughout his philosophical work, Strauss conspicuously says little about Spinoza's distinction between *natura naturans* (the aspect of nature that is closed to limited, human perception) and *natura naturata* (nature as already formed and thus available to human understanding). Spinoza develops this distinction in his posthumously published, major work *Ethics* that will be one of the focal points of discussion in this and the following chapters. Strauss, instead concentrates his attention on *The Theological-Political Treatise*.

The Theological-Political Treatise is a work of political philosophy and not of political theology. It clearly disappoints traditional theological conceptions of authority, dogma, and enforceability. Indeed, it diminishes eternal truth claims that religion had previously held concerning both politics and philosophy. *The Theological-Political Treatise* is a work of "biblical criticism, which was regarded as the major offense of Spinoza" (Strauss 1989: 258), because it diminished the divine authorship of the Bible. In this way, it historicized and naturalized theology: "The question, who wrote the Pentateuch, was traditionally answered as a matter of course, by Moses, so much that when Spinoza questioned the Mosaic origin of the Torah it was assumed that he denied its divine authorship" (Strauss 1989: 301). Because of the shocking disappointment Spinoza inflicted on the foundation of any revelatory truth, his name became synonymous with atheism, the disenchantment of the world, nihilism, and the death of God.

The scandal of Spinoza's critique of revelation came writ large in public awareness at the end of the eighteenth century, coinciding with the French Revolution and its initial set of secular or political hopes for social equality and diversity. Strauss wrote his doctoral thesis on F. H. Jacobi, the eighteenth-century philosopher, whose little book on Spinoza caused the so-called pantheism controversy.

Strikingly, Strauss's thesis abstains from any criticism of Jacobi's attempt to reinstate the validity of religious faith against the background of Spinoza's critique of revelation. The young Strauss argues that Jacobi, on the basis of David Hume's notion of belief, makes faith part of a principle of being, as instinct "Because belief, the force of belief, is grounded in a principal of being, (in the instinct), the value difference goes back to a difference in being" [*Gündet nun der Glaube die Kraft des Glaubens auf einen Seins-Prinzip, (in dem Instinkt), so is der Wertunterschied auf einen Seinsunterschied zurückführbar*] (Strauss 1997b: 287). By calling the theological category an instinct, Jacobi, in Strauss's account at least, naturalizes religion. This is exactly what Spinoza does, albeit with a radically different aim, namely that of disappointing the lofty expectations of endowing societal and political elevations with supernatural or divine blessings (such as the divine rights of kings).

By defending faith as a quasi-biological constitution of humanity, Jacobi wants to beat Spinoza at his own game, as it were. In doing so, he disavows Spinoza's disappointment concerning the validity of belief in revelation. As Strauss depicts it, Jacobi gives a naturalist explanation of the force of faith by claiming that a difference in the quantity of instinct explains why some tend to believe and some tend to doubt the presumed truth of religion/revelation (*Es ist dann das Mehr oder Weniger an* Stärke *des Instinkts, das zum Glauben oder Zweifel disponiert*, Strauss 1997b: 287). Strauss seems to be sympathetic to Jacobi's naturalizing of belief, and he clearly interprets it as "liberal" rather than orthodox. This becomes clear when he defends Jacobi against Moses Mendelssohn, who, he argues, "misinterpreted the former's liberal notion of faith (derived from Hume) as an attempted restitution of the Christian belief in revelation whom the latter had to reject with reference to the rational constitution of Judaism" [*misdeutet er (i.e., Mendelssohn) Jacobi's liberalen Versuch (sich von Hume herleitenden) Glaubensbegriff als Versuch einer Restitution des christlichen Offenbarungsglaubens, den er (i.e., Mendelssohn) unter Hinweis auf sein vernünftiges Judentum abweisen müsse*] (Strauss 1997b: 556). From the perspective of intellectual history, however, belief, as Jason Josephson-Storm has recently pointed out, was always thought to be a substantial part of human identity:

> Prior to Bayle's day, belief in God was thought to be an inborn trait and the existence of God such an obvious fact that atheism could only be asserted through a kind of bad faith or self-deception motivated by carnal passions. The sane human conscience would not allow God to be denied completely, and it was widely believed that libertine atheists must be either mad or profoundly racked by guilt. [. . .] It was believed that no one could rationally deny the existence of God because it was such a manifest and inescapable truth. (Josephson-Storm 2017: 71)

Spinoza, or more precisely his public image as mediated most influentially via Pierre Bayle's rather discriminatory equation of the Jewish philosopher with "Oriental" atheism and nihilism, radically disrupted this integration of belief (as a form of instinct) into human nature: "It is striking to the compulsive need to further Orientalize Spinoza, a figure whose very Jewishness rendered him already 'Oriental' in the eyes of many Europeans" (Josephson-Storm 2017: 70). Bayle's racist discourse constitutes a form of disavowed disappointment in the face of what would later, in the early twentieth century, go under Max Weber's famous expression "disenchantment of the world." In a way that anticipates other forms of discrimination against the Other, Bayle displaces his sense of disappointment onto the stranger, onto Spinoza as the figure of Otherness. According to Bayle, France and presumably Europe as whole would not face atheism and the threat of the void of nothingness, were it not for the presence of the Oriental, the Jew for which Spinoza increasingly stood as most powerful and specter-like symbol: "Bayle saw Spinoza as one representative of this vast system of nothing-ism or 'atheism' centred in the 'Orient'" (Josephson-Storm 2017: 70). In the early nineteenth-century Hegel would resurrect the specter of the "Oriental" Spinoza whom Hegel equates

Spinoza, Jacobi, and the Anthropocene 21

with negativity as such, the negative that in the progression of his dialectical movement morphs into the positive.

While Bayle displaced the threatening disappointment of a world empty of a transcendent God onto the Orient and the Oriental, Jacobi's so-called pantheism controversy raised the specter of Spinoza's presence within eighteenth-century German Enlightenment thought: "The pantheism successor controversies inspired heated discussions across the German philosophical world, and eventually Jacobi succeeded in making 'nihilism' the philosophical problem par excellence" (Josephson-Storm 2017: 73). In the late 1780s and the early 1790s Jacobi merged the threat of what he characterized as the "nihilism" (coining the very term; Gillespie 1995: 65–6) of Spinozist philosophy with the danger of the French Revolution justifying regicide and civil unrest: "the French Revolution if anything seemed to justify Jacobi's fears, as enlightenment came to evoke less rational Protestantism or enlightened absolutism than regicide" (Josephson-Storm 2017: 74). Jacobi's famous leap of faith (his *salto mortale*) disavows the disappointment with real-existing historical circumstances. Here we encounter the first instance of what I call disavowed disappointment. Disappointment first ensues from the hopes raised by the Enlightenment which either turn out to be disenchanting or destructive (as in the French Revolution's reign of terror) or a mere abject repetition of traditional hierarchies (as in Napoleon putting on the crown of an emperor).

In his book *The Myth of Disenchantment*, Jason Josephson-Storm rightly singles out Jacobi and the scandal around the figure of Spinoza as a turning point in intellectual history. Jacobi's so-called pantheism controversy not only introduced the new term "nihilism" but also prepared the ground for the conceptualizing of a break with the traditional past, which we now call (after Jakob Burkhardt and Charles Baudelaire) modernity:

> The Pantheism Controversy was one key moment—if not *the* key moment—when some Europeans convinced themselves that enlightenment rationality has initiated a treacherous slide toward the death of God and the de-animation of the world. From that point forward, it seemed to some that nihilism or atheism lurked in the heart of philosophy. When natural philosophy was cannibalized by the new notion of "science," it also came to seem that scientific progress pointed away from the divine. (Josephson-Storm 2017: 93)

To revert such a rather disappointing decline, Jacobi recast belief as a form of cognition coterminous with human instinct and reason. This revision of human rationality in terms of faith sets the stage for his famous *salto mortale*.

This term describes a leap of belief away from the negativity of a disenchanted and disappointed scene of secularization—that in Germany showed the impact of the French Revolution as "literal secularization as German states appropriated property previously belonging to the Church" (Josephson-Storm 2017: 75). By turning cognition into an organ of faith, Jacobi reverts the perceived threat of atheism and thus disavows the disappointment of reason as nihilist and disenchanting (showing the limits of human cognition as image of a traditional, transcendent God) or terrifying (as in the reign of terror).

Against this background of a disavowed disappointment in the wake of the French Revolution, this and the following chapters trace the ways in which Spinoza's reception by romantic poets and philosophers was slightly distorted through the so-called pantheism controversy, provoked by the publication of Friedrich Heinrich Jacobi's *On the Doctrine of Spinoza* toward the end of the eighteenth century. Albeit misleading in many ways, Jacobi's "little book" associates the name "Spinoza" with progressive tendencies which immediately become demoted as regressive (Jacobi's charge of fatalism) and subversive (Jacobi's charge of atheism).

The unease with Spinoza from the late seventeenth to the late eighteenth centuries crystalizes in Jacobi's term "specter." The specter of Spinoza is that of an Enlightenment version of modernity that rendered disappointing and inadequate not only the theology of revelation but also rationalist promises of immanent or secular teleology and philosophical foundations: "Romanticism was anti-foundationalist through and through; and it was so in an attempt to capture the inherent incompleteness of philosophy and knowledge" (Frank 2004: 10). It may sound odd to discuss Spinoza's philosophy within the context of a romantic sense of disappointment, incompleteness, and fragmentation. However, the fragmentary, the disappointed, and the incomplete are part of Spinoza's version of modernity. How so? While his notion of substance denotes completion, much of the philosophical endeavors in Spinoza's *Ethics* set out to render incomplete, disappointing, and limited various anthropocentric distortions of what substance or the universe truly is.

Spinoza's critique of anthropomorphic and anthropocentric notions of substance in fact marks the meeting point of his scientific and literary acumen: he uncovers as fictions various pseudo-scientific representations of the universe in terms of teleology and first principles. Teleology does not denote natural laws or goals. Instead, first principles are what humanity anthropocentrically and anthropomorphically projects into its image of what the universe or nature is supposed to be. These representations are disappointing: they are inadequate and fictitious, because they use anthropocentric wishes and anthropomorphic projections for the vast, and to our limited human understanding, incomplete, and fragmentary universe. We may thus discover in Spinoza the scientific and philosophical context for what would later become Schlegel's famous notion of romantic irony: "Irony is a sort of play that reveals the limitations of a view of reality that presumes to have the last word" (Elizabeth Millán-Zaibert 2007: 168). Irony here highlights a sense of disappointment with elevated conceptions of the human mind as a reflection of a transcendent God. By uncovering representations of the universe in terms of teleology as being limited— because they are grounded in a one-sided anthropocentric perspective— Spinoza subjects grand, foundationalist claims of human knowledge to ironic treatment. Here traditional philosophy no longer has the last word and, similarly "with the use of romantic irony, Schlegel showed that there were no last words" (Elizabeth Millán-Zaibert 2007: 168). Spinoza's deflation of purported keys to understanding the universe as anthropocentric and anthropomorphic deceptions or fictions feeds romantic philosophy's struggle with the foundationalism and the teleology that undergirds the knowledge claims of German idealism. Spinoza's scientific discovery of our limited, disappointing, and self-centered representation of substance or the universe provides the philosophical backbone for the romantic wariness and ultimate rejection of German idealism's claim "that the ultimate origin of Being is transparent" (Elizabeth Millán-Zaibert 2007: 32).

As I have shown elsewhere (Mack 2010), the ghost of Spinoza evokes a hidden enlightenment of diversity that deviates from the foundationalism and aprioristic paradigm of German idealism. Due to his unsettling and persistent haunting, Spinoza's thought shaped not only romanticism, skepticism, and anti-foundationalism but also the romantics' fascination with experiential science that is no longer grounded on the first principle of either teleology, the Cartesian cogito, Fichte's absolute *Ich*, or the Kantian *a priori*. As will be discussed in this and the following chapters, this non-teleological and anti-foundational heritage of Spinoza's approach to scientific inquiry might explain the unexpected modernity of romanticism.

In this respect, this and the following chapters further develop recent work on romanticism's modernism. As Frank has shown, the Nazis despised the early German romantics for aesthetic and ideological reasons:

> In the authors of early German Romanticism, the Nazis saw—and rightly so—ground breakers of the literary avant-garde, whose irony was biting and whose sincerity was doubted, enemies of the bourgeoisie, friends and spouses of Jews, welcomed guests and discussion partners at the Jewish Berlin salons, aggressive proponents of "the emancipation of the

Jewry," and finally "subversive intellectuals" (a slogan which the Nazis used indifferently to refer to members of the political left, to Jews as a group, and to intellectuals). (Frank 2004: 25)

As the following section will show, next to the literary avant-garde quality of romanticism, Spinoza's heritage also informs the fascination of the romantics with the philosophical and scientific implications of a modernity that has overcome the teleological foundations of traditional, representational methodologies, which Spinoza unmasked as anthropocentric and anthropomorphic fictions.

Jacobi's Leap of Faith: The Contamination of Idealism and Realism in Early Romanticism with a View of Later Disillusions and Disappointments

As has been intimated in the preceding section, Spinoza's legacy in romanticism could somewhat reductively be summarized by the term "modernity." The most striking aspect of Spinoza's modernity within romanticism is the so-called pantheism controversy in Germany at the end of the eighteenth century. This intellectual event caused not only a huge upheaval in the German-speaking world but the waves it set free also swept over into England, as will be discussed in the concluding section of Chapter 2 by mainly focusing on Coleridge's reception of the so-called pantheism controversy. As we will see, the word "pantheism" is actually a misnomer for Spinoza's philosophy, and the true target of Friedrich Heinrich Jacobi's 1785 publication *On the Doctrine of Spinoza* is what he calls atheism and, more importantly for how romanticism navigates its relationship with German idealism, fatalism: "Jacobi equated Spinozism to atheism and condemned the German Enlightenment thinkers for taking a path that led to fatalism and atheism" (Elizabeth Millán-Zaibert 2007: 21). As we shall see, from the late seventeenth to the early nineteenth centuries the name "Spinoza" was a red flag, signaling the disappointing prospect of disenchantment in terms of a secular and nihilistic age.

Jacobi's accusation of atheism refers to Spinoza as the symbol of the threating, atheist force of modernity. Following Elizabeth Millán's complex perspective on Jacobi's multilayered position, one could argue that he propounded a counter-modernity to the one outlined by Spinoza. This counter-modernity disavows disappointment by circumventing a confrontation between cognition and faith.

Instead, and as we have seen in the preceding section, Jacobi's *salto mortale* turns the potentially analytic and destructive work of reason into an element of belief. Belief disavows the disappointment of Spinoza's challenge to revelation and its accompanying anthropomorphism of the Anthropocene. As Daniel Tanguay has shown, Strauss's twentieth-century critique of philosophy in terms of societal impact or usefulness grows out of this unease with the Anthropocene subjugation of nature: "In addition to its disguised dogmatism, Strauss reproaches the modern Enlightenment for having transformed the meaning of philosophic enquiry by subjecting it to practical goals" (Tanguay 2007: 46). These practical goals are actually those of the Anthropocene: "The goal of this strategy was to make man master and possessor of the world, the creator of a world that would forever make the world as simply given—the natural world—disappear" (Tanguay 2007: 47). The significance of romanticism's Spinozist critique of teleology consists in preparing the ground for a twentieth century, and ultimately contemporary, postmodern questioning of Enlightenment rationality as the subjugation of nature.

Jacobi is crucial here. The specter of Spinoza that Jacobi's little book attempted to lay to rest reached a fever pitch of notoriety until it entered as the ghost of communism (in admittedly revised form). Marx's famous opening of his manifesto, which quotes Jacobi almost verbatim, will be discussed in the opening section of Chapter 2. Ironically, Jacobi's attempt to disavow the disappointing prospect of Spinoza's radical enlightenment—as introducing disenchantment and atheism into a new, modern world—only reinforced public consternation and concern.

What Jacobi sees as negative could appear less so from a romantic, Spinozist perspective. From this perspective, the scandal of Spinoza that keeps haunting our political and scientific life is that of a common world, free of hierarchies that cause the affects of envy and jealousy. In this new societal space, the dictates of reason demand respect and humility by openly avowing the disappointment with our epistemological limits that we share as a small part of an infinite universe. Restated, Spinoza's famous intellectual love of God includes an avowal of disappointment with our limitations. Crucially, this avowal of what we may experience as disappointing establishes an ethics of communality wherein reason makes us realize and understand our reliance on each other and on our environment.

There are different aspects to Spinoza. As will be discussed in more detail (in Chapter 2) twenty-first-century science has rediscovered one such aspect: namely, his significance for contemporary biophysics (emerging forms of life) and neuroscience. According to the neuroscientist Antonio Damasio, Spinoza anticipates modern findings of a parallelism—rather than a hierarchical opposition—between the mind and the body. Damasio shows that Descartes's one-sided idealist, hierarchical structure in which the mind has a position that enables it to control the mere matter of the body, is scientifically wrong, whereas contemporary science proves Spinoza's parallelism of mind and body to be prescient. Indeed, at the opening of Part V in his posthumously published *Ethics* Spinoza was quick to detect the anatomical nonexistence of the quasi-physiological organ that Descartes claimed facilitated the mind's controlling position over our affects and our embodied life.

Here Spinoza associates Cartesian idealism with stoicism and the stoic belief that the affects as bodily inclinations "depend entirely on our will, and that we can command them absolutely" (Spinoza 1996: 160). Spinoza goes on to show that "Descartes was rather inclined to this opinion" via what he posits as the physiology of the pineal gland:

> For he [i.e., Descartes] maintained that the soul or mind, was especially united to a certain part of the brain, called the pineal gland, by whose aid the mind is aware of all the motions aroused in the body and of external objects, and which the mind can move in various ways simply by willing.
> (Spinoza 1996: 161)

Spinoza here disappoints expectations of the mind's control over the body as a "simple" question of the will. Moreover, he, in an ironic mode, dwells on the nonexistence of an organ that Descartes idealistically posits to be real. Following such detailed questioning of the way in which Descartes stipulates the non-existing reality of the pineal gland, Spinoza undermines quasi-scientific attempts (à la Descartes) to unify our existence as mind and body "through recourse to the causes of the whole Universe, that is, God" (Spinoza 1996: 161). Spinoza here shows how Descartes disavows potential disappointment with the mind's reach over our embodied existence by subsuming the physical under the metaphysical. According to Spinoza's analysis, science in its traditional form partakes of metaphysics and willfully distorts empirical evidence in order to prove rather misleadingly its metaphysical assumptions. Indeed, from Spinoza's critical perspective, Cartesian science is, similar to Jacobi's leap of faith at the end of the eighteenth century, foundational in a theological sense: it is grounded in faith or belief in a god who guarantees—scientifically objectified through the hypothesis of the non-existing physiology of the pineal gland—the mind's assumed non-disappointing, controlling position over the body.

By showing how Cartesian science is actually a modern type of theology, Spinoza describes it as being foundational but crucially inadequate and inaccurate in advancing human knowledge of our environment and us. Descartes's totalizing union between the cerebral and the corporeal is thus not scientific. According to Spinoza, Descartes disappoints expectations of accurate empirical knowledge, because he shows the Cartesian method to be premised on the belief in the reality of an organ that ironically does not exists (i.e., the pineal gland). Underlying Spinoza's argument here, even though it is not clearly spelt out, is a distinction between rationalism that is empirical and non-foundationalist and a notion of reason that claims to be scientific but is ultimately idealist (based on the foundations of totality) and theological (grounded in the presupposition of God).

And here we witness Spinoza's complex methodology. First, he indeed engages in what Friedrich Schlegel calls "a negative, destructive system of highest knowledge" (*negativ vernichtendes System des höchsten Wissens*) (Schlegel 1971: 134). This is of course not the *Frühromantiker* but the Schlegel of 1828. However, the late Schlegel has a point here: there is a destructive or negative element in Spinoza's scientific methodology—one that fragments pseudo-scientific notions of the All or the Universe and makes us see their rather illusory and, for scientific purposes at least, rather disappointing proclivities for operating in the name of metaphysical and other ideological presuppositions, such as God.

It is precisely such impetus to destroy irreverently, unified structures that informs the early Schlegel and Novalis's romantic genre of the fragment. Moreover, this is not only true of the German case but, as Jerome McGann has shown, of early romanticism as a whole: "The earliest Romantic theories of Romanticism are always cast in polemical, incomplete, or exploratory forms" (McGann 1983: 47). The incomplete, disappointing, and at the same time explorative aspect of early romanticism will then inform modernism's suspicion of totalizing attempts to unify our experience of the world. The fragment disrupts and disappoints presumptions of completeness and totality. It renders inoperative the totalizing operations of Cartesian and, later on, Hegelian systems of human knowledge and science.

By unraveling the circle of knowledge, the fragment disappoints expectations of the hierarchical movement of the mind or spirit over the mere matter of our environment and our embodied existence that is the foundation of progress in Hegel's dialectics. Until recently (i.e., until the scientific rediscovery of Spinoza) the term "science" had been premised on the anthropocentricism of a human mind autonomously and systematically ordering and controlling nature.

Spinoza's intellectual love of God denotes the almost romantic longing of the incomplete for understanding the world and its soul in an, for us, unreachable state of completeness. Because each of us is fragmentary and incomplete and we rely on diversity, on interconnection, in short, on a sense of community—and Spinoza's notion of love denotes this interconnectedness and interdependence of the universe's fragmentary parts (of which humanity partakes):

> This love toward God is the highest good which we can want from the dictate of reason and, is common to all men; we desire that all should enjoy it. And so it cannot be stained by any affect of envy, nor by an affect of jealousy. (Spinoza 1996: 170)

This is not the rationality of a complete system. Rather the dictates of reason ask us to avow disappointment by engaging with an understanding of our limitations. It is this epistemological humility that guards against hostility toward our environment as manifested in envy when the self wants to usurp the life of others, or in jealousy when someone does not endure the well-being of others. Far from being absolute, scientific knowledge here operates in a self-critical or ironic mode. It remains fragmentary and disappoints expectations of its dialectical transformation into a system of purported completeness.

As we have seen, the fragmentation of empirically non-existing presuppositions of unity partakes of Spinoza's scientific methodology through which he undermines a stoic or idealist metaphysic of the mind's unifying control over the body. This fragmentary approach has previously been considered as anything but scientific. This is so because idealist philosophy from Descartes to Fichte and Hegel has until recently shaped our understanding of what science is. In this way Novalis, following Fichte, defines science as a generalizing and totalizing form of knowledge: "Science is the hypothesis—grasped in form of a sign—of the essence and character of a totality –science can only deal with the general and communal" (*Wissenschaft ist die—im Zeichen festgehaltene Vorstellung von dem Wesen und Eigenschaften Eines Ganzen—die Wissenschaft kann sich nur auf das Allgemeine und Gemeinschaftliche einlassen*) (Novalis 1999, Vol. 2: 138). This traditional, totalizing notion of science is, as McGann has accurately established, that of Hegel and the idealists; one that is opposed to romanticism as a mere fragmentary, non-scientific longing for rather than implementation of unifying and totalizing control of the cerebral over the merely material and corporeal:

> Hegel's theory of Romantic Art is important, then, precisely because it is a non-Romantic theory of its subject. Its non-Romantic character— the finishedness of its ideological presentation—highlights by contrast

a crucial aspect of Coleridge's theorizing, which searches (in vain) for a systematic reconciliation of its contradictions. (McGann 1983: 47)

There are indeed confluences of Hegel's idealism and Spinozist realism at work in romanticism. However, there is a tendency of critics such as Abrams and McGann to conflate the two.

Critics, especially in the Anglophone sphere, have neglected an important distinction between romanticism (despites its idealist ideology, as so impressively analyzed by McGann) and idealism. While idealism extols humanity into a position of ever-progressing knowledge of the universe in a systematic and complete form (reached at the stage of Hegel's absolute knowledge), romanticism keeps dangling this idealist promise only to leave us with a sense of disappointment. It is precisely this Spinozist cognizance of human limitations—of how our knowledge of the world is prone to be a mere representation of ourselves and our anthropomorphism and anthropocentricism—that Hegel's dialectics circumvents in its ever-progressing transmutation of the negative (the limited) into what the synthesis transmutes as the positive (the faultless).

McGann accurately describes exactly this moment of disappointment as the countermove to idealist promises of completeness at the end of Coleridge's poem "Kubla Khan": "The poem finally passes a most devastating judgement upon Coleridge's cherished belief that the realm of ideas provides the ground of reality" (McGann 1983: 106). The idealist foundations of romanticism collapse in the realist (Spinoza-inspired) disappointing recognition of our limited, mortal, and fragmentary condition. Hegel's dialectics, however, methodologically precludes such moments of disappointment by disavowing these in the endlessly progressive transmutation of the negative, the limited into the more complete, less limited. When this process reaches a state synthesis, then dialectics promises to transform the new, already-improved limitations into even more meliorated states and so on, until we reach absolute knowledge and the fulfilled state of completeness.

Romanticism approaches this idealist progression of dialectic's promise, from a perspective that has undergone and endured Spinoza's critique of anthropocentricism and anthropomorphism. The destructive element that informs romanticism's preoccupation with the incomplete and fragmentary partakes of a rationalism that is aware of its limits. Coleridge's poetics of disappointment and disillusionment would not be tolerated in Hegel's dialectics, premised as it is on the promissory note of progress toward absolute knowledge and completeness at the end of history.

McGann ignores that Hegel and Coleridge draw different consequences (for the former those of being completely involved in the dialects of idealist progress and for the latter those of recognizing the realist disappointment with it). On the contrary he maintains that the:

> "higher point of view" which Coleridge occupied would be the cherished goal of Hegel and the left-wing Neo-Hegelians after him. Marx would call their position and ideas the German Ideology to distinguish it from the original French Ideology associated with Destutt de Tracy. Where French ideology was critical, anti-religious, rational, and socially progressive, the German was synthetic, fideistic, speculative, and supportive of established power. In Hegel this was explicitly the case, but Marx argues that the position of the Neo-Hegelians was not fundamentally different. (McGann 1983: 8)

Critics like McGann refuse to realize that there is a fundamental difference to idealism in precisely the romantic recognition and avowal of disappointment and disillusion. It is a disappointing—disappointing from an idealist perspective, at least—recognition of incompleteness that is the realist, Spinozist heritage within romanticism. Realism is the destructive element in terms of rational critiques such as Spinoza's of the presumption of human knowledge implicit in anthropomorphic distortions that inform pseudo-scientific representations of the universe. Realism is romanticism's critical and disappointing counterpart to idealism which here emerges not as scientifically accurate but as Jacobi's spiritualism, as *Schwärmerei*: "Spiritualism is absolute idealism without realism" (Schlegel 1971, Vol. 9: 33).

At its most totalizing and idealistic, romanticism critically refuses to reach Fichte's and Hegel's heights of quasi-scientific unity. Here the disappointing awareness of embodied, material reality disturbs and perturbs the promise of idealism's controlling vision of the mind's ordering and unifying power. This perceived negative element is precisely the methodological foundation of Spinoza's non-idealist approach to scientific knowledge. Spinoza dismantles the totalizing unity of the cerebral control over the body by way of fragmentation, irony, and destruction. In this way, he renders illusory the promise of totality and the All. The body resists the stoic or idealist control of the mind: "Consequently, the forces of the body cannot in any way be determined by the mind" (Spinoza 1996: 162). However, this does not mean that Spinoza discredits mental work, such as awareness and analysis. His parallelism or, more precisely, his identity of body and mind means that the latter is intrinsically contaminated with the former. Our cerebral activity is itself part of our affect-ridden and embodied condition. This means that the mind needs to be critical of its own operations, and rather than trying to control embodied existence, we require of our mental work that it understands itself and the body of which it is a part. Spinoza contaminates his dictates of reason with those of the intellectual love of God. The outcome of such contamination is a notion of reason in terms of a dialogic of listening, of apprehension, of understanding—what Herder would later call *Vernunft* as *Vernehmen* (see Mack 2010: 145–6):

> Therefore, because the power of the mind is defined only by understanding, as I have shown above, we shall determine, by the mind's knowledge alone, the remedies for the affects. I believe everyone in fact knows them by experience, though they neither observe them accurately, nor see them distinctly. From that we shall deduce all those things which concern the mind's blessedness. (Spinoza 1996: 162)

The mind critically acquires knowledge, which remedies the shortcomings of the affects. The knowledge in question is empirical, based on experience but Spinoza makes clear that albeit we have experiences in common, the acquisition of accurate knowledge gained is a rather rare occurrence. This is so, because of our lack of adequate observation and of our deficiencies in the distinct understanding vis-à-vis our various experiences in the world. According to Spinoza, science does not control in a totalizing or idealist form our knowledge of our environment and ourselves. Instead, science provides us with a realist or empiricist understanding of how we can come to terms with the insufficiencies of our affective and embodied lives.

Spinoza is a rationalist with a difference, and the difference in question is his realist skepticism toward any form of idealism that elevates the mind into a controlling position over the body and the natural, mere material environment. Elizabeth Millán Brusslan has shown that there is an awareness of the limitations of reason in Schlegel's romantic philosophy that does not ensue in F. H. Jacobi's blind leap of faith. She has also analyzed (in her forthcoming chapter on Jacobi and the World Soul) how in his famous *salto mortale* Jacobi's faith assumes the mantel of the certainty that has been the prerogative of Descartes's *cogito ergo sum*. So while first contrasting feeling and reason, Jacobi dialectically transmutes the former as part of the latter in the synthesis that is the promised achievement of his quasi-Hegelian dialectic: reason finally grounded in faith.

Because of his rigid opposition between reason and the senses as well as feeling that, he argues, leads to faith, Jacobi accuses Spinozist thought of fatalism and atheism: here we find cold reason and there the affected and affecting senses that are the foundation of his notion of religion. This is a complete distortion of Spinoza's rationalism. Spinoza's rationalism differs from the idealism of Descartes, Kant, Fichte, Jacobi, and Hegel, precisely because it radically contaminates feeling and reason, affect and thought, body and mind. The affects are themselves part of a cerebral and corporal identity that instantiates what we are. The mind engages with and observes the affects of which it partakes and which it cannot autonomously control from the position of a quasi-physiological command center (i.e., Descartes's pineal gland). Contra Jacobi's underlying idealist position, Spinoza establishes a simultaneity and not a temporally or spatially spread-out opposition between these purportedly opposed entities.

We can see Schlegel's move away from Jacobi in the light of various Spinozist shifts that contaminate or, in other words, think simultaneously what are otherwise dialectically opposed categories, such as body and mind, faith and reason, rationality and affect. Walter Benjamin's modernism radicalizes Schlegel's Spinozist destructive element by arresting the movement of Hegel's idealist dialectics. Benjamin freezes Hegel's dialectical progression into an image where oppositions crystallize into being simultaneously at one with each other. Benjamin would thus define such a romantic divergence from the idealist progressions of the mind as "dialectics at a standstill" (Benjamin 2002: 462)—contaminated, frozen states wherein oppositions meet each other in ever-changing states of mutual entanglement. Such romantic-modernist and postmodernist dialectics at standstill outdoes the idealism of progress. Here we have reached Derrida's state of undecidability wherein we have, paraphrasing Strauss, to suspend judgment, unable to decide between what may strike us as mutually opposed positions. Benjamin's dialectics at a standstill thus grounds teleology "in the idea of catastrophe" (Benjamin 2002: 473) wherein "progression" gives way to a Spinozist simultaneity of an "image, suddenly emergent" (Benjamin 2002: 462). As Samuel Weber has shown:

> Benjamin's "dialectical image" thus heightens precisely what Hegelian dialectics seeks to overcome: the "disjunctive relation" of the "synthesis." The dialectical image does this by arresting the forward flow of time, but it can only do so by interrupting its "own" intentionality qua representation and signification. In short, the "dialectical" image disrupts the horizon of expectation to which it ostensibly responds and thereby makes way for something else. (Weber 2008: 120–1)

It makes way for an avowal of disappointment which Benjamin's arresting of Hegel's idealistic progression precisely instantiates, confounding expectations of teleology. Chapter 2 will first return to Jacobi and the Spinoza/pantheism controversy at the end of the eighteenth century. This will help set into relief the so far under-explored differences between romanticism and idealism in terms of the avowal (romanticism) or the disavowal of disappointments (idealism).

2

Rendering Dialectics Disappointing

Spinoza's Specter Haunting the Anthropocene from Romanticism to Postmodernism in Literature and Science

Introduction: Romanticism and the Disappointment of Idealism

This chapter explores the repercussions of Jacobi charging Spinoza with the twin evils linking atheism and fatalism. The reverberations of Jacobi's accusation shape idealism and romanticism differently in their respective responses to a sense of disappointment in the wake of the French Revolution's betrayal of Spinoza's democratic promise of equality and diversity. As has been discussed in Chapter 1, Jacobi proposes a leap of faith as a modern antidote, disavowing disappointment. Crucially, the allegation of fatalism does not so much go back to the late seventeenth century but is contemporaneous with the age of German idealism and romanticism.

One can trace this mutation of an atheist to a fatalist Spinoza in Hegel's development of Kant's idealist philosophy. In his *Religion within the Limits of Reason Alone* (1793), while hinting at an underlying charge of atheism (derived from the late seventeenth and early eighteenth centuries), Kant grounds his interpretation of Judaism in a reading of Spinoza, hypostasizing an atheist "religion without religion" wherein "the subjects remained attuned in their minds to no other incentive except the goods of this world and only wished, therefore to be ruled through rewards and punishments in this life" (Kant 1964: 735). Here Kant constructs what he calls a "Jewish theocracy" (Kant 1964: 735) on the basis of Spinoza's reading of the Hebrew Bible (for a detailed discussion of this point, see Mack 2003: 13–82).

At this point the charge of a worldly quasi-atheist religion fuses with that of fatalism: Kant describes subjects who are fatalistically ruled exclusively by "rewards and punishments in this life" and whose minds are passively attuned to "no other incentives except the goods of this world." Another word for such fatalist passivity is what Kant takes issue with under the term "heteronomy," whereas autonomy names the free and active workings of human rationality (Mack 2003: 73–89). In the ultimate footnote to chapter 1 of his *Hegel or Spinoza*, Pierre Macherey traces the image of Spinoza as fatalist and passive Oriental in Hegel's *Lectures on the History of Philosophy* to yet another source in Kant

> The orientalist interpretation of Spinozism is a common link in German philosophy. One can read in the opuscule of Kant on *The End of All Things*: "[. . .] the pantheism of Tibetans and of other oriental peoples, then later through metaphysical sublimation, Spinozism: two doctrines closely affiliated to one of the oldest systems, that of emanation, according to which all the human spirits after having emerged from divinity finish by reentering and being reabsorbed by it." (Macherey 2011: 223)

This quote highlights how in the misleading term "pantheism" the charges of passivity, fatalism, and being Oriental fuse with that of an atheist religion without religion (i.e., a religion that is not a proper religion but instead instantiates atheism). German idealists from Kant via Hegel to Fichte try to banish Spinoza's modernity by labeling it nonrational. They charge Spinoza with promoting a religion that is atheist without being properly religious but immanent-heteronomous—oriented toward the goods of this world—passive and hence fatalistic, fitting the prejudicial construction of a backward "Oriental" Spinoza who also happens to be the biblical, expert interpreter of Judaism as a worldly religion without religion.

In a highly disturbing and yet fascinating way, Jacobi's allegations against Spinoza's version of the Enlightenment do not contradict but instead partake of a German idealist project to advance a notion of modernity that is aprioristic, does away with heteronomous (experience-based) evidence, and hence relies on leaps of faith performed by the Kantian autonomy of the human mind. The highly derogatory term "fatalism" thus actually denotes a scientific, experiential approach (at the mercy of unpredictable outcomes) to the analysis of our world. Hence fatalism and realism are synonymous.

As we shall see in the following section, what made Spinoza such a crucial thinker of the anti-foundational, incomplete, and contingent for romanticism's struggle with idealism is exactly what has led to a scientific rediscovery of his work in the late twentieth and early twenty-first centuries. New neuroscientific and biophysical research has substantiated what from an idealist perspective appears to be Spinoza's disappointing account of the mind's failure to gain autonomy over the body and the external world.

Research—such as that of emergent forms of life that happen randomly rather than teleologically—has indeed discredited a foundational and aprioristic methodology in the sciences.

Against this background, it is not surprising that perhaps the most radical of German idealists, Fichte, explicitly endorsed Jacobi's leap of faith as idealism's defense against Spinoza's purported passivity and heteronomity:

> Like Jacobi before him, Fichte sees in Spinoza's philosophy a model of the sort of determinism/fatalism that he finds threatening to the wellbeing of philosophy. For Fichte, Spinoza was a thinker focused upon things rather than the I, on substance rather than the active subject. In Spinoza's system, the I is posited merely as a mode of being, subject to the laws of nature, with no access to the supersensible realm, and thereby robbed of its freedom. (Millán-Zaibert 2007: 81)

Jacobi's charge of passivity in terms of fatalism permeates the whole of German idealism's philosophical vilification of Spinoza. For German idealism, Spinoza represents the disappointment of heteronomy that undermines the progress of the human mind that must be autonomous to fulfill history's teleology. The idealists cast their philosophy of an active and autonomous modernity—a *Tathandlung* (Millán-Zaibert 2007: 74) as Fichte put it—in stark opposition to what they rejected as the backward, "Oriental" passivity and heteronomity, embodied in Spinoza's substance.

For the romantics, however, Spinoza's name signaled a glaring contrast to the foundationalist, aprioristic approach that has shaped idealism from Descartes to Kant, Hegel, and Fichte. As has been intimated above (and as will be discussed with a close focus on Spinoza's non-teleological philosophy of mind and body in the following section) a sense of disappointment with the unlimited powers of the human mind (not least with grand schemes and their disappointment in the French Revolution) made the romantics sympathize with a Spinozist suspicion of an idealistic version of humanity's centrality in the universe. In this idealist version, the autonomy of the mind is not subject to disappointments. However, this non-disappointing progression of human achievements is intrinsically one-dimensional and aprioristic: it dismisses the (heteronomous) evidence of experience. An experience-based model of neuroscientific and biophysical inquiry chimes with a contemporary rediscovery of Spinoza in the natural sciences. Here it is apposite to highlight how both modernist literature and contemporary sciences have rendered as regressive the purported non-disappointing progress story that partakes of the aprioristic foundationalism of Descartes and then the German idealist understanding of modernity and scientific advancements.

Contemporary scientific discoveries as well as a modernist abandonment of omniscience have called into question claims of all-encompassing comprehension. Such assertions of non-disappointment are grounded in the foundationalism of Fichte's radical development of Kant and Hegel's epistemological claims that render the autonomous human mind the foundation of absolute knowledge: Spinoza's notion of mind, nature, and

> form is not imposed on the body by the soul, as in Leibniz's model. Nor does it operate like an artificial machine, as in the Cartesian animal-machine, modelled on hydraulic or mechanical devices, in which a specific energy source, like an internal fire is needed to activate its parts. What is more, this form has no final causes and is not teleologically adapted to some function, unlike an artificial machine. (Atlan 2010: 174)

Spinoza abandons theologically conditioned aggrandizements of the human mind (theological as the image of God) and separates our environment from anthropocentric superimpositions such as mechanical functions serving human goals or end points that advance humanity's non-disappointing or grand role in the universe.

In eliminating teleology and the mechanical apparatus serving an anthropocentric as well anthropomorphic conception of nature, Spinoza advances anti-foundational ways of thinking which provide support for romantic philosophy's critical engagement with idealism's claims of the human mind's all-comprehensive consciousness. As we shall see in the following section, while encouraging such epistemological humility that allows for a sense of disappointment, Spinoza's skepticism is not relativist insofar as he does not dispute notions of scientific truth.

At issue is thus *not* a relativist questioning of the existence of truth. Instead, a romantic conception of philosophy critically investigates the delusions and fictions in self-centered, anthropocentric, and anthropomorphic notions of truth and reason. Such non-disappointing conceptions have become highly dubious in our contemporary age of the Anthropocene: "Prominent representatives of the modern European philosophical tradition such as Descartes and Fichte sought the foundation for philosophy in a lonely cogito or *Ich*, but Schlegel's rejects this move and any attempt to isolate a single, fixed principle (whether that principle is understood as an activity or as a fact) underlying all knowledge claims" (Millán-Zaibert 2007: 83). This rejection of a single, fixed foundation or principle deviates from the mainstream of European philosophy and reconnects to Spinoza's radical divergence from Descartes's cogito and the anthropocentricism of the Western philosophical and scientific tradition.

As Moa de Lucia Dahlbeck has recently pointed out, Spinoza's "philosophy is being vindicated by new scientific findings related to the Anthropocene" (Dahlbeck 2019: 1). Dahlbeck shows how a Cartesian idealistic episteme that enthrones the human mind in a position of not to be disappointed sovereignty provides the legal framework for our Anthropocene age: "The Anthropocene as understood as the ultimate empirical and physical upshot of having constructed and adhered to a modern episteme which is both ontologically erroneous and providing epistemological support for an unlimited exploitation of nature" (Dahlbeck 2019: 1). Crucial here is Spinoza's critique of an idealist, Cartesian conception of the human mind that avoids the disappointing condition of a mortal and frail human body over which it is supposed to be in control while being separate from it:

> As such, the Anthropocene is highlighted as a natural phenomenon that demonstrates the relevance of Spinoza's critique of Descartes's metaphysical explanation of the human being as a "dominion within a dominion" and his alternative explanation based on substance monism, philosophical naturalism and strict determinism. (Dahlbeck 2019: 1)

Descartes's idealist conception of the non-disappointing sovereignty of the mind over the merely embodied, natural body informs the German idealist notion of human autonomy and its unlimited power in the progression of our planet's history. This traditional sense of non-disappointment with humanity as a mentally supreme entity has recently been called into question with an emphasis on the destructiveness of idealist constructions of our environment that has rendered us humans a geographic force interfering with various ecosystems of our environment, with ozone levels rising in the air and plastic overwhelming organic and inorganic maritime systems.

It is against the contemporary background of not only the socioeconomic but also a planetary triumph of anthropocentric idealism (from Descartes's cogito to Fichte's absolute *Ich*) that we have come to see romanticism's difference to a Western philosophical tradition (see Morton 2013). That this difference is largely due to Spinoza's different, non-anthropocentric, and disappointingly non-teleological heritage within romanticism becomes apparent in the idealist vilification of his thought in the wake of the pantheism controversy that Jacobi's little book of 1785 provoked. As has been discussed in this section, the butt of such vilification was the equation of Spinoza's purported atheism with his assumed fatalism. Both atheism and fatalism are categories that function to vilify Spinoza's rather disappointing diminution of humanity's role in nature. Behind the charge of atheism is the aggrandizement of human achievements in the theological tradition of the West, wherein the human is famously the image of God. Fatalism is the logical consequence of such evisceration of the will as sanctioned by divine creation.

We are able to see a more nuanced perspective in which early German romanticism and German idealism are not indistinguishable as has been claimed by Frederick Beiser following the line taken by Isaiah Berlin who subscribes to Fichte's denigration of "Spinoza's system" as "at best [. . .] simply a rigid, logical unity in which there is no room for movement" (Berlin 2000: 88). To be fair to Berlin, his lectures of 1965 were a courageous attempt to extricate romanticism from the common post–Second World War association with irrationalism or, worse still, fascism and Nazism (see Millán-Zaibert 2007 and Mack 2010). Beiser has ceaselessly and admirably attempted to continue the rehabilitation of romanticism as first attempted by Berlin five decades ago. However, as Elizabeth Millán-Zaibert has shown, there is an underlying tendency in Beiser's work (here clearly following Berlin) to render romanticism acceptable by making it compatible with German idealism: "Beiser insists that the early German Romantics are absolute idealists" (Millán-Zaibert 2007: 37). This is in contrast to Manfred Frank's and Andrew Bowie's approach that sets out to show the ways in which romanticism informs the breakdown of totality, certainty, and omniscience in modern and postmodern writing and thought (see Bowie 1996 and Frank 1996). As it should be clear by now, the line of argument of this book is close to Franks's and Bowie's perspective and widens the scope of romanticism's modernity and contemporaneity by delineating how Spinoza's romantic heritage resurfaces in recent scientific discoveries.

With his admirable scholarly expertise Beiser has taken Berlin's open-minded approach toward the philosophical study of romanticism much further and has shown how much the romantics have learned from Spinoza's notion of nature whose monism diverges from the dualism that underlines various hierarchies—of nature and humanity, of body and mind, of autonomy and heteronomy—in idealist thought: "True to their anti-dualism, the romantics placed the self within nature, insisting that it is one mode of single infinite substance, one part of the universal organism. They were no less naturalistic than Spinoza: they too affirmed that everything is within nature, and that everything in nature conforms to law" (Beiser 2003: 15). However, by rendering idealistic the Spinozism of the romantics, Beiser implicitly accepts Jacobi's misnomer of pantheism which has informed the long confusion of Spinoza's position with that of the German idealists, which, as we shall see in the concluding section of this chapter, also spills over into the English reception of the Dutch philosopher: "What the romantics admired in Spinoza was his synthesis of religion and science. Spinoza's pantheism seemed to resolve all the traditional conflicts between reason and faith. It had made a religion out of science by divinizing nature, and science out of religion by naturalizing the divine" (Beiser 2003: 134). First of all it is imperative to make clear that Spinoza was not a pantheist. Were Spinoza's thought pantheistic it would render null and void his critique of various forms of anthropomorphism and anthropocentricism that forms a major part of his magnum opus, *Ethics*. How does pantheism clash with Spinoza's elimination of anthropocentric teleology? Beiser accurately describes pantheistic deifications of nature (and perhaps science too), but this is precisely what Spinoza takes issue with: he deflates deified and inflated notions of nature that do not allow for a sense of disappointment, human nature included. As pantheist Spinoza may well be compatible with Fichte's quasi-deification of human actions.

The distinctiveness of Spinoza's rationalism is that he precisely abstains from and, on the contrary, does away with deified, or, in other words, non-disappointing notions of nature of which humanity partakes. That he equates God with nature does not mean that he deifies the latter. His notion of God denotes not a personal or impersonal deity but substance which is another word for all there is, for the universe in its (for us humans) immeasurable immensity. The most striking difference to any form of pantheism goes back to Spinoza's distinction between a "naturing nature" (*natura naturans*) and nature as it appears to us (*natura naturata*). The former is the principle behind nature and the latter is its often deceptive formation and appearance which our senses tend to get wrong when, for example, we take the sun to be close to us simply because it makes a strong or close impression on us (because it is a hot and sunny summer day).

Clearly, Spinoza's huge distance from any form of pantheism makes possible his critique of a quasi-divine teleology which we in our anthropocentrism impute into the workings of nature. Rather than endorsing human goals as part of the telos of a pantheistically conceived nature, Spinoza sets out to separate our particular endeavors from any grand scheme of God or nature. Spinoza's outlook is sober and scientific, and he warns against any exuberant extolling of the natural and/or the human as supernatural or divine forces. As Stuart Hampshire has accurately argued, "Spinoza gives the strong impression of thinking like a biologist" (Hampshire 2005: xlvii). Spinoza's scientific way of thinking also cautions against making any hasty jumps that would reach deterministic conclusions about nature or positing laws within it.

A deterministic conception of the world as predictable is the offspring of a teleology created by the fantasies of anthropomorphism and anthropocentricism. Contrary to common perceptions, Spinoza is not a determinist, as the term is commonly understood (as in the Beiser quote earlier). As Hampshire has shown:

A determinist, as this label is commonly understood, has the single idea that any human behaviour is to be explained by well-confirmed natural laws which, taken together with a statement of initial conditions, exhibit the behaviour, whatever it may be, as always in principle predictable. This is not the kind of understanding, and of self-understanding that is proposed by Spinoza. (Hampshire 2005: 195)

Far from deifying science, as Beiser claims, Spinoza's critique of the theological tradition is directed against the elevation of human teleology—be it as "natural determinism" or as grand scheme of history's unfolding—into a quasi-divine sphere (i.e., what he calls anthropomorphism). As Hampshire has astutely pointed out, reflection, in contrast, "entails the suppression of egoism in our relation with the external world" (Hampshire 2005: xxiii). The issue at the heart of Spinoza's philosophy is not so much dualism and its purported overcoming—as we will see in the following section, Spinoza's strategy is at first dualistic so as to outdo various hierarchical command structures which presuppose forms of unity—but the deflation of teleology as a human fiction and delusion about humanity's place in the universe. Teleology is the driving force behind Descartes's cogito, Hegel's absolute spirit/intellect (*absoluter Geist*), and Fichte's absolute *Ich*. By idealizing Spinoza and the romantics, critics like Beiser only work into the hands of the idealists and undermine the difference of both Spinoza's and romanticism's rationalism.

Until recently, however, the idealists have managed to brand—ironically with the help of Jacobi's leap of faith—Spinoza with the vilification of backwardness; be it "Oriental" in Kant's and Hegel's discourse, or "pre-critical" as Slavoj Žižek has recently put it (Žižek 2010: 720). The early German romantics were ideal place holders for Spinoza's exteriority to mainstream scientific and philosophical inquiry. Romanticism "has been interpreted as *at best* a literary movement with excessive emphasis on the irrational forces of human life, in the words of no less an icon of German literature than Goethe, a sick movement to be avoided by anyone with a healthy spirit, and at worst, a movement sowing the seeds of something as diabolical as National Socialism" (Millán-Zaibert 2007: 1). As we have seen, this highly dubious, threatening, and even diabolic image surrounded the public perception of Spinoza from the late seventeenth century until Jacobi's *On the Doctrine of Spinoza* gave ammunition to the German idealist enterprise to turn the tables on a Spinozist radical enlightenment by relegating it to backwardness, to what the term "Orient" brought to mind as non-modern, non-enlightened, nonrational, and passively "pantheistic" (which Spinoza's philosophy, as shown in the preceding paragraphs, clearly is not).

Insidiously, "the renegade Jew who gave us Modernity" (Goldstein 2009) here becomes a caricature taken out of the worst of racist, Orientalist stereotyping. Behind this act of "philosophical" stereotyping is a strategy, a sociopolitical agenda: that of declaring "irrational" and "non-progressive" (backwardly "Oriental") what has been seen as the diabolical threat of Spinoza's radical enlightenment which does without the hierarchical as well as teleological structures that are part and parcel of idealist rationalism from Descartes to Hegel and Fichte and beyond (nowadays the "progressive" teleology of Pippin on the liberal right and Žižek on the left).

Jacobi employs the word "specter" to capture the all-pervasive danger of Spinoza's non-teleological and non-hierarchical philosophy. The term "ghost" seems to denote the sense of disappointment that becomes associated with the absence of grand theological conceptions informing our self-understanding as human species. Spinoza turns into a specter of disappointment, which Jacobi's leap of faith seeks to circumvent. The politics of such haunting become more than apparent when one pays attention to the historical itinerary of such ghosting.

Jacobi's phrasing as regards the specter of Spinoza precisely reappears in Marx's communist manifesto as the ghost which has been haunting Europe, that of communism itself (Mack 2010: 4–10). The specter is a figure of a disappointment. It disappoints established structures of power and knowledge, precisely because it comes—like Hamlet's ghost—out of the past to highlight ancient wrongs in the night of the present. The light the dark ghost sheds on the continuing perpetuation of traditional injustices and anthropocentric illusions (those of class included) disappoints established certainties.

The specter renders disappointing firm boundaries between the past and the present, the body and the mind, nature and humanity, master and slave. It disappoints by destroying established, "water-tight" notions of identity. It repeats such identities so that we see their deadly, *revenant* constitution. The ghost as *revenant* repeats, and what it repeats comes back to haunt us with a destructive difference that highlights as does Shakespeare's Hamlet that something is rotten in what he took to be homely (in Hamlet's familiar rendered unfamiliar or ghostly, home country Denmark).

Derrida invokes this repetition early in his book *Specters of Marx* without mentioning Spinoza's name. As becomes clear later on, the structure of repetitiveness that informs the haunting of specters includes a sense of avowed disappointment and the difference this sense makes: "A question of repetition: a spectre is always a *revenant*" (Derrida 1994: 11). Derrida goes on to imply that repetition always goes with a sense of disappointment whether explicitly avowed or disavowed: "One cannot control its coming and goings because it *begins by coming back*" (Derrida 1994: 14). Spectral beginnings disappoint notions of the new, because they are always a past that has uncontrollably come back to haunt us. As Derrida makes clear toward the end of his book, like Jacobi, Marx paradoxically invokes a ghost to put the ghost to sleep. The specter needs to rest for disappointment to be overcome or disavowed such as in Jacobi's leap of faith or in the Hegelian heritage of the dialectical negative that morphs into the positive in the Marxist progression toward the end of history where all human promises of teleology have come to fruition:

> One must take another step. One must think the future, that is, life. That is, death. Marx recognizes, of course, the law of this fatal anachrony and, finally, he is perhaps as aware as we are of the contamination of spirit (*Geist*) by spectre (*Gespenst*). But he wants to be done with it, he deems that one can, he declares that one should be done with it. He detests all ghosts, the good and the bad, he thinks that one can break with this frequentation. (Derrida 1994: 113)

The disappointment is that of human reason or spirit (*Geit*), which turns out to be dark, destructive, or ghostly. This contaminating simultaneity of the productive and counterproductive, of the adequate and inadequate describes Spinoza's conception of our human constitution. The ghostly trope of disappointment also explains an often-noted (Della Rocca 2008: 116; Nadler 2006 226; de Jonge 2004: 145 and Bennett 1984: 297) contradiction or division between Spinoza's showing the limits and inadequacy of the human mind (as being identical with a deception-prone and imperfect body), on the one hand, and his trust in the promissory politics of democracy's equality and diversity, on the other. According to Spinoza's account, any form of political practice accompanies some form of metaphysical or epistemological inadequacy: "In order to reach the level of adequate understanding that corresponds with one's highest expression of power to persevere—that is, wellbeing and freedom—it is inevitable that one will rely upon some form of irrational ideal" (Dahlbeck 2019: 156). Some form of disappointment inevitably haunts human endeavors. From this perspective, it becomes clear that the Anthropocene describes the destruction of both the non-human and the human environment. As Hasana Sharp has shown, from a Spinozist perspective, our age of the Anthropocene brings to the fore that the control of nature ultimately amounts to humanity's self-destruction:

> Climate change reveals the self-undermining effect of treating other beings as instruments and resources for human use. Surely human

beings frequently act as if we are lords and masters of nature, but the effects of our actions both exceed and undermine our intentions. (Sharp 2016: 276)

The ghost marks this paradoxical return or repetition (with a difference) of achievement as disappointment or the Anthropocene counter-productivity of human, industrialized production and consumption. The will to disavow such acknowledgment of the negative or disappointment partakes of extolling the powers of our cognition from Jacobi's *salto mortale* to Hegel's dialectics and its Marxist, as well as in the twentieth and twenty-first centuries neoconservative, notion of an end of history. Spinoza's sobering and Socratic reminder of the inadequacy of our knowledge—of our "self-assurance" as "a form of blindness, of self-deception" (Nehamas 1998: 40)—enters as specter that we may want to ignore or to disavow in the interest of keeping faith with our trust in progress and the prevalence of the non-destructive, positive eternity of our achievements.

In Jacobi's *On the Doctrine of Spinoza* this haunting is more geographically restricted to Germany rather than the whole of Europe as it is at the opening of Marx's *Communist Manifesto* (1848) where we encounter Jacobi's formulation almost verbatim—from "A spectre is haunting Europe—the spectre of communism" to:

> **A Ghost [Gespenst] has recently been haunting Germany in various shapes (I wrote to Moses Mendelssohn) and it is held by the superstitious and by the atheists in equal reference [. . .] Perhaps we will witness someday that an argument will arise over the corpse of Spinoza equal to the one which arose between the archangels and Satan over the corpse of Moses.** ([bold in the German original] Jacobi 1785: 168)

Jacobi makes clear that he endeavors to put an end to the haunting with which Spinoza's ghost seems to keep Germany and then later England and the whole of Europe (by the time it seems to have mutated to what Marx calls communism in 1848) enthralled. Jacobi composes and publishes the writings gathered together in *On the Doctrine of Spinoza* to exorcise the persistent impact of a figure that appears to be an anti-Moses of sorts. As we shall see in the concluding section in this chapter Jacobi's attempt at exorcism achieved the opposite result: it hugely increased the fascination with Spinoza to such an extent that the so-called pantheism controversy reached the rest of Europe, the shores of England included. The haunting of Spinoza is far from over by now. First it reemerged as Marx's specter of communism in the nineteenth century. The romantic kernel of such haunting might well be its scientific skepticism and its avoidance of one-dimensional, teleological reductions of our world—as Coleridge puts it in his Spinozist poem "Christabel":

> The maid, alas! Her thoughts are gone,
> She nothing sees—no sight but one!
> The maid, devoid of guile and sin,
> I know not how, in fearful wise,
> So deeply had she drunken in
> That look, those shrunken serpent eyes,
> That all her features were resigned
> To this sole image in her mind:
> And passively did imitate
> That look of dull and treacherous hate!
>
> (Coleridge 1991: 276)

There might be no better presentation of Spinoza's raison d'être for his deflation of the one-dimensional fixation that accompanies the workings of teleology. These lines focus on the cruelty—hatred, to be more precise—that partakes of such seemingly innocent—"The maid, devoid of guile and sin"—reduction of nature's and humanity's multilayered world to only one line which is that of teleology: "To this sole image in her mind." The next section discusses Spinoza's contemporary scientific relevance, and the conclusion to this chapter will revisit these lines to show how these partake of the Spinozist heritage in English romantic poetry.

Spinoza or Romanticism's Spectral and Socratic Modernity of Foucault's Care of the Self

As we have seen in the previous section, Spinoza is a spectral figure in the history of ideas. His legacy is multilayered. From the seventeenth and early eighteenth centuries onward, his name, however, first of all signified scandal: most of all the outrage of having written a "book forged in hell" (see Nadler 2011). The book in question is his *Theological-Political Treatise* of 1670. It made its author's name synonymous with that of the devil. What caused such strong invectives? Spinoza's treatise is indeed a breakthrough in a scandalous way, because it is the first book to introduce its readers to the literary or secular study of religious texts.

Here Spinoza first appears as a figure of disappointment that turns into the specter of Jacobi's and Marx's conception in the eighteenth and nineteenth centuries. What is the difference between the trope and the figure of disappointment? To address this question we need to attend to Alexander Nehamas's analysis of how Quintilian distinguishes in his work on *Rhetoric* between trope and figure. A trope "applies to words" (Nehamas 1998: 56). Its range is specific and clear. However, a figure has a much larger radius of meaning, because it "involves not just words but phrases and whole sentences" (Nehamas 1998: 56). Spinoza as a figure of disappointment anticipates the haziness of the specter of Spinoza and its connotations of scandal. As a figure of disappointment, Spinoza deflates expectations of sacred or revealed meanings that a premodern tradition has invested into religious texts as well as into the accompanying hierarchies, creeds and rituals, delineated and proscribed therein.

The Bible or, for that matter, any other form of holy script is not—as had been proclaimed at the time and in the centuries preceding the seventeenth and early eighteenth centuries—the word of God but an entirely human product. The Bible here turns into a fiction, into a work of literature. In his *Theological-Political Treatise* Spinoza thus stripped sacred texts of their transcendence. The philosopher here is both a philologist and literary critic, and he employs the skills of literary criticism in order to deflate inflated—fictional—notions of both sovereignty and transcendence. In his posthumously published magnum opus, *Ethics*, Spinoza radicalizes and further develops this new hybrid literary-philosophical approach and here not only as regards the theological and political sphere but also as it applies to the whole spectrum of human society and human knowledge. Spinoza uncovers as fiction what we have taken to be representations of truth not only in the sphere of religion but also in scientific and philosophical inquiry.

At this point, another aspect of Spinoza as a figure of disappointment appears, namely, his skepticism as regards human epistemology. What we take to be God or nature—and their purported teleology—or for that matter good or evil (morality)—might be nothing more than a product of our *figmenta*, our mental projections and wishes. In other words, it might well be that it is our fictions and inventions rather than our epistemological achievements that shed light on the real constitution of God, nature, good, and evil: teleological constructions about "all final causes are nothing but human fictions" (*omnes causas finales nihil, nisi humana esse figment*) (Spinoza 1996: 27; Spinoza 1925: 80). As I have shown elsewhere (Mack 2010: 11–47), Spinoza does not set out to abolish these fictions. If he did, he would be hostile to diversity, because it is exactly in the figuration of these *figmenta* that the imagination shapes the cultural formation of different ethnic groups. Instead, Spinoza analyzes an inability to detect the fictional element that underpins human modes of reasoning.

By skeptically unmasking sacred and other truths of purported rational operations as fictions of the human mind, Spinoza is the first thinker who attempts to theorize narrative (*figmenta*, fictions) as the constitutive fabric of politics, identity, society, religion, and the larger area that encompasses what goes under the rubric "human knowledge." Spinoza's hybrid literary-philosophical methodology is highly destabilizing. It disappoints traditional expectations of supernatural revelation. At the same time, it unhinges the supposedly solid foundations not only of political theology—that is, sovereignty, religion, political order—but also of what has been taken to be unquestionable scientific insights, discoveries, and sound (if not sacred) truths of purported rational inquiry. Spinoza's enlightenment is radical to the point that it subjects to critical observation that which we have taken to be rational. Are our cerebral operations not also caught up in the realm of human wishes and desires and the various fictions to which they give rise? Spinoza encourages us to take a critical approach toward human claims to reason and truth.

Spinoza's skepticism regards categories and representations of reality, but it does not question the scientific investigation of our world. As Pierre Macherey has shown, Spinoza uncovers the fictions that claim to be representations of truth which are then supposed to function as being representative of reason's operations. Macherey makes clear that Spinoza's break with Descartes's method results in a new understanding of science and rationality, one no longer premised on representations that "restore effects to their causes" (Macherey 2011: 56) but one that is grounded in what I would call contamination and what Macherey as well as Henri Atlan describe as simultaneity:

> It is on this precise point that Spinoza breaks absolutely with the Cartesian problematic of method. *The Meditations* restore effects to their causes: they go from the finite to the infinite, for example from the human soul to God, taking things in the inverse order to which they are actually produced, which goes necessarily from causes to effects. We understand from this point of view that knowledge is first determined as a representation, because it reflects the real in thought and from its point of view, confirming with criteria of validity that at the outset are given within it and that reproduce the order of the real by inverting it. For Spinoza, by contrast, an adequate knowledge, "explains" its object to the extent that it affirms itself as identical to it, not in the transparency of a conforming representation but in the likeness of the order of an equally necessary reality. This is the real order in which things were produced, and it must also be that of ideas: this is a generic order that

goes from cause to effects, and it is this that precisely expresses the *more geometrico*. (Macherey 2011: 56-7)

Spinoza's non-representational disruption renders disappointing the Cartesian methodology, which restores effects to their causes. In doing so Spinoza's figure of disappointment adumbrates structures for establishing the framework of modern and contemporary science as depicted in Thomas Pynchon's *Gravity's Rainbow*, a text that has come to epitomize postmodern literature (McHale 2011: 331; Mendelson 1976: 165). The opening sentence of Pynchon's novel relates to the non-teleological methodology of modern science, which Spinoza's philosophy first delineated theoretically by breaking with the representational paradigm of Descartes's approach to science: "A screaming comes across the sky. It has happened before, but there is nothing to compare it to now. It is too late" (Pynchon 1975: 3). This is non-representational *in nuce*: "It has happened before, but there is nothing to compare it to now," because each thing is identical to its idea and vice versa and thus cannot be compared to or represented by anything else.

Effects here precede causes and it is disappointingly "too late" to restore the former to the latter. Pynchon invents a word for such Spinozist reversal of the traditional, Cartesian paradigm of representation: "But among *Gravity Rainbow*'s untimely traits, the most prominent is surely its obsession with hysteron proteron, the figure of reversal in which effect precedes cause, response anticipates stimulus, sequelae predate injury" (Saint-Amour 2015: 309). Precisely because the order of things is identical with the order of ideas, we no longer need a representational framework wherein one would be representative of the other.

Disappointing expectations of mental control, Spinoza does away with the hierarchical command center of the mind. In mainstream idealist and Cartesian rationalism, the mind is supposed to control the movements of the body. Likewise the identity of the corporeal and the cerebral renders inoperative the hierarchy that is constitutive for a thinking grounded in representation: we no longer require the lowly sphere of matter to be representative of the higher sphere of the spirit; after all the two are identical, are contaminated with each other, or, in other words, are simultaneously one entity, through conceptually distinct.

How can we explain this strange meeting of romantic philosophy and a modernist as well as postmodernist sensibility à la Pynchon? As has been discussed at the opening of this section Spinoza's thought is at once literary critical/philological and scientific. This explains why it attracts poets, writers, and scientists as well as philosophers. Indeed, as has been argued earlier, Spinoza is fascinated by the concept of fiction and, significantly, he uses the term to question anthropocentric delusions about nature and the universe that claim to be scientific. In this way Spinoza refers to literature as a way to correct inaccurate forms of science. In his study of romantic philosophy and science Robert J Richards has rightly revised Heinrich Heine: "Heinrich Heine called Goethe 'the Spinoza of poetry.' He could have added 'the Spinoza of science' as well" (Richards 2002: 376). Goethe's reading of Spinoza was shaped by that of his mentor, the romantic philosopher, literary critic, and founder of the modern discipline of social anthropology Johann Gottfried Herder.

As I have shown, elsewhere (Mack 2010: 138–67), Goethe and Herder develop a non-teleological perspective on society and history (Herder's anthropological and historical writings) as well as on nature and the universe (Goethe's scientific and literary-theological work) that maintains the non-hierarchical and non-causal, non-representative interconnection of organic and inorganic being. As Richards has put it apropos Goethe: "An adequate idea would indicate why the individual had to exist; yet, he [i.e., Goethe] maintained, every individual is linked to every other, so that the conditions of the whole required the existence of each individual" (Richards 379). Herder's and Goethe's philosophy of diversity grows out Spinoza's notion of *conatus*. The *conatus* affirms each individual's and each state's and each moment's incomparable validity to exist within a non-teleological and non-hierarchical universe that is nevertheless interconnected (what Deleuze and Guattari would later call Rhizome).

As we have seen, in contrast to Descartes, Spinoza maintained that virtue was not superimposed on nature by reason, God, or political power. Rather the virtuous coincides with the joyful fulfillment of each individual's different natural potential. This appreciation of an infinite variety of different (but also subtly interconnected) forms of life makes for the *differentia specifica* of Spinoza's understanding of self-preservation (*contatus*) from that of Hobbes (Hobbes's political philosophy is based on a dualism between the state of nature and the politics of reason). Spinoza not only emphasizes radical difference (the incomparable and non-representational scream with which Pynchon's *Gravity Rainbow* opens) but also highlights how what differs interconnects in contaminated states of simultaneity—to neglect this contaminating element is to fall prey to the paranoia as presented in *Gravity's Rainbow qua* the destruction and self-destruction of colonial violence and warfare.

Spinoza renders disappointing expectations for gain if it comes at the cost for the life of the environment. Similarly, a paranoid gaze intent on the destruction of the other also destroys the self. Any form of violence outdoes

Spinoza's *conatus*. As in the lines quoted from Coleridge's poem "Christabel" at the end of the previous section, it fixates on one element but ignores the universe's interconnection. As in Spinoza's identity of body and mind, his conception of the *conatus* holds together at once two seemingly incompatible entities: it contaminates radical difference and intrinsic interconnection in ever-changing states of simultaneity.

By disappointing conceptual promises for clear and distinct representation, Spinoza inaugurates a scientific revolution that is so ground-breaking that it took centuries to be recognized as such by scientists such as Antonio Damasio and philosophers of science such as Hilary Putnam. What does Spinoza's rejection of representation entail then? An entirely new approach toward human knowledge that avoids hierarchical or representative models of truth such as Descartes's method or, much later, Hegel's dialectics. Instead of representing spirit in matter, or moving from the lowly sphere of the dialectical negative to the higher sphere of the positive—under which the negative becomes subsumed—Spinoza makes us see the identity of what we take to be hierarchically opposed entities.

As Macherey has shown, Spinoza's notion of *adequatio* renders disappointingly flat, contaminated and simultaneous what the operations of representation as well as dialectics separate and temporally dilate as the distance marking off the merely embodied (dialectically, the negative) from the cerebral (dialectically, the positive) which the former is supposed to represent. In the words of Macherey:

> The essential function of the category of *adequatio* is to break with the concept of knowledge as representation that continues to dominate Cartesianism. To know, in the sense to represent, to re-present, is literally to reproduce, to repeat; the idea is thus nothing more than a double, and image of the thing, for which it provides a representation, which exists and subsists outside of it. (Macherey 2011: 60)

According to Descartes, the mind controls the body and renders the merely material a representation or reproduction of its mental concepts or sense of order (nature's purported order and hierarchy). Spinoza shows how representations are mental constructions and fictions. They do not illuminate the world but are merely reproduced images of our anthropocentric (human and self-centered) approach to our environment.

Spinoza's abandonment of representation profoundly informs and shapes various romantic critiques of anthropocentrism. As Macherey has shown it not only counteracts the work of Spinoza's contemporary Descartes but also implicitly refutes the further development of Catesian method in Hegel's dialectics:

> It is thus possible, at the risk of chronological violence, to talk about the refutation to which Spinoza himself subjects Hegel: what awaits this refutation is the idealist presence of the dialectic, which bases its universality on the presupposition that thought, by reason of its internal reflexivity, is the form par excellence of the real, of all the real: it is as such that it presents itself as an absolute rational order that gathers, and absorbs, all other orders, in the process of its own totalization. The Hegelian dialectic, which presents itself as a circle of circles, presupposes a relation of hierarchical subordination between all the elements that it reunites, and this subordination is reflected through an ultimate term, from whose point of view the entirety of its progress can be understood, because it has a meaning. But it is exactly this presupposition that is immediately rejected by Spinoza, because he eliminates from his conception of the real, from substance, any idea of hierarchical subordination of elements. (Macherey 2011: 74)

Hegel's dialectics with its unity grounded in hierarchical subordinations of its elements indeed further develops and radicalizes the Cartesian priority of thought. For Spinoza, by contrast, "thought is identical to everything and therefore has nothing above it, but the sequence through which it is realized poses, at the same time, its absolute equality with all other forms in which substance is also expressed, and these are infinite in number" (Macherey 2011: 74). As we have seen in the preceding section, following Pierre Bayle's Orientalizing discourse, German idealists from Kant onward Orientalize Spinoza and equate the lack of hierarchy in his thought with passivity, which according to the prejudices implicit in German idealism, becomes equated with the Orient (as hierarchically inferior to the idealism of the Occident).

This Orientalized figure shapes the famous Spinoza controversy which Friedrich Heinrich Jacobi provoked through the publication of his 1785 book *On the Doctrine of Spinoza*. Elizabeth Millán-Zaibert has convincingly argued that Jacobi's first English translator, George di Giovanni, has a point in interpreting Jacobi's stance as that of Cartesian rationalist. She shows how di Giovanni "even goes so far as to compare 'the inner light' that Jacobi invokes, to Descartes' notion of reason" (Elizabeth Millán-Zaibert 2007: 56) and how di Giovanni's rationalist "reading of Jacobi cannot be ignored or easily dismissed" (Millán-Zaibert 2007: 56). Indeed this kind of reading would prove right Macherey's contrast between the idealist rationalism of Descartes and Hegel and the striking anomaly of Spinoza.

It is this anomaly which German idealists—be it Kant, Fichte, or Hegel—dismissively label disappointingly passive and fatalist. Indeed no one less than Hegel's absolute spirit appears in its true active and activated glory when configured as a stark contrast to the presumed "Oriental" passivity of Spinoza's substance: "By contrast, Hegel thinks of Spirit as subject and as entirely within a perspective of eminence, which constrains and subordinates unto itself all that is produced as real and which would appear as its manifestation" (Macherey 2011: 74). As has been discussed earlier, Spinoza's notion of the *conatus* establishes the simultaneity of the subjective and the objective; a subject—most prominently Hegel's absolute spirit itself—that sets out to subordinate its objective, "merely material" environment would destroy not only that but also itself (it would be autoimmune, as Derrida would call it).

Indeed, the moot point in this context of subjectivity and objectivity or spirit and matter is Spinoza's prescient and scientifically accurate approach toward the mind-body divide. As Henri Atlan has recently shown, the American philosopher of science Hilary Putnam's notion of a *"synthetic identity of properties"* (Atlan 2010: 176; italics in original) partakes of a contemporary rediscovery of Spinoza in the natural sciences. As Atlan explains Putnam's notion of a *synthetic identity of properties*

> is from a study on "mind and body" in which Putnam traces the history of theories of the identity of body and mind in modern philosophy, Spinoza's theory, and those of other authors, like Diderot, who were inspired by it, were not taken seriously until the second half of the twentieth century, because philosophers considered them to be a priori false. In the absence of empirical arguments for or against identity, it was untenable, because it was implausible and inadmissible *a priori* for rational thought. The situation changed when the philosophical mainstream stopped being *aprioristic* and actually become *anti-aprioristic*, under the effect of the blows dealt by the natural sciences to various rational axioms, such Euclid's postulate, or the nature of physical magnitudes in the nineteenth and twentieth centuries. (Atlan 2010: 177ff. 16)

Spinoza's approach anticipates modern non-aprioristic science that is grounded in experience.

Aprioristic procedures presuppose order, purity, and teleology as foundation of our universe (Mack 2016: 77–107). Spinoza's skepticism apropos categorizations of rationality in terms of order and purity preconditions his experiential approach to science. Cutting edge modern science has abandoned various notions of an *a priori* order or teleology and has shown that Spinoza was right: teleology is a fantasy of the human mind. Instead of a plan there is chance and randomness. There is no control or causation between mind and body because the two entities are identical.

Against this background, Spinoza's spectral philosophy emerges as that of (from an idealist perspective at least, disappointing) impurity. Spinoza is the thinker of the impure, or, in other words, of the contaminated and contaminating. Related to the issue of impurity is that of destruction. It may sound strange to associate Spinoza with the destructive or negative element. However, this was Spinoza's public image as the spectral figure of disappointment from his portrayal by Pierre Bayle as "Oriental" atheist and his identification with nihilism in the so-called pantheism controversy onward. As will be discussed in the following paragraphs, for Hegel, Spinoza's negativity is passivity, which he contrasts with the activity of a dialectical movement that progressively moves from any given negative toward its transmutation into a positive entity. In his *Lectures on the History of Philosophy*, Hegel differentiates his Lutheran faith from Spinoza's notion of substance, which here appears to be part of a romantic, fragmentary, negative, or incomplete account of the universe. Hegel differentiates his notion of reason as universal comprehension from Spinoza's avowal of humanity's limited or disappointing incapacity of cognizing the universe in entirety. Similar to Jacobi's cognition as form of positive faith, Hegel identifies belief and comprehension:

> This comprehension has been called faith, but it is not a historical faith. We Lutherans—I am a Lutheran and will remain the same—have only this original faith. This unity is not the substance of Spinoza, but the apprehending substance in self-consciousness which makes itself eternal and relates to universality. The talk about the limitations of human thought is futile; to know God is the only end of religion. (Hegel 1997: 277)

In Hegel's account the negativity of mere Spinozist substance dialectically morphs into the positivity of an apprehending one, which is that of the active subject. Hegel's idealist subject rejects Schlegel's romantic irony with its Socratic and Spinozist connotations of a limit to human knowledge.

Alexander Nehamas has traced Schlegel's concept of romantic irony back to Plato's figure of Socrates. However, an uncertain, impure state between knowledge and ignorance also characterizes Spinoza's conception of an imperfect human mind that is identical with the frailty and mortality of the body: "Human beings are constantly oscillating between the desire to understand things fully and the realization that complex understanding is impossible" (Nehamas 1998: 92). The limits of our precarious, embodied mind may sometimes appear negative, if not destructive. Schlegel's conception of romantic irony avows such disappointment with life: "Acknowledging that predicament and being able to live with it is, very roughly, what he [i.e., Schlegel] understands by irony" (Nehamas 1998: 92). What Plato's Socrates conceptualizes as ignorance, Spinoza explores as the inevitable inadequacies of human cognition that pertain to even the greatest of our mental achievement.

Spinoza is certainly not a Platonic thinker. Indeed, Spinoza was banned from contact with the Amsterdam Jewish community (the famous *herem*), because he denied the Platonic and Christian doctrine of the immortality of the soul. While being somewhat Platonist in his rationalist, Cartesian critical stance toward the imperfections and misleading inclinations of the body and its affects, unlike Plato, Spinoza does not argue that our embodied life is a disease. Whereas he diverges from what Nietzsche would later criticize as the otherworldly, ascetic, and proto-Christian dogmas of the Platonic Socrates, Spinoza's rationalism nevertheless embraces a Socratic commitment to telling the truth—albeit cautiously. Being cautious helps safeguard the individual (Spinoza's famous motto was *caute* or "be cautious") from political and doctrinal threats. Spinoza is indeed the first modern philosopher who practices Socratic rationalism not as universalist dogma (applicable to everyone) but as a way of life for those who want to extricate themselves from political pressures to conform to society (as will be discussed in Chapter 3 as Foucault's Socratic theory of the care of the self).

Indeed Spinoza's capacity to live as double outsider—first as member of a minority that has been persecuted in Spain and Portugal as so-called *Marranos* and then as outcast from his family and his native (minority) Jewish community—attests to his willingness to live outside pre-given societal definitions of what an individual is supposed to be. From Foucault's perspective of social outsiders, there is a Socratic element about Spinoza's delicate ability to navigate a distinctive course for himself remaining a Jew (by not converting to the majority religion of a Christian denomination) while casting himself outside traditional forms of belonging to the Jewish community. It is this abnormality that makes Spinoza the first modern Jew.

To be able to live as double outsider Spinoza had to be able to care for himself outside all forms of societal definition. He had to create a new—now we would say modern—selfhood that had freed itself from traditional demarcations and expositions. The late Foucault would call it Socratic care for the self, such work of self-extrication from society's various networks of power and knowledge (ranging from schools, universities to prisons and psychiatric clinics). Foucault's rediscovery of the Socratic care of the self partakes and completes his earlier analysis of how power and knowledge creates individuals or subjects.

The crucial and in the early and middle Foucault unacknowledged point is that such individuals are not true to what they could be. Rather they are mere copies of what societal forms of power and knowledge define them to be; as Nehamas has put it apropos Foucault's critique of authorship and subjectivity: "What counts as individual, who one is, is whatever our many varieties of information regarding people describe" (Nehamas 1998: 172). While the early and middle Foucault spent over twenty years analyzing how societal power and knowledge creates individuals, authors, and subjects, the late Foucault's rediscovery of the Socratic care for the self points to ways in which this process could be turned on its head. To do this the self has to engage in what Spinoza would call the cautiously subversive or destructive work of telling truth to religious and societal forms of established power and knowledge. Indeed, Spinoza and his ethics of self-preservation and perseverance (*conatus*) instantiates the first modern form of what Foucault calls the ancient Socratic technique of extricating oneself—as a therapeutic care for the self—from being pre-and endlessly redefined by societal pressures.

Foucault himself singles out Spinoza as the last philosopher who dedicated his entire life to the care of the self. In his 1981–82 College de France lecture *The Hermeneutics of the Subject*, Foucault analyzes with regard to Spinoza the Socratic element of a kind of knowledge that is not used as a utilitarian instrument for the exercise of power but as an encounter that transforms and cures the self from exposure to societal pressures and regimentations:

> You can see quite clearly there [i.e., in the first nine paragraphs of Spinoza's *Treatise on the Correction of Understanding*]—and for well-known reasons that we don't need to emphasize—how in formulating the problem of access to the truth Spinoza linked the problem to a series of requirements concerning the subject's very being: In what aspects and how must I transform my being as subject? What condition must I impose on my being as subject so as to have access to the truth, and to what extent will this access to the truth give me what I seek, that is the highest good, the sovereign good? This is a properly spiritual question and the theme of reform of the understanding in the seventeenth century is, I think, entirely typical of the still very strict, close, and tight links between, let's say, a philosophy of knowledge and a spirituality of the subject's transformation of his own being. (Foucault 2005: 27–8)

The term "spiritual" describes this inner transformation which Socratic knowledge unleashes in the self, untying the ties that societally restrict and regiment it. As a double outcast Spinoza was a striking figure for such destructive and at the same time liberating refashioning of the self after having voluntarily severed its precarious ties to society. In his 1983-4 lecture series *The Courage of Truth* Foucault expands on the pivotal role of Spinoza as the last philosopher whose life radically breaks away from its prearranged itinerary shaped as it is by family and community ties: "And, subject to much more precise analyses, we might say that with Spinoza we have, as it were, the last great figure for whom philosophical practice was inspired by the fundamental and essential project of leading a philosophical life" (Foucault 2011: 236). In Spinoza's case, there is clearly a choice to offend public opinion and have his own, minority Sephardic (and highly precarious) Jewish community impose a ban (*herem*) on him so as not to endanger its own position faced with the Christian majority of Amsterdam. Thinking of Spinoza and Socrates (who equally choses societal offense that leads to his execution in Athens) Foucault goes on to define what he understands under "the problem of the philosophical life" as "a problem of a choice which may be identified through biographical events and decisions" (Foucault 2011: 236). Socrates's courage to truth destroyed some of the sacred truths of his society, and his choice to persevere in his philosophical ways led to his execution in his native city. Spinoza embarked on his decision not to rescind his calling into doubt the immortality of the soul at the start of his philosophical life. And it was the scandal of this choice that untied him from established, societal truths.

As modern and individualist Socratic thinker practicing a new, "geometric" version of the "the elenchus—the devastating question-and-answer method by means of which he [i.e., Socrates] tries to puncture his interlocutors' self-confidence" (Nehamas 1998: 47), Spinoza introduces a certain destructive element. This avowedly disappointing, destructive element has become a driving force for the courage to engage the fragmentary and incomplete in romanticism, modernism, and postmodernism.

Spinoza's destructive element demolishes not only the purity of religion but also that of science. What Descartes establishes as the autonomy of the mind and its control over the body, Spinoza contaminates with the often misleading work of the affects of which our rational workings are ineluctably a part. This is not as straightforward as it may first sound, because Spinoza separates body and mind, perhaps most famously in his *Ethics*, Part III, Proposition 2 which states that "The body cannot determine the mind to thinking, and the mind cannot determine the body to motion, to rest, or to anything else (if there is anything else)" (Spinoza 1996: 71). This proposition is not to argue for a dualism of mind and body but rather to confound a Cartesian notion of an interaction between the two entities wherein the cerebral commands and controls corporal actions with which Spinoza takes issue under Proposition 2 writing: "They are so firmly persuaded that the body now moves, now is at rest, solely from the mind's command, and that it does a great many things which depend only on the mind's will and its art of thinking" (Spinoza 1996: 71). While not being able to determine each other, the mind and the body are nevertheless (paradoxically) contaminated with each other. As Spinoza puts it, they are "the same thing" (Spinoza 1996: 73).

We come to this state of contamination wherein body and mind are the same thing from what Spinoza describes as that which reason has learned from experience, namely that the mind, being ignorant of the causes by which it is conscious of its own actions, does not understand how it is prompted by the irrational sphere of appetites. The appetites are the unknown causes of consciousness, as Spinoza says in the following passage worth quoting in full:

> So experience itself, no less clearly than reason, teaches that men believe themselves free because they are conscious of their own actions, and ignorant of the causes by which they are determined, that the decisions of the mind are nothing but the appetites themselves, which therefore vary as the disposition of the body varies. For each governs everything from his affect; those who are torn by contrary affects do not know what they want, and those who are not moved by any affect are very easily driven here and there. (Spinoza 1996: 73)

Our consciousness of our own actions does not mean that we are free agents, because being conscious is not the same as being cognizant of the causes by which we are determined. The true cause of our action—of which we may well be aware but this awareness says little here—resides in the contamination of mind with appetites, with affects. Hence, there is no parallelism but, as Henri Atlan has shown, an identity of body and mind: "In fact, Spinoza himself never uses the word 'parallelism' and explicitly refines his position as an ontological monism manifested in a conceptual dualism" (Atlan 2010: 170). Or, as Spinoza puts in the paragraph following the one cited earlier:

> All these things, indeed, show clearly that both the decision of the mind and the appetite and the determination of the body by nature exist together—or rather are the same thing, which we call decision when it is considered under, and explained through, the attribute of thought, and which we call a determination when it is considered under the attribute of extension and deduced from the laws of motion and rest. (Spinoza 1996: 73)

Here we have not a parallelism, but—from a rationalist and/or idealist perspective, at least—a rather disappointing and more far-reaching, identity of body and mind. There is a simultaneity rather than a spread-out opposition between the two entities. The figure of contamination instantiates simultaneity and thus moves beyond Hegel's paradigm of dialects which is still holding a firm grip on political and philosophical inquiry from Robert Pippin to Slavoj Žižek. The premise of Hegel's dialectics is a dualism that, as Henri Atlan has shown, has formed much of our scientific heritage. Atlan has analyzed the ways in which Spinoza differs from the mechanical and dualistic premises of philosophers of science who have shaped our understanding of what it means to be scientific, most notably Leibniz and Descartes:

> Spinoza's physics has nothing to do with mechanics. Unlike the physics of Descartes and Leibniz, it is not a theory of motion that can be judged in the light of modern physics. These statements in *Ethics* II, outlining a theory of simple and compound bodies are more relevant to what we would consider chemistry or biophysics; that is, they constitute a physical theory about the nature of compound entities, with no fundamental difference between the living and the nonliving. (Atlan 2010: 171)

Simultaneity defines the state of compound bodies.

The romantic philosopher Novalis reads Spinoza in terms of this monistic simultaneity of what idealist thought separates: Spinoza contaminates nature with its purported opposite, namely, reason. In his letter of January 20, 1799, to Caroline Schlegel, Novalis maintains that in "Spinoza lives already this divine spark of nature's reason" (*in Spinotza lebt schon dieser göttliche Funken des Naturverstandes*) (Novalis 1999, Vol. 1: 686). Following and deflecting Spinoza's one substance monism, Novalis contaminates what idealist rationalism separates in opposition to each other: nature and reason. By contaminating reason with its purported opposite, nature, he declares as foolish the antagonism between realism and idealism. From the perspective of Spinoza's monism, oppositions are illusory and it is only thinking that makes them so: "All real conflict (*Streit*) is an illusion (*Schein*)—therefore is the question of idealism and realism so foolish, so *illusory* (*scheinbar*)" (Novalis 1999, Vol. 2: 141). Novalis argues that there is a methodology of correlation—what he calls an "infinite idea of love"—in Spinoza's philosophy, which he misses in the idealist philosophy of Fichte:

> Spinoza [. . .] has grasped the infinite idea of love (*die unendliche Idee der Liebe*) and has adumbrated its method—to realize oneself for it and realize itself for oneself on this thread of dust (*Staubfaden*). It is a pity

that I do not see any indication of this idea in Fichte and that there I do not feel the breath of creation. (Novalis 1999, Vol. 1: 602)

The idealism of Fichte and Hegel is from the romantics' perspective one-sided. Idealist cognition lives the illusion of taking one half—or one part of an opposition—to be the whole truth. Idealistic (à la Fichte) and fideistic (à la Jacobi) cognition turns out to be disappointingly illusory. In a Spinozist and Socratic vein, Novalis destroys the rationalist illusion of a mind fully in charge of comprehending our universe:

> The illusion (*Schein*) is always the half (*ist überall die Hälfte*)—the half of a whole is exactly illusion (*das Halbe eines Ganzen allein ist Schein*)—because everything, however, cannot simply be halved, we encounter illusion everywhere. The illusion of cognition originates in the elevation of the half to being the whole (*Der Schein unsrer Erkenntnis ensteht aus dem Erheben des Halben zum Ganzen*)—or, in the making half of what is inseparable, of that whose *mere existence consists* in its correlation (*oder aus dem Halbiren des Untheilbaren, desjenigen, des* Wesen blos in der Zusammensetzung *besteht*)—in the counter-natural (*widernatürlichen*) abbreviation or division of transcendence and immanence. (Novalis 1999, Vol. 2: 88)

Because Spinoza makes us see the world in correlated, contaminated ways as the monism of one substance, he is, for Schlegel and Novalis, not operating in the field of thought but that of love or what the late Foucault would call the Socratic "care for the self." The care for the self as Nehamas has shown is a form or precondition of love, because it "precedes, or perhaps constitutes, the care for others" (Nehamas 1998: 167).

Idealist thought, however, is "the art of illusion" (*Alles Denken ist also eine Kunst des Scheins*) (Novalis 1999, Vol. 2: 89). As will be discussed in the following, concluding section, Spinoza's scientific notion of the simultaneity of purported opposites or contrasts constitutes what romantic poets and philosophers discuss as love, nature, and the correlating force of the imagination—terms that here denote the contaminating chemistry that is romantic poetry.

Conclusion: Coleridge's Imagination and Other Contaminations of Spinoza's Rationalism

Much of this chapter has been dedicated to tracing the struggle between idealism and romanticism as well as to delineating how Spinoza's rational, scientific thought has encouraged romantic as well as postromantic thinkers and poets to embark on a non-foundational, non-teleological, and non-aprioristic path of writing and thinking (prefiguring what Deleuze and Guttari would call the Rhizome in the twentieth century). As we have seen in the first section of this chapter, the romantic reception of Spinoza was preconditioned by Jacobi's theological and idealist charge of both fatalism (heteronomy and passivity) and atheism.

Jacobi's term "pantheism" distorted how Coleridge, Hölderlin, Novalis, and Schlegel potentially perceived Spinoza's conception of the simultaneity of self and Other, of body and mind. Despite the misleading term "pantheism," which the romantics inherited from Jacobi's *On the Doctrine of Spinoza*, the contours of a philosophy of simultaneity and contamination emerged as an alternative to the teleological paradigm of the purity of the thinking subject (Descartes's cogito, Kantian autonomy, and Fichte's absolute *Ich*). As Nicholas Halmi has recently pointed out: "Coleridge recognized in Spinoza's monism the only intellectually viable alternative to Kant's transcendental idealism" (Halmi 2012: 196). Here we encounter the divergence between ontology and anthropology, realism and idealism which has been discussed throughout this chapter. For the romantics, Spinoza proffered a realist alternative to the idealist philosophy of Descartes's *cogito*. But this is not the whole story of Spinoza and romanticism.

As we have seen in this chapter, there is, however, more to Spinoza's heritage within romanticism than this broad appeal as an avenue out of the aprioristic foundationalism of idealism. Critics who focus on the philosophical and theological issues only come to the conclusion that a romantic poet à la Coleridge finds Spinozist monism appealing, while shying away from Spinoza's abandonment of a personal, transcendent God: "While satisfying what reason demanded, the dissolution of subject-object dualism, Spinozan monism, denied what morality required, a voluntaristic conception of God" (Halmi 2012: 203). The specter of Jacobi's atheistic Spinoza looms large here, and Coleridge seems indeed to have been torn by a purported conflict between religion and reason, between the heart and the head as he describes it in the *Biographia Literaria*: "For a long time indeed I could not reconcile personality with infinity; and my head was with Spinoza, though my whole heart remained with Paul and John" (Coleridge 1991b: 112). Even though Spinoza eliminates both teleology and a personal, transcendent deity, his philosophy is not necessarily hostile to religion. As has been discussed in this chapter, he undermines anthropocentric and anthropomorphic conceptions of nature, God, and the universe but he does not dispute the ethical and moral role of religion (see also Mack 2010: 25–30).

Rather than residing in the conflict between religion and reason, Coleridge's preoccupation with Spinoza springs from an underlying demand for holding together what seem to be mutually exclusive entities or tendencies. Spinoza fascinated the romantics due to the figure of contamination that emerges from his ontologically monistic, though conceptually dualistic, philosophy. Paradoxes here no longer come across as they traditionally have done, as impasse, as aporetic. The specter of Spinoza signals both the threat and the promise of collective change toward liberal democracy (French Revolution) or later on, Marx's specter of communism.

Both Jacobi and Marx attempt to lay to rest the contaminating and paradoxical working of a spectral Spinoza who, as a figure of disappointment, oxymoronically promises and forestalls what has been promised. As a specter, Spinoza's destructive element concerns not only his scandalous denying of the soul's immortality and his unveiling of revelation as, in truth, a human, anthropocentric, and anthropomorphic fiction or construction. Spinoza's spectral gaze also retrospectively disappoints all forms of collective promises. In doing so, the ghostly life of Spinoza's future interaction with the nineteenth and twentieth centuries paradoxically points still further backward, away from modern collectives to the Socratic individual who, as in Foucault's work, extricates the self from its entanglement in rather disappointing networks of societal regimentation.

As we have seen in this chapter, the specter of Spinoza allows thus for the simultaneity of collective promises and the Socratic retreat from such collectives and their oppression. This specter-like here and at the same time there, or, in other words, this contamination of what dialectics separates as mutually opposed entities, allows us to avow disappointment as not singularly disappointing but as also promising. Spinoza as thinker of the paradoxical enables us to see the promise in disappointment and the disappointment in promises. As a rationalist Spinoza disappoints expectations of the mind's autonomy over the body and the environment.

However, this disappointment of the mind also promises a more nuanced, experience-based, modern scientific approach to more accurate knowledge of us—as having a mind that is embodied—and our universe. Similarly, Spinoza's destruction of traditional hierarchies that partakes of his critique of revelation, which as political theology, sanctioned and sanctified a traditional social order divided unequally in a feudal way, also holds out the hope for a new democratic form of government. The disappointment of such collective promises turns attention to the societal pressures which we face as individuals in a modern social order that takes itself as being unquestionable rather than as fallibly and embodied (affect-ridden, from Spinoza's rationalist perspective) human.

After the failed promises of the French Revolution and after romanticism, Spinoza's spectral life in the nineteenth and twentieth centuries pivots around how we deal with historical, collective disappointments. Are we able to avow disappointment and see its contaminated potential of promise? Or, do we impatiently reject the prospect of being liable and likely to undergo disappointing experiences as part of our limited, not always autonomous, human condition? Through its contaminating spectral thinking together of what we might otherwise dialectically separate and oppose as mutually exclusive opposites, the ghost of Spinoza allows us to avow disappointment not necessarily as the absence but as the precondition for genuine hope and promise. The authenticity of a hope that had been contaminated by disappointment consists in its experience of negativity. Here we no longer need to expel what we may define as negative, because we have come to understand negativity as part of ourselves. In concrete historical terms, we thus do not displace our disavowed sense of disappointment onto the Other or what Coleridge's "Christabel" describes as the single-minded teleology of hatred.

Spinoza's thought then makes possible insight into the ever-changing simultaneity of what seems otherwise mutually exclusive and diametrically opposed. This is why Goethe, Herder, Schlegel, Novalis, and Hölderlin associate Spinoza with a philosophy of love, and in Coleridge's case, rather misleadingly, with mysticism. Halmi is justified in being astonished at Coleridge's fusion of Spinoza's rationalism with mysticism: "The differentiation of Spinozan monism from conventional pantheism figures in the *Biographia Literaria*, where Spinoza is unexpectedly aligned with the theosophist Jakob Böhme and the Quaker George Fox, 'mystics' whom Coleridge credits with having enabled him 'to skirt, without crossing, the sandy deserts of utter unbelief'" (Halmi 2012: 200). Could it be that the figure of contamination implicit in Spinoza's philosophy allows us to hold in a state of simultaneity what has traditionally been rendered paradoxical and mutually exclusive or aporetic? As we have seen in this chapter, Spinoza is at once a dualist and a monist, affirming difference while at the same time insisting on the intrinsic interrelation of what differs. It is this contaminating paradigm of simultaneity which makes Coleridge compare Spinoza to the mystics. As regards the history of ideas, this is a misleading term for Spinoza who was of course a rationalist philosopher. But he was a rationalist with a difference, and it is this contaminating difference that Coleridge has in mind when he puts Spinoza in the company of Fox and Böhme: "For the writings of these mystics acted in no slight degree to prevent my mind from being imprisoned within the outline of any single dogmatic system" (Coleridge 1991b: 83). In this avoidance of one exclusive perspective we witness Spinoza's contaminating thought of simultaneity which holds together what traditional philosophy separates and opposes.

Chapter 3 explores how a Spinozist, romantic avowal of disappointment informs modernism. The itinerary of such romantic-modern enthrallment of disappointing disenchantment traces Joseph Conrad's modernist notion of the destructive element back to its inception in Keats's poem "To J. H. Reynolds, Esq." (1818).

3

The Destructive Element

Keats and Conrad or How Romanticism Avows Idealism's Disavowed Disappointment

Questioning the Notion of the Romantic as a Subcategory of the Idealistic: The Long Life of Hegel's Progressive Idealism Throughout Literary History

As we have seen in the preceding chapters, the critical consensus conflates romanticism with idealism. In the German case, there is a pronounced tendency to subsume the work of romantic poets and thinkers under the term "German idealism." This conflation of romanticism and idealism also shapes early-twentieth-century conceptualizations of hopes for a future that could remake the damages of the past. As will be explored in Chapters 5 and 6, this congruence of idealism and romanticism prominently re-emerges in the romantic promises of Scott Fitzgerald's *The Great Gatsby*, a novel that critically reflects on the consequences of disavowed disappointment for both the individual and society at large.

The subsuming classification of the romantic as subcategory of the idealist ignores how Goethe, Herder, Schlegel, Novalis, and Hölderlin in different ways question the denigration of embodied experience (or, in philosophical terms, realism) that partakes of an idealist position in which the mind has been given sovereignty over the merely embodied, material world. In Anglophone criticism there is a similar tendency to focus on what Raymond Williams has defined as one of his key terms in the romantic period, namely, "*idealist* (= visionary)" (Williams 1993: xvii). According to Williams, the visionary romantic poet is an idealist. There is a clear development here from Williams's broad equation of romantic visions with the rather vague term "idealist" to Jerome McGann's more firmly established identification of romanticism with the idealism of Hegel.

What is true of Byron's work is true of romantic poetry in general. It is a poetry of ideas and ideals, and—ultimately—of ideology, which is why displacement and illusion are its central preoccupations and resorts. Consequently, its greatest moments of artistic success are almost always those associated with loss, failure, and defeat—in particular the losses which strike most closely to the ideals (and ideologies) cherished by the poets in their work (McGann 1983: 132).

McGann here touches upon a crucial element that distinguishes romantic realism from the promissory teleology of idealism which culminates in Hegel's world spirit whose manifestation Kojève's Hegelian interpretation in 1930s of the last century would locate in the establishment of Soviet communism which he saw coincide with the end of history.

As Kojève makes clear Hegel himself witnesses the arrival of the world spirit at the end of history with his sight of the future emperor Napoleon horse-riding his triumphant victory that closes the Battle of Jena in 1806: "According to Hegel, Man is nothing but Desire for recognition (*der Mensch ist Anerkennen*), and History is but the progress of the progressive satisfaction of this Desire, which is fully satisfied in and by the universal and homogenous State (which for Hegel was the Empire of Napoleon)" (Kojève 1969: 192). Napoleon's victory illustrates "*human* Desire" that is "realized by the Action of the Fight to the death for prestige" (Kojève 1969: 144). From this Hegelian, idealist perspective, history manifests the reality of reason, created by humanity's dialectical negation of the merely given, natural world: "Man, on the other hand, *essentially* transforms the World by the negating Action of his Fights and his Works, Action which arises from *non-natural* human Desire directed toward another Desire—that is, toward something that does not exist really in the natural World" (Kojève 1969: 138–9). By dialectically negating merely embodied nature, humanity creates the rational teleology of the future.

This is the end of history where reason triumphs fulfilling the desire for recognition of the most rational form possible, thus finally assuaging human desire for absolute perfection or, in Hegelian terms, absolute spirit/intellect (*absoluter Geist* or *wirklicher Welgeist* Hegel 1973: 551). As "the *negation* of Space (of diversity)" (Kojève 1969: 137) time is always human in this Hegelian account, directed toward the promise of a future homogenous state wherein all diversity or natural negativity morphs into the end-synthesis of the total and absolute recognition of the triumphant master at the end of history—be that Napoleon (for Hegel) or communism (for Kojève) or free market capitalism after the collapse of the Soviet Union (for Fukuyama).

Hegel renders historical the ancient Socratic form of dialectics: "For 'dialectical' understanding is nothing other than the historical understanding of the real" (Kojève 1969: 192: 145 note 35). Whereas the elenchus of Socratic dialectics shows the limits of human knowledge—making clear how Socrates's conversation partners are ignorant where they claim to be insightful (Nehamas 1998: 72–9)—Hegel's dialectics renders the negativity of our rather (from a rationalist perspective, at least) disappointing embodied, material existence into the positive reality of future-oriented time (what the term "teleology" describes). The human centered and thus anthropocentric desire for recognition creates the will to negate the merely embodied, natural and create a fully rationalist future reality which is that of the triumphant conquest of homogenous power subduing the diversity of both humanity and nature at the end of history (which nowadays takes the form of the Anthropocene). This conflation of history with humanity, of reality with idealist reason, Kojève clearly explicates in his reading of Hegel's *Phenomenology of Spirit*:

> Now, in Chapter IV of the *Phenomenology*, Hegel shows that Desire that is directed toward another Desire is necessarily the Desire for *Recognition*, which—by opposing the Master to the Slave—engenders *History* and moves it (as long as it is not definitively overcome by Satisfaction). Therefore: by realizing itself, the Time in which the Future takes primacy engenders History, which lasts as long as *this* Time lasts: and this Time lasts only as long as History lasts—that is, as long as human acts accomplished with a view to social *Recognition* are carried out. (Kojève 1969: 135)

Crucial here is the starting point of history's anthropocentric teleology (pivoting around humanity's recognition and its idealist satisfaction at the end of history) in the rationalist desire to negate Cartesian extended matter or, in Hegel's terms, the immediacy of nature or mere embodied, empirical reality: "And the *reality* of Desire comes from the *negation* of given *reality*" (Kojève 1969: 135). In this crucial sentence Kojève rather underhandedly acknowledges the bifurcation of two realities in idealism.

Most importantly, rationalist desire denies the existence of one, namely, of immediate, empirical reality. This denial makes desire rational or idealist: it overturns and disavows the disappointing limits of our embodied conditions. Dialectical movement enacts such disavowal by morphing whatever resists as negatively given into the positivity of human-made social reality wherein we all compete for recognition until, in the final state of synthesis, there is only one, homogenous winning combatant ruling the triumphant state at the end of history.

So the dialectical is congruent with the real in a promissory sense of anticipating a fully rationalist future wherein human desire has been completely assuaged and identity has come into its own as total social recognition: "Therefore, it is the Real itself that is dialectical, and it is dialectical because it implies in addition to Identity, a second fundamental constituent-element, which Hegel calls *Negativity*. Identity and Negativity are two primordial and universal ontological categories" (Kojève 1969: 199). Negativity is nothing other than positive in that it disavows the reality of the merely given disappointment of embodied reality and thus, as work of desire, opens up the space that we call humanly made time, or, in other words, Hegel's idealistic history, which functions as a synonym here for the real as ideal.

Now romanticism, albeit playing with the language games of idealism—with what McGann calls romantic ideology—instead of disavowing, avows the disappointing dissonance rather than idealist coincidence between the real and the ideal. As McGann has shown in Keats "these moments" of what I would call avowed disappointment with idealist expectations and romantic promises "are typically related to the apparent failure of poetry and the imagination" (McGann 1983: 132). McGann clearly shows that the romantic consciousness of Keats or Shelley or Byron is one of disappointment rather than of triumphant recognition of the real in terms of the ideal. Avowed disappointment constitutes a conscious refusal to engage in dialectical rationalizations that render positive (ideal and autonomously intellectual/spiritual) the negative (real, empirical reality) by way of an included exclusion. Hegel's dialectics begins with negativity and thus includes the negative for the time being only with a view of excluding its negative element in any given synthesis: that is, that of positivity (which then of course turns into another negative to be included for another synthetic exclusion and so on):

> Of course, Keats's "fancy" has not failed him at all, it has simply refused to submit to the final ideological appropriation of which the poem itself has proposed. The displacement efforts of Romantic poetry, its escape trails and pursued states of harmony and reconciliation —ultimately, its desire for process and self-reproduction ("something evermore about to be")—are that age's dominant cultural illusions which Romantic poetry assumes only to weigh them out and find them wanting. (McGann 1983: 133)

One could characterize romanticism in this sense as idealism's truly critical consciousness. Understood in this way, romanticism avows what idealism disavows, namely, a sense of disappointment with history's decidedly non-idealist, messy, and violent itinerary not toward the teleology of an harmonious end but toward the circular, self-productive insistence of various manifestations of desire for superior recognition that are seemingly endlessly fighting one another.

Idealism is a relentlessly progressive movement which is that of Hegel's historical and historicist dialectics. Along idealist lines, literary critics have come to view literature in strictly historical terms. As literary historians they implicitly follow—be it consciously as Jameson (as we will see in Chapter 4) or unconsciously as McGann)—a teleology of history as most clearly pronounced by Hegel and Hegelians. This and the following chapters explore the contamination, or, in other words, simultaneity of what has often been seen as historically and theoretically opposed elements of literary periodization: that of romanticism and modernism. Even though recent scholarship has analyzed convergences between the two periods, this departure from a notion of literary history premised on Hegelian conceptions of progress is still confined to a specialist discourse of periodization rather than of larger conceptual expositions.

Moreover, and as will we see soon, it is not so much a philosophical but a historical element that recent scholarly discussions have discovered as the missing link between romanticism and modernism: namely, the period of decadence; a word whose obviously non-progressive connotations had been previously veiled under the term "symbolism," which as Vincent Sherry has recently shown is "not merely a polite word for 'decadence'; it is a replacement with political implications and ideological content" (Sherry 2015: 15). From Edmund Wilson's 1931 book *Axel's Castle: A Study in the Imaginative Literature 1879–1930* the term "symbolism" functions to hide the disappointment that goes with the history or story of decline, as inscribed in the term "decadence." In other words, "symbolism" as heading for this same literary period serves to obfuscate the fall or decline of "decadence." Following Wilson, influential critics such Frank Kermode and Hugh Kenner established an opposition between the romantic as "the decadent condition of history and the renovating work of modernism" (Sherry 2015: 14). Wilson's periodization of the time separating romanticism and modernism under the heading of symbolism elides "decadence" as a late romantic, counter-progressive element to the progress under which the modern and the modernist have been subsumed. After the failed promises of the French Revolution, actual history may be on a declining or decadent trajectory. However, the idealism behind the conception of literary history assumes a Hegelian, dialectical morphing of the negative into the positive, of which the eluding of decadence within the term "symbolism" partakes.

Literary scholars (such as Vincent Sherry) who set out to questions a previously assumed opposition between romanticism and modernism have to refer to another rubric of a specific period to be able to establish connections. Following an established idealist approach to the study of romanticism, they locate a modern element in the promises the first generation of romantics attached to the French Revolution. As we have seen in the preceding chapters, these were, however, the Spinozist hopes for a liberal democracy, based on social, religious, and gender equality.

Unlike Hegel, Spinoza does not ground notions of a diverse as well as egalitarian modern, democratic society within a framework of historical necessity, inevitability, or teleology. Spinoza's difference to modern contractual theories—from Machiavelli and Hobbes, via Rousseau and Kant to Hegel and Marx—consists in his ancient Socratic focus on the self. As Pierre Hadot has put it: "One could say that Spinoza's discourse, nourished on ancient philosophy, teaches man how to transform, radically and concretely, his own being, and how to accede to beatitude" (Hadot 1995: 271). However, Spinoza intriguingly combines this ancient philosophical tradition of a therapeutic self-transformation with a radically democratic political vision of a modern diverse society. Hence the self, according to Spinoza, includes the community of other selves. The self is much more than itself.

Contrary to Emmanuel Levinas's charges, Judith Butler has recently shown that Spinoza is not an individualistic but a communal thinker of the care of the self. This is so, because Spinoza's famous notion of self-preservation (*conatus*) presupposes and embraces the preservation of the other. If it did not do so, it would be autoimmune or self-destructive, because, according to Spinoza, the self depends for its survival on the well-being of others (Mack 2010: 29–45): "The Levinasian tendency to reduce the *conatus* to a desire to be, which is reducible to self-preservation, attempts to lock Spinoza into a model of individualism that belongs to a contractarian tradition to which he is opposed" (Butler 2015: 80). The self is at the same time other than itself, or, put differently, our actions and thoughts always depend on and include those of our community and environment. We are never only ourselves. Spinoza's self is thus simultaneously communal:

> The multitude does not overcome or absorb singularity; the multitude is not the same as a synthetic unity. To understand whether Levinas is right to claim that there is no Other in or for Spinoza, it may be necessary first to grasp that the very distinction between self and Other is a dynamic and constitutive one, indeed, a bind that one cannot flee, if not a bondage in which ethical struggle takes place. Self-preservation for Spinoza does not make sense outside the context of this bind. (Butler 2015: 80)

Spinoza's reason is neither teleological nor contractual. Instead, Spinoza's rationality describes the self's awareness of the umbilical cord that inextricable binds herself or himself to others, to the community. In contrast to idealism's structure of oppositions—autonomy versus heteronomy; mind versus body; negative versus positive—Spinoza's rationality contaminates what we have become accustomed to oppose as binary opposites. Thinking here is not of contrasts but of simultaneities: "Here again we are asked to consider the *simultaneity* of these desires. Just as in desiring to live well we also desire to live, and the one cannot quite be said to precede the other, so here, what one desires for oneself turns out to be, at the same time, what one desires for others" (Butler 2015: 81). Spinoza's *Ethics* reconnects with an ancient understanding of philosophy as an art of life—which Conrad's Stein in *Lord Jim* will summarize with the succinct phrase "how to be?" (Conrad 1986: 200), as will be discussed at the end of Chapter 4. Rather than oppose being with nothingness or self with other, Spinoza establishes a nonconfrontational sense of rationality and modernity wherein we contaminate opposites—such as destruction and survival; being and nonbeing—rather than establish distances and priorities between them which historical dialectics attempts to bridge over time (in the course of what is posited as history's necessity or teleology).

This teleological, dialectical conception informs current accounts of literary criticism and theory so profoundly that romanticism can only be discussed in the context of modernism through the progressive itinerary marked by the French Revolution, which historically defines the time of the first romantics. Wordsworth's spots of time thus denote this romantic promise that carries into what has been defined as the modernist value of novelty: "The earlier poets, Wordsworth and Coleridge most notably, were sufficiently young to have undergone their poetic formations at a time when the optimism of the Continental possibilities was still in the ascendant, and their work with the imaginative temporality that is evident in the spot-of-time consciousness reflects this earlier circumstance" (Sherry 2015: 39). The problem for a progressive line of modernity arises with the disappointment of romantic promises invested into the French Revolution, when the same had turned into a reign of terror: "These conditions shift for poets of the second generation, for Shelley most representatively, where the spot of time loses its integral force and so foregoes its transformative power" (Sherry 2015: 39). Here history as progress turns into its opposite: a story of decline, of decadence. However, decadence is itself a literary periodization to which recent historical accounts refer in a new attempt to establish connections between the romantic and the modernist. Moreover, the implicit but unacknowledged disappointment of a decline still partakes of an overall dialectical framework of progress as Sherry makes clear:

> To follow that progress along this particular line of inquiry is to rediscover and reclaim the middle and turning term in the literary

> history bridging romanticism and modernism. This is "decadence," which represents a sense of historical loss that was experienced first in the second generation romanticism but then accepted and subsequently reified, stylized, by the writers affiliated with this term. This is the decadence that Edmund Wilson, Frank Kermode, and others have most emphatically and categorically written out of the account. Reinserted in the medial position and mediating role it properly occupies, decadence returns to alter our fundamental sense of this legacy, drawing on a new volume and resonance from the political history we may restore to its developing and changing iterations. (Sherry 2015: 40)

Moving the term "decadence" beyond its periodization—beyond being a more disturbing or uncomfortable term for the literary movement of symbolism—still leaves it not in a central but mediating position.

What does "decadence" here mediate? It mediates between the opposite positions of progress (modernism and its "new" modernity) and decline (romanticism and its sense of lost promises after the failure of the French Revolution). Going back to the issue of periodization this mediating position is the point "where an identifiably nineteenth-century poetic decadence turns into a discernibly modernist poetics" (Sherry 2015: 154). As a literary period as well as a poetic ingredient, decadence "serves as turning fork for a poetics that registers the pressure of the previously impermissible and unsaid on the language of available record" (Sherry 2015: 138). As a mediator, despite having decline or fall written into the term, "decadence" nonetheless partakes of the progressive history which dialectically moves from romanticism to modernism. As the modernist ingredient of the previously tabooed, the decadent is the newness or progress of modernism.

We will see in the following section how Stephen Spender theorizes modern writing and writers precisely in these heroic terms of a mission that has previously been thought to be impossible. Spender describes this new accomplishment of the modernist literature in terms of what Conrad's Stein in chapter 20 of *Lord Jim* calls "the destructive element" (the title of Spender's 1935 book on modernism). As we will see in the following section, undermining such heroism of the modern and modernist is the recognition that the very term derives from the romantic poet Keats. The new is indeed the disappointingly old. Here we encounter Keats's dissatisfaction rather than Hegel's satisfaction. Moreover, this sense of dissatisfaction and disappointment gives rise to an apprehension of terror at the sight of destructive rather than productive progression throughout history and nature.

From Romanticism to Modernism: Keats's Destructive Element and Joseph Conrad

Keats's romantic sense of avowed disappointment with ideas and ideals in their empirically real historical formations in a so far unexplored way informs a key trope of modernism: that of the destructive element. In his seminal study *The Destructive Element: A Study of Modern Writers and Beliefs* Stephen Spender explores modernist writers—with a main focus on Henry James—under what I would call the trope of disappointment. The phrase "the destructive element" derives from the Stein episode of Joseph Conrad's early-twentieth-century novel *Lord Jim*. As we will see in the concluding section of Chapter 4, this is a crucial text in the genesis of what will be first explored in this and the following chapters as the new genre of a male-centered novel of disavowed disappointment.

Crucially, the destructive element that gives rise to a modernist and postmodernist sense of disappointment—either avowed or disavowed—in so far undiscovered ways grows out of romanticism's disillusionment with idealism, or, more precisely, with what Keats calls in his epistle poem "To J. H. Reynolds" the elemental heart "of an eternal fierce destruction" (Keats 1970: 325). Conrad would transform this romantic trope of destructive disillusionment with idealism into a key phrase for Spender's momentous definition of the modern and its ongoing reach beyond postmodernity.

Why is Spender's approach to modernism still relevant for our contemporary situation? Because it describes a continuing public concern with a post-idealist, post-romantic, and post-modern form of the void. As we have seen in Chapter 2, Jacobi first brought this modern vacuum to scandalous attention in the ghostly form of nihilism, or, in other words, the assumed atheism and fatalism of Spinoza's unceasing specter-like haunting of Germany and Europe at large. Spender calls this ghostly presence of nihilism "the consciousness of a void in the present" (Spender 1935: 15). Far from being an isolated issue for a few troubled and perhaps haunted individuals, this disappointed consciousness of a spiritual and moral void has become a public issue, a matter of politics in the mid-1930s. Spender implies that this modern topic may contaminate in spectral ways traditional separations between past and present.

Against the background of the earlier discussion of post-idealist romantic ghostly presences which is the destructive element in modernist writing, Spender's effort to defend the new (modernism) from the old (romanticism and perhaps realism) seems to be itself an anxious manifestation of unacknowledged disappointment. His avowed focus on the new represses an awareness of the actual ghostly presence of the old (literally Keats's romantic haunting of "eternal fierce destruction" informing Conrad's modernist "destructive element"):

> What interests me here is what writers write about, the subjects of literature to-day. So that in the last section I am not defending the young writers from the old writers, I am defending what is, in the widest sense, the political or the political-moral subject in writing. To me the lesson of writers like James, Yeats, Eliot and Lawrence is that they are all approaching in different ways, and with varying success, the same political subject. Their subject may sometimes seem impossible, for in the chaos of unbelief the time lacks, or has seemed to lack, all moral consistency. (Spender 1935: 15)

Spender is at pains to demarcate the radical break of the contemporary, the new, the modern and modernist. There is a sense of an heroic mission of the impossible to deal with this perceived utter novelty of a political situation which is that of emptiness, of a void, left behind by the destructive work of what Jacobi first coins "nihilism" (Gillespie 1995: 65–101) at the end of the eighteenth (and not in Spender's early twentieth) century. Indeed, J. Hillis Miller has traced the ways in which post medieval literature recorded the increasing absence of a communion with nature and God long before Spender's writing about a modern void. According to Miller there is a growing divide between the promises of culture and an isolated, empty reality:

> Reality is conceived of as gross, heavy, and meaningless, the desert of the world before man. But the values which man has created by transforming the world into his own image are mere subjective illusions. They exist only as fragile forms of consciousness, ready at any moment to evaporate, leaving man face to face once more with the desolation of reality. Culture in all its forms is the insubstantial foam upon a great ocean of shapeless matter. (Miller 1963: 11)

The modern city is the symbol of this meaningless reality of humanity's own, anthropocentric making: "The city is the literal representation of the progressive humanization of the world" (Miller 1963: 5). Miller does not take into account the non-anthropocentric, Spinozist promise of a new world in which old, religiously sanctioned hierarchies and their accompanying injustices and inequalities to do with gender, class, and so forth were going to gradually disappear (as to a limited extent has gradually and sporadically been the case in at least parts of our modern post–Second World War world).

Reality not so much disillusioned us but disappointed Spinozist social promises (such as in the French Revolution and in Napoleon becoming a new emperor), while still keeping them alive so that Jacobi's specter of Spinoza reappears as the specter of communism in Marx's famous mid-nineteenth-century manifesto (as discussed in the preceding chapters). Critics and theorists (apart from Laura Quinney's more specialized study of the formal aspects in *The Poetics of Disappointment* [1999]) have so far not discerned a sense of avowed disappointment with these social rather than religious developments and that not in Spender's heyday of modernism but at the height of second-generation romanticism. Miller and also McGann refrain from exploring the modernist starkness of this sense of disappointment in a romantic poet such as Keats.

On the contrary, for Miller, romanticism establishes a return to a transcendent God in the form of the artist or the poet: "The romantics still believe in God, and they find his absence intolerable. At all costs they must attempt to re-establish communication" (Miller 1963: 13). After the collapse of established, traditional forms of religion, "romanticism therefore defines the artist as the creator or discoverer of hitherto unapprehended symbols, symbols which establish a new relation, across the gap, between man and God" (Miller 1963: 13). However, these new relations are quite tenuous and, more importantly, this precariousness informs the poetic consciousness of romanticism.

Crucially, what Miller characterizes as the romantic poet's role as "discoverer" concerns a void which Spender anachronistically singles out as Conrad's destructive element which he places at the foundation of the problematic modernism is struggling with. This assumed radically new destructive element in actual fact derives from Keats's romantic poem "To J. H. Reynolds Esquire" (1818). The modern and the modernist is not that new or modern: paradoxically novelty turns out to be that of a revenant, or return of an old, already last century, romantic sight of a dark rather than divine discovery. As we will see in Chapter 4, in Conrad's destructive element we indeed witness the return of Keats's ghost. At the end of his poem "To J. H. Reynolds Esquire," Keats establishes a setting with which we are by now familiar from Conrad's Marlow narrations: that of a home location. It is one that opens up outward to the destructive force of the sea:

I was at home,
And should have been most happy, but I saw
Too far into the sea—where every maw
The greater on the less feeds evermore . . .
But I saw too distinct into the core

> Of an eternal fierce destruction,
> And so from happiness I far was gone.
> Still I am sick of it; and though today
> I have gathered young spring-leaves, and flowers gay
> Of periwinkle and wild strawberry
> Still do I that most fierce destruction see:
> The shark at savage prey, the hawk at pounce,
> The gentle robin, like a pard, or ounce,
> Ravening a worm . . .
>
> (Keats 1970: 325)

This long passage is worth quoting at length in order to bring to the fore the implicit sense of haunting that animates it. The at-home opening promises fulfillment and happiness ("should have been most happy") which then undergoes a sense of rude disappointment with the experience of a too deep sight of the destruction at sea. The ensuing rhyme of evermore with core highlights the relentless character of an ever-increasing discovery and awareness of a destructive core rather than a benign revelation at the heart of creation. The core of existence, what Conrad would later call its element, is an "eternal fierce destruction." This discovery renders the home ghostly and uncanny. As part of this destructive, ghostly visitation, the promise of happiness evaporates: "And so from happiness I far was gone." The poetic self has fallen under what could be called the modern, spectral enthrallment of disenchantment. Acknowledging the presence of this romantic and modern spell of disenchantment amounts to avowing a sense of disappointment from Keats's promise of happiness to the rude awakening in the ghostly haunting or the empirical destruction at work at sea, which the poetic voice then defines as its discovery of the true elemental core of life and nature.

Such discovery does not elevate. It literally sickens Keats's poetic voice and that in a haunting way that does not seem to let go: "Still I am sick of it; [. . .] Still I do that most fierce destruction see." The "Still" anaphora reinforces the temporal dimension of a haunting that persists over time. There is also a sense of pain that comes across in the elongated, piercing alliterations in the cumulative sound pattern of "fierce," "still," "destruction," and "see." Haunting here is clearly an experience of pain and disappointment. This painful incident thwarts the promise, which the gathering of flowers holds out for the poetic voice, of either happiness or, at the very least, a cure from suffering inflicted by the sight into destruction's core. The romantic promise symbolized by flowers here radically disintegrates into what Conrad's Stein calls "the destructive element."

The description of the putative circumstances surrounding Jim's jump from the ship of which he is in charge precedes Stein's formulation of the "destructive element" in chapter 20 of *Lord Jim*. Jim's betrayal of the British colonialist and bourgeois idea of doing one's duty, by forsaking the vessel and its passenger, leaves the narrator, Marlow, distraught. The first part of Conrad's novel consists in coming to terms with the painful truth of lofty ideas torn into the destructive drift of real events such as Jim's disloyal jump into the sea: "He was there before me, believing that age and wisdom can find a remedy against the pain of truth, giving me a glimpse of himself as young man in a scrape that is the very devil of a scrape, the sort of scrape greybeards wag at solemnly, while they hide a smile" (Conrad 1986: 138). The repetitive gerund ("believing," "giving") structure of this sentence reinforces a sense of paralysis in the wake of destruction. Indeed, Marlow's act of conjuring the young Jim in front of his mental eye moves from a sense of motionless, gerund-like stasis to that of death or self-destruction: "And he had been deliberating upon death—confound him! He had found *that* to meditate about because he thought he had saved his life, while all its glamour had gone with the ship in the night" (Conrad 1986: 138). In contrast to Keats's poem "To J. H. Reynolds Esquire," here the focus is not on the destructive in nature—birds of prey and fishes—but on the human self and its violence. Jim, as he informs the narrator, Marlow, had succumbed to suicidal ideation after his jump from the ship. In Hegelian terms, his deserting of the ship and its passengers diminishes his social standing and thus endangers his position in the struggle for recognition.

The crucial point here is that Jim seems to be concerned about himself and his societal estimation rather than reflecting on the death of the passenger carried by the *Patna*; (as will be further explored later in this chapter as well as in Chapter 4) the passengers consist of 800 Muslim pilgrims. Jim declares that he only thought of saving the passengers and not himself at the moment of crisis, but we know from the quotations earlier that his reflections pivot around his own reputation. So the following assertion might only serve to uphold his good image of himself in front of Marlow and society in general: "He protested he did not think of saving himself. The only distinct thought formed, vanishing, and re-forming in his brain, was eight hundred people and seven boats; eight hundred people and seven boats" (Conrad 1986: 138). This consideration of only 7 boats for 800 people might imply that not all could be saved, but at least attempts could have been made by Jim and his fellow crew members to save some. Clearly Jim is most concerned with defending his reputation and this comes most clearly to the fore when he invokes risking his life, which, as we have seen in the opening section to this chapter, is the touchstone of Hegelian social recognition. He clearly states that he would have been glad to risk his life in order to maintain or even increase his social recognition:

> He leaned towards me across the little table, and I tried to avoid his stare. "Do you think I was afraid of death?" he asked in a voice very fierce and low. He brought down his open hand with a bang that made the coffee cups dance. "I am ready to swear that I was not—I was not... By God—no! He hitched himself upright and crossed his arms; his chin fell on his breast." (Conrad 1986: 138)

Strikingly, Jim calls upon God to clear his name. Religion and secularized religious language indeed play an important role in depicting crucial differences between the colonizing male antihero of disavowed disappointment and the colonized (the passenger of the *Patna*) who entrust their lives to his and his fellow crew's safe-keeping of the ship. Frederic Jameson misreads *Lord Jim* by not taking seriously the role of these Muslim pilgrims and their difference, not only in regard to religion but also, more importantly, in terms of the colonialist or imperialist hierarchy (i.e., to the British commanding crew of which Jim of course partakes).

For Jameson's progressive or, as he calls it, "Utopian" (Jameson 2002: 271) reading the topic of Islam invokes religion in general (and Max Weber's account of Protestantism, in particular) rather than the political role of Eastern Muslim pilgrims on a ship chartered by British, Anglican colonizing officers: "So at length we find ourselves interrogating, as though it were the fundamental concern of this sea story and adventure tale, the clearly secondary and marginal phenomenon of religion and religious belief" (Jameson 2002: 236). "Clearly secondary and marginal," is this really the role of Islam as the belief of the colonized compared to the Anglican colonizers? As we will see in Chapter 4, Conrad strikingly marks off as "exacting" and genuine the religion of the Muslim pilgrims from the rather selfish and feeble one of Jim and his colonizing class.

Conrad in fact radicalizes the division in Keats's poem "To J. H. Reynolds Esquire" between those who are prey and those who preyed upon, in the quite explicit hierarchical architecture that constitutes the normative dwelling arrangements on the ship, long before the crisis, the moment of its sinking. In this description the novel lays out socioeconomic and political hierarchies of colonial life of which religion serves only as a marker of secularized cultural difference:

> Below the roof of awnings, surrendered to the wisdom of white men and to their courage, trusting the power of their unbelief and the iron

shell of their fire-ship, the pilgrims of an exacting faith slept on mats, blankets, on bare planks, on every deck, in all the dark corners, wrapped in dyed cloths, muffled in soiled rags, with their head resting on small bundles, with their faces pressed to bent forearms: the men, the women, the children; the old with the young, the decrepit with the lusty—all equal before sleep, death's brother. (Conrad 1986: 56)

While Jim himself invokes the term "belief" in a secularized sense as trust in the ideas of courage and duty, that serves to justify the idealist superiority of his colonizing British bourgeois class and of course his own self-image of disavowed disappointment, this passage strikingly characterizes the "white men" by "the power of their unbelief."

The term "unbelief" here denotes the powers of human-made, anthropocentric technology ("the iron shell of their fire-ship") which upholds their position of power over the "backward," colonized believers. Belief seems to diminish the modern, idealist struggle for recognition. The colonized "believers of an exacting faith" appear to live in noncompetitive society. Their depiction in terms of the social equality of sleep anticipates their role as victims, equally exposed to death by drowning, due to the sinking of the *Patna*. The underlying theme of *Lord Jim* is the paradoxical belief in unbelief: the disavowed disappointment with the progress of human, idealist, and secularized history as it plays out both socioeconomically and ideationally in the contrast between "primitive" and modern; between "progress" and return; between unbelief and an "exacting belief."

The duplicity of "belief" is quite pronounced: "You must remember," Marlow instructs us, "he [i.e., Jim] believed, as any other man would have done in his place [as part of the British colonial crew], that the ship would go down at any moment; the bulging, rust-eaten plates that kept back the ocean, fatally must give way, all at once like an undermined dam, and let in the sudden and overwhelming flood" (Conrad 1986: 106). The powers of unbelief seem to be built on shaking, literally, "rusting" grounds. Belief here is the opposite of "exacting." It does not demand any courage or obligation, religious or ethical. Instead of at least trying to prevent disaster (literally a shipwreck), it attempts to save its own skin letting in the destruction that Keats in his poem "To J. H. Reynolds Esquire" locates in the sea.

Belief here centers around not the isolated self but its struggle for recognition within its own class-based, colonial society, letting others, which here are clearly culturally and religiously colonial Others, fall prey to a death by drowning: "He [i.e., Jim] stood still looking at these recumbent bodies, a doomed man aware of his fate, surveying the silent company of the dead. They *were* dead! Nothing could save them! There were boats enough for half of them perhaps, but there was no time. No time! No time!" (Conrad 1986: 106). As we will see in the following paragraphs, Jim's account contradicts itself at the point at which it turns most insistent: namely, on the proclaimed lack of time in the moment of crisis. The belief in himself hinges on the momentary absence of consciousness. Jim's reference to a loss of consciousness here helps to disavow disappointment in himself, because being not fully himself, he excuses the absence of his conscience, which would have reinforced the importance of duty, responsibility, and ideational uprightness in one's conduct.

Contrary to Jameson's marginalization of religion, or at least religious language, in Conrad's *Lord Jim* here we encounter not only the verb "believe" but also that of "save" on a single page! All of this in the ironic context of colonization, because the colonizers were—as Christian missionaries or in a more secularized form as modernizers—proclaiming to "save" the colonized. Moreover, in this quote in which Marlow reflects Jim's perspective, those Muslim pilgrims who are going to drown in Keats's waters of destruction figure as mere background, as almost reified "recumbent bodies"; instead the focus is on Jim himself and his failed struggle for social recognition which then explains the rather exaggerated self-description as "a doomed man aware of his fate" having lost his "glamour" (but not his life itself) with the sinking ship: "he had indeed jumped into an everlasting deep hole. He had tumbled from a height he could never scale again" (Conrad 1986: 125). This is the height of Jim's social position in Hegel's struggle for recognition.

Sickness here responds to societal pressures, not to a relationship with nature that turns out to be disappointing rather than elevating. The realization of his declining social recognition makes Jim feel sick. This precisely recalls the sense of sickness which Keats's poetic voice undergoes after having witnessed the destruction animals inflict on each other. In Jim's case sickness does not result from the suffering of Others (the Muslim, Eastern passengers of the *Patna*) but the reaction of falling sick merely reflects on what his peers now "believe" him to be and with it his standing in Anglican society:

> "They made up a story, and believed it for all I know. But I knew the truth, and I would live it down—alone with myself. I wasn't going to give in to such a beastly unfair thing. What did it prove after all? I was confoundedly cut up. Sick of life—to tell you the truth; but what would have been the good to shirk it—in—in—that way? That was not the way. I believe—I believe it would have—it would have ended nothing."
>
> He had been walking up and down, but with the last word he turned short at me. "What do *you* believe?" He asked with violence. (Conrad 1986: 140)

The question of belief here turns violent and that in a pronounced, secularized, hierarchical, bourgeois societal context. Jim repeats the word "believe" until he turns it "violently" toward the narrator, Marlow. This is about not religious truth, but Jim's standing within the secular social order of British colonial society.

Whereas the poetic voice of Keats's poem "To J. H. Reynolds Esquire" falls sick after having seen too far into the destructive life at sea, Conrad's Jim is himself implicated in what he witnesses. The sickness here is far more personal. It is a sickness of the self and its relation to its societal environment and its associated ideas, ideals, pressures, and expectations. Moments before this violent turn on Marlow, questioning whether he believes his version of what has occurred moments before his jump from the ship, Jim actually acknowledges that his account is unbelievable. He clearly contradicts his earlier insistence that he had not had time to reflect on his actions, when he admits that there was time to deliberate and save at least some passengers of the *Patna* (who were fast asleep in the moments before shipwreck):

> "Jumped," he corrected me incisively, "Jumped-mind!" he repeated, and I wondered at the evident but obscure intention. "Well, yes! Perhaps I could not see then. But I had plenty of time and any amount of light in that boat. And I could think too. Nobody would know, of course, but this did not make it any easier for me. You've got to believe that too. I did not want all this talk... No... yes... I won't lie... I wanted it: it is the very thing I wanted—there. (Conrad 1986: 139)

There is truth revealed as an implicit disappointment of the self with itself. This extraordinary quotation from Jim anticipates the more veiled, ironic narrative tone of Conrad's *Heart of Darkness*. Jim makes obvious his sense of uncertainty, of concealment, of unreliability. He puts a statement forward and immediately withdraws it literally as "No... yes." Moreover, by admitting that he had time to think and that there was light enough to see and develop a plan in regard to how to rescue at least some of the passengers who as Muslim pilgrims were asleep and thus ignorant of the impeding danger, Jim acknowledges not only his guilt of not acting to save lives but also his deliberate distortion of the "truth" within his preceding pleas to the narrator such as this one: "You think me a cur for standing there, but what would you have done? What! You can't tell—nobody can tell. One must have time to turn round. What would you have me do?" (Conrad 1986: 111). This ad hominem appeal turns out to be false, and the narrator anticipates the revelation of Jim's disappointing relationship not only with the practical issue of saving lives entrusted to him but also with his deceptive usage of language. For Marlow,

Jim's actions and words highlight the dubiousness of colonial society at large: "I was made to look at the conventions that lurks in all truth and on the essential sincerity of falsehood" (Conrad 1986: 111). Disappointingly and highly paradoxically the false turns out to be the true. In other words, in order to narrate the falsehood of the society he is depicting, Marlow needs to present "truths" in the sense of the historical reality of their falsehood. This is the true topic of *Heart of Darkness* whose narrative illuminates the ethical falseness of colonialism's proto-totalitarian racism.

The issue of "truth" in a secularized colonial society is bound up with the inability to acknowledge disappointment. This is the subject matter of *Lord Jim*. Without spelling it out, Marlow characterizes an oxymoronic rendering of the true as the false in terms of colonial inflections of what it means to belong to the male gender. As Judith Butler has argued, gender "ought not to be constructed as a stable identity or locus of agency from which various acts follow; rather, gender is an identity tenuously constituted in time, instituted in an exterior space through a *stylized repetition of acts*" (Butler 2007: 1919; italics in original). These habituated, repetitive acts create the illusion of being "natural." In truth, they are constructions. Butler differentiates expression from performance in this context of gender as social construction rather than a naturally given entity:

> If gender attributes, however, are not expressive but performative, then these attributes effectively constitute the identity they are said to express or reveal. The distinction between expression and performativeness is crucial. If gender attributes and acts, the various ways in which a body shows or produces its cultural signification, are performative, then there is no pre-existing identity by which an act or attribute might be measured; there would be no true or false, real or distorted acts of gender, and the postulation of a true gender identity would be revealed as a regulatory fiction. That gender reality is created through sustained social performances means that the very notions of an essential sex and a true or abiding masculinity or femininity are also constructed as part of a strategy that conceals gender's performative character and the performative possibilities for proliferating gender configurations outside the restrictive frames of masculinist domination and compulsory heterosexuality. (Butler 2007: 192–3)

If gender were expressive, as has traditionally been held, then it would signify a biological or naturally given predisposition. However, Butler's notion "performative" does not merely denote gender's fictive or socially constructed constitution but it also adumbrates the larger horizon of societal expectations and disappointments. There is a general expectation (perpetuated through repetitions and their stylized habituation) to live up to one's gender role.

In the case of Conrad's colonial context, Jim should fulfill what the phantasmal coordinates of his male gender role stipulate: to act dutifully and to be ashamed at the prospect of nonperformance to such an extent as to disavow rather admit to disappointment. Here disappointment denotes precisely the failure to perform what societal norms and regulations constitute as appropriate (dutiful, non-disappointing) male behavior. By disavowing disappointment, Jim tries to confirm his socially constructed gender role. Gender thus vibrates in the tension of societal expectation and their potential, performative disappointment.

Indeed, it is expectations that produce the gendered phenomena they anticipate. Disavowal of disappointment conjures the object after it has already proven to be elusive, fictive, and phantasmal which it indeed is, because it is societally performative rather expressive of a biological or naturally given constitution. The kernel of the hierarchically instituted male gender is the Hegelian struggle for social recognition and hence the readiness to risk life and limb for safeguarding the status quo as superior or master (Jim's title role is that of "lord"). Nalin Jayasena traces to Carlyle the construction of a male identity as the willingness to risk one's life in order to gain social recognition: "Jim seems to subscribe, even in fantasy, to a notion of masculinity inscribed by Carlyle, which requires that a man perform death-defying tasks, displaying no fear in the face of danger" (Jayasena 2007: 29). However, Carlyle inherited this conception of male identity from Hegel's idealism (as discussed in the first section of this chapter).

Against this background of an idealist construction of male gender as intrepid in the face of death, Conrad's *Lord Jim* unmasks the dubious and constructed or fictive nature of such a conception. It is not only his jump that cast into doubt Jim's intrepidity but also his refusal to acknowledge his fears and disappointments. Jim's equivocation of what he insists to be "believable truth" highlights a disavowal of disappointment which Conrad's Marlow narrated, male-centered novels first introduce as a new genre that has shaped the itinerary of the novel from modernism to the contemporary (as will be discussed in Chapters 5 and 6 that will analyze this new genre in Scott Fitzgerald's *The Great Gatsby* and Saul Bellow's *Ravelstein*).

Critics have explored in various ways the central role of male gender in Conrad's work but so far the critical consensus has overlooked Conrad's significance as inventor of a subgenre of what I call the novel of disavowed disappointment. This genre is male centered in a critical way: it is usually a male narrator who, like Marlow, is fascinated but at the same time detached from the main male protagonist of his narration. As Katherine Snyder has clearly shown, Marlow's relationship to the central character of his story telling is highly ambiguous, be that Jim or Kurtz: "Motivated by a desire for self-preservation as much as by a sense of 'jealous guardian'-ship, Marlow affirms that Jim 'achieved greatness,' much as in *Heart of Darkness* he affirms that Kurtz was a 'remarkable man': valiantly or perhaps desperately maintaining as true what he has seen and shown to be patently false" (Snyder 1999: 189). Crucial here is what we as readers see.

Conrad's novels clearly set up their male protagonists as champions for great ideas of duty and empire and at the same make us recognize how they fail to live up to any form of ideal conduct. Marlow's narrations are about actual disappointments and their idealistic declarations sound ironic in the context of what we as readers are experiencing and witnessing. As Snyder puts it, "Marlow doggedly maintains the fiction of masculine plenitude in the face of obvious masculine lack" (Snyder 1999: 189). However, the important point is that Conrad's texts make us see the discrepancy between Marlow's expectations and the disappointing narratives that actually materialize in the course of his narrations. Snyder has come close to discovering what I call the subgenre of the male-centered novel of disavowed disappointment when she describes "bachelor narrators" as follows:

> Much of the energy of these "off-centered" or ex-centric first person narratives is expended in negotiating the honorific modifier: the greatness, goodness, or lordliness of the cipher-like anti-heroes at the heart of these novels. Indeed, the primary anxiety of these novels' bachelor narrators is that their exemplars of authentic manhood may prove to be "hollow men," men whose outward form hides inward emptiness, or worse, a heart of darkness. The fear of a moral vacuum behind the façade is a preoccupation of modern life and modernist literature, but in these texts it insistently expresses itself, or is formed by, these bachelors' identification with and desire for other men. (Snyder 1999: 174–5)

The importance of "belief" in a secular Western colonial society of the British Empire consists in in its subscription to the colonialist story line pivoting around unfailing duty. "Belief" here disavows disappointment. "Desire" might be too strong a word here. It would be more accurate to say that there is an ambivalent fascination with the idealist hopes or, as in Jay Gatsby's case, romantic promises which the male narrator has invested into the main protagonist of his narration. These expectations then unravel in form of various disappointments which we as readers bear witness to but, and this is the most important note-worthy part, which the main male character abstains from characterizing as disappointing. The moot point is that the male protagonist disavows the disappointment which the male narrator clearly shows to take place during the itinerary of his narration.

At this point the literary subject matter of the male-centered "genre" of the novel of disavowed disappointment becomes indistinguishable from the philosophical theme of idealism. Idealistic conceptions of progress—which then serve as ideational justifications for the rather materialistic interests of colonialism—are a fraught topic for gender issues, because idealist thinkers from Hegel to Carlyle identified masculinity as vector of history's progression. Conrad's new subgenre of the novel sets into relief male gender constructions that accompany idealist accounts of modernity's teleology.

Most strikingly, Hegel genders the (progressive) state as masculine and the private family setting as feminine (Mack 2003: 48–53). In the final part of his *Phenomenology of Spirit*, Hegel goes so far to differentiate between a *divine* (*göttliches*) and mere *human* (*menschliches*) force of moral law, and he characterizes the former as *masculine* (*männliche Character*) and the latter as *feminine* (*weibliche* Hegel 1973: 536). True to his dialectical method that includes what it ultimately excludes, Hegel does not expel female gender. However, a woman functions as the included Other: she helps to produce life and also supports its growth.

A pronounced gender hierarchy pervades idealist accounts of progress from Hegel to Carlyle and beyond. The narrative of the West's modern progress then shapes colonialism's justification of itself. Here gender, idealist progress, and colonialism form a whole which literary critics tend to see in isolated terms (i.e., focusing their specialized attention only on one term). The male-centered narrative of disavowed disappointment disturbs the progressive drift of this fusion toward an ever better future. It does so by showing through its narrator deflected concern with one character—be it Kurtz, or Jim—how progress fails to acknowledge its own dark side: that is, its disappointment.

From Hegel onward, the refusal to avow disappointment partakes of the construction of male identity. Hegel thus clearly contrasts the "feminine principle of nutrition" from the "masculine principle of the driving force of selfconscious being" (*zum weiblichen Prinzipe der Ernährung, hier zum männlichen Prinzipe der sich treibenden Kraft des selbstbewussten Daseins gediehen*) (Hegel 1973: 526). Jayasena has pointed out that criticism of "*Lord Jim* has either focused on the formal aspects of the novel (and, subsequently praised it as modernist classic) or examined its political themes" (Jayasena 2007: 22). Frederic Jameson's misreading of the novel is symptomatic of what Jayasena is discussing here. Those critics, like Padmini Mongia and John McClure, who explore male gender issues in *Lord Jim* fail to link them to the colonial, imperial theme of the novel (Mongia 1992: 183; McClure 1981: 120–30). However, Jayasena does not pay attention to the larger philosophical and societal implications of this construction of masculinity as the driving force behind the West's self-proclaimed progress or historical teleology which serves as idealist justification for its colonialist exploitations. Conrad questions both the idealist construction of male gender (as in Hegelian terms not fearing death in the struggle for recognition) and the ideas of colonialism as progress of Western civilization.

He does so by shifting Keats's core of destruction from the animal life of the sea to that of the male, colonial-imperial self who fails to live up to idealist aspirations. In order to account for Jim's failure to not even attempt the rescue the lives of the Muslim passengers of the ship he is entrusted to safeguard, Conrad's narrator feels compelled to explore Jim's psyche. However, Marlow, Conrad's narrator, constantly shifts ground.

First he sympathizes with Jim's attempt to comply with the demand to provide a factual account of his failure of duty affirming that "only a meticulous precision of statement would bring out the true horror behind the appalling face of things" (Conrad 1986: 65). Facts would illuminate horrible events: "The facts those men were so eager to know had been visible, tangible, open to the senses" (Conrad 1986: 65) as the destruction at sea infiltrates the sensual life of Keats's poetic voice rendering it sick.

Then, however, Marlow deflecting the position of Jim turns inward. This is the point where Keats's destructive element as instinctively exerted by the feeding mechanisms of birds and fishes living off the sea turns inward into the life of the mind, to "something invisible, a directing spirit of perdition that dwelt within, like a malevolent soul in a detestable body" (Conrad 1986: 65). *Lord Jim* invokes Keats's destruction within natural life and sees this increased within humanity whose grand ideas of duty and progress it renders hollow and satirical thus preparing the way for the ironic deflation of "modern" colonialist ideology in *Heart of Darkness* which will be explored in Chapter 4: "An unthinking and blessed stiffness before the outward and inward terrors, before the might of nature and the seductive corruption of men—backed by a faith invulnerable to the strength of facts, to the contagion of example, to the solicitation of ideas" (Conrad 1986: 75). This is a highly ironic way of writing that celebrates what must appear intellectually dubious ("unthinking") and ridiculously rigid ("stiffness").

However, the mindless, blessed stiffness in the face of outward and internal pressures points to Stein's genuine question of wisdom, of "how to be" as a way of embracing rather fighting what we consider to be negative, or contaminating or contagious. This will be discussed at the end of Chapter 4 which will return to Keats's core of destruction via the Stein episode of

Lord Jim and its formulation of the modernist "destructive element" as a philosophy of life or art of living. Anticipating Stein's embrace of the negative, the destructive element, Marlow in this quotation deflates outward, social, and environmental pressures and goes on to dismiss ideas and idealisms that justify colonialist exploitations: "Hang ideas! They are tramps, vagabonds, knocking at the back-door of your mind, each taking a little of your substance, each carrying away some crumb of that belief in few simple notions you must cling to if you want to live decently and would like to die easy!" (Conrad 1986: 75) Here literature meets philosophy: philosophy not of ideas but in terms of an art of living.

What Conrad proposes is not philosophy as an academic discipline. Instead he connects his literary work to an ancient, Socratic conception of wisdom that differs from "modern University philosophy" where "philosophy is obviously no longer a way of life or form of life" (Hadot 1995: 271). By evoking the art of living decently and dying easily, Conrad's Marlow describes the subject matter of ancient philosophy which, following Socrates, engaged with the life of individuals: "There was a Socratic style of life (which the Cynics were to imitate), and the Socratic dialogue was an exercise which brought Socrates' interlocutor to put himself into question, to take care of himself, and to make his soul as beautiful and wise as possible" (Hadot 1995: 269). Hang ideas and engage with life and death, this is Marlow's advice in the quotation earlier. Avowing disappointment destroys the pretense of ideas and makes possible a genuine engagement with the art of living and dying. Marlow here avows a sense of disappointments with ideas; an acknowledgment of destruction, which neither Jim nor Kurtz is able to do.

Having "hanged ideas" Marlow embraces the disappointment of sober simple notions as to how to swim with rather than overcome the destructive element, which will be Stein's advice to Jim later on in chapter 20 of the novel. Conrad's narrator here makes clear the butt of his ironic way of writing: it is ideas that disavow real-existing disappointment and that eat away at our life, which serve to cover exploitative practices or render euphemistic human works of destruction. Rather than abandon all philosophical notions, the passage appraises a few—from an idealist perspective—simple ones that support the art of living and dying. Here thinking or philosophizing is, similar to the Stein episode on the destructive element, a response to the ancient Socratic question of "how to be?": "This life of *theoria* is thus not opposed to the practical, since it is a life of philosophy, lived and practiced; it is precisely the '*exercise of life*'" (Davidson 1995: 29). Literature here meets the ancient Socratic meaning of philosophy as a way of living as well as a preparation for dying. Conrad's Marlow attempts to grasp the art of "living decently" and "dying easily." From its ancient, Socratic foundations, this art requires a transformation of the self. Hence, the emphasis on inwardness.

Against this background, Marlow's disappointment with not only lofty ideas but also facts or, in other word, the acquisition of knowledge, appears in a new light—namely, that of the art of living and dying that is premised on the inner transformation of the self: "Rather than aiming at the acquisition of a purely abstract knowledge, these [i.e., spiritual] exercises aimed at realizing the transformation of one's vision of the world and a metamorphosis of one's personality" (Davidson 1995: 21). It is this new, destructive vision of the world that renders sick the poetic voice of Keats's poem "To J. H. Reynolds Esquire." As we have seen the sickness in question here amounts to a disappointment with the lofty idea of progress as propounded in an idealist understanding of romanticism in terms of progress, hope, and promise. Keats thus avows disappointment with an idealized or romanticized nature which excludes recognition of its destructive core.

Sickness partakes of a spiritual exercise that makes one realize the void inherent in lofty ideas of progress. Decadence is thus only a moment within a modernist as well as romantic notion of self-renewal through the disappointing recognition of the destruction at work in nature and, in a greatly enhanced way, human society—in what Conrad calls "crowds" in the following quotation from the close of *Lord Jim*'s chapter 7:

> Which of us here has not observed this, or maybe experienced something of that feeling in his own person—this extreme weariness of emotions, the vanity of effort, the yearning for rest? Those striving with unreasonable forces know it well—the shipwrecked castaways in boats, the wanderers lost in a desert, men battling against the unthinking might of nature, or the stupid brutality of crowds. (Conrad 1986: 108)

The "yearning for rest" recalls Freud's death drive and what Nietzsche seemingly dismissingly labeled "decadent." Sickness is related to the fall or jump inscribed into the word "decadence." As Vincent Sherry has recently shown in a brief reading of *The Secret Agent*, Conrad's modernism may appear to be affiliated with decadence. Conrad may well have been sympathetic to *The Secret Agent*'s anarchists "who are attacking the Progress mythology for which the imperial plan was the promissory agent" (Sherry 2015: 123). As we have seen in this chapter, idealism and its gendered construction of progress gives rise to what I call a male-centered disavowed sense of disappointment. Strikingly, Conrad's novels avow disappointment at moments of acknowledged or obvious failure. Indeed, *Lord Jim*'s first part consists of a long contemplation of its main protagonist's shortcomings, epitomized by the decadence of his fall or jump from the ship when and where it would have been his task to save at least some of the lives entrusted to it.

Sherry reads decadence a crisis of modernism. The anarchists of *The Secret Agent* enact such crisis by attacking the agent of progress (imperialist or otherwise) which, in this novel, is science (the Greenwich Observatory as symbol for the scientific measurement of time): "Anarchism may be read in this novel [i.e., *The Secret Agent*] then as a most vivid and specific instance of a crisis of modernization, which, in turn, defines the moment and opportunity of modernism" (Sherry 2015: 123). How could a crisis of modernization be an opportunity of modernism?

Sherry leaves this question unaddressed in his detailed and fascinating historicist study of decadence within mainstream modernism (such as Conrad's). Rather than consciously reflecting on the conditions of its own time, the modernism of Conrad calls upon the trope of disappointment in order to establish a literary-philosophical point of wisdom that attempts to free the self from various pressures. These pressures are precisely what Keats's poetic voice in the poem "To J. H. Reynolds Esquire" identifies as "the core/ of an eternal fierce destruction" (Keats 1970: 325) as visible in the creaturely life at sea. Conrad's Stein will rephrase what Keats's poem sees happening at sea, as the "destructive element." This destructive element may actually be benevolent, if one does not attempt to overcome or try to fight it, but swims with it in an acknowledged way of disappointment. As will be explored in Chapter 4, wisdom consists in avowing rather than—in a stereotypical male, idealist-imperialist way—disavowing disappointment.

4

Modernity's Promise and Its Disavowed Disappointment

Hannah Arendt's Analysis of Totalitarianism Out of the Sources of Conrad's *Heart of Darkness*

The Destructive Element in *Heart of Darkness*: Conrad's Irony

As we have seen in Chapter 3, Conrad practices a destructive deflation of lofty ideas and romantic promises in an ironic style of writing that leaves the reader on dangerous, shifting ground. Chapter 3 has also explored how Keats locates what he calls "the core/of an eternal fierce destruction" in nature, to be more precise in the sea. Now in Conrad's male-centered narratives of *Lord Jim* and *Heart of Darkness*, the sea hauntingly transfers destruction from nonhuman nature into the core of humanity's civilization. An instance of such transposition from the nonhuman into the human sphere takes place in the last cry of Kurtz which manifests itself as a visitation of a romantic vision turned hollow. The natural sense of touch here transmogrifies into a spectral one of fascination with ghostly presences of disappointment which in yet another set of disturbing swerves then have to rely on the idealism of ideas for their uneasy and unconvincing exorcism:

> Oh, I wasn't touched. I was fascinated. It was as though a veil had been rent. I saw on the ivory face the expression of sombre pride, of ruthless power, of craven terror—of an intense and hopeless despair. Did he [i.e., Kurtz] live his life again in every detail of desire, temptation, and surrender during that supreme moment of complete knowledge? He cried in a whisper at some image, at some vision—he cried twice, a cry that was no more than a breath—"The horror! The horror!" (Conrad 1973: 111)

Ambivalence pervades this quotation as irony does in fact set the tone for the whole texture of Conrad's *Heart of Darkness*. This stylistic or tonal awareness has so far evaded the theoretical and critical consensus.

Indeed, Conrad's novella serves as a mouthpiece for various ideological, philosophical, and political or historical positions. To name the most striking of these: as a defense of racism (Achebe 2006) or as its refutation (Said 1994), as a metaphysical revelation of the violence and destruction inherent to the West's metaphysics (Lacoue-Labarthe 2012) and, more radically, still, as a general apocalyptical uncovering of "horror" as a universal ontology, which is not limited to one political or philosophical tradition such as that of the Occident as argued by Lacoue-Labarthe (Miller 2012). What has evaded the critical consensus, however, is the irony inherent in Conrad's trope of disappointment which proclaims nothing while promulgating a plethora of possible meanings ranging from imperialism's pride and its "ruthless power" to the "craven terror" it inflicts on its subjects. All these manifestations ironically withdraw into the meaninglessness of annulled promises in Kurtz's "hopeless despair." Irony is indeed *Heart of Darkness*'s "destructive element." Being destructive, it is constructive precisely through its destruction of myths of idealism, imperialism, and progress. It is this diminution, if not extinction of meaning, which displaces Kurtz's cry into "no more than a breath" of spectral horror whose real presence is as ambivalent as anything else about Conrad's *Heart of Darkness*.

Conrad's novel immediately withdraws what it has put forward. This is how ambivalence and irony work: "Irony is acknowledged concealment" (Nehamas 1998: 67). What irony conceals might be nothing, a void: "Irony often communicates that only a part of a picture is visible to an audience, but it does not always entail that the speaker sees the whole. Sometimes it does not even imply that the whole picture exists" (Nehamas 1998: 67). The uncertainty of whether there is any meaning or reality to be discovered characterizes the ironic style of narration which is that of Conrad's Marlow. Lacoue-Labarthe accurately explores how the West partakes of what it projects as its Other: "But this horror is less the *de facto* horror of savagery than the power of fascination that savagery exerts over the 'civilized' who suddenly recognizes the 'void' upon which their will to ward off the horror rests—or fails to rest. It is its own horror that the West seeks to dispel" (Lacoue-Labarthe 2012: 119). Yet, even this horror of the West dissipates into an exorcism of a "saving idea."

The spectral haunting of Kurtz's horror evaporates with the apparition of another fleeting and ironically self-cancelling ghostly presence of the "redeeming idea." Conrad's Marlow avows disappointment with Kurtz's genocidal colonialism ("exterminate all the brutes" Conrad 1973: 87) while at the same time disavowing it, again creating the sense of ironically concealing an empty entity. Idealism paradoxically or, in other words, in a self-cancelling manner serves to justify the horror of exterminatory conquests of the Other:

> The conquest of the earth, which most means the taking it away from those who have a different complexion or slightly flatter nose than ourselves, is not a pretty thing when you look into it too much. What redeems it is the idea only. An idea at the back of it: not a sentimental pretence but an idea: and an unselfish belief in the idea—something you can set up, and bow down before, and offer sacrifice to . . . . (Conrad 1973: 31–2)

As in Keats's sight far into the destruction at sea, we encounter an excessive look, here however, into the depth of human destruction rather than animal feeding habits. Emblematic of the trope of disappointment, the passage pulls the rug under what it is saying: colonial occupation and theft thus serves to realize the unselfish belief in the idea behind such extremely selfish action. Keats's sight far into the destruction at sea here turns into an excessive look into the horrors of colonialism. The idea itself turns into a superstitious object of worship, a fetish of sorts to whom one bows down before to "offer sacrifice to." Progress contaminates with what is supposedly its opposite and the assumed rationalism of idealism evaporates in the atavistic practice of sacrifice.

Via the preceding analysis of an empty kernel at the heart of Conrad's *Heart of Darkness*, which ironically promises to reveal what it conceals only to continuously cancel or withdraw the meaning which has been put forward, idealism mutates into colonial exploitation as well as unlimited selfishness and the progress (of rationalism and ideas) appears to be a radical regression. Indeed, rationalism turns out to be the superstition of occultism. The enlightener Kurtz—the "prodigy" and "an emissary of pity, and science, and progress" (Conrad 1973: 55)—is an irrational believer in ghosts. As Jonathan Dollimore has recently argued, Conrad indeed follows Max Nordau's famous theory of degeneration: "In *Heart of Darkness*, the over-civilized is seen to have an affinity with the excesses of the primitive. Kurtz embodies the terrible paradox that contemporary degeneration theorists like Max Nordau tried to explain but only exacerbated, namely that civilization and progress seem to engender their own regression and ruin" (Dollimore 2012: 68). Dollimore here avoids drawing the consequences from Conrad's radically ironic cancellation of meaning: it is not so much that progress over-refines itself and thereby mutates in its opposite but that it is its opposite.

This is precisely the topic of *Heart of Darkness*: how the light of Enlightenment is at the same time its self-cancellation or withdrawal in darkness. The promise of modernity is simultaneously its disavowed disappointment. This is the significance of the connection between Conrad's novella and Nordau's degeneration theory—as Jason A. Josephson-Storm has recently shown, the modern was indeed enamored to the atavism of spiritualism and its belief in ghosts: "In one significant respect, though, Nordau was right—not in his idea of degeneration, but in his simpler observation that Western Europe was in the midst of an occult revival. [...] in late nineteenth-century England, full-blown spiritualist movements and occult revivals were in place" (Josephson-Storm 2017: 184). This paradoxical—and from a truly rationalist perspective, disappointing—cohabitation of the scientific with the occult arises from the sobering non-anthropocentric, Spinozist implications of Darwin's discovery of evolution: "In Russia as in Britain science was used to evade Darwin's lesson: humans are animals, with no special destiny assuring them a future beyond their earthly home" (Gray 2011: 3). In order to avoid "the key fact about evolution as described by Darwin," namely, "that it has no aim" (Gray 2011: 39), science became pseudoscience and attempted to "purge" humanity of its imperfections.

Darwin's evolutionary findings prove right Spinoza's critique of teleology as nothing else but a projection of humanity's wishes and desires (appetites). Being an animal contradicts anthropocentric concepts of humanity's teleology of perfection with its divine origin as image of God. Here we encounter the disappointing presence of Spinoza's specter and the immediate demand to exorcise its presence through the practice of pseudoscience masquerading as the science of eugenics and spiritualism: "Eugenics aimed to rid the world of defective human beings, while Spiritualist believed that the body that awaits in the afterlife would be purged of defects. Eugenics and spiritualism were both of them progressive creeds, claiming that by using new knowledge humankind could attain a level of development higher than anything achieved in the past" (Gray 2011: 81–2). The turn from science into pseudoscience is social and political. It springs from the populist desire to avoid acknowledging disappointment. In spiritualism's case, there is the clear wish to overcome the disappointing fact of our mortality. In a similar way, eugenics attempts to redo our frail—subject to disability—and often limited constitution which we share, as Darwin's discovery of evolution has shown, with our origin, that of animals, of apes, rather than that of an eternal and perfect deity.

In the figure of Kurtz, Conrad depicts such a conflation between science, art, progress, and a populist politics that displaces real-existing disappointment with any given ontological or economic or social condition onto the Other—the disabled person, the primitive or savage (the "brutes"), the immigrant, the Jew, or the Muslim. Marlow does not know the profession of Kurtz: "and to this day I am unable to say what was Kurtz's profession, whether he ever had any—which was the greatest of his talents" (Conrad

1973: 115). As readers we are again left with uncertainty and with the possibility dangling in front of our eyes, that there is nothing and what poses as hidden or concealed may well be the absence of any profession. Such a lack then ironically turns into overabundance: "He was a universal genius" (Conrad 1973: 115). The all-embracing capacity of the "universal genius" manifests itself in the rather dubious realm of public demagogy.

A visitor informs Marlow about Kurtz's real talent while again concealing the disappointing absence of any admirable qualities, saying that Kurtz should have been what he clearly was—a demagogue in populist, colonial politics (proclaiming "Exterminates all the brutes!" Conrad 1973: 87):

> This visitor informed Kurtz's proper sphere ought to have been politics "on the popular side." He had furry straight eyebrows, bristly hair cropped short, an eye-glass on broad ribbon, and, becoming expansive, confessed his opinion that Kurtz really couldn't write a bit—"but heavens how that man could talk. He electrified large meetings. He had faith—don't you see?—he had the faith. He could get himself to believe anything—anything. He would have been a splendid leader of an extreme party." "What party?" I asked. "Any party," answered the other. "He was an—an—extremist." (Conrad 1973: 115)

Progress is a form of regression here, and the irrationalism of myth persists in what has been assumed to be a demythologized modernity. The emissary of science and progress believes in ghosts. Talent paradoxically consists in educational ignorance. According to this quotation, Kurtz lacks any scholarly or scientific knowledge (he is an analphabet) and his only talent is a destructive, extremist one: that of a public demagogue who electrifies large populist audiences and persuades them of extremist, violent views.

From Colonialism to Totalitarianism: Conrad's *Heart of Darkness* and Hannah Arendt's *Origins of Totalitarianism*

Hannah Arendt indeed advances her theory that fascism and totalitarianism developed out of imperial colonialism with direct reference to Conrad's Kurtz, the populist demagogue:

> Like Mr. Kurtz in Conrad's "Heart of Darkness," they [i.e., colonialists and fascists] were "hollow to the core," "reckless without hardihood, greedy without audacity and cruel without courage." They believed in nothing

and "could get [themselves] to believe in anything—anything." Expelled from a world with accepted social values, they had been thrown back upon themselves and still had nothing to fall back upon except, here and there, a streak of talent which made them as dangerous as Kurtz if they were ever allowed to return to their homelands. For the only talent that could possibly burgeon in their hollow souls was the gift of fascination which makes a "splendid leader of an extreme party." (Arendt 2004: 247)

In what, however, consists Kurtz's populism and extremism? In a fascinating way Kurtz, the populist, extremist politician, informs Arendt's theory of totalitarianism as the terror of dialectical idealism that does away with any superfluous, natural imperfection inherent in the diversity of nature. Here we encounter Conrad's contamination of idealism and exterminatory terror, all closely related to the Hegelian progression of dialectics whose relentless transformation of the negative by the positive in ever more perfect syntheses displaces onto the Other and thereby disavows any disappointing imperfections:

The movement of history and the logical process of this notion are supposed to correspond to each other, so that whatever happens, happens according to the logic of one "idea." [...] Dialectical logic, with its process from thesis through antithesis to synthesis which in turn becomes the thesis of the next dialectical movement, is not different in principle, once an ideology gets hold of it; the first thesis becomes the premise and its advantage for ideological explanation is that this dialectical device can explain away any factual contradictions as stages of one identical, consistent movement. (Arendt 2004: 605)

Factual contradictions are visitations of Jacobi's specter of Spinoza, or Marx's specter of communism. The ghost is the diversity of new beginnings that hinder the progressive movement of dialectics.

Spectral hauntings highlight the regressive return of the past and they thus do not fit into the grand progressive scheme of nature/history defined in dialectical-idealist terms. Unlike Conrad, Arendt does not refer to ghosts and Kurtz's spectral "The horror! The horror." However, in a figurative sense, Arendt's notion of diversity included ghosts as revenants that connect the past to the present and vice versa. She defends the project of modernity not in ideological terms that narrow down the plurality of nature and history in the interest of what she calls the logic of one single and thus totalitarian and extremist idea: "An ideology is quite literally what its name indicates: it is the logic of an idea. Its subject matter is history, to which the 'idea' is applied; the result of this application is not a body of statements about something that *is*, but the unfolding of a process that is constant change" (Arendt 2004: 604). She critiques a version of modernity that banishes not so much the occult sphere of ghosts but the empirical plurality and unsystematic messiness of our embodied minds.

Whereas ghosts, as *revenants*, make the past return uncannily and disappointingly in the midst of the lived presence, Arendt insists on the continual renewal of birth, of the renaissance, or, what she calls, recalling and secularizing Augustine, new beginnings. It is with the early medieval theologian Augustine and new beginnings that her critique of modernity gone astray as totalitarian terror ends:

> Beginning, before it becomes a historical event, is the supreme capacity of man; politically, it is identical with man's freedom. *Initium ut esset homo creatus est*—"that a beginning be made man was created" said Augustine. This beginning is guaranteed by each new birth; it is indeed every man." (Arendt 2004: 616)

By connecting her notion of the new and modern to an old, sacred, or theological thinker (Augustine), Arendt implicitly allows for the spectral presence of the past within the radical break of new beginnings, of modernity.

Elsewhere, in her book *On Revolution* (1963) she indeed insists that every revolution to be sustainable requires ghostly roots in some form of constitutional past or tradition. The American Revolution thus sustains itself constitutionally through its ghostly tie to ancient Rome and Roman constitutionalism (*lex*). The founders of the American Revolution were the founding fathers of America's constitution. They connected themselves backward in a spectral *revenant* of "Roman *pietas*" which "consisted in being bound back to the beginning of Roman history" (Arendt 1990: 199). For Arendt, modernity's sustainability consists in this spectral copresence of the foundational past, of the binding constitutional law (*lex*) within the individuality of new, revolutionary beginnings: "and the outstanding characteristic of the modern age was that it turned once more to antiquity to find a precedent of its own occupation with the future of the man-made world on earth" (Arendt 1990: 230). In *Between Past and Future* Arendt thus insists that human actuality or presence in the world depends on a grounding in the past that could be interpreted as spectral.

Thinking acknowledges and relates to the ghosts of the past: "Only insofar as he thinks, and that is insofar as he is ageless—a 'he' as Kafka so rightly calls him, and not a 'somebody'—does man in the full actuality of his concrete being live in this gap of time between past and future" (Arendt 1977: 13).

It is this spectral gap between the past and the present that hinders and disappoints dialectical attempts to force or terrorize the diverse course of natural and/or human history into the linear shape (from negative to positive to synthesis and then turning the latest synthesis into a negative again and further progressing thus on this line of dialectics' logical idea) of what Arendt understands by ideology as the logic of one dialectical idea.

In her early American work *The Origins of Totalitarianism* she responds to the violence inherent in Kurtz's colonial and, for Arendt proto-totalitarian, logic of the idea that makes him exclaim in the name of historical progress "Exterminate all the brutes" and then in the ghostly setting of what Arendt would read as a paradoxical modern foreclosing of new beginnings "The horror! The horror!" Struggling with the unacknowledged myth or ghost within a single-mindedly future-oriented version of modernity that gives rise to totalitarian specters of populist politics such as Conrad's Kurtz, Arendt (as will be discussed in the following paragraph) strikingly employs the term "miracle." Arendt explicitly contradicts mainstream rationalist approaches that read fascism in terms of what George Lukács has called "the destruction of reason." Conversely, Arendt's breaking down of the term "ideology" as the logic of the idea, locates it in close vicinity to the rationalism of idealism.

Rather than lacking reason or idea, ideology does not allow for any form of ideational disappointment or hindrance that goes with the arrival of the unexpected or the long forgotten. By precluding the surprising element of the miracle, ideologies close the door to anything that deviates from an *a priori* linear arrangement of time, which forces the diversity of our world to conform to its prearranged outline: "Ideologies are never interested in the miracle of being" (Arendt 2004: 604). Here it is not the uncertain, ironic, or quasi-miraculous entry of a ghost (as in Shakespeare's *Hamlet*) but the miracle of thinking which in fact describes what Arendt means by the terms "natality" (birth) or "new beginning." Thinking is not isolated. It is plural in so far as it is open-ended rather than predetermined by teleology. Being open it allows for miracles and the return of the past, however, disappointing such *revenant* of the old may be (such as Hamlet's ghost who depicts both family life and the larger state of Denmark as a major disappointment, as something "rotten").

It is against this open-minded and open-ended background of the plural practice of thinking, that Arendt defines logic rather than premodern or somewhat occult or opaque forms of belief or rituals as the kernel of modern terror and irrationalism: "The only capacity of the human mind which needs neither the self nor the other nor the world in order to function safely and which is as independent of experience as it is of thinking is the ability of logical reasoning whose premise is self-evident" (Arendt 2004: 614). By being cut off from empirical experiences of the world (human and otherwise), logical reasoning is in a position of sovereign terror over what it has separated and cut itself off from.

Dialectics *qua* the logic of the idea rules ruthlessly over the human and natural world in terms of what Arendt's friend Walter Benjamin depicts in thesis IX of his "Theses on the Philosophy of History" as the storm of rapidly onward-moving progress. Benjamin's angel would like to save lives and awaken the dead. However, progress in terms of logical necessity is merciless. Against his or her will, the storm of progress ruthlessly forces the angel to witness its work of destruction rather than intervene and save those who have been ravished. So it is the contemplation of disaster that remains as the messianic remainder of redemption in our "progressive" world of logical and dialectical inevitability:

> Where we perceive a chain of events, he sees one single catastrophe which keeps piling wreckage upon wreckage and hurls it in front of his feet. The angel would like to stay, awaken the dead, and make whole what has been smashed. But a storm is blowing from Paradise; it has got in his wings with such violence that the angel can no longer close them. This storm irresistibly propels him into the future to which his back is turned, while the pile of debris before him grows skyward. This storm is what we call progress. (Benjamin 1999a: 249)

The sheer force of progress's storm metaphorically describes the brutal inevitability of logical necessities that operate in Hegel's dialectics of history's teleology (as inscribed into the notion "end of history" which has been explored at the opening of Chapter 3). Such a storm blowing from paradise renders the same a hell of catastrophic destruction. Here we gain insight into what Benjamin means by his notion dialectics at a standstill, as discussed at the closing of Chapter 3. Benjamin's arrested dialectical movement forms an image that holds presumed mutually opposed entities—such as catastrophe and paradise—in a state of contaminating simultaneity. In contrast to Benjamin's apocalyptical framework, in Arendt the work of destruction grows out of a rationally conceived teleology that destroys any form of nonconforming and thus disappointing diversity.

The terror of dialectics' logic destroys the disappointing, unforeseen negativity of new beginnings taking its cue from Conrad's Kurtz and his "the horror!" after having ruthlessly pronounced his slogan "Exterminate all the brutes": "A terror is needed lest with the birth of each new human being a new beginning arise and raise its voice in the world, so the self-coercive force of logicality is mobilized lest anybody ever starts thinking—which as the freest and purest of all human activities is the opposite of the compulsory process of deduction" (Arendt 2004: 610). It is this forward-moving compulsory force of logical deduction which is Kurtz's "devotion to efficiency" (Conrad 1973: 31). Arendt in yet unexplored ways establishes her differentiation between the terror of dialectical logic as efficient "brute force" (Conrad 1973: 31) and the practice of thought or what she calls the activity of thinking.

Crucially, Conrad uses the term "thoughtless" (Conrad 1973: 93) for Kurtz's "unreflective audacity" (Conrad 1973: 93), and it is precisely this term which Arendt will employ for her provocative analysis of how someone could do what the main administrator of the Nazi-genocide did in Arendt's famous account of it in *Eichmann in Jerusalem*. I have shown elsewhere (Mack 2009) that in her provocative "report on the banality of evil" Arendt employs an ironic style of writing which the earlier discussion here has analyzed as Conrad's way of establishing uncertainty about any form of truth or meaning in Marlow's narration of his main male character's (i.e., Kurtz's) disavowed disappointment so that we are never faced with his terrifying ghost but only with the whisper of breath tenuously exclaiming "The horror! The horror!" That Arendt employs the term "thoughtless," directly taken out of Conrad's Marlow narration of Kurtz, for characterizing Eichmann's facilitation of the most horrendous genocide in human history is itself ironic, because it self-consciously conceals more than it brings into the open. In the context of history's most shocking mass murder, the word "thoughtless" sounds like an appalling understatement (Mack 2009). Within the context of Arendt's and Conrad's linguistic register, however, it denotes the utter disregard of diversity which categorically makes possible ruthless genocidal deeds as proclaimed in Kurtz's "Exterminate all the brutes!"

Because he is a force of efficient, logical deduction, Conrad's Kurtz is lonely and thoughtless. As we have seen, Marlow's narration disappoints promises of certain, verifiable actions. We only receive glimpses of characteristics, capacities, and fragments of exclamation. Being lonely and thoughtless, Kurtz does not partake of community. He does not seem to have a viable relationship. Not thinking of others, Kurtz separates himself ruthlessly from diversity, which is to say, from the diverse human communities that constitute humanity.

Conrad's Marlow thus describes Kurtz's "loneliness" and his "essential desolation" (Conrad 1973: 93) and, even more to Arendt's point about ideology as the efficient but thoughtless logic of the idea, how "there he was thoughtlessly alive, to all appearance indestructible solely by the virtue of his few years and of his unreflective audacity" (Conrad 1973: 93). The "gifted Kurtz" (Conrad 1973: 84) does his public, political work "in utter solitude" (Conrad 1973: 85). We do not hear of or know any details and there might indeed be nothing substantial—because the efficiency of dialectical logic keeps erasing immediate, concrete particulars that obstruct or disappoint its onward rush to ever greater syntheses—except that whatever it is, epitomizes modern Europe in what Arendt later, relying on *Heart of Darkness*, theorizes as the terror of logical deduction imposed on the diversity of being from the post-Hegelian mid-nineteenth century onward: "All of Europe contributed to the making of Kurtz; and by-and-by I learned that, most appropriately, the International Society for the Suppression of Savage Customs had entrusted him with the making of a report, for its future guidance" (Conrad 1973: 86). Here is indeed the deductive, single-minded futurity of promise and hope resulting from the logic of Hegelian dialectical movements that suppresses any uncanny ghostly apparitions which might hinder or disappoint its predetermined movement.

The disappointment of what early anthropologists of religion like Edward Burnett Tylor and James Frazer labeled tellingly as "survivals" (Strenski 2006: 78) has to be done away with, or as Conrad calls it "suppressed":

> The tremendous intellectual change which took place in the middle of the nineteenth century consisted in the refusal to view or accept anything "as it is" and in the consistent interpretation of everything as being only a stage of some further development. Whether the driving force of this development was called nature or history is relatively secondary. In these ideologies, the term "law" itself changed its meaning: "from expressing the framework of stability within which human actions and motions can take place, it became the expression of motion itself" (Arendt 2004: 598).

Having done with the old, modern progression abandons the ground on which the diversity of the new could arise. Law in the traditional sense is the legal framework of a constitution, which Arendt singles out as the achievement of the American Revolution whose respect for tradition she contrasts with the single-minded terror fixated on a future promise that she locates in the French Revolution. Law as Roman *lex* establishes community. In doing so it binds the present to the past and, according to Arendt, constitutional law does the work of memory which prevents a thoughtless, lonely rush of progress that ruthlessly erases what preceded the contemporary moment. Crucially, the legal preservation of the past enables the development of new beginnings. It does so by safeguarding diversity from any attempt at dialectically superseding what may be categorized as negative or disappointing into a line of promising progression which violently erases what preceded it, resembling Benjamin's storm blowing from paradise:

> The laws hedge in each new beginning and at the same time assure its freedom of movement, the potentiality of something entirely new and unpredictable; the boundaries of positive laws are for the political existence of man what memory is for his historical existence: they guarantee the pre-existence of a common world, the reality of some continuity which transcends the individual life span of each generation, absorbs all new origins and is nourished by them. (Arendt 2004: 600)

Instead of protecting the diversity of old and new beginnings, what Arendt would call the totalitarian law of Hegelian dialectical motion disregards any content or context, being singularly fixated on the promise of a future. Conrad's seafaring narrations from the West to the East are crucial for Arendt's formulation of a critical theory that challenges a modernity that has intensified preceding forms of violence precisely by its dialectical inclusion of the negative (of spectral pasts) only to have them all the more efficiently expelled in final, synthesizing movements. Synthesizing formations are short-lived and dialectical movements relentlessly repeat their own motion, because they subsume the negative into the positive. Any given positive moment in dialectical transit has already passed its moment and becomes a new negative in form of a spectral synthesis that awaits another subsuming and so forth.

The geographical movement on the seas from the Occidental to the Oriental reenacts the categorical and temporal law of dialectical motion that leaves the spectral past behind as disappointment and thus negativity which makes room for hope and promise. Disappointment logically has to disappear here. Should there be a lingering sense of disappointment remaining somewhere, it has to be disavowed. The non-Western, colonial subjects of *Heart of Darkness* which might potentially thwart or disappoint the onrush of progress are linguistically deprived of any resisting force (a force implicit in the term "enemies") that could put up a fight. They have been rendered bare categories of a progressive law of motion that excludes difference in terms not of resistant enmity but of subdued and incarcerated criminality: "but these men could by no stretch of the imagination be called enemies. They were called criminals, and the outraged law, like the bursting of shells had come to them, an insoluble mystery from the sea" (Conrad 1973: 43). Instead of the protective law (Arendt's constitutional law, safeguarding old and new beginnings), the proto-totalitarian, colonial law of Conrad's *Heart of Darkness* is "the outraged law" that, by resembling the violent speed that is the "bursting of shells," metaphorically describes Arendt's cultural theory of dialectical motion or what she calls terror (recalling the French Revolution's reign of terror):

Terror, therefore, as the obedient servant of natural or historical movement has to eliminate from the process not only freedom in any specific sense, but the very source of freedom which is given with the birth of man and resides in his capacity to make a new beginning. In the iron band of terror, which destroys the plurality of men and makes out of the many the One who unfailingly will act as though he himself were part of history and nature, a device has been found not only to liberate the natural and historical forces but to accelerate them to a speed they would never reach if left to themselves. Practically speaking, this means that terror executes on the spot the death sentences which Nature is supposed to have pronounced on races or individuals who are "unfit to live," or History on "dying classes," without waiting for the slower and less efficient processes of nature or history themselves. (Arendt 2004: 601)

This relentless movement of efficiency and progress operates through categories that turns people into the excluded or eliminated either as criminals or as nonhuman insects (ants).

For Conrad's narrator the colonial subject of *Heart of Darkness* appears as ants: "A lot of people, mostly black and naked, moved around like ants" (Conrad 1973: 43). In the spectral shadow of Kurtz's colonialism of "The horror! The horror!" we encounter for the first time human life spread bare to the nakedness of mere life that is specter-like indistinguishable from being lifeless or undead, which Giogio Agamben calls "bare life" (Agamben 2002: 158). Agamben refers the notion of bare life to Foucault's critique of biopolitics as biopower: "The ancient right to kill and let live gives way to an inverse model, which defines modern biopolitics, and which can be expressed by the formula *to make live and to let die*" (Agamben 2002: 82–3; italics in original). Arendt calls terror, this efficiency in denying or affirming—strictly in accordance with the logic of the idea that separates those who are worthy from those who are unworthy of being alive—the right to live. Those who have logically and thus categorically been rendered naked or bare reside in the ghostly sphere in between life and death, being neither alive nor dead. They are what in Auschwitz went under the name *Muselmann*. According to Agamben the *Muselmann* inhabits a spectral sphere of uncertainty, blurring the distinction between life and death and rendering both unstable and uncanny:

> In one case, he appears as the non-living, as the being whose life is not truly life; in the other, as he whose death cannot be called death, but only the production of a corpse—as the inscription of life in a dead area and, in death, of a living area. In both cases, what is called into question is

the very humanity of man, since man observes the fragmentation of his privileged tie to what constitutes him as human, that is, the sacredness of death and life. (Agamben 2002: 81)

As will be explored in the concluding part to this chapter, Conrad's Stein, in chapter 20 of *Lord Jim*, engages with an ancient Socratic concern about the sacredness of life and death, which Arendt perceives to be under attack in logical, dialectical movements with "progress" disregarding humanity's frailty and its precarious condition.

The horror that Conrad depicts as a modern, colonial, proto-totalitarian unacknowledged specter is an early form of a dialectical and efficient stripping down of life and death's sacredness, rendering both uncertain and ironic in the sense of unstable. As we have seen earlier, Conrad employs the term "naked" to describe this lack of distinction between thing and living being, between life and death. In *Heart of Darkness*, colonial subjects are thing-like—a "mass"—and naked, alive ("breathing"), and yet almost inanimate like a flowing mass of fluid or a resting piece of metal ("bronze"): "the crowd, of whose presence behind the curtain of trees I had been acutely conscious all the time, flowed out of the woods again, filled the clearing, covered the slope with a mass of naked, breathing, quivering, bronze bodies" (Conrad 1973: 108). In ways that have not been explored Agamben's notion of naked, "bare life" takes up Arendt's concept of superfluous life that she extracted out of a critical engagement with *Heart of Darkness*.

Now we come to see how the sense of ghostly uncertainty, which pervades Conrad's Marlow narration in terms of irony, establishes the trope of disavowed disappointment. The disappointing fact (from the perspective, at least, of what Arendt calls the terror of progressive logical motion) is that "savages" are not yet fully suppressed, that they are still alive. Conrad's narrator Marlow disavows the presence of "races and individuals who are" categorically defined in negative terms of disappointment as "unfit to live" (in the Arendt quote earlier) and are thus legally condemned to a ghostly, zombie-like existence where the differences between being dead and alive have become blurred: "They were dying slowly—it was very clear" (Conrad 1973: 44). The narrative disavows disappointment by casting what it describes (the ruthless brutality of colonialism and Kurtz as its hero or antihero) in a self-concealing, ironic, and highly uncertain mode, where, as readers, we are not sure about whether we encounter objects, animals, or human beings, either dead or alive:

> The thing looked as dead as the carcass of some animal. I came upon more pieces of decaying machinery, a stack of rusty rails. To the left

a clump of trees made a shady spot, where dark things seemed to stir feebly. I blinked, the path was steep. A horn tooted to the right, and I saw the black people run. A heavy and dull detonation shook the ground, a puff of smoke came from out of the cliff, and that was all. No change appeared on the face of the rock. They were building a railway. The cliff was not in the way or anything; but this objectless blasting was the work going on. (Conrad 1973: 42)

Objectless is the blast of Arendt's relentless terror of motion. It moves forward and uproots whatever might resist or disappoint it. This objectless teleology of ever-increasing positivity renders the world world-less or as Conrad's Marlow calls it unearthly: "The earth seemed unearthly. [. . .] It was unearthly, and the men were—No, they were not inhuman. Well, you know, that was the worst of it—this suspicion of their not being inhuman" (Conrad 1973: 69). In this key text of early modernism we already are face to face with our current posthumanist position after what has been called postmodernism.

As in the Ishiguro's *Never Let me Go* (or in postmodern and posthumanist films such as Ridley Scott's *Blade Runner* or Steven Spielberg's *Artificial Intelligence*; Mack 2016: 191–215) the suspense here revolves around what we know to be the thrill of the obvious which is here the unexpected: that those, who are by way of nomenclature or category, nonhumans (similar to the clones in Ishiguro's *Never Let me Go*) feel and behave exactly like us. Those defined as such are perhaps not inhuman or nonhuman as they are proclaimed to be by what Arendt calls the logic of the progressive dialectical idea. This means that what has been conceived of as disappointment, as negative to be subsumed by the movement of the positive, might actually not be disappointing after all. If this were the case, the presumption of the logical ideal would disintegrate and the whole dialectical edifice would collapse with it.

This suspenseful, or "thrilling," as Conrad's Marlow puts it in the following short quotation, recognition of the promise in what has been written off as disappointing, this realization that the colonial subjects are what they are, by dialectical logic, denied to be, namely humans, arises slowly only to be disavowed in the customary stereotyping of the Other as nonhuman, ghostly, animalistic disappointment: "It [i.e., the realization that colonial subjects 'were not inhuman'] would come slowly to one. They howled and leaped, and spun, and made horrified faces; but what thrilled you was just the thought of your remote kinship with this wild and passionate uproar" Conrad 1973: 69). These ghostly apparitions of caricature resemble Kurtz's brutes who, being negative or superfluous—hindering or disappointing dialectics' movement of the "redeeming idea"—are all or totally subject to the terror of extermination.

As Arendt makes clear, colonialism operates on the ghostly logic of economical transactions wherein there is no such thing as a stable, abiding form of value. Here everything is ceaselessly in process as in dialectics where the logical necessity of synthesizing movement renders any moment transitory. What turned into a (positive) synthesis a moment ago now has to be discarded and superseded as disappointment that we included only to exclude and disavow. Men like Kurtz "were representatives of an economy that relentlessly produced a superfluidity of men and capital" (Arendt 2004: 247). Arendt's analysis of ideology in terms of the logic of the idea refers ironically to the "redeeming idea"—"What redeems it is the idea only" (Conrad 1973: 32)—of *Heart of Darkness* that makes possible the violence of extermination.

It is the idea of progress as "the suppression of savage Customs" that creates what Conrad calls (in the quote earlier) the "unearthly" and what Arendt describes as the "uprooted" as well as "superfluous" reality of exploitation: "To be uprooted meant to have no place in the world, recognized and guaranteed by others; to be superfluous means to not belong to the world at all" (Arendt 2004: 612). Superfluous life is stripped of dignity, down to the state of being utterly naked that often precedes exterminations. The precondition of such denuding of any sense of dignity is the logical work of categorization: "The most persuasive argument in this respect, an argument of which Hitler like Stalin was very fond, is: You can't say A without saying B and C and so on, down to the end of the murderous alphabet. Here the coercive force of logicality seems to have its source; it springs from our fear of contradicting ourselves" (Arendt 2004: 609). Arendt elaborates on the paradoxical connection between the lonely totalitarian leader and his followers, arguing that what ties the two together is precisely the compulsory force of dialectically synthesizing, forward-moving logic, which ruthlessly disregards what actually resists its ideational framework.

What questions such dialectics of the end of history is precisely the unforeseen, the contradictory illogicality of diversity, and new beginnings. Within the logical settings of ideology and dialectics, the plurality of new beginnings appears to be negative or disappointing. This is why diversity has to be synthesized away, done away with, and banished from this world that has been, in Conrad's terms, rendered "unearthly": "Totalitarian rulers rely on the compulsion with which we can compel ourselves for the limited mobilization of people which even they still need; this inner compulsion is the tyranny of logicality against which nothing stands but the capacity of men to start something anew" (Arendt 2004: 609). Diversity consists of new beginnings. As such diversity's plurality is contradictory and it may thus appear to be negative and disappointing.

Kurtz's spiritualist whispering "The horror! The horror!" conjures the Spinozist and disappointing ghost of nature whose imperfect, diverse manifestations have been (exterminatory or genocide-like) rationalized as superfluous life: as life of the Others that have to be killed, just as negativity has to turn into a positive synthesis in the anthropocentric cosmos of perfection.

Romanticism and Modernism as Post-Idealist Forms of Disappointment: From Keats to Conrad's Destructive Element

Whereas idealism refrains from acknowledging disappointment in its unceasing dialectical forward-moving line of reason, it is time to distinguish romanticism from such idealist, promissory thrust. As we have seen in the opening section of Chapter 3, a broad equation of romanticism with idealism in terms of the visionary gives the impetus to Jerome McGann's late-twentieth-century critique of what he calls, following Heinrich Heine, the romantic ideology. McGann relates the term "ideology" via Heine and romanticism to Marx's critique of idealism as the German ideology. As McGann clearly shows, Marx uses the German case to differentiate it from a more socially critical French perspective:

> Where French Ideology was critical, anti-religious, rational, and socially progressive, the German was synthetic, fideistic, speculative, and supportive of established power. In Hegel this was explicitly the case, but Marx argued that the position of the neo-Hegelians was not fundamentally different. (McGann 1983: 8)

According to Heine and Marx, romanticism is a form of idealism that covers up real-existing economic injustices and social inequalities. Romantic here is the idealistic notion of history's progress and teleology which is also part of Marx's Hegelian heritage. McGann overlooks this crucial difference between Heine and Marx (as will be explained in the following paragraph). As we have seen in Chapter 3, Derrida analyzes Marx's fear of ghosts in terms of a past that keeps disappointing not only a present but also the promises of a better communist future. Marx's critique of what he calls the German ideology is focused on the promise of history's teleology toward the establishment of a communist society that has been freed from the ghostly shackles of past injustices and inequalities.

Heine, by contrast, remains enthralled by the specter of Spinoza which he reads as the ghostly presence of an open-minded conception of a non-anthropomorphic God, as Other of humanity's Anthropocene. Countering Jacobi's accusation of Spinoza's name as synonym of atheism, Heine defends the first modern Jewish thinker as preserving the ghostly presence of an ancient, deistic conception. "Only lack of understanding (*Unverstand*) and malicious intent (*Böswilligkeit*) could impute into this teaching (*Lehre* i.e. Spinoza's) the epithet 'atheistic'" (Heine 1968: 95), with these words Heine resurrects the ghost of Spinoza whom Jacobi intended to lay to rest by labeling his philosophy atheist and fatalist and thus unworthy of further attention. Rather than being an atheist, Heine proclaims Spinoza to be the true guarantor of God's ancient presence in modern, that is, anthropocentric if not Anthropocene times:

> No-one has ever spoken more sublime about the deity than Spinoza. Instead of saying that he denies God, one could say that he denies humanity (*Statt zu sagen, er leugne Gott, könnte man sagen, er leugne den Menschen*). All finite things are only modification of an infinite substance. All finite things partake of God, the human intellect is only a small ray of light of the infinite thinking (*nur eine Lichtstrahl des unendlichen Denkens*), the human body is only a small atom of the infinite extension (*der menschliche Leib ist nur ein Atom der unendlichen Ausdehnung*); God is the infinite cause of both, the spirits and the bodies (*der Geister und der Leiber*), natura naturans. (Heine 1968: 95)

This spectral presence of a deism within the assumed atheism of the first modern Jewish thinker relates to Heine's interpretation of history and the ghostly role of the Jews within it. According to Heine, the Jews were the guardians of antiquity, of a past which has often been used to stigmatize them as Oriental, or primitive embodiments of a disappointment that refused to embrace the future-oriented redemptive message of Christianity: "Like a ghost, who guards a treasure, which has once been entrusted to it while still being alive, so resided this slaughtered people (*dies gemordete Volk*), this ghostly people (*dieses Volk-Gespenst*), in its dark ghettos and preserved the Hebrew Bible there" (Heine 1968: 78). Heine depicts the Jewish people in a language that anticipates the description of colonial subjects in Conrad's *Heart of Darkness*.

First of all, there is a striking, almost chiastic, parallelism of being a murdered or "slaughtered" and being a "ghostly" people—residing in the uncertain state between life and death. Moreover, Heine ties the survival of the seemingly dead past to the presence of a specter-like people which

Conrad's narrator Marlow depicts in a derogatory tone in *Heart of Darkness*. As we have seen in the previous section, the very humanity of the Other is ironically (that is to say, self-consciously) called into question. The uncertainty of *Heart of Darkness*'s ironic tone alerts us to the discrimination and the racism that partakes of what Arendt would later call the idealism of ideology wherein the logic of the "progressive" idea becomes drawn out in all its murderous consequences.

The evolutionary and colonialist context of *Heart of Darkness* relegates non-Western people to the assumed "primitive" or savage stage of pre-modernity. With his native, Polish background, Conrad must have been as critical of such evolutionary, Hegelian dialectical approaches to history as his contemporary compatriot, the British-Polish anthropologist Bronislaw Malinowski (Mack 2001: 90–106). Similar to colonialized as well as stateless Jewish people, the Poles were relegated to an inferior status in Hegelian and evolutionist approaches: "Given that Poland was victimized by a 'historic' nation and state, it was implied that Poland must for Hegel be of 'non-historic' nature. All this was totally inadmissible for Poles" (Jerischna 1988: 132). As Ernest Gellner has shown, the progressive movement implicit in the early social anthropology of Frazer grows out of the dialectical structure of Hegel's approach to the past that becomes disavowed as disappointing and as such relegated to the negative and its ensuing inclusive exclusion within a newly formed positive synthesis:

> Though Frazer's pervasive evolutionism is clearly inspired by Darwin rather than Hegel, nonetheless he too sees the global pattern of development as passing an ultimate moral verdict. *Weltgeschichte* still remains *Weltgericht*. Reason, though of British empiricist variety this time, still guides history, albeit loosely. How pleasing can these world-historical verdicts be for a member of a nation whose political institutions have apparently *not* been fit to survive? (Gellner 1988: 170)

One way to articulate displeasure with superseding, progressivist accounts of history is to introduce ghosts into the narrative—such as Kurtz's spectral whispering "The horror" which disappointingly deflects his horrendous genocidal command "Exterminate all the brutes." Drawing on Nietzsche's critique of historicism, Mark Sandy has recently argued that spectral apparitions recall disappointing moments which we have been appointed not for memory's recall but for the act of forgetting: "A wilfully forgotten moment [. . .], Nietzsche reminds us, 'returns as a ghost' and disturbs the peace of a later moment" (Sandy 2013: 6). It is in such spectral and rather unexplained context of displeasing disturbances in which acts of failure materialize in what I call the new genre of Conrad's Marlow narrated and male-centered novels of disavowed disappointment.

The most pronounced early novel of such new genre is Conrad's *Lord Jim*. As Hillis Miller has pointed out, the narration of this novel is as unreliable as the tone of voice is ironic and uncertain and ambiguous in *Heart of Darkness*: "In *Lord Jim* no point of view is entirely trustworthy. The novel is a complex design of interrelated minds, no one of which can be taken as secure point of reference from which the others may be judged" (Miller 1982: 32). There are narrations within the narration but Marlow is the narrator who presents them all. Marlow has a special interest in proving the heroic character of Jim and "Jim's desertion [i.e., of the ship *Patna*] seems especially deplorable to Marlow because Jim looks so trustworthy, so perfect an example of the unassuming nobility of the tradition from which he has sprung" (Miller 1982: 27). This is the tradition on which the British Empire was built.

The proto-totalitarian context of colonialism within *Lord Jim* will return in amplified, horrified form in *Heart of Darkness*. Because some of the themes surrounding the topic of disavowed disappointment within the narration of *Lord Jim* (1900) will resurface in *Heart of Darkness* (1902), the concluding part to this chapter now returns to the former, earlier novel: "*Lord Jim* would offer a counterpoint to *Heart of Darkness*: again, an imaginative European would become a trader in a tropical outpost, but this time the adventure would be apparently redemptive: he would atone for past disgrace and largely vindicate his romantic aspirations" (Watts 1986: 17). How can *Lord Jim* offer a counterpoint to *Heart of Darkness* taking into account that it was published two years before (1900, with *Heart of Darkness* being published two years later in 1902)?

This raises the more crucial question of whether Jim indeed redeems himself, which is highly doubtful. This promissory or redemptive reading of *Lord Jim* becomes even more questionable if we take into account that Jim's failure on the *Patna* already repeats an earlier disappointment in regard to the fulfillment of duties as Fredric Jameson has pointed out: "There was indeed an earlier scene that contained the elements of this one: lifeboat, people in distress, hesitation at the abyss of the instant and on the break of the leap to freedom. The point is that in that earlier scene Jim *failed* to jump" (Jameson 2002: 252). Critics keen to disavow this sense of disappointment in their redemptive readings of *Lord Jim* thus ignore earlier repetitions of failure. These repetitions make the romance or fairy-tale-like ending of Conrad's novel literally appear like the self-consciously produced illusions of *Heart of Darkness*'s saving idea that ironically resurrects "faith" in promises and redemptions. In doing so they lay to rest spectral disturbances. Seen from this perspective, *Heart of Darkness* ends like *Lord Jim* with faith and redemption cast into the questioning light of irony and disappointment. Facing Kurtz's widow, Marlow's knowledge is ironic or Socratic:

> "But you have heard him! You know!" she cried.
> "Yes, I know." I said with something like despair in my heart, but bowing my head before the faith that was in her, before that great and saving illusion that shone with an unearthly glow in the darkness, in the triumphant darkness from which I could not have defended her—from which I could not even defend myself. (Conrad 1973: 119)

The glow of light in the darkness is itself ambiguous, because it is spectral or unearthly, recalling Kurtz's and his fellow colonialists' horror which denudes the earth, rendering it and its populations naked or in Arendt's terms "superfluous." Conrad's male-centered Marlow narrated narratives of disavowed disappointment end with the paradoxical triumph of the spectral glow of darkness. Readers seem to expect a triumph at the close of the novel, especially at *Lord Jim*'s whose romance-like second part explicitly raises such expectations only to disappoint them:

> The longing for the second chance, for the return of a situation in which you can prove yourself, this time triumphantly, is, when it declares itself in Jim's agony after the *Patna* episode and his trial, merely the repetition of a repetition: the real second chance, in the event the only one, is the *Patna* crisis itself, in which Jim is now given the unexpected opportunity to complete his long-suspended act, and to land in the cutter over which he was poised so many years before. (Jameson 2002: 252)

Yet even in Jameson's critical reading of the romance-like, promissory aspect of *Lord Jim*, disappointment must not show its face. How come? Jameson's attempt at reading Conrad's novels in terms of romance and reification is part of a larger promissory, dialectical framework which he delineates in *The Political Unconscious* (of which the chapter on Conrad is the concluding part).

Jameson interprets Jim's failure as the deficiency of his capitalist-colonialist class (in Marxist parlance, the bourgeoisie). By historicizing Nietzsche's disappointment with ethics as mere social conventions and fictions serving the bourgeoisie's will to power, Jameson reads *Lord Jim* with particular reference to the Stein episode, whose passage on the destructive element he does not mention, as historical manifestation of a declining class. The whole of Conrad and, more generally, all forms of literature become legible for Jameson only within this historicist, dialectical framework, which functions to lay to rest any romantic (Keats's or Heine's) specters of destruction and disappointment.

Religions and their ideas partake of such dialectical rationalizations and Conrad's disappointing romance appears as document of an outdated past, fitting Max Weber's sociology of religion as charismatic stage that will itself be superseded: "In Weber's scheme of things, all social institutions describe a fatal trajectory from the traditional to the rationalized, passing through a crucial transitional stage which is the moment—the vanishing mediation—of so called charisma" (Jameson 2002: 238). Jameson establishes interesting connections between Conrad's novel and Weber's sociology of religion by invoking an early passage from *Lord Jim* describing 800 Eastern Muslim pilgrims whose safe passage over the sea Jim abandons when he jumps from the *Patna*. The narrative describes them as "eight hundred men and women with faith and hopes, with affections and memories [. . .] coming from north and south and from the outskirts of the East" (Conrad 1986: 53). Here is faith, as it will reappear in the Western setting of Kurtz's widow at the end of *Heart of Darkness*.

In *Heart of Darkness* the idea is extraneously superimposed on the Western "colonialists" (Conrad 1973: 31) who are "conquerors, and for that you want only brute force" (Conrad 1973: 31). In his contact with these colonialists the narrator Marlow becomes so disillusioned and dispirited that he seems to find solace only in "the redeeming facts of life" (Conrad 1973: 52). Kurtz's widow might have faith, but her husband's followers appear in the sinister light of "faithless pilgrims bewitched inside a rotten fence" (Conrad 1973: 52). The same contrast between the genuine faith of the colonized (the Muslim pilgrims journeying on the *Patna*) and the secular faithlessness of the colonizers (the British officers who do not care for the life of those entrusted with them on the *Patna*) emerges in *Heart of Darkness* that already features in the earlier and longer novel *Lord Jim*.

However, in *Lord Jim* the Eastern pilgrims are faithful and they appear in the light of genuine human affections and memories. Their faith partakes of an idea but it is an authentic one which does not need to be superimposed to deflect the spectral shadow of its disappointing reality. Here the idea is not an illusory cover (an ironic euphemism for the ultimately disappointing promise of the West's efficiency and superiority over the Eastern, or premodern so-called "primitive" or "savage" stage of history) for exterminatory practices but is itself performative.

For the Eastern pilgrims in *Lord Jim* the idea is a call: "At the call of an idea, they had left their forests, their clearings, the protection of their rulers, their prosperity, their poverty, the surroundings of their youth and the graves of their fathers" (Conrad 1986: 53). In contrast to the clear economic interests that drive Western colonialists, the Eastern pilgrims of *Lord Jim* are classless or at least indifferent to social hierarchies. Faith here is a call, a vocation and not a deceiving cover for an ideology, for the ruthless perpetration of the logic of the dialectical idea, as Arendt would call it.

Whereas Conrad's novel sets in relief the contrast between these "unconscious pilgrims of an exacting belief" (Conrad 1986: 54) and the consciously ironic usage of faith as concealing colonialist brutality, Jameson disavows this sense of disappointment with the modern West by making his theoretical approach partake of a larger dialectical historicized account of progress, guided by the Hegelian notion of history's presumed teleology or "inevitability" (Kojève's "end of history"): "Clearly, notions such as 'progressive' and 'regressive' are simply ethical categories projected onto political and historical phenomena in classical Marxism (but also in Hegel), these categories are maintained but fused into a whole new order of thinking by the concept of historical inevitability" (Jameson 2002: 223–4). From such dialectical perspective of the historicized idea, modernism turns idealist and loses its rather disappointing spectral moment of Keats's destructive core: "Yet modernism can one and the same time be read as Utopian compensation for everything reification brings with it" (Jameson 2002: 225). Keeping faith with Hegel's dialectics, Jameson only allows for the momentary presence of the negative that almost immediately morphs into a compensatory positive synthesis (that here goes under the name of utopia whose presence is historically inevitable). Reification is the disappointing and destructive remnant that imperialist and capitalist modernity carries to the shores of modernism, which dialectically compensates this negativity and turns the same into the triumphant progress implicit in the notion "historical inevitability." Modernism, according to promissory or dialectical accounts of it such as Jameson's highly influential one, disavows disappointment by laying to rest specters of the thing-like remnant associated with the passé, the bygone, the imperfect past.

In true Hegelian dialectical fashion Jameson uses the term "negative" as the foundation of the abolition or transubstantiation of negativity. Hence:

> A negative hermeneutics, then, would on the contrary wish to use the narrative raw material shared by myth and "historical" literature to sharpen our sense of historical difference, and to stimulate an increasingly vivid apprehension of what happens when plot falls into history, so to speak, and enters the force fields of modern society. (Jameson 2002: 117)

When in this dialectical framework "plot falls into history," we encounter, as in Jameson's interpretation of *Lord Jim*, Weber's sociology of disenchantment as well as Lukács's Marxist literary theory of reification. Jameson separates this disappointing moment where we are left with the mere materiality of things deprived of any meaning (sacred or secular) from any connotations of what I would call the promise within disappointment.

Following Jameson, scholars of modernism have taken exception to the paradox of promise residing in disappointment and vice versa. Similar to George Lukács's discovering in the disappointing consciousness of the proletariat (which is that of reification) simultaneously as well as paradoxically the hope of a better future, Walter Benjamin contaminates the disappointment of the reified with the promise of desire attached to commodification in his reading of Paris as capital of the nineteenth century which constitutes his *Arcades Project*. Such contamination of the abject and the appealing has, however, caused much consternation in the field of literary criticism and theory. Related to the way in which Jameson has faulted Lukács for a lack of utopianism, Bill Brown takes Benjamin to task for cohabitating Marx's critique of "commodity fetishism" with the libidinal economy of Freud's promissory agent of desire:

> Benjamin's appropriation of Marx, which serves here to mark a long history of such appropriation, misrepresents Marx because it seems to insist on understanding our desire for objects as more primary than understanding the structure through which they become commodities. Insofar, then, as accounts of commodity fetishism describe an aesthetics fascination with objects—the projection of an aesthetic value considered to be the property of a thing—they depart from Marx's theory. But such departure has become second nature in literary and cultural study no doubt because those institutions of a rapidly developing consumer culture (developing rapidly even as Marx wrote) have made the human fascination with objects seem the more pressing object of our historical attention. Indeed, it is hardly possible to think seriously about material objects in the closing decades of the nineteenth century without beginning to think about the department store, where people were meant to circulate through a newly theatricalized world of goods, where anyone was welcome to merely browse, where management's idea was not simply to sell merchandise but also to inculcate desire. (Brown 2003: 31)

Can we separate structures and the desires we might read into them? The economics of our consumer society (evolving from Benjamin's department stores of the Paris Arcades) would prove that we should be wary of such dialectical compartmentalizations. The structural aspect would be sober and disappointing, whereas desire denotes pleasure and promise.

How can we understand economics without taking into account the psychology of affects and their interaction with seemingly lifeless objects or things? For Lukács as well as for Benjamin our attempt to establish clear distinctions between the disappointing moment of reification (which makes us see the structures that make possible commodification) and the promissory call of desire partakes of dialectics wherein the negative becomes invisible through its erasure in the positive. Whereas dialectics compartmentalizes and spreads out disappointment and hope into two distinct moments, a new way of thinking would insist on the copresence of these commonly juxtaposed entities. This simultaneity of the negative and the positive, of the disappointing and the promising manifests itself in the spectral *revenant* of the past. Stein in *Lord Jim*, recalling Keats, calls it "the destructive element." Jameson does not allow for such simultaneity. Instead he advances the dialectical concept of historical movement grounded in teleology, or, as Jameson calls it "historical inevitability" (Jameson 2002: 224) which he characterizes as purely positive, as "necessarily Utopian" (Jameson 2002: 276).

Lukács's critical theory is not dialectical enough for Jameson, because here reification might remain negative or destructive and thus resists history's posited turn toward utopia. For Jameson, at least, Lukács's analysis of reification comes dangerously close to avowing disappointment and Conrad's Keats derived destructive element. This is why Jameson singles out Lukács as a critical theorist in the Marxist tradition, whose modernist critique of reification courts the danger of embracing, like Conrad's Stein, the negative or destructive:

> So Lukács is not wrong to associate the emergence of this modernism with the reification which is its precondition; but he oversimplifies and deproblematizes a complicated and interesting situation by ignoring the Utopian vocation of the newly reified sense, the mission of this heightened and autonomous language of color to restore at least a symbolic experience of libidinal gratification to a world drained of it, a world of extension, grey and merely quantifiable. (Jameson 2002: 48)

While the term "libidinal" might evoke Benjamin's peculiar contamination of Freud's psychoanalysis with surrealism, Jewish messianism, romanticism, and an apocalyptical questioning of progress recast as destructive "storm blowing from paradise," Jameson has a rather uncomplicated dialectical notion of history in mind that actually manifests the ruthless necessity and inevitability with which Benjamin takes issue: "History is therefore the experience of Necessity, and it is this alone which forestall thematization or reification as mere object of representation or as one master code among many others" (Jameson 2002: 87). Jameson's utopia is dialectical and hence historicist and as thus manifests "rather the inexorable *form* of events" (Jameson 2002: 87) disregarding any content.

Apprehensive of such idealist disavowal of disappointment the romanticism of Keats and the modernism of Conrad dwells on a destructive core in terms of on an elemental negativity. In a reified way, Conrad's destructive element insists on its thingness, on its materiality (reification is a translation of Lukács's term *Verdinglichung*). In doing so, it is the very irresolvable negativity of destruction's core that resists, by way of reification, any dialectical transubstantiation into any form of posited positivity (be that Jameson's Ernst Bloch-inspired utopia or Kojève's or Fukuyama's Hegelian end of history).

According to Lukács, the dialectical utopianism which Jameson advocates is like its supposed opposite, that is, empiricism, itself a product of reified consciousness: "Reified consciousness must hopelessly (*hoffnungslos*) remain beholden equally to the radical extremes of rude empiricism (*rohen Empirismus*) and abstract utopianism" (Lukács 1968: 164). Paradoxically Jameson's utopia here appears to lack any grounds for hope. This is so, because it is itself an abstraction: an idealist offshoot of imposing *Heart of Darkness*'s redeeming idea onto the rude, empirical reality of exploitation.

Arendt's analysis of ideology as the logic of the idea benefits from Lukács's complementary approach. Lukács argues that the ideological is abstracted or cut off from life (*vom Leben abgeschnittenen Ideologie* Lukács 1968: 151). As a separate entity the logic of the idea has been superimposed on everyday life and history. Separation does not preclude impact. On the contrary, as ideology the idea all the more forcefully determines empirical life and thus gives rise to a what Lukács calls a spectral materiality (*gespenstiger Gegenständlichkeit* Lukács 1968: 194). As has been discussed throughout this and the preceding chapter, far from being, as common knowledge holds, a way of re-enchanting or spiritualizing life, the spectral partakes of the disappointment that accompanies Keats's and Conrad's destructive element. In Lukács's materialist deconstruction of idealist vestiges within Marxist dialectics, the ghostly is the destructive core of reification:

> The transformation of the commodity relationship into a thing of "spectral materiality" can therefore not come to a rest in the commodification of all objects which are required for the satisfaction of needs (*Gegenstände der*

Bedürfnissbefriedigung). It [i.e., this transformation] imposes its structure on the entire consciousness of humanity: humanity's characteristics and capacities no longer form the organic whole of the person, but appear as "things" (*"Dinge"*) which the human being possesses (*"besitzt"*) and sells (*"veräussert"*) like the various things of the environment (*wie die verschiedenen Gegenstände der äusseren Welt*. Lukács 1968: 194)

In this crucial quotation, Lukács (similar to Benjamin's desire-based approach as critiqued by Brown in the quotation earlier) extends Marx's notion of the spectral from the material sphere of objects to that of human consciousness. More importantly, it is this spectral consciousness of the reified that defines Lukács's conception of the proletariat. This introduction of the spectral within the core of the carrier of hope, which is the proletariat in Marxist thought, renders the same at the same time disappointing and destructive. As Derrida has clearly shown, Marx does not like ghosts: "He [i.e., Marx] detests all ghosts, the good and the bad, he thinks one can break with this frequentation" (Derrida 1994: 113). By placing the spectral within the core consciousness of the proletariat, Lukács radically recasts materialism. He achieves this by outdoing materialism's idealist, Hegelian heritage. In a romantic as well as modernist way, disappointment thus becomes the ground of hope and promise.

As we will see in the concluding part of this chapter, Conrad's Keats-derived destructive element partakes of what Lukács conceptualizes as the negative, reified consciousness of the proletariat. Crucially, negativity here does not undergo a dialectical transubstantiation into the positive. It remains adamantly negative but in doing so it also gains a liberating force that sets it free from all traditional pressures of societal conformity. The destructive, disappointingly reified consciousness of the exploited, proletarian class here emerges as the modern precondition for establishing ancient spiritual, Socratic exercises in new form that Foucault, following the ancient historian Pierre Hadot (Nehamas 1998: 164), has rediscovered as the care of the self. This chapter will close in a state of simultaneity wherein Conrad's romantic-modernism of the destructive element freezes in a state of contamination with the ancient Socratic practice which the late Foucault has theorized as the care of the self. How can the abject or destructive simultaneously be liberating or redemptive? Negativity in its non-transubstantiated state before dialectically morphing into the positive, precisely through its society defying, through its antisocial affects and effects, promises in its collapse—its breakdown or breakage—a break with the continuity of exploitation. It is this break with hegemonies and homogeneity that establishes a turn toward new conceptions of promise which are at the same ancient ones. They are no longer grand or all-encompassing societally but revolve in a Spinozist way around the self's preservation (*conatus*) which is here simultaneously that of a society that no longer defines itself in opposition to the negative or abject or destructive element.

Conrad's Keats-Inspired Destructive Element and Lukács's Conception of the Proletarian Consciousness as Negative, Disappointing Platform for Non-conforming Forms of the Care of the Self

The way out of the inhumanity of capitalist commodification is its disappointing and destructive contemplation within the disappointed consciousness of the proletariat. Lukács in fact contaminates Marx's command to change the world with a radical contemplative position, which is that of the consciousness of the proletariat: "the meaning of actions in terms of changing reality is in its materialist substrate even more contemplative than, for instance the cognitive ideal of Greek philosophy" (*auf das materielle Substrat des Handelns dieses Verhalten noch viel kontemplativer ist als etwa das Erkenntnisideal der griechischen Philosophie*) (Lukács 1968: 237). In other words, contrasting with dialectical, and in Jameson's terms, utopian, Hegelian traditions within Marxism, Lukács renders the promissory term "proletariat" (as in revolutionary proletariat) itself ghostly, disappointing, and destructive. As in Marx, the proletariat constitutes the only hope for Lukács, as he put in italics in the original German: "Only the consciousness of the proletariat can show the way out of the crisis of capitalism" (*Aus der Krise des Kapitalismus kann nur das Bewusstsein des Proletariats den Ausweg zeigen*) Lukács 1968: 163). Yet this bearer of hope resembles what Stein in Conrad's *Lord Jim* calls "the destructive element."

Out of the preceding triangular reading that moves from Jameson's idealist disappointment with Lukács's missing utopianism (informing Jameson's misreading of *Lord Jim*) to a neglected form of non-idealist modernism (that takes its cue from Keats's romanticism of a destructive core), we can now better understand Conrad's critique of idealism as ideology *qua* "romantic promises" in *Lord Jim*.

Jim fits the standard congruence of idealism and romanticism. He believes in and propagates the ideas and the ideology of the British bourgeoisie and the British Empire. As we have seen, Conrad's narrator, Marlow, has invested so much trust and hope into Jim's character partly because of his belief in the logic of the ideas of ideology that makes Jim an idealist romantic who trusts, promises, and hopes as promulgated by the popular literature of his class: "the source of all Jim's trouble is his romanticism, that childish image of himself as a hero which has its source in the fraudulent literature and sticks with him all his life" (Miller 1982: 29). This is romantic ideology which is idealist (as discussed in Chapter 3) and it needs to be distinguished from the romanticism of avowed disappointment with "that most fierce destruction" (Keats 1970: 325) at sea as formulated at the end of Keats's poem "To J. H. Reynolds Esquire."

Indeed, Conrad continues with Keats's descent from being "at home" (Keats 1970: 325), surrounded by the comforts of hope, to the haunting sight "too far into the sea" (Keats 1970: 325), and he turns this movement into a major modernist trope of disappointment in the Stein episode of *Lord Jim*. Critical approaches to Conrad's novel have been preoccupied with factual, historical accounts (Watt 1979) of a ship that has been abandoned by its colonial crew such as the steamship *Jeddah* (see Sherry 1966: 299–309). As Miller has pointed out: "In all these cases knowledge of the historical sources makes the story based on them not less but more inscrutable, more difficult to understand" (Miller 1982: 37). It is time to discover the literary and philosophical genre of Conrad's male-centered novels of disavowed disappointment and locate their conception in the romantic-modernist critique of such disavowal.

Stein in Marlow's narration of *Lord Jim*'s chapter 20 coins Conrad's notion of the destructive element. The destruction is precisely that of romantic promises and hopes, which the poetic voice of Keats's "To J. H. Reynolds Esquire" encounters while straying from the happiness of home by looking too far and deep into the rather disappointing ravenous appetite at sea "where every maw/the greater on the less feeds evermore" (Keats 1970: 325). Conrad keeps the location of the sea. However, he shifts the attention away from the nonhuman world of animals feeding on each other to the human and, in a performative, socially constructed way (as discussed in Chapter 3), a male-centered will to power.

A class of Western colonialists like Lord Jim and Mr. Kurtz exerts this domination over those which are categorically or ideologically defined as inferior as colonized like the 800 Eastern pilgrims of an exacting faith whom Jim abandons to their death in the destructive waves of the sea. The "saving ideas" justifying this rapacious colonialism constitute the disavowal of disappointment in the ideology of domination. *Heart of Darkness* and *Lord Jim* bring to the fore the irony and ambiguity of such ideationally and socially constructed, male-centered disavowal of actual horror and exploitation.

The term "lord" emerges in the full irony of its usage, at least here— comparable to the exclusivity of the "idea only" in *Heart of Darkness* which becomes revealed as a cover for the brutality perpetrated in its name. The courage of colonial lords like Jim is yet another romantic veil hiding the disappointing, spectral reality of what factually keeps taking place in Western history's exploitative actuality, as *Lord Jim* clearly states: "There was always a doubt of his courage. The truth seems to be that it is impossible to lay the ghost of a fact" (Conrad 1986: 187). The spectral occurrence of the fact avows its disappointment which the "idea only"—the romantic promise—has sought to disavow (the ideology that keeps the likes of Mr. Kurtz and Jim going). In *Heart of Darkness* the hard-to-lay-to-rest ghost of a fact manifests itself in Kurtz's whispered, spectral last words "The horror! The horror!" that point to his actual colonialist proto-totalitarian exclamation "Exterminate all the brutes!" In *Lord Jim* Conrad describes the male-centered ethos of disavowed disappointment apropos the whole class of Western colonialists as follows:

> They were all equally tinged by a high-minded absurdity of intention which made their futility profound and touching. To fling away your daily bread so to get your hands free for a grapple with a ghost may be an act of prosaic heroism. Men had done it before (though we who have lived to know full well that it is not the haunted soul but the hungry body that makes an outcast), and men who had eaten and meant to eat every day had applauded the credible folly. (Conrad 1986: 187)

This quotation from the opening of *Lord Jim*'s chapter 19 highlights the reified, materialist consciousness that partakes of Lukács's conception of the proletariat. There is a double disappointment here of thing as well as ghost which Lukács, as we have seen earlier, has characterized as reification of a spectral thingness. Once we assuage the need for material necessities, they keep haunting us in ghostly forms. This seemingly never-ending circle of needs and their satisfaction causes disappointment.

However, Conrad's male-centered and Marlow narrated novels of disavowed disappointment illuminate the absurdity of high-minded intentions by casting them into the spectral light of their destructive actuality (thus displacing Keats's birds and fishes of prey into a more horrendous human reality). *Lord Jim*'s chapter 19 reveals the spectral as the disappointing *revenant* of the factual, namely, as "the ghost of a fact" and thus prepares for Stein's embrace of disappointment in terms of "the destructive element" in the following chapter:

> Yes! Very funny this terrible thing is. A man that is born falls into a dream like a man who falls into the sea. If he tries to climb out into the air as inexperienced people endeavour to do, he drowns—*nicht wahr*? . . . No! I

tell you! The way is to the destructive element submit yourself, and with the exertion of your hands and feet in the water make the deep, deep sea keep you up. So if you ask me—how to be? (Conrad 1986: 200)

Critics and theorists have so far ignored how this passage critiques the genre of the male-centered novel of disavowed disappointment which Conrad first develops in a highly ambiguous and ironic manner. As we have seen, Conrad transposes Keats's core of destruction from the natural to the human sphere: to that of society, colonialism, and, in a more general sense, exploitation and reification. Stein's sea imagery for the description of the destructive element is thus metaphorical. However, the image of someone struggling not to drown in the sea has a striking reference (in the first part of Conrad's novel) in the 800 Muslim pilgrims whom Jim and his fellow colonialists abandoned in the ship wreck of the *Patna*. Those who drown are thus victims of societal and historical injustices.

The struggle for survival at sea has a larger historical and societal point of reference in the death at sea of the 800 Muslim pilgrims. The Stein episode in chapter 20 links back to the opening chapters of *Lord Jim* where the hierarchies between colonizers (the British crew of the *Patna*) and colonized (the passengers on the *Patna*) are set into relief (see Chapter 3). Yet, Stein seems to be advising an individual rather than a group of people; it is Jim after his failure to save the lives on the *Patna*. The setting of the Stein episode in chapter 20 might obscure the larger societal and historical points of reference in Conrad's novel. It is the self that is apparently the center of Stein's advice regarding the destructive element.

In this context it is illuminating to cross-reference Michel Foucault's intellectual itinerary from a concern with the social and political topics of power and knowledge to that of the care of the self, which is the context in which Stein gives his advice to Jim instructing him on "how to be." As Nehamas has put it: "It took Foucault a long time—most of his life—to come to think of himself as a philosopher who had always been concerned with the care of the self and whose project, despite its general applications, was essentially individual" (Nehamas 1998: 169). However, neither Stein's advice to Jim (within the larger context of Conrad's novel) nor Foucault's theory of the Socratic care of the self is simply addressed to an individual. Both Stein's and Foucault's address to a self has larger political implication as Nehamas acknowledges when he argues that it is "useful to excluded, oppressed groups that have not been able to speak in their own voice so far" (Nehamas 1998: 168). How can a self-centered advice as to Stein's question "how to be" have political implication for those who are excluded or stigmatized as "disappointments" by society at large?

To address this question, it is helpful to show that Foucault's more explicit political work on power and knowledge has been concerned with the self too. However, in this case he traced how power constructs and creates versions subjectivity which are then reified. In this process of reification, the subject turns into an object, an object of disappointment. Foucault's theory of the care of the self returns to an ancient Socratic version of knowledge which is not that of power over people but how the self might find ways out of such societal and political pressures wherein she or he becomes reified as a subject in terms of an object of power. According to Foucault, our modern notion of knowledge subjects the subject to obedience to the objectified measures of truth, whereas the ancient understanding of the care of the self enables the individual to find his or her own truth. Nehamas calls into question whether Foucault's conception of Plato's Socrates (the opposite of Nietzsche's critique of an otherworldly Socrates) as not being hostile to worldly, embodied life is entirely accurate: "Foucault's case against the otherworldly interpretation of Socrates's last words would be stronger if the *Phaedo* never presented life as sickness" (Nehamas 1998: 160). Be that as it may, Foucault clearly differentiates modern ways of control, performance measurement, and other forms of surveillance from what he theorizes as the Socratic care of the self: "Foucault argues that the vocabulary of 'caring' is always positive; it suggests not the surveillance of prison guards or the solicitude of parents" (Nehamas 1998: 160). I would argue that it addresses Stein's question of "how to be."

Stein advises Jim not to fight but to embrace the disappointing or destructive element. By not trying to reach above the waves, Stein's self engages in a form of ascesis which Foucault has singled out as the ancient Socratic form of self-knowledge rather than knowledge that conforms to power or society at large. The self that embraces the destructive element and thus diminishes itself does not renounce but finds itself. Self-renunciation is indeed the modern form of reified and objectified selfhood which is conforming to societal norms of power: "We understand ascesis as progressive renunciation leading to the essential renunciation, self-renunciation. We hear it with these resonances" (Foucault 2005: 319). Not so the Socratic embrace of the destructive element wherein, as Stein metaphorically describes it, the self gains knowledge of how to swim and how to be:

> I think ascesis (*askěsis*) had a profoundly different meaning for the Ancients. First of all, because obviously it does not involve the aim of arriving at self-renunciation at the end of ascesis. It involved, rather constituting oneself through *askěsis*. Or, more precisely, let's say it involved

arriving at the formation of a full, perfect, complete, and self-sufficient relationship with oneself, capable of producing the self-transfiguration that is the happiness one takes in oneself. (Foucault 2005: 319–20)

Through the ascetic embrace of Stein's destructive element the self disentangles itself from societal pressures that demand success and power, or, in Stein's terms, a reaching above the waves. Rather than fight or disavow the destructive and disappointing, work along with it and thus abandon quests for domination (such as colonialism and other forms of exploitation). The Stein quotation from *Lord Jim*'s chapter 20 is dense, not to say, elliptical. Crucially, the formulation of the destructive elements in abbreviated form responds to the Socratic and spiritual question of how to swim on the waves of life or, as Stein puts it, "how to be."

By not reaching above to obtain societal norms of knowledge and power, the ascetic self establishes a self-sufficient relationship with itself and with the waves on which it swims. Crucially, here it transforms itself, rather being changed and expelled as part of a dialectical process shaping history's progression toward a larger political teleology (the "end of history" in Kojève and Fukuyama). The ascetic self-transformation consists in an avowal of disappointment which enables Stein's embrace of the destructive element. In the following chapters we will see how Conrad's new genre of the ideationally and socially constructed male-centered novel of disavowed disappointment engages with the critique of historical promises that willfully ignore history's and society's destructive element.

5

The Trajectory of Conrad's Novel of Disavowed Disappointment

Hegel's Dialectics, F. Scott Fitzgerald's *The Great Gatsby*, and Saul Bellow's *Ravelstein*

Introduction: Disappointment and the Gender Dynamics of the Novel

Is there a human cost to modernity? A cost would assume a price—perhaps a heavy one—for achievements accomplished through the course of human history. What if the price is too high or the demands involved are too painful? It would be worse still should there be a cost and no recompense for the price stipulated for goods that never show up, or only arrive in parts, or exclusively reach addressees that are quite remote and out of touch with the commoners whose hopes for modernity's promises of equality and inclusivity were understandably quite high.

This chapter discusses the ramification of Hegel's idealistic dialectics for social and intellectual life in the twentieth and twenty-first centuries, and in doing so it contributes to a new understanding of the genre that is about the life of commoners, of ordinary people. As Terry Eagleton has argued, the "novel was born at the same time as modern science, and shares its sober, secular, hard-headed, investigative spirit, along with its suspicion of classical authority" (Eagleton 2005: 7). Along with this suspicion of authority comes the promise of social, economic, and political equality. As Eagleton makes clear the novel is indeed about the life of common people, disregarding any traditional social hierarchies, which as Walter Benjamin has famously shown in his work of art essay, structure the production as well as the reception of aesthetics in a pre-secular world before the dawn of Spinozist modern science. George Lukács has been the first to differentiate the novel from its premodern form, the epic. Eagleton draws on this distinction when he characterizes the novel as the genre of and for commoners:

> The epic deals with a world of nobles and military heroes, whereas the novel deals with common life. It is the great *popular* genre, the one mainstream literary mode which speaks the language of the people. [...] It is not the first literary form in which the common people stage an appearance. But it is the first to treat them with unwavering seriousness. Our contemporary version of this is no doubt the soap opera, which we enjoy not so much for the occasional dramatic turn of plot but because we find the familiar and everyday a strange source of fascination in itself. (Eagleton 2005: 7)

Because the novel originates with the Spinozist promise of a common, nonhierarchical, and scientific modern world, it has almost exclusively been characterized by an unwavering optimism. This chapter will introduce a new genre of the novel not of promise and optimism but of disappointment. The disappointment in question partakes of a history of unfulfilled promises for common people.

After the betrayal of the French Revolution's Spinozist promises of equality in Robespierre's reign of terror and the otherwise continuing hold of hierarchical and exclusive structures on modern societies in the eighteenth, nineteenth, and twentieth centuries, disappointment has become a political topic. In Sara Ahmed's words: "It is the subject who feels bad, who is curious, who wonders" (Ahmed 2010: 190). Conversely, "much happiness is premised on, and promised by, the concealment of suffering, the freedom to look away from what compromises happiness" (Ahmed 2010: 196). Therefore, disappointment and unhappiness are not solely negative experiences, because they can be an adequate reaction to an injustice. As such, they help promote change. The lack of promised goods—not necessarily objects but also social structures and forms of behavior that are conducive to the good life, inclusive to all—might stipulate the recognition of disappointment and unhappiness.

The no-show of promised and fully paid for goods is disappointing. It is a striking illustration of disappointment in action. What if the intellectual elite disregards such disappointments, which the public at large keeps experiencing, by proclaiming that all held out in promise, has indeed been fulfilled? This has been a so far ignored pattern within modern history, shaping a rather disturbing form of interaction between intellectual and political history. Intellectuals of all colors and shades have been greeting rather disappointing manifestations in economics, politics, and society as if these were the golden dawn of a new century wherein the costs demanded for progress were now paying big dividends for everyone concerned.

Bellow's usage of the term "human cost" within the context of a better understanding of modernity indeed opens up a new perspective on his last novel *Ravelstein*. It does so by evoking Alexandre Kojève's *Introduction to the Reading of Hegel*—a text, as we shall see, which the historical figure of the intellectual Allan Bloom (on whom the main character of the novel is based) first introduces to the American audience. Bellow opens his last novel in the setting of Kojève's Paris where he delivered his public lectures on Hegel's master-slave dialectics in the late 1930s. Bellow makes implicit the connection between the main protagonist of his novel and the Hegelian, revolutionary philosopher: Ravelstein "himself had studied in Paris years ago under the famous Hegelian and high official Alexandre Kojève, who had educated a whole generation of influential thinkers and writers" (Bellow 2000: 45). The term "high official" evokes a contamination of political power and ideas, which Kojève embraced as a communist and Ravelstein (aka Allan Bloom) imported from the leftwing European continent to America in the form of neoconservatism. This contaminating force of ideas and their political ramifications is interrelated to the thematic of a cost that goes with human civilization and the progress of history. It in fact preoccupies Kojève in his *Introduction to the Reading of Hegel*. Right from the start (in chapter 1 entitled "In Place of an Introduction") the author dwells on Hegel's interpretation of the master-slave relationship in his *Phenomenology of the Spirit*.

It is significant for the larger historical horizon of the novel that through its concern with the human costs of modernity, Bellow's *Ravelstein* implicitly evokes Hegel. This is so because together with this nineteenth-century philosopher, the novel also highlights the idealist coloration of what we now take to be "modernity." Our modernity is not so much Spinoza's radical enlightenment of diversity that has done away with teleology and hierarchy as one that has been shaped by what for Hegel is the foundation of all human progress: the radically unequal and violent interaction between master and slave. Bellow's *Ravelstein* thus unfolds a two-pronged time horizon: that of the inceptions of an idealist modern world in the late eighteenth and early nineteenth centuries and that of the twentieth century. Hegel unites these two time horizons through his most powerful afterlife in the intellectual and social history of the second half of the last century, and Kojève's *Introduction to the Reading of Hegel* may be largely responsible for the continuing waves and aftershocks of idealism's immeasurable impact on modern economic, philosophical, and political life.

While engaging with an idealist modernity, Bellow's last novel does not so much belong to philosophical discourse as partake of a literary legacy, at least in its form. In its first part, this chapter traces such literary legacy by analyzing the contaminating simultaneity of promise and disappointment—and not, as the critical consensus has so far assumed, a Hegelian, temporally spread-out opposition between the two—in Fitzgerald's novella *The Great Gatsby* (1926). This interpretation breaks with the received scholarly and popular perception—powerfully reinforced through Baz Luhrmann's 2012 Hollywood film version putting 1922 morally loose glamour front and center—of Fitzgerald's novel as celebration of the Jazz Age. Bellow's *Ravelstein*, in turn, refers to the Great Gatsby not only through the glamorous and yet flawed character of its main protagonist but also in more explicit references to the American Jazz Age when describing the Glyph couple: "The Glyphs were no ordinary academic couple—they were at home in London as well as in Paris. In Saint-Tropez, or some such place, the Scott Fitzgeralds had been their close neighbours. Glyph and his wife were not your common name droppers. They had been a rich American Jazz-Age couple" (Bellow 2000: 38). Like the ambience of Fitzgerald's novel of the Jazz Age, Bellow's *Ravelstein* seems to avoid what is ordinary or common. As we shall see, this first impression is, however, highly misleading as regards both novels. Bellow actually sets out to democratize his main protagonist extraordinary life. Ravelstein's death becomes the occasion to meditate on the death of millions of European Jews in the Nazi genocide.

Indeed, Bellow's last novel traces the way in which his main protagonist approaching the end of life confronts the same within the larger historical twentieth-century context of violence and death. Against this background Ravelstein's fate embraces that of European Jewry in the first half of the twentieth century. Part of Ravelstein's personal appeal to the narrator Chick is his depersonalization of mortality, his anti-bourgeois evasion of the fear of death. While Ravelstein lives by ideas, Bellow's narrative focus does not pivot around an ideational kernel. Instead Bellow's last novel explores how its main protagonist's personality as educator makes ideas accessible for a nonacademic audience: "He lived by his ideas. His knowledge was real, and he could document it, chapter and verse. He was here to give aid, to clarify and *move*, and to make certain if he could that the greatness of humankind would not entirely evaporate in bourgeois well-being, et cetera. There was nothing of the average in Ravelstein's life" (Bellow 2000: 53). This going beyond the average relates Ravelstein to Gatsby. Like Gatsby, Ravelstein embraces risks and rejects bourgeois concerns with health and longevity: "But to prolong his life was not one of Ravelstein's aims. Risk, limit, death's blackout were present in every living moment" (Bellow 2000: 54). Strikingly, in both *Ravelstein* and *The Great Gatsby*, a non-bourgeois lifestyle that endangers well-being comes into being through a contamination of love and risk.

Hope enables such contamination of eros and death. Gatsby embarks on his beyond average parties in his multimillion-dollar mansion not to seek social approval but to impress and win the heart of his first love. In doing so, he courts disappointment and death. Ravelstein, the educator, democratizes extraordinary ideas driven by love for his students. Ravelstein

> took an unusual interest in his student [. . .]. He would have said, that if asked about this, that given the sort of education they were getting, with its unusual emphasis "on the affects"—on love, not to beat around the bush—it would have been irresponsible to pretend that the teaching could be separated from the binding of souls. That was his old fashioned way of putting it. Naturally there was a Greek word for it, and I can't be expected to remember every Greek word I heard from him. *Eros* was a *daimon*, one's genius or demon provided by Zeus as a compensation for the cruel breaking up of the original androgynous human whole. (Bellow 2000: 82)

On a personal level, love—as in *The Great Gatsby*—moves Ravelstein to risk his life and court death. Bellow's narrator explicitly contaminates the idea of *eros* with the individuality of the novel's main protagonist: "He was HIV positive, he was dying from complications from it. Weakened, he became the host of an endless list of infections. Still he insisted on telling me over and over again what love was—the neediness, the awareness of incompleteness, the longing for wholeness, and how the pains of Eros were joined to the most ecstatic pleasures" (Bellow 2000: 94–5). However, the narrator is not concerned with the idea of Eros but how it relates to Ravelstein's life and personality. *Ravelstein* contaminates idea and life, eros and sex, love and risk/death: "He was doomed to die because of his irregular sexual ways. About these he was entirely frank with me, with all his close friends" (Bellow 2000: 160). Risk of death relates Gatsby's and Ravelstein's love life.

One could describe death as the disappointment of love. However, there is more than the individual dimension in Bellow's and Fitzgerald's respective novels. Anti-Semitism pervades as a historical and political theme in *The Great Gatsby*, and *Ravelstein* focuses on anti-Semitism writ large in the Nazi genocide. The occasion for such reflection on the historical is Ravelstein's risk-induced, eros-driven experience with death. At this point the novel goes beyond the extraordinary main protagonist and opens up to the common experience of European Jews (that of anti-Semitism and death in the Nazi genocide). Anti-Semitism and the Nazi genocide have not been predominant themes in the intellectual and political work of Allan Bloom. Bellow's novel strikingly departs here from the published ideas of the historical figure on which his main protagonist is based here.

Rather than being concerned with the dark disappointment of mass killings, Bloom's real contamination of ideas and politics have become a driving force for Alexandre Kojève inspired promises of Hegel's glorious end of history either in the non-disappointment of a hoped-for universal communism or, in the neoconservatives case, a globally redemptive free market combined with liberal democracy—and this is exactly the point of references to the Iraq War in Bellow's novel wherein Ravelstein clearly enjoys being in charge at his Chicago command center, his famous switchboard, that keeps him connected in an eros-ideational and at the same time political telephone line to his students now running W. H. Bush's White House. Chick, the narrator of Bellow's novel, seems to agree with neoliberalism when he appears to praise the genius of capitalism, to have made it possible for Ravelstein to become fabulously rich merely through the appeal of his theory: "His intellect had made a millionaire of him. It's no small matter to become rich and famous by saying exactly what you think—to say it in your own words, without compromise" (Bellow 2000: 4). Yet, the narrator seems to be little interested in the actual politics of Ravelstein's ideas. He makes clear that Ravelstein himself did not request of him any engagement with his ideas: "He clearly didn't want me to write about his ideas" (Bellow 2000: 129). As we shall see, Chick articulates a measure of disappointment with the presumed predominance of idea over what he calls nature and "real reality" (Bellow 2000: 97).

On a formal level, Fitzgerald's *The Great Gatsby* and Bellow's *Ravelstein* share a captivated and yet critical narrator who, modeled on Conrad's Marlow, mediates our encounter with a glamorous, admirable, risk-taking male protagonist who ultimately experiences the disappointing aspect of the human condition: death. Both novels have a political and historical dimension wherein the disappointment that the male protagonist undergoes reflects critically on quasi-redemptive promises of glamour and wealth. In *Ravelstein* the death of the individual triggers various reflections on the gravest political disappointments of the twentieth century: Hitler's concentration camps and Stalin's gulags. Anti-Semitism and the Nazi genocide make Ravelstein and his German Jewish friend Herbst question: Why the Jews? Ravelstein tries to find an answer to this question in a Jewish sense of justice that guards against the exuberance of limitless promises and hopes:

> So he was dying and thinking of these questions [i.e., anti-Semitism and the Nazi genocide], Ravelstein formulated what he would say but was not able to deliver his conclusions. And one of these conclusions was that a Jew should take a deep interest in the history of the Jews—in the principle of justice, for instance. (Bellow 2000: 179)

The principle of justice disappoints limitless expectations of promises such as wealth, health, or redemption. The Jews are both historical and (from a Christian and Muslim perspective) theological place holders for disappointment, and this is the case to an unconscious extent in the anti-Semitic passages of *The Great Gatsby* and in a more thoughtful manner in *Ravelstein*: "The Jews, Ravelstein and Herbst thought, following the line laid down by their teacher Davarr, were historical witnesses to the absence of redemption" (Bellow 2000: 179). Bellow here actually quotes from Leo Strauss's lecture "Why We Remain Jews: Can Jewish Faith and History Still Speak to Us?" (1962). It is worth referring to the passage in Strauss's public lecture of 1962 from which Bellow imports this quotation into *Ravelstein*:

> Judaism is not a misfortune (I am back to my beginning) but, let us say, a "heroic delusion." In what does this delusion consist? The one thing needful is righteousness and charity; in Judaism these are the same. This notion of the one thing needful is not defensible if the world is not the creation of the just and loving God, the holy God. The root of injustice and uncharitableness, which abounds, is not in God, but in the free acts of his creatures—in sin. The Jewish people and their fate are living witness for the absence of redemption. This, one could say, is the meaning of the chosen people; the Jews are chosen to prove the absence of redemption. (Strauss 1997c: 327)

Significantly, in this part of his lecture, from which Bellow lifts his quotation in *Ravelstein*, Strauss discusses anti-Semitism. The injustices inflicted upon the Jews throughout history result from the free, sinful acts of God's creatures. These creaturely misdeeds are proof of the absence of redemption. Due to violent and unjust actions of humanity disappointment pervades our world.

Strauss goes so far to interpret the notion of the chosen people in this abject and disappointed mode: the Jews are chosen to be living witness to the absence of redemption, and the various injustices they have to endure are proof of precisely such precarious election. On a more general or abstract level, absence of a once promised redemption (be it in a theological or secular sense such as money or wealth through which one can redeem and exchange material goods) instantiates disappointment. Both *The Great Gatsby* and *Ravelstein* let us experience the disappointment of wealth, glamour, and grand political ideas after which their respective main male protagonist seems to hanker, at least at first sight.

Rather than extolling the high life of wealth and fame, *The Great Gatsby* highlights the collapse of the Spinozist promise of modern equality and diversity. It does so by the persistent presence of racist discourse and racist representation within it and, associated with racism, a chauvinism that is actually symptomatic of a so far not fully discovered genre of the literary disavowal of disappointment, focused on a promising but ultimately flailing and failing male protagonist.

Next to the literary formal element of a male narrator fascinated by but also critically removed from the male protagonist of the narration, the theme of racism is a discordant and disturbing content that traverses from *The Great Gatsby* to *Ravelstein* within a force field that here does more than cast a shadow on the supposed innocuousness of high society. In Bellow's last novel the early-twentieth-century racism pervading Fitzgerald's depiction of the Jazz Age disturbs the supposed innocence of ideas as the reflective presence on the crimes perpetrated in the Nazi genocide, not only as mental but also as physical shock that "goes straight to your bones" (Bellow 2000: 178). Here again Bellow quotes from Strauss's essay and this from the very opening. Strauss here strikes a personal note:

> I could not prepare this lecture, for entirely private reasons, as I would have wished to prepare it. But nevertheless I did not cancel the lecture, because I thought I am prepared, if not indeed for this lecture, then for its subject. I believe I can say, without any exaggeration, that since a very, very early time the main theme of my reflections has been what is called the "Jewish question." May I only mention this single fact perhaps, going very far back in my childhood. I believe I was about five or six years old in some very small German town, in a village, when I saw in my father's house refugees from Russia, after some pogroms which had happened there, women, children, old men, on their way to Australia. (Strauss 1997c: 312)

Strauss here unpeels layers of his personal connection to Jewish studies and its hidden, personal sphere that precisely unfolds in Bellow's *Ravelstein* when the public life of glamour (Ravelstein's switchboard connection to the White House and so forth) recedes. For some private reason Strauss admits to be ill prepared for his lecture and yet fully prepared for it due to the subject matter's intricate imbrication in his own personal life from early childhood onward. The repercussions of anti-Semitism cling to him from this age onward and they stick to his inner mark. As in *Ravelstein* anti-Semitic injustice and violence goes to the bones:

> At that time it could not happen in Germany. We Jews there lived in profound peace with our non-Jewish neighbors. There was a government, perhaps not in every respect admirable, but keeping an admirable order everywhere; and such things as pogroms would have been absolutely impossible. Nevertheless this story which I heard on that occasion about pogroms in Russia made a very deep impression on me, which I have

not forgotten to the very day. It was an unforgettable moment. I sensed for a moment that it could happen here. That was overlaid soon by other pleasing experiences, but still it went to my bones, if I may say so. (Strauss 1997c: 313)

Acquaintance with the victims of Russian pogroms has shaped Strauss's personality from early childhood onward. This moment can only be overlaid but not forgotten. It presages horrors to come that could happen in the deceptively safe German environment of Strauss's provincial upbringing, seemingly distant from the troubles of Russia and pogroms.

Bellow took Strauss's oscillation between private experiences of history's anti-Semitic violence and "more pleasing" experiences from Strauss's lecture. The meditation on the horrors of the Shoah unravels the male protagonist's—Ravelstein's—preoccupation with the intriguing relationship between intellect and power, between the elation of ideas and the nightmarish history of Germany and the European continent in the 1930s and 1940s.

Not as starkly as in *Ravelstein*, discrimination and the violence that ensues from various forms of inequality—that of gender, class, and race—dampens and challenges the dream component of hope and romantic readiness in *The Great Gatsby*. On the level of ideas, this contamination of promise and disappointment shapes the formal arrangement of the campus novel, *Ravelstein*. The exploration of the simultaneity of these apparently mutually opposed characteristics sheds light on the novel as a genre that still awaits discovery by literary critics.

As has been explored in Chapter 4, this genre could be called the novel of disavowed disappointment. The combination of the two words "novel" and "disappointment" may strike some readers as oxymoron, because, as intimated earlier, the critical consensus seems to claim a certain optimism as characteristic of this genre and its to-be-expected "upbeat endings." To associate the novel with disappointment flies in the face of what one of its most astute critics has highlighted as perhaps the genre's most distinguishing characteristics: a good-natured trust in life of which the narration is proof, showing that despite difficulties all is well that ends well. According to Terry Eagleton, fiction from the Victorian age onward aims to inspire hope and to edify its audience:

If the Victorians were especially disconcerted by dejection, it was not least because gloom was felt to be disruptive. In an age of social turmoil, one of art's primary purposes was to edify. The point of fiction, as Freud argues of fantasy in general, was to correct the blunders of an unsatisfying reality. The English novel lent support to the status quo not only in its respect for rank or regard or social order but also in its insistence on upbeat endings. (Eagleton 2015: 13)

Eagleton's assessment holds true to a certain extent. However, his reading of the Victorian novel tends to be one-dimensional. As Gillian Beer has shown, the Victorian novels of George Eliot end not so much on an upbeat note but with the disappointment of the female protagonists of the novel (Beer: 2018: 5–30). The Victorian novel thus includes disappointed experiences. It allocates these, however, to female characters. There is thus a well-known nineteenth-century genre of the novel of disappointment from George Eliot's *The Mill on the Floss* via Flaubert's *Madame Bovary* to Fontane's *Effie Briest*. The nineteenth-century novel avows disappointment in its depiction of gender relations.

This chapter analyzes a new type of the novel of disappointment, which originates with some of Joseph Conrad's male characters. As is well known, Fitzgerald's *The Great Gatsby* takes its model of narration from Conrad's *Heart of Darkness*. Whereas some nineteenth-century novels avow the disappointment of their female characters, Conrad's Marlow narrated texts highlight how societal constructions and their concomitant expectations motivate male characters to strive unsuccessfully to disavow their disappointment. Fitzgerald's Gatsby radicalizes such disavowal of disappointment. By connecting *The Great Gatsby* to what I call the novel of disavowed disappointment, this chapter analyzes the historical ramifications within the critique of male gendered promises and their implication for politics at large in Bellow's *Ravelstein*.

As a result of such analysis, we will be able to locate Fitzgerald's *The Great Gatsby* in a lineage of Conradian narratives performed by a male narrator about a flawed but nevertheless fascinating male protagonist whose itinerary through life ends in some form of disappointment. The most striking case is the male protagonist's failure to perform his duty in Conrad's *Lord Jim*. Fitzgerald consciously takes up the theme of a delusory and failing male protagonist when he has a Marlow-like voice narrate Jay Gatsby's exuberant but bound-to-be disappointed hopes of rearranging the past (a more recent example is Philip Roth's last work entitled *Nemesis*).

The Great Gatsby and Conrad's Disappointing Male Protagonists

As we shall see, Bellow's *Ravelstein* follows Fitzgerald's *The Great Gatsby* in that it formally adopts the view of a narrator who allows for a mildly critical perspective on the main character of the respective novel.[1] As has been well established in the critical literature, Fitzgerald's narrator is grounded in Conrad's Marlow figure, who narrates both his *Lord Jim* and *Heart of Darkness*. Robert Wooster Stallman first noted what he called "the obsessive hold of Conrad in shaping Fitzgerald's greatest novel" (Stallman 1955: 5). Stallman argues that Fitzgerald inherited from Conrad an ambivalent narrator, oscillating between fascination and critical distance: "Fitzgerald's romantic idealism *and* satiric detachment are patterned upon the characteristic Conradian ironic combination employed in the creation of Jim, Nostromo, and Kurtz" (Stallman 1955: 9). Toward the opening of *The Great Gatsby*, Fitzgerald establishes this ambivalent position of the narrator on the main character. He does so in the following highly nuanced way: (a) by first proposing a nonjudgmental position, (b) then moving to do the opposite—passing on judgment—and (c) then articulating a sense of unlimited admiration for the hero who is at the same time the antihero of the narration:

> When I came back from the East last autumn I felt that I wanted the world to be in uniform and at a sort of moral attention forever; I wanted no more riotous excursion with privileged glimpses into the human heart. Only Gatsby, the man who gives his name to this book, was exempt from my reaction—Gatsby, who represented everything for which I have an unaffected scorn. If personality is an unbroken series of successful gestures, then there was something gorgeous about him, some heightened sensitivity to the promises of life, as if he were related to one of those intricate machines that register earthquakes some thousand miles away. (Fitzgerald 2006: 2)

The narrator's fascination with the main character of the novel counteracts the opposed feeling of revulsion or "unaffected scorn." Why the fascination then, in spite of the initial reaction of disgust? Like Bellow's Ravelstein, Gatsby's character overflows the boundaries of personhood: he is larger than his appearance.

How can this be the case? What causes the narrator's fascination with the gorgeousness of Gatsby is a proclivity in his character that is greater than he

---

[1] I owe this insight into the formal, narrative parallel between Fitzgerald's *The Great Gatsby* and Bellow's *Ravelstein* to Michael O'Neill who in an email of November 3, 2018, compared the two novels, writing: "I meant something that's in there from the narrator's perspective (a bit Great Gatsby like?) that's fascinated by legacies and Influence."

is, as manifested in his giving the impression as if he were "related to one of those intricate machines that register earthquakes some thousand miles away." The image of Gatsby's personality in terms of a seismographic sensory machine might imply some powers of prolepsis or historical anticipation on his part. This impression is misleading, because the gorgeousness of Gatsby is not of dark, ominous colors but of bright, promissory ones, and indeed the crucial point in the important quote earlier is the consternation about "some heightened sensitivity to the promises in life." Gatsby's character in quasi-allegorical manner bodies forth or symbolizes what the concept of hope denotes. The narrator goes on to define this larger than life element in Gatsby as "an extraordinary gift for hope, a romantic readiness such as I have never found in any other person and which it is not likely I shall ever find again" (Fitzgerald 2006: 2). Romantic here does not necessarily relate to the literary periodization of romanticism but to something fantastic, fanciful, imaginary, and idealistic. The imagination in question here partakes of Gatsby's "gift for hope" and his "heightened sensitivity to the promises in life."

Yet the term "romantic" might also assist us in contaminating what so far has been taken to be two distinct phases of Scott Fitzgerald's oeuvre. The critical consensus first establishes a lyrical, dreamy phase—belonging to the era of the so-called Jazz Age—of which *The Great Gatsby* has become the most famous example. The late phase—after the Great Depression—follows this where dreams and promises have turned into disarray, into various disappointments. Could it be that the harsh realities of Fitzgerald's *The Crack-Up* are already informing the promissory hopes of *The Great Gatsby*? Morris Dickstein sees the late Fitzgerald's preoccupation with disappointment and disintegration in terms of detoxification apropos the heavy alcohol consumptions that goes with the Jazz Age. This perspective ignores that Fitzgerald's own experience as an alcoholic intensified with his growing realization of disappointment, as Dickstein himself acknowledges:

> There is no doubt how much he really *did* suffer during this period [i.e., the late, disappointed one following the dreamy one of *The Great Gatsby*], when his golden marriage was all but over, when drink and disappointment often made him behave strangely, when his stories were no longer welcome in the magazines that had provided most of his income, when even Hollywood could find no real use for his talent. (Dickstein 2005: 80)

Nevertheless, critics like Dickstein establish too stark a separation between the illusory bliss of romantic possibilities and the purported phase of disappointment following such promises. From this perspective, Fitzgerald's last phase is closer to what Dickstein rightly describes as our dystopian age:

> This suggests that it may not be the lyrical, romantic Fitzgerald of the 1920s who most claims our attention today but the shattered, disillusioned Fitzgerald of the 1930s; not the poet of early success, romantic possibility, and nostalgic regret but the hard-edged analyst of personal failure and irretrievable loss, the man who redeemed in his work what was slipping away in his life, who achieved a hard-worn maturity even as he described himself as a failure, and exhausted man, a spent force. (Dickstein 2005: 82)

Can we not see in the Fitzgerald of *The Great Gatsby* the hard-edged analyst of disappointment? Does the narrator of this novel not establish a delicately poised form of narration that contaminates promise and disappointment? It is exactly this simultaneity of the affectionate and the critical, of the promissory and the disappointed through which *The Great Gatsby* has created a novelistic form of its own and which serves as template for Bellow's last novel *Ravelstein*. Literary critics like Dickstein implicitly follow Hegel's temporalization of knowledge by establishing phases and periods as regards not only literary history but also that of individual authors, such as contrasting early with late Fitzgerald. Would it be more insightful to contaminate the two and see the late Fitzgerald of disappointment already present in the early one of hope and romantic possibilities? Instead of separating the two and contrasting one with the other, we might come to recognize them simultaneously as intricately entangled with each other.

Against this background, the term "romantic readiness" might refer to the romanticism not only of promises but of disillusions and disappointments too, which informs—contra Dickstein—not only the late but also the early Fitzgerald of *The Great Gatsby*. Dickstein characterizes this romantic moment as "the moment of clarity when the dreamer, the visionary, is humanized by loss, by suffering, by fellow feeling—when the mental traveller, no longer adrift in 'fairy lands forlorn,' turn homeward, in Keats's words, to the 'sole self,' the self without romantic illusions" (Dickstein 2005: 88). Contrary to the implicit temporalization and separation, following Hegel's dialectical pattern of thought, that still holds sway over the theory and practice of literary criticism, it is precisely the doomed darkness of disappointment that generates the colorful gorgeousness and glamour of larger than life figures such as Fitzgerald's Gatsby and Bellow's Ravelstein.

Time, future time, preoccupies both novels in a way that we come to see promise already as disappointment. This simultaneity of the promissory and the disappointed may also change the way we recognize and experience what comes to strike us as disappointment. Because of such contamination of opposites, we may realize that there is promise in disappointment too. From its opening pages onward, *The Great Gatsby* contaminates promise with disappointment, letting us see gorgeousness sitting side by side with the dark matter of ashes and dust: "No—Gatsby turned out all right at the end; it was what preyed on Gatsby, what foul dust floated in the wake of his dreams that temporarily closed out my interest in the abortive sorrows and short-winded elations of men" (Fitzgerald 2006: 2). The narrator is deeply ironic—if not bitter—here, for Gatsby turns out all right at the end of the novel, after his murder.

It is disappointing when one realizes that "turning out all right" means being dead. Adding to this pervasive sense of disappointment is the narrative circumstance that it is the Gatsby while being still alive which causes the narrator to lose interest in the sorrows and short-lived elations of humanity. This is certainly not the stance of promissory hope. Clearly, Fitzgerald's *The Great Gatsby* contaminates romantic readiness with romantic disappointment. Gorgeousness here intermingles with the foulness of dust and ashes.

The novel deliberately casts Gatsby's exclusivity and exuberance as being intrinsically bound up with the shallowness and triteness of modern crowds—evoking the London crowds of Eliot's "waste land" (Fitzgerald 2006: 24), which is "contiguous to absolutely nothing" (Fitzgerald 2006: 24). The critical literature has established the ways in which Fitzgerald's *The Great Gatsby* has been shaped by the depiction of modern city life in Conrad's *Heart of Darkness* and Eliot's "The Waste Land," with the former being a major influence on the latter, as Long has pointed out. Long is exemplary of the critical literature on *The Great Gatsby* that has so far ignored the contamination of promise and disappointment, which permeates this novel.

The critical focus has so far been on moral and sociohistorical components rather than on the novel's destabilization of categories such as hope and disappointment through the way it contaminates one with another. Recent studies continue to be preoccupied with the historical context of the Jazz Age. In *Careless People*, Sarah Churchwell thus acknowledges disappointment only with respect to the decline of this age: "*The Great Gatsby* made manifest precisely what Fitzgerald's contemporaries couldn't bear to see, and thus it is not only the jazz age novel par excellence, but also the harbinger of its decline and fall" (Churchwell 2013: 7). Before the more recent historicist approach, influence studies such as Stallman's and Long's have abstained from discussing such confounding usage of opposed terms focusing instead on legacies of literary representations of evil for which Baudelaire is indeed an important writer and thinker shaping the work of not only Conrad but also Eliot and, following him, Fitzgerald:

> Baudelaire was among Conrad's favorite poets, and he had used a passage from one of Baudelaire's poems, "Le Voyage" (which contains the phrase "the horror!") as an epigraph to one of his own works. Baudelaire had written that evil, though destructive, is more *human* than passive nonentity; and this vision of evil forms a criticism of the spiritual inertia of modern culture. The same criticism applies to in *Heart of Darkness*, where the infinite potentialities of the human soul are evoked by Kurtz, contrasted with the complacency of the "monstrous town." The theme of the dehumanization of contemporary society appears later in the century in T. S. Eliot's "The Waste Land" (1922), which is again focused on a great modern city, in this case London. As in Conrad's "city of the dead," the inhabitants of Eliot's London lead an existence that is a form of death-in-life. Eliot has *Heart of Darkness* in mind when he wrote "The Waste Land," and even intended to use a passage from the novel as the poem's epigraph. Fitzgerald had read and admired "The Waste Land," and its influence had been attributed to him in *The Great Gatsby* in his social attitude and in the wasteland idea of the valley of ashes. (Long 1966: 415 note 4)

Rather than being opposed to the supposed promissory excitement of Baudelaire's evil (summed up in his famous term *"fleur du male"*), is the dreariness of a modern life-in-death existence not its contaminating other side? Fitzgerald embeds Gatsby's exuberant and evil—in Baudelaire's sense of *fleur du male*—gangster mansion into the ambience of a drab valley of ashes in order to illustrate geographically the contamination of what we take to be opposed sides of excitement and sterility, of promise and disappointment.

The ecstatic life of Gatsby's excessive party permeates the border to the absoluteness of being nothing, of being dead, evoking the empty state of modern drabness, highlighted in Eliot's "The Waste Land":

> A crowd flowed over London Bridge, so many,
> I had not thought death had undone so many.
>
> (Eliot 1969: 62)

The exuberance of *The Great Gatsby* borders on the exhausted un-deadness of Eliot's "so many" in the flow of crowds over London Bridge in "The Waste Land." The narrator describes his sense of Gatsby's exclusive aura as being at heart contaminated with the dreariness of mechanical reproduction when he regrets ever having "set foot upon his over-populated lawn" (Fitzgerald 2006: 68). Extravagance here gives way to disappointment of the "so many" as articulated in Eliot's "The Waste Land."

Gorgeousness and foulness, the elevated and the drab contaminate each other here rendering promise a disappointment—a peculiar state of contaminating simultaneity, which might also turn disappointment into a promise. Seen from the vantage point of the foul valley of ashes, which is a metaphor for the desolation that is the collateral by-product of mass consumption and mechanical reproduction, Gatsby's mansion evokes the hollowness of Joseph Conrad's "The horror! The horror!" in *Heart of Darkness*. It also recalls the paralysis between death and life of Eliot's "Waste Land": "A sudden emptiness seemed to flow now from the windows and the great doors, endowing with complete isolation the figure of the host, who stood on the porch, his hand up in a formal gesture of farewell" (Fitzgerald 2006: 56). There have been numerous studies showing that Fitzgerald reworked themes and materials from Eliot's "The Waste Land" and adopted the narrative style of Conrad's perspective on the main character Mr. Kurtz in his *Heart of Darkness* (Long 1966). However, what has so far evaded theoretical illumination is that this literary tradition from Conrad onward of a contamination of a promising male hero with the lethal violence of an antihero, of so-called progress and so-called regression, of excitement and monotony highlights disappointment as lying at the heart of promise. The valley of ashes that surrounds his mansion externalizes Gatsby's inward geography wherein death and disappointment simultaneously enfolds hope and promise. Rather than waxing lyrical about the excessive wealth of Long Island, the locality of *The Great Gatsby* makes us see exuberance side by side with the foulness of decay, of ashes.

Strikingly Fitzgerald deliberately fuses romantic and German idealist notions while describing Gatsby's mansion. The mansion embodies romantic promise, because "Gatsby bought that house so that Daisy would be just across the bay" (Fitzgerald 2006: 79). Crucially, the narrator contaminates personal romantic longings with the sociohistorical manifestation of Kant's modernity, premised as it is on capitalist and bourgeois hierarchies. Gatsby's promising mansion dominates the otherwise drab and disappointing valley of the ashes: "There was nothing to look at from under the tree except Gatsby's enormous house, so I starred at it, like Kant at his church steeple, for half an hour" (Fitzgerald 2006: 89). Romantic promise and idealist (non-materialist, Kantian) freedom make room for the real-existing circumstances of disappointment.

Promises here emerge as a desperate way to disavow disappointing facts of class and poverty. The description of the arranged meeting between Gatsby and his childhood love Daisy suddenly takes on romanticism's darker and realistic colors citing the gloom of real-existing poverty from Keats's "Ode to a Nightingale": "He [i.e., Gatsby] lit Daisy's cigarette from a trembling match, sat down with her on a couch far across the room, where there was no light save what the glooming floor bounced in from the hall" (Fitzgerald 2006: 96). The phrasing about light darkly generated from gloom has here been cited from the last three lines of the fourth stanza of Keats's "Ode to a Nightingale":

> But here there is no light,
> Save what from heaven is with the breezes blown
> Through verdurous glooms and winding mossy way.
> (Keats 1970: 528)

Romanticism contaminates promise with disappointment and darkness with light. Fitzgerald's novel of disappointment thus relates back to Keats's realistic awareness of social injustices and failures. However, it is noticeable that in Fitzgerald's passage citing key phrases from Keats's ode any reference to heaven or other transcended entities is missing. The perspective here is purely immanent and secular. In Fitzgerald gloom paradoxically and immanently generates the shaded, dark light of a modernity which bifurcates in stark sociopolitical hierarchies of class, exclusion, and inequality, as the following two lines closely following the cited phrase from Keats amply make clear:

> One thing's sure and nothing's surer
> The rich get richer and the poor get—children.
> In the meantime,
> In between time—
> (Fitzgerald 2006: 97)

The real-existing grounds for Gatsby's romantic promise (or, illusion) and at the same time its disappointment reside in economic and social inequality. Daisy was in love with Gatsby in the first place. However, Gatsby was poor. She married the obnoxious and racist millionaire Tom whose body was "capable of enormous leverage—a cruel body" (Fitzgerald 2006: 7). From the opening of the novel onward he propounds racist ideas and their scientific validity: "The idea is if we don't look out the white race will be—will be utterly submerged. It is all scientific stuff; it's been proved" (Fitzgerald 2006: 13). At a crucial exchange toward the end of the novel, Gatsby confronts Tom making clear that it is social and economic inequality that hindered Daisy's authentic love life: "'She never loved you, do you hear?' he cried. 'She only married you because I was poor and she was tired of waiting for me. It was a terrible mistake, but in her heart she never loved anyone except me!'" (Fitzgerald 2006: 131). As a poor young man, wealth promised the fulfillment of Jay Gatsby's love life: "She had caught a cold, and it made her voice huskier and more charming than ever, and Gatsby was overwhelmingly aware of the youth and mystery that wealth imprisons and preserves, of the freshness of many clothes, and of Daisy, gleaming like silver, safe and proud above the hot struggles of the poor" (Fitzgerald 2006: 151). Gatsby is no average person, because he single-mindedly and scrupulously builds his enormous wealth not so much as to escape from the struggles of the poor as to gain the love of Daisy. Fulfillment of love is the hope and the promise here.

Crucially hope here does not lie in the future but in restoring a marred past, ruptured and broken by social and economic inequalities. This is precisely what the famous exchange between Gatsby and the narrator is about—and at the heart of it is what unspoken social inequality remains:

> "I wouldn't ask too much of her" I [the narrator] ventured. "You can't repeat the past.'"
>
> "Can't repeat the past?" he cried incredulously. "Why of course you can!"
>
> He looked around him wildly, as if the past were lurking here in the shadow of his house, just out of reach of his hand.
>
> "I'm going to fix everything just the way it was before," he said, nodding determinedly. "She'll see."
>
> He talked a lot about the past, and I gathered that he wanted to recover something, some idea of himself perhaps, that had gone into loving Daisy. His life had been confused and disordered since then, but if he could return to a certain starting place and go over it all slowly, he could find out what that thing was. (Fitzgerald 2006: 111)

Gatsby's present accumulation of wealth cannot change his adolescent poverty, which drove Daisy into the arms of the repulsive but wealthy Tom. Repeating the past here is a promise and what hinders its fulfillment or redemption disappointingly relates back, as in a vicious circle, to its actual failure in the past in the first place: social, economic, ethnic, and political inequalities. Social gender rules interdict Daisy to leave her husband Tom.

Strikingly, Gatsby and Ravelstein are love-driven characters who flounder at the structure of society. No wonder that Ravelstein asks his students to repudiate their parents and their families in order to free themselves from social inhibitions and inequalities. Both Gatsby's and Ravelstein's quests end in disappointment and mortality. Gatsby's and Ravestein's extraordinary material success takes second place to their respective idealism. Ideas triumph over life here, and the force of the idea is its promise of redemption either to regain and remake an imperfect and socially and economically unequal childhood or, as in Ravelstein's case, to project hope into the future of a globally liberated (like Iraq) democratic, prosperous world of liberal free markets. Drawing on the anthropological research of Marilyn Strathern and Carol MacCormack, Judith Butler has analyzed the way we have become culturally and socially accustomed to associate "reason and mind" (Butler 2007: 50) with "masculinity and agency, while the body and nature are considered to be the mute facticity of the feminine, awaiting signification from an opposing masculine subject" (Butler 2007: 50). In keeping with the societal construction of a rationalist, idealist masculinity (Lacan's famous law of the father, or, in other words the symbolic), the idea driven male protagonists lose their sense of the real world in their quest for a promised one. It is the promise of either the reshaped past or the redemptive future which makes us disavow what has already been lost. And this even after promises have clearly been seen to be outdone by stark social circumstances (such as that Daisy cannot dissolve her marriage to Tom):

> I have an idea that Gatsby himself didn't believe it would come, and perhaps he no longer cared. If that was true he must have felt that he had lost the old warm world, paid a high price for living too long with a single dream. He must have looked up at an unfamiliar sky through frightened leaves and shivered as he found what a grotesque thing a rose is and how raw sunlight was upon the scarcely created grass. A new world, material without being real, where poor ghosts, breathing dreams like air, drifted fortuitously about... like that ashen, fantastic figure gliding toward him through the amorphous trees. (Fitzgerald 2006: 163)

At the end of his life, Bellow's Ravelstein wonders whether we all pay a high price for buying into the various promises and hopes of modernity. One of such hopes is Gatsby's: that the ills of the past can be redeemed in a materially improved circumstance such as his own as self-made millionaire. The high price of modernity's promise is the loss of a sense of reality. Losing "the old warm world" means paying "a high price for living too long with a single dream" as Gatsby does and his later Hegelian idealist fellow traveler Ravelstein, whose real historical figure introduced the traditional left-wing idealism of a future liberated world into American conservatism as neoconservatism.

In the foregoing passage material improvements paradoxically lack reality; they are stuck in a ghostly sense of being objectified. However, paradoxically disappointment contaminates promise. In other words, there is promise in disappointment. And this consists in realizing the arbitrary, socially enforced hindrance to the non-objectified, true relationship of love. This realization helps to strengthen one's reserves against various pressures which society exerts. As has been discussed in Chapter 4, this is what the late Foucault has theorized as the ancient Socratic "care of the self." As we will see in Chapter 6, this ancient conception of selfhood plays a crucial role in modern attempts to extricate ourselves from our entrapment in cultural and societal constructions (such as the ones of gender allocations and various other stereotypes).

6

Political Promises and History's Disappointments

Leo Strauss as the Esoteric Center of Bellow's *Ravelstein* and the Critique of Grand Political Promises

At any rate, I have concerned myself with men and women whose moorings have been cut, and who are swept away from their native shores and out to sea, sometimes on a tide of their own righteousness or resentment.
Philip Roth, *Reading Myself and Others*

Introduction: The Loss of Moorings, Foucault's Care of the Self, and the Modernist Return to a Premodern View of Philosophy as an Art of Living

In this quotation Roth evokes Conrad's modern condition of having lost one's mooring. This loss of foundations describes the crisis of traditional coordinates. As we have seen in Chapters 3 and 4, Conrad's *Lord Jim* and *Heart of Darkness* highlight how lofty ideas serve as a cover for most heinous crimes in sociohistorical practices (such as colonialism). Conrad's ironic usage of the "ideas only" unmasks the disappointment with their realization.

The collapse of traditional values in their colonialist and lethally exploitative historical manifestation causes a sense of disappointment. Avowing a sense of disappointment with modern ideational distortions of traditional coordinates stipulates a renewed concern with wisdom as guide to how to be. As will be explored in Chapter 7, in a mode similar to Conrad, Kafka addresses a modern loss of valid traditions. As Benjamin has put it in his letter of June 12, 1938, to his friend, the historian of Judaism, Gershom Scholem, "Kafka's work instantiates the illness of the tradition" (*Kafkas Werk stellt eine Erkrankung der Tradition dar*) (Benjamin 1978: 763). According to Benjamin, Kafka's narratives are parables without a spiritual point of reference. For this reason Kafka was a "writer of parables but he did not found a religion" (Benjamin 1999b: 805). The irony of their colonialist, exploitative usage depletes the validity of ideas in Conrad's novels.

In a more radical way, the signs of Kafka's parables are empty of any spiritual or redemptive signification; they exclusively refer to the corrupt politics of an immanent, capitalist, quasi-religious system: "The gate to justice is study. Yet Kafka doesn't dare to attach to this study the promises which tradition has attached to the study of the Torah. His assistants are sextons who have lost their house of prayer; his students are pupils who have lost the Holy Writ [*Schrift*]" (Benjamin 1999b: 815). Benjamin here describes the loss of both Hagada (the practiced, acted law as illustrated by Talmudic narrations) and the ignorance of Halacha (the spiritual guidance that Talmudic law offers).

In a society in which the spiritual guidance proffered by law is ignored, a dedication to the study of this unpracticed law might work for justice. Yet even the contemplative life of study, rather than praxis, has lost its validity in a society that has become so corrupted that even the texts of the scriptures have not escaped corruption. As Benjamin puts it in his letter of June 12, 1938, to Scholem, "what has been lost is the consistency of truth" (Benjamin 1978: 763). Hagada is the narrative element of Talmudic law (Halacha). These narratives transmit the wisdom of truth as inscribed in Halachic law. This loss of both the validity of ideas and the consistency of truth is not peculiar to Kafka, as Benjamin goes on to point out. However, what is new in Kafka is the complete focus on the narrative element that has been deprived of any spiritual, Halachic truth: "Kafka's true genius was that he got rid of the truth in order to save its remaining element which is haggadic" (Benjamin 1978: 763). There is a surplus to Kafka's parabolic narrative, and this is precisely the glaring absence of truth.

Kafka's parables "do not submit to the teaching of truth [*Lehre*] as the Hagada has lain at the feet of the Halacha" (Benjamin 1978: 763). It is this discrepancy between narrative and truth element that accounts for the absence of wisdom in Kafka's work. According to Benjamin, wisdom only appears in random form throughout Kafka's novels and short stories: "once in form of a rumour of true things [*Gerücht von wahren Dingen*]" and "the other product of this random slide show [*Diathese*] of wisdom is foolishness [*Torheit*], which admittedly has completely done away with the content of wisdom [*welche zwar den Gehalt, der der Weisheit zueigen ist, restlos vertan hat*], but has instead preserved its calm and pleasing element which is completely absent in rumour [*aber dafür das Gefällige und Gelassene wahrt, das dem Gerücht allerwege abgeht*]" (Benjamin 1978: 763). Kafka's narratives thus present wisdom reduced to a zero point of significance.

As pleasing and uncertain rumor, Kafka renders truth disappointing, as a topic for and of humor or amusement. Similar to Conrad's sense of irony, Kafka's usage of humor serves to highlight the modern condition of a loss of moorings that turns urban landscapes into disorienting seascapes for Conrad's destructive element, where the question is how to swim or how to be without any form of guidance. The modernist literature of both Conrad and Kafka attempts to come to terms with the loss of traditional spiritual and scientific points of orientation—be they truth (science) or wisdom (as guide to everyday life). Out of this awareness of a modern void in meaning and truth, modernist, postmodernist, and contemporary writers approach the topic of literature in terms of what Foucault has rediscovered as the Socratic care of the self. This does not turn the literary into a substitute for religious forms of spirituality. Instead a modernist, postmodernist, and contemporary revision of this ancient practice establishes literature as well as philosophy as a novel space, wherein the self becomes capable of building new worlds outside various forms of sociopolitical oppression. These literary and philosophical spaces contaminate the contemplative with the sphere of praxis: the self can here practice his or her life outside traditional forms of meaning and truth which have lost their validity and consistency.

The following returns to the discussion of the care of the self in the Stein episode in Conrad's *Lord Jim*. As has been explored at the end of Chapter 4, Stein evokes the Socratic concern of how to be. Addressing the question of how to be, literature rediscovers a Socratic conception of philosophy as an art of life. Here modernist literature reconnects with the premodern in order to help liberate the self from exploitative social practices (such as colonialism in which Stein and Jim are implicated). This chapter continues to analyze the underlying notion of what Foucault has theorized as the premodern, Socratic practice of the care of the self: Leo Strauss, the historical figure behind Ravelstein's teacher Felix Davarr takes issue with a Hegelian account of history wherein the modern overcomes the premodern in a teleological manner. The following section explores how Davarr/Leo Strauss's political philosophy conceptualizes disappointment with Hegel's struggle for recognition, setting it in relief against a Socratic tradition of the care of the self, as modernity's dark side of power.

Leo Strauss's Critique of Hegel Struggle for Recognition

I had learned from Spinoza to appreciate the clarion call of the Fifteenth Chapter of the *Principe*.
(Leo Strauss, Preface to the American Edition of *The Political Philosophy of Thomas Hobbes*)

In this sentence Leo Strauss articulates his sense of discovery in detecting Machiavelli and not Hobbes (who merely speaks out explicitly what is already implicit in Machiavelli) as the "originator of modern political philosophy" (Strauss 1963: XV), and thereby as the ground of modernity's break with antiquity. First, a shift from nature (outside and beyond the control of politics and society) to real or factual societal human conventions shapes this departure of the modern from the premodern.

Later in the eighteenth and nineteenth centuries German idealism submerges the remainder of non-anthropomorphic nature into the progress of human history whose laws now govern the planet in an increasingly, industrialized, Anthropocene age. According to Strauss, Machiavelli introduced the struggle for power, for recognition. In *The Prince* Machiavelli argues that those who want to preserve power have to observe how humans realistically behave. What has humanity in common? According to Machiavelli, the longing for power over others and over nature. The ruler has thus to make sure to eliminate any potential competitors so "that whoever is responsible for another's becoming powerful ruins himself" (Machiavelli 1961: 16). What motivates Strauss to investigate the genealogy of modernity? He wants to understand how the struggle for social recognition and power turns individuals into conformists who support the exertion of violence and totalitarian power (the modern form of tyranny) in the century preceding ours.

As we have seen in Chapter 5, Fitzgerald's *The Great Gatsby* and Bellow's *Ravelstein* trace the itinerary of their respective main male protagonist in order to set in relief the struggle for social recognition. That the present cannot redress or redo the societal invisibility of the early Gatsby—that precluded his marriage to his childhood sweetheart—is the form of disavowed disappointment specific to Fitzgerald's famous novel of the Jazz Age.

Bellow's *Ravelstein* lays the emphasis not so much on personal but historical disappointment concerning a public intellectual who implicitly disavows the disappointing experience with power in the first half of the twentieth century, by enthusiastically embracing the role of adviser to those who hold power at the close of the twentieth century. In disavowing the historical disappointments of politics, the main male protagonist also ignores the lessons of his teacher in political philosophy, Leo Strauss (Davarr). This chapter explores how Leo Strauss and his critique of value-free science informs Bellow's last novel of the disavowed disappointment with history implicit in the neoconservative (Strauss's pupil Allan Bloom) Kojève-like Hegelian alliance of power and intellect, philosophy and politics.

Leo Strauss resides in the background of Bellow's *Ravelstein*. He does so as the teacher of Allan Bloom (the historical figure for whom Bellow promised to write his last novel as a memoire). Critics have so far not explored the ways in which Bellow's last novel thematizes the disappointment of historical promises, which is the major theme of Leo Strauss's critical engagement with Kojève's Hegelian notion of the end of history. Strauss here emerges as a crucial interrogator not only of an idealist alliance between philosophy and politics but also of one of the products of such alliance. Strauss indeed questions the predominance of human ideas and their productive manifestation as the rule of the Anthropocene that reaches into and substantially changes the geological outlook of our planet nowadays via global warming and its consequences.

As is clear from the recent publication of Strauss's 1965 seminar on Hegel's *Philosophy of History*, humanity's subjugation of nature played a major role in his encounter with the idealist nineteenth-century philosopher. As we will see toward the end of this chapter Strauss's concern with Hegel's master-slave dialectics relates to his concern with Hobbes's contrast between civilization and the presumed irrational state of nature. Hegel radicalizes the Anthropocene hierarchized divide between a disappointing realm of nature and the promising horizon of humanity's end of history: "His world, the man-created world, becomes more important than the given world. Also something which Marx took over" (Strauss 2019: 121).

Theorists and historians of the Anthropocene have not recognized the significance of Leo Strauss's return to both nature and the ancient Socratic tradition of what Michel Foucault has called "the care of the self." In a fascinating way Foucault's work on knowledge and power shares with Strauss's critique of modern forms of power and conformity (or, in other words, what Carl Schmitt calls "sovereignty") a rediscovery of Socrates, creativity, and philosophy as a liberation and refuge from the pressures of the Anthropocene. These pressures are not only visible in their impact on nonhuman nature (by destroying the biodiversity of our planet). They are also noticeable as the homogenizing apparatuses within first modern political philosophy—as most explicitly laid out in Hobbes's modern political philosophy and its Machiavellian preoccupation with political realism in regard to the "actual experience of how men behave in daily life and in 'public conversation'" (Strauss 1963: X). How men behave in everyday life and according to political, economic, and social conventions has become a defining feature of the novel as a literary genre: "The epic deals with a world of nobles and military heroes, whereas the novel deals with the common life. It is the great *popular* genre, the one mainstream literary mode which speaks the language of the people" (Eagleton 2005: 8). As has been analyzed in Chapter 5, the hidden content of Fitzgerald's *The Great Gatsby* is the rise of a common, poor male protagonist to extraordinary wealth and status in early-twentieth-century America.

Through his rise on the social and economic ladder, Gatsby hopes to redeem his ordinary past, when his poverty prevented him from marrying his beloved. Economic inequality thwarted the ambitions of his personal life in the first place. The male protagonist of Fitzgerald's novel sets out to remedy and disavow disappointment by winning over the now married Daisy. At this point in time, however, social conventions preclude Daisy leaving her unloved and rather brutish and brutal husband Tom. The reader of the novel senses that Daisy might be disappointed in her marriage of convenience, but the narrative focuses on Jay Gatsby's disavowal of disappointment—on his determined quest to redo or remedy the past and its inequality and injustices by dint of his rise to economic success. The pressure to become fabulously rich for one personal reason results in further levels of unfairness for society and the narrator of *The Great Gatsby* makes clear that the male protagonist's disavowal of disappointment involves incurring the social cost that partakes of organized crime.

Fitzgerald's *The Great Gatsby* accentuates time through the allegory of its main character—future time, to be precise (the promissory, the fanciful expectation of what is to come in terms of "romantic readiness"; hopes and expectations). In *Ravelstein*, Bellow transforms this focus on hope and on the future in an ideas-driven way, changing the topic from that of a dubious businessperson (Jay Gatsby) to that of a glamorous intellectual (Abe Ravelstein) endeared to the high life of influence and power. However, this does not mean that Bellow's last novel extols the promises of redemption proclaimed within political ideas such as communist or neoconservative ones. There is a tension between the narrator's (Chick's) fascination with the person Ravelstein and a critical stance toward a preoccupation with the promissory abstractions of political philosophy. As Chick makes clear, seeing the person is different from explaining his politics and ideas: "But I would rather see Ravelstein again than to explain matters it doesn't help to explain" (Bellow 2000: 231). The novel *Ravelstein* pivots around how life and death intrudes into the abstraction of ideas, displacing them and thereby often proving them wrong or inadequate.

If Gatsby overflows the limits of one single person, Ravelstein's character bursts the boundaries of time, or limited periodization: "Mixtures of archaism and modernity were especially appealing to Ravelstein, who could not be contained in modernity and overflowed all ages" (Bellow 2000: 69). Closely related to Fitzgerald turning Gatsby into a quasi-allegory of future time, hope, and the promissory, Bellow's narrator sums up the character of his main protagonist as this overflowing of temporal boundaries, going on to state: "Oddly enough, he [i.e., Ravelstein] was just like that" (Bellow 2000:

69). Reading Bellow's last novel within the context of the Great American novel of the Jazz Age that formally shaped its outline (i.e., Fitzgerald's *The Great Gatsby*) prepares for a new and more accurate reading of its narrator's positioning vis-à-vis its main protagonist. This is an important step for a better understanding of *Ravelstein*, because critics have identified Bellow's approach with that of the historical figure that lies behind its main protagonist—that is, Allan Bloom aka Abe Ravelstein (Hitchens 2000). Critics have thus reduced Bellow's last novel to being an espousal of neoconservatism (the intellectual position of Allan Bloom).

As we shall see, Bellow's *Ravelstein* indeed reflects issues of Bloom's neoconservatism but it does so in ways that are critical rather than merely affirmative. There is a sophisticated relationship between the thematic of promises and hopes in *The Great Gatsby* and the neoconservative preoccupation with a better, globally democratic world of the future. At this point, Allan Bloom's role of introducing Kojève's *Introduction to the Reading of Hegel* to an American audience is significant, because it translates a traditionally utopian and revolutionary agenda of a European provenance via transatlantic transfer to a conservative clientele. From such vantage, *Ravelstein* reflects on the pitfalls within a modern world that is our current state of affairs (constructed through and in Hegel's idealism) and of which Kojève is such an important thinker not only for the historical intellectual "Ravelstein" but also for Lacan, Judith Butler, and so much of postmodern literature and theory.

As for Gatsby, there is nothing average about Bellow's Ravelstein. Both are larger-than-life figures. Both live the life of romance; in Gatsby's case, it is a life-long obsession with a sweetheart from adolescence for whom he builds his dubious wealth and for whom he is willing to sacrifice his life. Similarly, Ravelstein "was doomed to die because of his irregular sexual ways" (Bellow 2000: 160). The specific narrators of the two novels both acknowledge the respective flaws of the character they are extolling, while sometimes referring to ironical distance or articulating a different perspective, that of the society at large: "Others saw him [i.e., Ravelstein] as bizarre, perverse—grinning, smoking, lecturing, overbearing, impatient, but to me he was brilliant and charming" (Bellow 2000: 160). As has been explored in Chapter 5, the narrator (Mr. Carraway) of *The Great Gatsby* calls into doubt the main protagonist's hope for redeeming a disappointed, disjointed, objectified past. On a much larger historical scale, Bellow's last novel critically distances itself from Ravelstein's prioritization of grand concepts such as Hegel's "History" over the disappointingly grim particulars of historical experiences that individuals had to endure as witnessed in the anti-Semitic massacres in

Nazi-occupied Bucharest. Facing death, the late Ravelstein increasingly turns the drift of his conversations with Chick to the historical horrors of anti-Semitism and the Nazi genocide:

> "You haven't brought it up. So you have any memory of the massacre in Bucharest when they hung people alive on meat hooks in the slaughterhouse and butchered them—skinned them alive?" One rarely heard Ravelstein speaking of such things. He would now and then refer to "History" in large Hegelian terms, and recommend certain chapters of the Philosophy of History as great fun. With him gloomy conversations on the "full particulars" were extremely rare. (Bellow 2000: 124)

Chick, the narrator, here establishes a distance between the main protagonists' Kojève-inspired grand Hegelian scheme of politics and philosophy and the historical particulars of the Nazi genocide. There is a noticeable contrast between the promise of ideas ("great fun") and the shock of and disappointment with historical events ("gloomy").This critical distance to Allan Bloom's ideas and his politics might well have been part of Bellow's friendship. In this context, it is noteworthy that in his unpublished eulogy speech at Bloom's funeral, Bellow differentiates between the person and his ideas. Moreover, he describes his friend as paradoxically separated from the Hegelian (Enlightenment) ideas Bloom upheld in his role of intellectual adviser, in the footsteps of Kojève, of those in charge of political events (i.e., Thatcher and Reagan): "He is *free* from the Enlightened ideas he holds" (Bellow papers/Regenstein Library/University of Chicago). Isn't that amazing? In real life, Bellow clearly distances himself from Bloom's Enlightenment (Hegel) derived ideas and turns the man into a work of art, as a way of avoiding "nihilism." At his funeral, Bellow renders Bloom the thinker and cofounder of neoconservatism an artist, a Stendhal of sorts:

> The artist is not necessarily bound by his summation, because as artist he acts with freedom. His abstractions, his *cerebral* principles will splinter and give way to forces that make a work of art. Stendhal, who presents himself as a disciple of Locke actually is a great wit and ingenious interpreter of human behaviour. He is *free* from the Enlightenment ideas he holds. They are little more than a convenience to him. The most advanced ideas of an artist are, in the end, not declarations but questions. Shakespeare is free even from the ideas that tempt him most. He cannot be seduced by his own most powerful summations. We can no longer derive our summation from the definitions of humankind set by enlightened democracy. They have been used up entirely. Those of us

who are called, or call themselves artists, must turn again to the sources of their strengths, to the stronghold of the purest human consciousness. Only the purest human consciousness, art-consciousness, can see us through this time of nihilism. (Bellow eulogy speech of Allan Bloom/ Bellow papers/Regenstein Library/University of Chicago)

The term "nihilism" evokes the specter of Leo Strauss and his critique of modernity as intrinsically nihilistic. It is a nihilism of promising ideas of power and their rather shocking political perpetration throughout modern history. What Bellow calls the purest human consciousness—or, art consciousness—Strauss describes as wisdom: as the artistic liberation from societal and political pressures. Stark disappointments of real-existing history seem to change late Ravelstein's outlook on politics and ideas: "When he [i.e., Ravelstein] was dying he seemed to feel it necessary to speak more openly about matters [i.e., anti-Semitism and the Nazi genocide] we had never felt it necessary to discuss" (Bellow 2000: 125). Extraordinary as Ravelstein's life and idea may have been, the main part of Bellow's last novel describes his experience of illness and mortality.

This painful experience shifts the emphasis in an ideational and at the same time actual historical framework, from the promise of a globally redeemed world to the stark disappointments and horrors of real-existing history, economics, and politics. Critics have ignored how Bellow's last novel takes issue with Hegelian promises of politics, as most influentially formulated by Alexandre Kojève, whose ideas the real-existing Ravelstein introduced to an American audience (see Allan Bloom's "Introduction" Kojève 1969: vii–xii). Kojève's notion of an end of history, which he formulated in the 1930s in his lectures on Hegel's *Phenomenology of the Spirit* and which were first published in English in Allan Bloom's US edition *Introduction to the Reading of Hegel* (1969) have been taken up by the left and the right spectrum of politics.

From Kojève's perspective Hegel's term of the end of history promised the future reality of a global communist state. Allan Bloom translates this left-wing promise into the neoconservative ideal of a unified world in which all countries of the globe share a liberal democratic constitution and free market economy. The communist and the neoconservative ideas are both twentieth- and twenty-first-century versions of Hegel's promised reign of the fully redeemed world spirit, inaugurating the immanent, political reign of peace, security, and freedom on a universal scale. More than disappointing, traumatic historical experiences here contaminate what seems to reside beyond average hope: the promise of the end of conflict, poverty, envy, and rivalry once history will have ended. Implicitly referring to the traumatic historical experiences of the Nazi concentration camps and Stalin's gulags, in his intellectual exchange with Kojève of the early 1950s, Strauss questions the connivance of philosophers with the actual crimes committed by politicians as follows:

> Tyranny is a danger coeval with political life. The analysis of tyranny is therefore as old as political science itself. The analysis of tyranny that was made by the first political scientists was so clear, so comprehensive, and so unforgettably expressed that it was remembered and understood by generations which did not have any direct experiences of actual tyranny. On the other hand, when we were brought face to face with tyranny—with a kind of tyranny that surpassed the boldest imagination of the most powerful thinkers of the past—our political science failed to recognize it. (Strauss 2000: 23)

The crimes committed in the Nazi genocide have indeed surpassed the "boldest imagination" of writers and thinkers in the early 1950s. Strauss characterizes himself as one of the "contemporaries, disappointed or repelled by present-day analyses of present-day tyranny" (Strauss 2000: 23). He goes on to differentiate the modern form of political terror as perpetrated in the Nazi genocide and in Stalin's gulags from what preceded it.

In this context, Strauss calls "science" the striking missing ingredient in pre-modernity and characterizes this term by an advance in ideological and technological means of domination: "In contradistinction to classical tyranny, present-day tyranny has at its disposal 'technology' as well as 'ideologies'; more generally expressed, it presupposes the existence of 'science,' i.e., of a particular interpretation, or kind, of science" (Strauss 2000: 23). This modern "kind" of science is political as far as it changes nonhuman nature concerning what now goes under the concept of the Anthropocene.

Strauss broadens the notion of the rule of the Anthropocene to include the modern transformation of human nature and society "by a science" (Strauss 2000: 23) which in modernity "is applied to 'the conquest of nature'" and thereby "popularized and diffused" in the societal realm. The promise of the scientific, *a priori* or idealist domination first in regard to human nature, progressively then—as a new advance in a perpetual and universal development of "progress"—increasingly broadens out into a global reach over nonhuman nature in its entirety (what the term "Anthropocene" indeed denotes): "We are now brought face to face with a tyranny which holds out the threat of becoming, thanks to 'the conquest of nature' and in particular of human nature, what no earlier tyranny ever became: perpetual and universal" (Strauss 2000: 27). The modern scientific refrain from value judgment enables this popularization and diffusion of the Anthropocene, which Strauss calls the "control of nature."

Science and the social sciences, in particular, are in the grip of what Max Weber has famously called the freedom from values. Strauss takes issue with this modern approach to science as being value-free: "Our political science is haunted by the belief that 'value judgements' are inadmissible in scientific considerations, and to call a regime tyrannical clearly amounts to pronouncing a 'value judgment'" (Strauss 2000: 23). Strauss's larger argument here is of direct concern to Bellow's last novel and its main male protagonist. How so?

The underlying historical background of *Ravelstein* is the relationship between the intellectual and power, between philosophy and politics, between science and ethics. The image that exemplifies this historical background is the almost comical obsession of Ravelstein with his switchboard in his Chicago apartment that establishes his "special relationship" with his former students (the "old boys" of Bellow's novel) in the White House. Here clearly emerges the interplay between intellect and power. Leo Strauss questions how modern science and politics render the intellectual a "value-free" participant (rather than a critic) of the Anthropocene will to power.

Is the inconspicuous protagonist Davarr (Strauss) the secret center of *Ravelstein*? He is the teacher of Ravelstein. The narrator of Bellow's last novel introduces him in a generalized way, stating: "We are a people of teachers. For millennia, Jews have taught and been taught. Without teaching Jewry was an impossibility. Ravelstein had been a pupil or, if you prefer, a disciple of Davarr" (Bellow 2000: 101). What does the teacher teach, however? Strauss is famous for his rather rigid formulation of a radical break between modernity and antiquity. Like his friend Walter Benjamin, Strauss casts modernity's break with the premodern not in an ideological mold but as part of what Nietzsche analyzes as the consequences resulting from the death of God: nihilism in terms of the *ennui*, the void, and suppression of creativity.

However, there is more elasticity and sophistication in Strauss's contrast between the premodern and the modern than might seem at a first glance. As has been discussed in the introduction to this chapter, Benjamin explores in Kafka's work modernity's reduction of teaching to a zero point of significance. The remainder of this emptying out of meaning is the mere story deprived of any wisdom or traditional instruction (as law or Halacha) or meaning. Strauss highlights Benjamin's division between ancient wisdom and modern amusing forms of mere rumors about it. Strauss's nuanced approach comes to the fore in the way he consciously selects an ancient text, namely Xenophon's *Hiero or Tyrannicus*, in order to address the problem of a presumed break between the ancient and the modern. An increase in the technological and ideological exertion of power resulted from the modern break with the Socratic care of the self.

It is this topic of an ever-increasing power apparatus which suppresses and oppresses diversity as well as idiosyncrasy which calls forth Strauss's intense predilection for Socratic wisdom. As Richard Velkely has clearly shown, Strauss here diverges from Heidegger's preoccupation with Being and beings in terms of the priority of history and practical, political usefulness (for a discussion of Benjamin's related critique of Heidegger, see Mack 2014a):

> In other words, Strauss agrees with Heidegger that Being, as the ground of the openness to beings, is coeval with man and history. But something crucial to the human is not coeval with its history, namely, its coming into being, its prehistory. The need to bear in mind the question of the prehistorical origin seems connected to Strauss's appreciation of Socratic philosophy as open to questions that transcend altogether the moral and political realm, while being aware of the difficulties such questions cause for practical human life. In this way Socratic questioning exposes the duality in the human—as both belonging to the moral and political realm and transcending it. (Velkley 2011: 61)

According to Strauss, Socrates inaugurates philosophy's break with societal pressures (what Velkely calls the "moral and political realm"). Philosophy's divergence from various forms of the collective exertion of power becomes all the more urgent after the totalitarian violence perpetrated in the first half of the twentieth century. So in his letter of September 4, 1949, to Kojève, Strauss makes clear how much he would "welcome it if the Xenophon-Strauss-Kojève book appeared" (Strauss 2000: 244). It becomes apparent that in Strauss's framework there is a contamination rather than a rigid contrast between antiquity and modernity, when he thereby includes Xenophon's ancient text in his late 1940s and early 1950s controversy with Kojève. For Strauss, Kojève is of special importance here, because his pronounced modern position is delightful in its clarity and thereby provocativeness. Strauss conveys this to Kojève in the same letter (of September 4, 1949): "Besides that I am glad that finally someone represents the modern position intelligently and in full knowledge—without Heidegger's cowardly vagueness" (Strauss 2000: 244). The revealing reference to Heidegger's vagueness is to the German philosopher's silence after the war about his early intellectual support of Nazism's modern tyranny. Heidegger's speech about "the self-assertiveness of the German university" (1933) as rector of Freiburg University—where his first administrative deed was to follow political orders and expel Jewish academics (his teacher Edmund Husserl included) from the university—is surely the prime striking example of what Strauss interrogates as the problematic alliance (rather than critical distance) between philosophy and politics.

From its opening onward, Bellow's last novel depicts Ravelstein's allure to the promise of power and politics, which runs parallel to Gatsby's hope of resetting the past by means of gaining social and economic standing. Ravelstein's fascination with the appeal of political might makes him turn his artistic apartment into a military command station of sorts, where he is keen to receive the latest news before anyone else does in the public at large. This rendering porous of the borders between politics, on the one hand, and philosophy and creativity or art, on the other, is exactly the theme of Strauss's critique of positivist or value-free science against which he defends a Socratic understanding of philosophy that unties the philosopher from political and social pressures.

In Bellow's last novel this liberation from the attraction of political as well as the social and economic power, by means of which Gatsby hopes to redo his own disadvantaged and impoverished past, occurs through the narrator's Chick and Ravelstein's growing preoccupation with the disappointment of past promises in the course of twentieth-century history. Ravelstein's illness and impending death shift the novel's narrative observation away from the glamour associated with the intellectual's impact on actual power games (as confident and adviser to both Margaret Thatcher and Ronald Reagan) toward a recognition of the shock and disappointment with the history of European anti-Semitism and the Nazi genocide, in particular. Strauss implicitly performs a sense of disappointment with history, when he undoes a division between antiquity and modernity. He does so when he argues that the one who founded the modern notion of the realistic predominance of adapting to what is most opportune for the increase in political power or, sovereignty, namely Machiavelli, learned this lesson from an ancient text: namely, Xenophon's *Hiero or Tyrannicus*. Crucially, Strauss chooses this Socratic piece of wisdom as the starting point for his controversy with Kojève. The argument between Strauss and Kojève concerns precisely the moot point of Bellow's *Ravelstein*: the glamorous prospect of political influence whereby the intellectual stands in a receptive relation to the allure held out by any tangible impact on the real-existing exercise of power (Ravelstein's having a direct line or special relationship with the White House).

Here the almost invisible figure of Ravelstein's teacher, who appears in Bellow's novel under the esoteric name Felix Davarr, becomes the hidden center of the narrative. Davarr or Leo Strauss not only taught the art of writing as an esoteric practice, he also advised that intellectuals keep a critical and disappointed distance to current forms of political and social pressures and fashions. From Strauss's perspective, the pressure to buy into the allure of political promises and social success is as ancient as history. Hence, Strauss somewhat dismantles his contrast between the ancient and the modern. Indeed, he interprets an ancient text as the foundation of Machiavelli's modern intellectual version of affirming the validity of a realistic and opportunistic as well as conformist practice of politics in terms of what Hobbes and later Carl Schmitt (as intellectual collaborator of Nazi Germany) would call sovereignty:

> There is only one earlier work on tyranny to which Machiavelli emphatically refers: Xenophon's *Hiero*. The analysis of the *Hiero* leads to the conclusion that the teaching of that dialogue comes as near to the teaching of the *Prince* as the teaching of any Socrates could possibly come. By confronting the teaching of the *Prince* with that transmitted through the *Hiero*, one can grasp most early the subtlest and indeed the decisive difference between Socratic political science and Machiavellian political science. If it is true that all premodern political science rests on the foundation laid by Socrates, whereas all specifically modern political science rests on the foundation laid by Machiavelli, one may say that the *Hiero* marks the point of closest contact between premodern and modern political science. (Strauss 2000: 24–5)

The point of closest contact between the premodern and the modern also marks the position where they differ from each other most glaringly. Indeed, in his reading of Xenophon's *Hiero*, Strauss contaminates antiquity with modernity to render negative or disappointing the timeless appeal of political power for intellectuals like Bellow's Ravelstein or Strauss's friend and interlocutor Alexandre Kojève.

In a highly sophisticated way Strauss presents philosophy as the scandal of or the obstacle to political promises and ambitions. While, at first sight, it may seem as if Strauss's political philosophy separates one term from the other, he actually contaminates the two to render each aporetic of the other. Socratic wisdom teaches the art of living. It does so by turning philosophy into the disappointment rather than the fulfilling servant of political aspirations:

> Socratic rhetoric is emphatically just. It is animated by the spirit of social responsibility. It is based on the premise that there is a disproportion between the intransigent quest for truth and the requirements of society, or that not all truths are always harmless. Society will always try to

tyrannize thought. Socratic rhetoric is the classic means for ever again frustrating these attempts. (Strauss 2000: 27)

In an intriguing way, Strauss here connects two terms that have traditionally been opposed to each other: justice and disproportion. Traditionally, the just is the fitting or proportionate. Virginia Woolf highlights the political violence—what Strauss would call social irresponsibility—of what she calls the goddess of proportion in *Mrs Dalloway*. In Woolf's novel a scientist, a leading psychiatrist, worships "proportion." This form of worship advocates social and political conformism. It validates a societal structure that separates the mad from the sane, the powerless from the powerful, the knowledgeable from the ignorant, and the colonized from the colonizers. Moreover, it attempts to establish a homogenous, universal state of the globe premised on the superiority of the Christian faith (to which everyone will have been converted in Woolf's satire of the Hegelian end of history). The episode in Woolf's *Mrs Dalloway* about the psychiatrist Sir William Bradshaw's worship of proportion highlights the social irresponsibility of the traditional political order, premised as it has been—and still is—on aligning political justice with any given socially dominant conception of what is "fitting" or acceptable (proportionate).

Woolf's satire of the traditional standard of proportion for measuring social responsibility helps a better understanding of Strauss's contaminating and yet aporetic conception of philosophy's relationship with politics. In a truly responsible way, philosophy is political as long as it remains frustratingly disappointing of any attempts to render it compatible with any given program or social impact agenda: "Mostly forgotten in modernity, in Strauss's view, are not doctrines of teleology and natural law, but the duality of the human, the tension between law and *eros*, which entails the permanent 'homelessness' of philosophy in practical affairs" (Velkley 2011: 23). In this sense, philosophy is negative, contaminating, or "tyrannical." Crucially it remains disproportionate and negative in a radically non-dialectical way: its aporetic position concerning political promises or hopes hinders any process toward its self-overcoming into the positive, the proportionate, the politically, socially, or economically impactful or useful.

Philosophy engages with politics in a disproportionate way on another level too: that of intellectual history. This may indeed help to explain why an ancient text (Xenophon's *Hiero or Tyrannicus*) becomes the foundation of modern political philosophy in Machiavelli's *Principe*. Society and politics may always try to tyrannize thought but true philosophy is also tyrannical or, in other words, aporetic toward politics and the social order. Xenophon's *Hiero* could serve as a handbook for how to be a good tyrant. Machiavelli did indeed read it in this way. However, this reading of the ancient text presupposes a proportional perspective between intellect and power—the setting of Ravelstein's apartment in Bellow's last novel, wherein the intellectual seat of art and thought becomes a command center for the exertion of political power with the switchboard as line of direct communication between the philosopher and those in power in Paris, London, and at the White House.

Leo Strauss or Davarr—the teacher, hidden in the background—is indeed the esoteric center of *Ravelstein*. His teaching critically interrogates the main male protagonist's cozy relationship with those who try to enact political promises and hopes (neoconservatives who attempt to bring about notions of an end of history by homogenizing in a Kojève-like sense the remainder of the world). From Davarr's perspective of justice and disproportion, Ravelstein's intellectual support of practically political, social, and economic agenda appears comical at best. The first part of Bellow's last novel has farcical elements depicting the way its main male protagonist enjoys the role of an adviser at Margaret Thatcher Chequer's PM retreat as well as at Ronald Reagan's White House. Comical too is the way Ravelstein turns from teacher and thinker into a general of sorts, with the switchboard in his apartment always ready at the beckon and call function. This slightly comically distanced mode of narrating switches into one of empathy with the dying Ravelstein which significantly accompanies a sense of historical disappointment with which the novel ends by reflecting on the history of anti-Semitism in Europe.

Similar to his post–Second World War exchange with Kojève Davarr/Leo Strauss would respond to Ravelstein/Allan Bloom's preoccupation with having an impact on politics with an aporetic contamination between intellect and power, between society and thought, between philosophy and politics. In his interpretation of Xenophon's *Hiero* Strauss indeed provides an explanation of the mutual disappointment that characterizes the disproportional relationship between politics and philosophy, keeping them in a scandalous state of contamination: "The reason why the city as such cannot lay claim to man's ultimate attachment is applied in Xenophon's 'tyrannical' teaching" (Strauss 2000: 99). On a literal, proportionate, or non-esoteric level, Xenophon seems to advise on how to govern at one's best as a tyrant (and this is Machiavelli's modern reading). However, the city so governed also tyrannizes those who live in it and try to practice the Socratic art of living. From this esoteric perspective, the philosophical, Machiavellian advice on how to be a good tyrant calls into question the entire political enterprise. It is disproportionate, tearing the rug out under the feet of what the text says on its exoteric surface: hence,

The "tyrannical" teaching, we shall answer, serves the purpose, not of solving the problem of the best political order, but of bringing to light the nature of political things. The "theoretical" thesis which favors beneficent tyranny is indispensable in order to make clear a crucial implication of the practically and hence theoretically true thesis which favors rule of law and legitimate government. The "theoretical" thesis is a most striking expression of the problem, or of the problematic character, of law and legitimacy: and legitimate government is not necessarily "good government" and almost certainly will not be government by the wise. Law and legitimacy are problematic from the highest point of view, namely, from that of wisdom. In so far as the city is the community kept together, nay, constituted, by law, the city cannot so much as aspire to that highest moral and intellectual level attainable by certain individuals. Hence the best of city is morally and intellectually on a lower plane than the best individual. "Individualism" thus understood is at the bottom of Xenophon's "cosmopolitanism." (Strauss 2000: 99)

By arguing for the greater potential deficiency in any form of government, Strauss seeks to delineate the creativity of the individual. The larger community or the state might impinge or threaten personal creativity. In the quotation earlier, Strauss puts Machiavelli's proportional or literal reading of Xenophon's *Hiero* in quotation marks. The "tyrannical" teaching exoterically brings to light the despotism when a legitimate regime confronts certain aspects of philosophical and artistic life. According to Strauss, the prime example of such harshness is the fact that the democratic government of Athens decided to put to death the bearer of wisdom, of the art of living, namely Socrates. The particular charge against Socrates was that he affirmed the theory of "tyrannical" teaching—that is, he made the audience aware that any form of government has some deficiency, some unjust, or "tyrannical" aspect at some point. This is potentially subversive, highlighting—in a theoretical but not practical way—the deficiency of even the best form of government (democracy as practiced in Athens). For this philosophical (here in the sense of theoretical) act of subversion, the democracy of Athens legitimately executes Socrates and sends Xenophon, one of his students, into exile: "Socrates' and Xenophon's acceptance of the 'tyrannical' teaching would then explain why they became suspect to their fellow citizens, and, therefore, to a considerable extent, why Socrates was condemned to death and Xenophon was condemned to exile" (Strauss 2000: 76). Full awareness of inviting societal disapprobation raises the question why those associated with wisdom (such as Socrates) do not counteract their social exclusion, which may even lead to their execution by the community at large. This question goes indeed to the heart of what Strauss and, later on, Foucault, single out as the hallmark of living well or living wisely. It is what Foucault calls "the care of the self," which consists in being able to disentangle oneself from societal and political pressures, precisely by establishing a distance to various demands for social recognition.

Theorists and critics have so far failed to recognize that Strauss's notion of Socratic wisdom and Foucault conception of the "care of the self" counteract Hegel's standard of human achievement, namely, that of societal recognition. As Franco has recently shown, Strauss correlates what for Hobbes constitutes the civilizing moment of fearing death with Hegel's desire for social recognition:

> Like radical doubt, the fear of violent death springs from a distrust of nature rather than grateful acceptance of it, and it leads to an effort to actively control nature rather than a mere contemplation of it. According to Strauss, Hegel agrees with Hobbes on this foundational point when he locates the origin of self-consciousness in the slave's fear of violent death in his life-and-death struggle with the master. (Franco 2019: 2)

As Franco has pointed out, while making clear that he is not a Hegelian, Strauss tries to be fair to Hegel, depicting him as a liberal who is not a democrat: "While Hegel was a liberal in his defence of the rights of man, his belief that government should be run by a trained bureaucracy showed that he was not a democrat" (Franco 2019: 11). The undemocratic notion of a ruling, bureaucratic class that partakes of Hegel's notion of social recognition is indeed the butt of Strauss's controversy with Kojève concerning antiquity and modernity.

Strauss clearly argues that Kojève's 1930s *Lectures on the Phenomenology of the Spirit* provides an honest and clear exposition of the modern position in regard to how the individual remains inextricably bound to societal and larger political pressures. For Strauss these pressures are clearly conformist and restrict the leeway for wisdom, the art of living, or, in other words, what Foucault calls "care of the self." Kojève refers to Hegel's master-slave relationship in *The Phenomenology of the Spirit*. According to Hegel, a struggle for recognition creates and perpetuates social cohesion. Those who are at the lower levels of the social order—Hegel's *Knecht* or servant, or worker/laborer, or, in the most extreme case, slave—are wholeheartedly driven to gain the recognition of those at the top—Hegel's *Herr* or master/superior. Kojève calls this relationship one of master and slave.

In doing so, he shifts Hegel's emphasis on war to one of work. In Kojève's Marxist account (Benjamin would characterize this extolling of work as vulgar Marxism) the act of labor binds the slave to the master. Dialectically this negative act of enslaving is also one of liberation or perfection, wherein one foregoes oneself and becomes one with the social whole, which now illuminates the true meaning of the term "master":

> Perfection (which is always conscious of itself) can be attained only in and by work. For only in and by work does man finally become aware of the significance, the value, and the necessity of his experience of fearing absolute power, incarnated for him in the master. (Kojève 1969: 23)

Strangely enough, critics and theorist have so far failed to notice that Kojève in fact tones down the more martial tone of Hegel's discussion of what the *Herr* or master truly means. In Hegel's account mastery is the destruction of immediate being as exemplified individually in the act of eating or socially in the waging of war (Mack 2003: 42–62).

Far from promising any form of fulfillment or perfection, work in Hegel denotes potentially death-bringing activity. The master is lethal, and mastery consists in showing the individual its insignificance in the face of the larger societal and political whole. Hegel indeed takes issue with what Strauss appraises as individualism—as the "cosmopolitan" capability to extricate oneself from the limitation of any given societal arrangement—when he reprimands "individuals (*Individuen*) who aim at being inviolably for themselves (*unverletzbaren* Fürsichsein) and reaching the security of personhood" (*der Sicherheit der Person* Hegel 1973: 335). The master renders those individuals slaves by making them feel the deadly experience precisely through the imposition of work: "in that imposed form of labour, they are made to recognize their master, namely death itself" (*in jener auferlegten Arbeit ihren Herrn, den Tod, zu fühlen zu geben*) (Hegel 1973: 335). The negative here dialectically morphs into the positive precisely through negating what Strauss calls cosmopolitan individualism (that steps outside the limits of any given society) and transforms individuals into laborers or slaves (Hegel's *Knecht*) that absolve their lives in and through (ultimately lethal) work for the greater benefit of society at large.

Hence, the master is ultimately the community, which subordinates its constitutive individuals: "The negative essence reveals itself as the true *power* of the communal essence and the *force* of societal self-preservation" (*Das negative Wesen zeigt sich als die eigentliche* Macht *des Gemeinwesens und die* Kraft *seiner Selbsterhaltung*) (Hegel 1973: 335). Hegel here most directly and explicitly claims the superiority of the political and communal over that of the individual. Indeed, it has become clear by now that Hegel's *Herr* symbolizes the death bringing might of the community's collective force and power over the threat of any potential deviation an individual might pose.

Against this background Strauss positions himself vis-à-vis Kojève as radically non-Hegelian. He associates such a position with that of Socratic wisdom. Intriguingly by contaminating his Socratic individualist mode of argumentation with that of cosmopolitanism, Strauss does not reject community or politics as such. He only takes issue with the potential pressures of communal and political claims on the creativity and elusiveness, which constitutes for Strauss human life at its best. Consequently, according to Strauss there definitely exists a community of free spirits that transcends national and religious boundaries and in doing so constitutes what one could call a cosmopolitan republic, wherein humanity's elusive inventiveness and wisdom "may live as a stranger" (Strauss 2000: 90).

Strauss's cosmopolitan community is only in a vague sense religious. Hence he uses not a religious but an elusive English notion, describing it as "gentleman-like" (here clearly Strauss's love of England comes to the fore). The term "gentleman" denotes for Strauss a loose, non-compulsory socioreligious environment, wherein, unlike Hegel's community, individuals feel free to choose their affiliations, freed from any pressures to which they might otherwise be exposed. This vague notion of religion, which offers the prospect of unbinding—rather than binding—the individual from communal oppression seems to be part of Strauss's German Jewish intellectual heritage and its Spinoza inflected (via Goethe and Heine) revision of nature/God.

The Spinoza-inflected turn is also part of Strauss's rediscovery of nature and natural right, and it informs his contamination of the traditional divide between Jerusalem and Athens. As a result of such contamination, religion—rather than enforcing societal pressures—loosens the after all only humanly managed grip of sacred or divine creeds so that if "the natural order is traced to the gods, the compulsory character of the law recedes in the background" (Strauss 2000: 105). The term "gentleman" describes this non-compulsive, Spinozist, or free-spirited appraisal of humanity's Other, God, or the pagan gods of nature: "The notion linking 'praise' and 'gods' is gentlemanliness. Praise as distinguished from compulsion suffices for the guidance of gentlemen, and the gods delight at gentlemanliness" (Strauss 2000: 105). Strauss distinguishes his peculiar term "gentlemanliness" from compulsion that accompanies Hegel's master-slave relationship.

Kojève identifies the compulsion for a struggle of recognition between Hegel's master and slave as the foundation for an homogenous modern state. In his response to Strauss's account of Socratic wisdom as a quiet space that allows for the unbinding of social and political pressures (as most prominently holding sway in the struggle for recognition), Kojève first states that this act of unbinding threatens the homogeneity of the modern state, which binds irrevocable and totally all its members. He then applies the term "madness" to Strauss's Socratic self that has extricated itself from societal and political pressures.

Whoever steps out of the homogeneity of the state and no longer engages in the struggle for recognition has succumbed to insanity and is thus no longer a member of humanity, according to Kojève's rather discriminatory account. Here Strauss's Socratic wisdom of the individual, who with Melville's Bartleby says "I prefer not to" facing peer pressure, appears as the negativity denoting madness and thus requires to be dialectically removed from Kojève's account of the homogenous modern state: "And we can call this knowledge [i.e., of Strauss's Socratic wisdom] madness" (Strauss 2000: 153). The tyranny of modern busyness and conformity is the rule of Hegel's state or, in Kojève's term, the end of history over the diversity of nature (which here includes humanity), wherein everyone fully human (in Kojève's term "sane" and not "mad") bows to the struggle for recognition and fuses with politics (conforms to it). The homogeneity of Kojève's rational state of the end of history demands compulsion of a rather illiberal kind of politics. Here, in Kojève's rather dismissive reply to Strauss, wisdom and tyranny depend on each other: "the coming of the wise man must necessarily be preceded by the revolutionary action of the tyrant (who will realize the universal and homogenous State)" (Strauss 2000: 175). Kojève indeed affirms the validity of the intellectual as adviser and supporter of politics, of power, however tyrannical it may be.

According to Kojève's account, the rational individual enacts what Bellow's novel describes (with some comical distance) as Ravelstein's glamorous role as adviser to those who are the masters of the universe (Thatcher, Reagan, and those in the White House to whom Ravelstein has a direct, switchboard access from his Chicago apartment). Such a cozy relationship between intellect and power has always been "reasonable" in Kojève's Hegelian identification of history/politics with rationality:

> When I compare the reflections prompted by Xenophon's Dialogue and by Strauss's interpretation with the lessons that emerge from history, I have the impression that the relations between the philosopher and the tyrant have always been "reasonable" in the course of historical evolution: on the one hand the philosophers' "reasonable" advice has always been actualized by the tyrants *sooner or later*; on the other hand, philosophers and tyrants have always behaved toward each other "in accordance with reason." (Strauss 2000: 175)

Kojève maintains that it is tyranny which installs the promising state of a world governed by homogeneity. As Strauss put it in his response: "He [i.e., Kojève] does not hesitate to proclaim that present-day dictators are tyrants without regarding this in the least as an objection to their rule" (Strauss 2000: 185). Bellow's Ravelstein shapes the American foreign policy by introducing Kojève's originally left-wing, Hegelian notion of the end of history as the universal homogenous state into neoconservative republicanism. Ravelstein's political, financial, and public success endows him with a Gatsby-like aura of glamour that outshines "reasonable" expectations of social recognition. However, both Fitzgerald's *The Great Gatsby* and Bellow's *Ravelstein* make us see the delusions of public eminence. The two novels in different but related ways unmask the futility and vanity of social recognition. They do so by turning our perspective away from societal standards of benchmarked achievements to that of what Strauss calls wisdom—genuine knowledge of us and our world wherein we come to realize how what we commonly and dialectically oppose with each other is actually contaminated with each other.

The Great Gatsby and *Ravelstein* outdo dialectical oppositions such as the one between, "reasonable" and "unreasonable," hope (positive) and disappointment (negative). Beyond average promise simultaneously embodies the abjection of poverty and social exclusion. Like Gatsby, Ravelstein is an extravagant figure. You might call him the intellect's version of the shady businessperson. In contrast to Fitzgerald's novel, Bellow's has tangible intellectual coordinates in the setting of the University of Chicago with clearly identifiable historical characters such as Felix Davarr (i.e., Leo Strauss) and Abe Ravelstein (i.e., Allan Bloom). The real Ravelstein was indeed extravagant in his writings and established a clear affiliation with Kojève's identification of Hegel as beginning and end of history and modernity. Bloom clearly does so in *The Closing of the American Mind*, when he provocatively posits a parallel between the inception of Nazi Germany and what he describes as the end of the Enlightenment in the America of the 1960s. Following Kojève, Bloom identifies Hegel with progress, modernity, and civilization: "Whether it be Nuremberg or Woodstock, the principle is the same. As Hegel was said to have died in Germany in 1933, Enlightenment in America came close to breathing its last during the sixties" (Bloom 1987: 314). Characterizing itself as "memoir," which the narrator "had promised to write" (Bellow 2000: 160) Bellow explicitly blurs distinctions between fact and fiction, between history and literature.

It might be appropriate to call *Ravelstein* a novel of intellectual history or of the history of ideas. As such, it has been analyzed in this chapter: as a fascinating work of literature situated in between history and philosophy; facts and ideas. Not only is its subject matter extravagance à la *The Great*

Gatsby, but it also engages the intellectual strategy of esoteric illusions as championed by Ravelstein (following his teacher Davarr/Leo Strauss) of esoteric reading:

> The products of their great minds have been in print for centuries and accessible to a general public blind to their esoteric significance. For all great texts had esoteric significance, he believed and taught. This, I think, has to be mentioned, but no more than mentioned. The simplest of human beings is, for that matter, esoteric and radically mysterious. (Bellow 2000: 22)

Here and in related passages, the narrator clearly distinguishes his narrative interests from the male protagonist's promissory involvement with ideas and their political exclusivity. The narrator democratizes the esoteric philosophy of the celebrated academic.

The hero of Bellow's last novel *Ravelstein* indeed takes pride in shaping actual political events, through inspiring his former students now working in Washington, from his secret intellectual base of power at the University of Chicago:

> It was very pleasant to win Ravelstein's approval, and his students kept coming back to him—men now in their forties, some of whom had figured significantly in running the Gulf War, spoke to him by the hour. "These special relationships are important to me—top priority." [. . .] Possibly Ravelstein's views or opinions sometimes worked their way into policy decisions, but that wasn't what mattered. What mattered was that he should remain in charge somehow of the ongoing political education of his old boys. (Bellow 2000: 12)

The point is not the political detail but that the intellect should remain in charge. Being called upon by those in power proves that the intellectual enjoys social recognition in an extravagant, Gatsby-like manner. The intellectual may not be a tyrant but his preoccupation with social recognition rather than wisdom moves Ravelstein away from Strauss and closer to Kojève who came to acknowledge the violent or tyrannical foundation of what he calls Hegel's master-slave relationship. In his response to Kojève, Strauss highlights the violence (rather than the value-free work) that Hegel's *Herr* inflicts on the *Knecht*:

> There is such a thing as devotion to one's work, or to a cause, "conscientious" work, into which no thought of honor or glory enters.

> But this fact must not induce us to minimize hypocritically the essential contribution of the desire for honor or prestige to the completion of man. The desire for prestige, recognition, or authority is the primary motive of all political struggles, and in particular of the struggle that leads a man to tyrannical power. (Strauss 2000: 189)

Political impact thus endows the intellect with promise and hope. It is a hope that disavows disappointment because it is in charge of events spiritually regardless of what actually happens.

The neoconservative revolution is a case in point, because neoconservatism does not so much offer a political program as offer an idea which should redeem reality. Whether it is the right or left, politics has turned idealist and perfectionist. Donald Trump's populism has only increased the momentum of a quasi-messianic idea of perfection and redemption—where the costs for modernity are to be redeemed for everyone—that has characterized the interaction between idea and actual political manifestation from the French Revolution onward. Whereas in the past conservatives were wary of these promises, with Ronald Reagan, George W. Bush, and, more radically so, Donald Trump the right has fully recognized and embraced the promises of modernity for everyone either in the globe (neoconservatives) or nationally (every American, "Make America Great Again").

The actual existing Ravelstein of Saul Bellow's novel under the same name was an early intellectual of what John Gray has analyzed as the new right of Margaret Thatcher and Ronald Reagan. As Gray has clearly shown, the new right claims the utopian hope and promise which fuelled revolutionary movements and inspired Hegel's end of history (coinciding with the French Revolution and Napoleon's conquest of Jena in 1806), merely applying it to the supposed panacea of free markets and liberal democracy spread throughout the globe. The new right is, like Kojève's and Allan Bloom's belief in the beneficence of the intellectual's impact on realistic, factual politics, an offspring of the hopes fostered by the Enlightenment:

> Enlightenment thinkers believed they served the cause of civilization. But when the political movements they spawned adopted terror as an instrument of social engineering—as happened in revolutionary France, communist Russia and China—it was barbarism that ensued, and a similar process is underway today. In a curious turn the world's pre-eminent Enlightenment regime has responded to terrorism by relaxing the prohibition on torture that was one of the Enlightenment's true achievements. Neo-conservatism—which is still, despite its ruinous record, the predominant political tendency in a number of Western

countries—may be the last of Enlightenment ideologies; but it too is ready to use terror to realize its utopian goals. (Gray 2007: XVII)

Even though it might hide its name, the utopian promise of Hegel's political philosophy still governs contemporary world politics. Some of its intellectual proponents (having turned from neoconservative to liberal) have merely changed the emphasis from the chiliastic "end of history" to what Fukuyama has recently proclaimed as the timelessly given human essence which he now defines as "the principle of universal and equal recognition" (Fukuyama 2018: 90). Allan Bloom's bestselling book *The Closing of the American Mind* (for whose 1987 book Bellow wrote a foreword) in fact anticipates this chiliastic liberalism of the former neoconservative. He does so by claiming that the hope held out at the inception of modernity has been redeemed by mutual agreement of recognition. This agreement consists in a pact between political rulers and those governed, which is crucially sustained by Enlightenment promises of freedom and equality: "Modernity is constituted by the political regimes founded on freedom and equality, hence on the consent of the governed, and made possible by a new science of nature that masters and conquers nature, providing prosperity and health" (Bloom 1987: 158). It seems Bloom succeeded in instructing the new conservative leaders of this dialectic between rule and consent achieved through promises of equality and freedom. Science is important here as a quasi-empirical guarantor of the realization of these promises, anticipating the delivery of "prosperity and health" to everyone. Ironically, the narrator of Bellow's *Ravelstein* bows out and lets Margaret Thatcher and Ronald Reagan in, as the intellectual's disciples (Bellow 2000: 15). The new right which Thatcher and Reagan introduced onto the world political stage took Bloom's utopianism—what Bellow refers to as the combined redemptive ideas of "Jerusalem and Athens" (Bellow 2000: 15)—very seriously. Not least, because of the electoral appeal of such utopianism that promises full prosperity and health, the golden age of equality and freedom to all. What is crucial here is that the appeal in question is grounded in an ideal whose realization is posited as already existing due to the disavowal of disappointments, that is to say, due to the willful neglect of past failed promises (such as the French Revolution or the Stalinist revolution).

Bellow's novel distances itself from such impactful fusion of ideas, politics, and economics and their redemptive promise. It does so through its focus on Ravelstein's reflection on the Shoah and on the question as to what could have given rise to such genocidal hatred: "The war made clear that almost everybody agreed that the Jews had no right to live. That goes straight to the bone" (Bellow 2000: 178). As has been discussed in Chapter 5,

Bellow lifts the "straight-to-the-bone" metaphor from Strauss's 1962 lecture "Why We Remain Jews" where he recalls early childhood encounters of anti-Semitic pogroms as going "straight to my bones" (Strauss 1997c: 313). This physical sense of going straight to the bone counterpoises the abstractions of a scientific Archimedean view that levers the redemptive promises of politics. Toward its end, Bellow's *Ravelstein* elaborates on this sense of physicality that avoids various political, economic, and scientific abstractions through which we risk losing our experience of worldly reality, however, material and disappointing it may be:

> Under the debris of modern ideas the world was still there to be rediscovered. And his [i.e., Ravelstein's] way of putting it was that the grey net of abstraction covering the world in order to simplify and explain it in a way that served our cultural ends has *become* the world in our eyes. We need to have alternative visions, a diversity of views—and he meant views not bossed by ideas. He saw it as a question of words: "values," "life-styles," "relativism." I agreed up to a point. We need to know—our deep human need, however, can't be satisfied by these terms. We can't climb out of the pit of "culture" and the "ideas" that supposedly express it. The right words would be great help. But even more, a gift for reading reality—the impulse to put your loving face to it and press your hands against it. (Bellow 2000: 208)

The narrator distances himself from Ravelstein's intellectual preoccupation with ideas and words and argues for a reading of reality inclusive of the wordless. Here it is a sensual and empiricist pressing of hands against reality. This image might recall Wilson's pressing of his face against the window, when he delusionarily identifies the face in the Doctor J. Eckleburg's advertisement for seeing glasses with the omniscience of God:

> walked to the rear window and leaned with his face pressed against it [...] looking at the eyes of Doctor T. J. Eckleburg which had just emerged, pale and enormous, from the dissolving night. "God sees everything," repeated Wilson. "This is an advertisement," Michaelis assured him. (Fitzgerald 2006: 161)

Bellow's narrator presses his hands against the thingness of reality. In *The Great Gatsby*, the deluded and misled Wilson (who will mistakenly kill Gatsby for the death of his wife at the end of Fitzgerald's novella) presses his face against a window and develops the image of an advertisement into the idea of God's omniscience and justice that will eventuate in his act of murder.

Not only words, but images and pictures are thus symbolic as well. Facing pictures or images, we are at a remove from our physical experience: like Wilson, we press our face against a window; a screen of ideas and images that may elevate and delude us about physical reality, precisely by putting us at a remove from it. We thus remain in a literally imaginary world, prone to being deceived and disappointed: "Of course we see pictures, not the real thing, but the pictures are dear to us, we come to love them even though we are aware how distorting an organ our mirror-brain is" (Bellow 2000: 208). Why, however, should pictures be less misleading than promising ideas and abstractions? Precisely because they are less promissory, they are less grand, more attached to what they are a mere image of. Images without accompanying words and ideas are not capable of promising redemption. Images, or "pictures" as Bellow puts its (Bellow 2000: 149), depict mere external circumstances such as the weather in which Ravelstein, as political philosopher of neoconservative global promises, takes little interest:

> It wasn't like Ravelstein either to bother with the weather, the weather would adapt itself to whatever the people that mattered were thinking, and he would sometimes criticize me for "checking out the externals"— keeping an eye on the clouds. "You can count on nature doing what nature has been doing forever. Do you think you're going to rush in on Nature and grab off an insight?" he would say. (Bellow 2000: 177)

Ravelstein here delineates the classic idealist cum rationalist dialectical opposition between Kantian autonomy and heteronomy, between external, irrational nature and the internal, rational workings of the mind. As I have shown in *German Idealism and the Jew*, this opposition turns troublesome when we come to attend to how it partakes of socially discriminatory mechanisms wherein the Jews and other Others ("Orientals" and so forth) become placeholders for the negative aspects of this dialectics.

Against this background, a crucial passage toward the ending of *Ravelstein* disappointedly identifies the unprecedented violence of the Nazi genocide as partaking of the rationalism of idealistic promises: "There were also the Jews who had lost the right to exist and were told as much by their executioners— 'There is no reason why you should not die'" (Bellow 2000: 168). The reason of exclusionary, dialectical ideas shapes the lethal ideologies of various quasi-redemptive ideologies in the first part of the twentieth century that witnessed Kojève's first formulation of the later neoconservative phrase "the end of history" in the Paris of the 1930s:

> And so from the Gulag in Russian Asia to the Atlantic Coast, there was a record of destruction or something like a death-disseminating anarchy.

> You had to think of these hundreds of thousands of millions destroyed on ideological grounds—that is, with some pretext of rationality. A rationale had considerable value as a manifestation of order or firmness of purpose. (Bellow 2000: 168)

It is the idea of a kind of redemption that lies at the heart of the genocidal violence with which the avowed disappointment with history and politics of Bellow's last novel is concerned. Why could the promissory idea of redemption give rise to the unprecedented mass murder of the Nazi genocide? Addressing this question, we encounter the trope of disappointment that has to hide from the surface of reality. It becomes displaced onto the category of the negative, and the word "the Jews" comes to denote and symbolize the negativity of disappointment so that actually existing Jews can be identified with what is perceived to be responsible for redemption not materializing:

> Such a volume of hatred and denial of the right to live has never been heard or felt, and the will that willed their death was confirmed and justified by a vast collective agreement that the world would be improved by their disappearance and their extinction. [...] The Jews, Ravelstein and Herbst thought, following the line laid down by their teacher Davarr, were historically witnesses to the absence of redemption." (Bellow 2000: 179)

As we have seen in Chapter 5, in this key passage, which is worth re-quoting, Bellow cites Strauss verbatim. Here, at the point of avowing disappointment with the course of history and politics in the course of the twentieth century, Davarr as esoteric teacher turns into the exoteric center of the novel at its close. Here Bellow adapts Strauss's insight that the esoteric is actually the exoteric (and vice versa):

> The supreme cunning of esoteric writing is in fact to create the belief that the most important doctrines are always hidden, in this way leading the reader to miss what is sometimes said quite clearly on the surface of the text. One then searches the depths of the text for what appears quite naturally on the surface. (Tanguay 2007: 83)

Perhaps via Strauss, Bellow's *Ravelstein* adumbrates a critique of the idealism, which Bloom's advocacy of Alexandre Kojève's Hegelian disavowal of disappointment perpetuates by transporting it from Europe to Ronald Reagan and later to the White House of President Bush senior and junior.

Indeed, Allan Bloom—the historical figure of Ravelstein—may have been the first intellectual to translate Hegel's dialectics of a disavowed disappointment that posits the end of history as promissory synthesis into the dawn of neoconservatism in the United States. The 1992 manifestation of such transatlantic translation of Hegel's promissory idealism into the end of cold war political ambience is Francis Fukuyama's *The End of History and the Last Man*. The main title of this book in fact cites Kojève's famous interpretation of Hegel's hope in the fulfillment of all promises at a world-historical moment (such as Napoleon's victory at the Battle of Jena at the time of which Hegel was completing his *Phenomenology of Spirit*).

In his introduction to an American audience of Kojève's *Introduction to the Reading of Hegel*, Bloom indeed highlights the end of history as the main interpretative achievement of the translated book: "Now, the most striking feature of Kojève's thought is his insistence—fully justified—that for Hegel, and for all followers of Hegel, history is completed, that nothing really new can happen in the world" (Kojève 1969: x). Crucially, here Bloom indicates that the promise of the end of history is itself disappointing, precluding the emergence of the new. At the opening of his preface to *The End of History*, Fukuyama emphasizes that his "'End of History' would never have existed, either as an article or as this present book," without "the invitation to deliver a lecture by that title during the 1988-89 academic year, extended by Professor Nathan Tarcow and Allan Bloom of the John M Olin Center for Inquiry into the Theory and Practice of Democracy at the University of Chicago" (Fukuyama 1992: ix). Fukuyama goes on to single out Bloom and Tarcov as his teachers and friends "from whom I have learned an enormous amount over the years—starting with, but by no means limited to, political philosophy" (Fukuyama 1992: ix). Fukuyama's 1992 book establishes clear connections between the historical figure of Ravelstein, Kojève's Hegel, and its translation via Bloom into the formation of neoconservatism and its promissory revolutionary populism from the Iraq War to Trump's hope to make America great again.

Apropos neoconservatism and writing about the inception of this century, John Gray maintains that during "the past generation the Right abandoned this philosophy of imperfection and embraced Utopia" (Gray 2007: 32). In his book *Black Mass*, Gray traces the way in which the promises of Spinoza's radical enlightenment have lost their hold on European politics during the horrors of the twentieth century, while migrating to the shore of America. The move from Kojève's Hegelian idealism to the new, idealist conservatism of Allan Bloom, on which Bellow's character Ravelstein is based, epitomizes such migration of ideas and their contaminated *Realpolitic* across the Atlantic from the end of the twentieth and the dawn of the twenty-first centuries onward. In a passage worth quoting in full, Gray singles out the main character of such transatlantic importation of Hegel, on whom Kojève famously lectured in the Paris of the 1930s and 1940s and whom Allan Bloom first introduced to an American audience:

> As an intellectual movement neo-conservatism originated on the Left, and in some ways it is a reversion to a radical kind of Enlightenment thinking that has disappeared in Europe. Europe is not without its own illusions—as the idea that the diverse countries that compose it can somehow be welded into a federal super-state capable of acting as a rival power to the United States—but it has abandoned the belief that human life can be remade by force. Even in France—the home of the Jacobins—the faith in revolution was killed off by the history of the twentieth century, but when it died in Europe it did not vanish from the world. In a flight that would have delighted Hegel it migrated to America where it settled on the neo-conservative Right. Neo-conservatives are noted for their disdain for Europe but one of their achievements is to have injected a defunct European revolutionary tradition into the heart of American political life. (Gray 2007a: 32–3)

Nearly half a century before Francis Fukuyama famously declared the "end of history" at the end of the Cold War (Fukuyama 1992), Alexandre Kojève did the same during and at the end of the Second World War. The end proclaimed here is far from being a doomsday. On the contrary, it posits a golden culmination of human progress where everything promised has reached the point of quasi-miraculous fulfillment.

His teacher Leo Strauss established contact between Bloom and Kojève. Bloom adopted Kojève's demand that the intellectual struggles for honor and Gatsby-like glamour by gaining the social recognition of world leaders. While reflecting on the horrors of the Nazi genocide, Bellow's Ravelstein ceases to disavow disappointment with history and politics. At this point he embraces Strauss's critique of Kojève, when he maintains that "insofar as the philosopher, owing to the weakness of the flesh, becomes concerned with being recognized by others, he ceases to be a philosopher" (Strauss 2000: 203). Strauss here might have had Jay Gatsby in mind and his rather unwise struggle for unmaking a past of failed promises and inadequate social recognitions. Chapter 7 analyzes how an unacknowledged sense of disappointment informs our contemporary politics of fear. Strikingly, it is a fear of immigrants and an angst-ridden concern with borders that accompanies current political promises and nationalist manifestations of hope.

7

Disappointment in the Age of the Anthropocene

How D. H. Lawrence and Kafka Render Dialectics Inoperative

Introduction: The Symbolism of Numbers or from Financial to Political Crises— Populism and the Struggle for Distinction in Hegel's Master-Slave Dialectics

Apprehensions of crises go hand in hand with a fear of contaminations. The fear of deteriorating circumstances, of a decline in our living conditions causes the felt need for a tightening of borders in order to keep out those who are perceived to be "Other": strangers, the poor, immigrants, the mentally ill, and so forth. The financial crisis of 2008 has by now already turned into a political crisis where issues of policing borders, identity, race, and nationality are the exclusive focus of public discussion while concerns for economic benefits such as employment, tax income, and trade have almost become irrelevant. Or, so it seems.

In *Philosophy and Literature in Times of Crisis* I have proposed the provocative thesis that after the financial crisis a certain economist paradigm which reduces diversity to the spurious and identifying "evidence" of numbers has become the exclusive consideration which subsumes all aspects of life from health to ethics. By comparing two early-twentieth-century classics— D. H. Lawrence's *Women in Love* and Kafka's *Das Schloss*—this chapter analyzes why and how an economist obsession with numbers determines contemporary politics and policy. The current populist preoccupation with immigration and the building of border walls is not so much a break with an economist paradigm of numbers as a mere shift within it. A new reading of the immigrant stranger K. in Kafka's *Das Schloss* will illuminate how numbers are not so much economic indicators as symbols denoting distinction or the lack thereof.

Kafka refers to Hegel's master-slave dialectic when he describes K.'s dread about the hierarchical subordination in work relationships. Here K. as a stranger occupies the lowest social position of being socially inferior, of being a mere working tool wherein like a slave the sphere of work coincides with that of existence as such in the state of *Arbeiterseins* (*die gefürchteten Folgen des Untergeortetseins, des Arbeiterseins*) (Kafka 1926: 66). Kafka's stranger, migrant K., here embodies a feared negativity (*gefürchteten Folgen*) which the master-slave dialectics of an economy premised on distinctions (of which numbers are indicators) includes merely to exclude. Seemingly paradoxical, this paradigm is all the more relevant at those times when the general population faces disappointing prospects vis-á-vis promises of prosperity. At this point economist reductionism avows to diminish the role of business or, in other words, economics as such—when leading Brexiteers claim that they are not interested in the economic benefit of immigrants from EU countries but instead attempt to restore the integrity and purity of English culture which is apparently threatened by these immigrants. How can we explain such blatant rejection of material interests?

This book analyzes the ways in which such misleading and disingenuous abnegation of economic benefits partakes of a disavowal of disappointments at times of economic crises. Once the markets have disappointed public expectations, because their potential promises have not materialized, financial crises turn into political ones as witnessed by the current rise of various forms of populism and nationalism. In order to maintain hope, political expectations shift from the apparent material to the immaterial sphere of identity politics. The latter in fact reinforces concrete measures such as the construction of a wall between Mexico and the United States or the closure of borders (between the United Kingdom and the EU). A deceptive evasion of economic interests in the face of market declines indeed disavows real-existing material disappointments by emphasizing form over substance. Formal concerns to do with the purity of, say, English culture obfuscate objectified circumstances that have financially shaken large parts of the population (such as nearly nine years of austerity in the UK).

By touting formally anti-immigrant measures, populist politicians operate a bourgeois prioritization of form over material substance, and this most strikingly at a time when the latter has become a source of disappointment. This raises the question whether a bourgeois preoccupation with free markets has immaterial rather material motivations. Is the concern with economic benefits actually about the material improvement of livelihoods? Is it not rather to do with the symbolic quest for distinctions and recognitions? Here it becomes apparent that numbers, like words or images, are symbols. They promise something but are in themselves immaterial, mere strokes of the pen or printing press.

The economist prioritization of quantity over quality partakes of the attempt to reach symbolically higher "qualitative" levels of value or significance. Distinctions, however, unfold via a structure of oppositions. As Pierre Bourdieu shows in the following quotation, the hierarchy of such structure relies on the dialectical movement of Hegel's master-slave opposition:

> Verbal virtuosities or the gratuitous expense of time or money that is presupposed by material or symbolic appropriation of works of art, or even, at the second power, the self-imposed constraints and restrictions which make up the "asceticism of the privileged" (as Marx said of Seneca) and the refusal of the facile which is the basis of all "pure" aesthetics, are so many repetitions of that variant of the master-slave dialectic through which the possessors affirm their possessions. In doing so, they distance themselves still further from the dispossessed, who, not content with being slaves to necessity in all its forms, are suspected of being possessed by the desire for possession, and so potentially possessed by the possessions they do not, or do not yet, possess. (Bourdieu 2010: 254)

Bourdieu here implicitly contaminates the seemingly opposed spheres of materialism and aestheticism, of privilege and asceticism. Developing further Bourdieu's approach we may come to see economic concerns in terms of symbolic ones to do with social and class distinctions. Economics drafts a network of distinctions and the populist opposition between natives and foreigners, between citizens and immigrants partakes of such symbolization of the innocent and the negative.

The immigrants here embody the negativity, which Hegel's dialectic of the master and slave transmutes into a new synthesis of the positive, when the slave internalizes his inferiority to the point at which he actively overcomes it by risking all his material possessions, which remain in his state of lack and abjection: his bare life. Only by completely dispossessing his life, the slave may gain mastery of the master's possessions, according to the mutations of Hegel's politics of mutually opposed social and economic roles. Current populist oppositions between ethnic and national identities follow such dialectical promises of overcoming negativity (the stranger) in structurally the same dialectical way as the free market expectations of turning poverty into wealth.

The content differs, however, having moved from the blatantly material sphere of wealth creation to the cultural sphere of identity. Even though populist politicians sometimes downplay the importance of economic considerations, their discourse still pertains to a dialectical movement in which deficiencies transmute into promised outcomes: from poverty to wealth and from cultural alienation in a multicultural society to a future state of ethnic and national purity wherein the native population has been awarded its "country back." We need a theory of contaminations (such as attempted in my book Contaminations [2016]) in order to arrive at a more nuanced understanding of why the political focus on policing borders and keeping out foreigners obfuscates its specific economist motivation: one that reduces human beings to numbers. Crucially, numbers are not "objective." They are themselves fraught with symbolic significance. The greater the number of immigrants, the worse for the native population. This is exactly how the press and the home office has reported and framed immigration numbers in the wake of the Brexit referendum in the UK, and this is still continuing.

Why, however, turn to early-twentieth-century classics in order to illuminate our current, twenty-first-century situation? As we will see in the following, perceptions of crisis have haunted modernity from the failed promises of the French Revolution onward. Around 1900, sociologists first attempted to think through the contaminating paradoxes of modernity. Their sense of modernity was individualistic and at the same time adumbrated a social formation that gave rise to the crowd (le Bon, Simmel, and Freud). Modernity contaminated tradition with the absence of tradition, the cult of the individual (what Weber would call Charisma) and collectivism.

How can we explain the simultaneity of opposed tendencies that characterizes modernity and which I theorize in literary terms with the figure of contamination? In his study of Henry James the philosopher Robert Pippin focuses on the loss of traditional values when he discusses the crisis of modernity to which modernist literature responds. Modernity ushers in a radical change in traditions that have so far determined social relations: "Everything of significance in the basic manner of civilized life known heretofore, in the role of history, hierarchy, sensibilities, gender relations, social power, is about to change" (Pippin 2000: 32). While Pippin raises an important point, it is worthwhile to contextualize this issue within a larger historical framework. Against this background, the change in significance and traditional forms of meaning with which Pippin is concerned here is not entirely new at the beginning of the twentieth century. At the dawn of the twentieth century the loss of traditional coordinates of significance is, indeed, a striking feature in literary, religious, and sociological texts: Weber's writing on the Protestant work ethic and Walter Benjamin and Gershom

Scholem's letter exchange about Kafka's characters as religious students, who have lost the whole script, are powerful instances of this (as discussed in the introduction to Chapter 6).

As we have seen in Chapters 1 and 2, long before 1900, however, with Spinoza's radical enlightenment in the seventeenth century and the French Revolution at the end of the eighteenth century, there has been the promise of equality and diversity, holding out the hope of a non-sovereign kind of politics that will have abandoned hierarchical structures that could give rise to the affects of envy and jealousy. It is precisely those hierarchically symbolic points of inclusion and exclusion which have determined not only the economic but also the social, political, and cultural network of relationships and this all the more pronounced after the financial crisis and the ensuing rise of populism (as discussed earlier). These hierarchies are not new and in order to better comprehend their deleterious repercussions it is imperative to analyze early-twentieth-century literary attempts to come to term with them. Kafka's *Das Schloss* lays out the harsh and bare structure of such hierarchical relationships that pinpoint the stranger or immigrant as the most negative point whom, like Hegel's slave, society includes only to exclude. While Kafka's narrative leaves out historical coordinates, Lawrence's *Women in Love* foregrounds the post-First World War context of a contamination between class, national, and economic rivalries and hierarchies.

However, on a theoretical level at least, by the early-twentieth-century hierarchies and their associated traditional significations of value lose their societal validity. This apparent dissipation of traditional structures of hierarchy accompanies an even more pronounced diminution of the promise of freedom and social equality. This sense of disappointment with the hopes for social inclusion plays a notable role in a late nineteenth-century thinker who in the first place has not invested much trust into the political ideal of egalitarianism. Robert Pippin has intriguingly reconceptualized this thinker, Nietzsche, in literary and psychological terms. As we will see in the following section, D. H. Lawrence takes issue with Nietzsche's attempt to establish his famous will to power as a way toward the construction of new sociopolitical hierarchies. Nietzsche's new strong individual would countenance any remaining hopes for a nonhierarchical version of modernity premised on Spinoza's radical enlightenment of diversity (as taken up in Marx's *Communist Manifesto* and held out by socialism at the end of the nineteenth and in the first part of the twentieth centuries). In Pippin's reading, however, Nietzsche not so much propounds a position or program but describes the dilemma of a world that has lost traditional forms of signification, while not being prepared to found or believe in new ones (such as equality or freedom).

Nietzsche, the literary thinker, is concerned with the psychological situation of what he calls nihilism as the void of value and as the loss of established sign systems of meaning. This loss offers itself as new pawn in an ever renewed master-slave dialectics. In the current populist context, immigrants denote an absence of native meanings and the erasure of a nation's significance. The loss is symbolic and cultural but this does not diminish its substantive implication for politics. Proving right Spinoza's critique of traditional theology as anthropocentric projections of human ideals and wishes, the loss of transcending meanings in actual fact diminishes a given community's image of itself and its role in the world.

The loss of belief in God and associated traditional meanings hence appears to be disappointing and negative. Nietzsche's famous death of God embraces the whole world of human knowledge and its ramification for given communities. To avoid such a void, Nietzsche seeks to overcome the nihilism of pale, enervated atheists who do not have the courage to invest into affective and significant relationships either new or old:

> So we need to understand why if the death of God signals a general end to the possibility of transcendence, religion, morally significant truth, and so forth, the successor culture would not simply have to be a culture of such pale (joking, ironic) atheists, people for whom nothing much is important beyond their own immediate happiness and their security in achieving happiness. (Pippin 2010: 51)

According to Pippin, Nietzsche's psychological question is the "possibility of sustaining a commitment to any such value in the current historical condition, a condition of cultural and spiritual death" (Pippin 2010: 52), which is the condition of nihilism.

Nietzsche's question opens up nightmarish visions and fields of destruction and dissatisfaction which the currently prevailing populist discourse displaces onto the immigrants as placeholders for all kinds of real-existing disappointments (financial and otherwise). On the psychological level of the individual, the world's nihilistic void of significance plunges the subject into the paralyzing state of boredom. Pippin urges us to take seriously Nietzsche's vivid metaphors and metonymies for such destruction that renders ideas and ideals uninteresting and boring:

> that we treat the phenomenon of nihilism in a way closer to Nietzsche's images and figures and tropes, many of which have been cited often; images of death, decay, illness, the absence of tension, a "sleep" of the

spirit (as in his beautiful claim that what is needed now is "an ability to dream without having to sleep"), and perhaps the most intuitive metonymy of failed desire: boredom. (Pippin 2010: 54)

On a sociopolitical level, various populist ideologies displace the disappointing negativity of such voids of boredom and meaninglessness on to the stranger, the immigrant, the Jew, or Muslim.

Concerning the psyche of the individual, the psychology of fin-de-siècle ennui places the cause of political and intellectual uncertainties in "the failure of desire that" Nietzsche calls "nihilism" (Pippin 2010: 58). Nietzsche's term "nihilism" articulates the sense of self-dissatisfaction, boredom, and all the social phenomena ensuing from such destructive voids of validity, meaning, and significance that we find in major modernist classics from Henry James to Joseph Conrad, Virginia Woolf, Kafka, Benjamin, Scholem, D. H. Lawrence, and Thomas Mann.

These voids of validity still stick to traditional entities but empty them of meaning: "Nietzsche described all modern moral philosophy, together with its psychological assumptions, as a doomed attempt to cling to the fundamental precepts of Christian morality but without the authorizing force that made the system credible—a creator God" (Pippin 2010: 67). Hegel's progressive dialectics, whose synthesis transmutes any given negative into a positive, is a powerful form of such secularized Christian morality. The Hegelian Pippin comes to see the void of Hegel's secularized Christian vision of a satisfied, economically enriched bourgeois life, from the perspective of Nietzsche's withering psychological critique of its boredom and void:

> Hegel was, understood historically, wrong ("psychologically wrong," let us say) and a good deal of later European high culture has to do with in just *what* sense he was wrong. The psychological sense suggested by Nietzsche is clear enough by now. This sort of world, Hegel's world, both disguises from itself, in massive strategies of self-deceit, its own hidden brutality. (Pippin 2010: 123)

By the twenty-first century, Nietzsche's psychological critique of dialectics seems to have inflected American middlebrow art too. In modern and contemporary culture, mental illness often epitomizes a void of meaning and significance that comes with the loss of transcendence. Let me provide an exemplary case from a recent US TV series about borders, the loss of meaning, and a curious critique of dialectics from the pen of a mentally ill protagonist.

In the first season of the US TV show *The Bridge* we encounter a mentally ill character who rages against dialectics. The main culprit diverts the attention of the police to this disturbed man. In perhaps the best joke of the series, Hank, one lead detective, complains that he still does not know what the term "dialectics" means and this after a long search on the internet. The role of the border is the main subject matter of *The Bridge*: the border separating Mexico from the United States. One of the weaknesses of its first season becomes apparent when we realize that what the mentally ill person says about dialectics turns out to be anything but deranged. Instead, what he says goes to the heart of what the show is trying to depict as the violence of hierarchies and distinctions and how this violence operates through various oppositions and borders.

Why take issue with dialectics in the context of borders? The mentally ill protagonist attacks dialectics as a way of thinking, which creates oppositions whose demarcations, need to be controlled. He says that the violence and the injustice that haunts the borderland between Mexico and the United States highlight what is wrong with dialectics: it operates within the structure of oppositions. Within the context of *The Bridge* we are faced with contrasts between negative (evil or corrupt) Mexico and positive (law abiding) United States. In an intriguing and sociopolitically important manner the show questions the validity of such facile antagonism.

As part of his critique of dialectics, the mentally ill character of season one argues that the violence that seems to be restricted to the Mexican border will spill over into the US side, because the dialectical opposition between the positive and the negative will come home to roost: the negative will contaminate the positive and vice versa. Dialectical ways of thinking that separate our world into distinct and contrasting elements deceive ourselves about the contaminated constitution of our world where borders are illusory sign systems that aim to control or police our lives but eventually these and similar structures of separation break down and their porosity emerges in plain sight. This is exactly what takes place in season 2. It is perhaps a bit misleading to put the theoretically as well as practically moot point of the *The Bridge* into the mouth of a so-called madman but then this very reversal of madness and truth might be another sophisticated way of questioning separations and contrasts.

The issue of mental health is all the more relevant to Nietzsche's problematic of nihilism, because nihilism undermines our capacity to act and interact. Nihilism paralyzes. How so? It does so by deflating our image of God and ourselves and by thus confronting us with negativity, with loss, lack, and disappointment. Ethnic and other populist ideologies gain their attraction and force by precisely disavowing such realities of loss and disappointment.

They do so by first symbolically constructing the image of an Other, the stranger (the immigrant, the Jew, the Muslim), which the counter-image of sanity and selfhood opposes. The Other now bears the negative markers of failure, loss, and disappointment. Once the self is without the Other, negativity has dialectically morphed into the promise of success.

A critical reader might wonder, however, whether dialectics is not concerned with such reversals. Is such mobility not its appeal in modern and contemporary social theory from Hegel to Judith Butler, Robert Pippin, and Slavoj Žižek? Crucially, the movement in question here is away from what is considered to be negative: it is the journey from "evil" Mexico to "positive" United States where the former becomes abolished or subsumed (*aufgehoben* as Hegel puts it) in the latter. Negativity does not disappear completely but it undergoes, nevertheless, a transformation into something else wherein some of its elements inform a new, positive identity. As Judith Butler has shown in her recent critique of Hegel's dialectics of recognition:

> There is lots of light in the Hegelian room, and the mirrors have the happy coincidence of usually being windows, as well. This view of recognition does not encounter an exteriority that resists a bad infinity of recursive mimesis. There is no opacity that shadows these windows or dims that light. In consequence, we might consider a certain post-Hegelian reading of the scene of recognition in which precisely my own opacity to myself occasions my capacity to confer a certain kind of recognition on others. It would be, perhaps, an ethics based on our shared, invariable, and partial blindness about ourselves. (Butler 2005: 41)

Butler's ethics of blindness diverges from Hegel's dialectics where the light—referred to in the preceding quotation —demarcates boundaries clearly. The opacity Butler appraises allows for the porosity of borders which would dissolve in what I call a theory of contaminations. Contaminations question the clearly divided entities which the light of dialectics illuminates, while playing off the negative against the positive and eventually dissolving negativity into positivity, Mexico into the United States, as it were.

Butler attempts to render opaque the clearly demarcated oppositions of dialectics in order to alleviate the violence that sometimes accompanies such contrasts. As we have seen in Chapter 6, one famous contrast is Hegel's confrontation between master and slave. The slave overcomes his negativity, his inferiority, by staking his life in the struggle for recognition. The violence that goes with such an extreme readiness to risk one's own life in order to overcome one's perceived negativity (as slave) prompts Butler to assert

Spinoza's *conatus*—the right or urge; Agamben has recently called it "the demand"[1]—of each living being to persist in staying alive:

> Spinoza marks for us the desire to live, to persist, upon which every theory of recognition is built. And because the terms by which recognition operates may seek to fix and capture us, they run the risk of arresting desire, and of putting an end to life. As a result, it is important for ethical philosophy to consider that any theory of recognition will have to give an account of the desire for recognition, remembering that desire sets the limits and the conditions for the operation of recognition itself. Indeed, a certain desire to persist, we might say, following Spinoza, underwrites recognition or, indeed, forms of judgment that seek to relinquish or destroy the desire to persist, the desire for life itself, undercut the very precondition of recognition. (Butler 2005: 44)

By counterbalancing Hegel's dialectics with Spinoza's *conatus*, Butler attempts to level the playing field between master and slave. She sets out to neutralize terms of prioritization such as "master" or "enjoyment."

Does such equalization of the playing field not, however, outdo the very kernel of Hegel's dialectic? Dialectics depends on the hierarchical oppositions of symbols, of terms such as master and slave, native and stranger, positive and negative. Do we need to render inoperative the operations of Hegel's dialectics? Indeed, Agamben has recently conjoined Hegel's dialectical opposition between master and slave to one between enjoyment and labor. The master enjoys the labors of the slave and even though Hegel allows for a reversal of such terms, as Butler has analyzed, the two are nevertheless clearly distinct and opposed to each other.

More importantly, dialectical structures set one above the other (master over slave; positivity over negativity). Both Butler and Agamben attempt to obscure such oppositions. Agamben argues that such rendering obscure or undifferentiated of hierarchical oppositions has been lost in modern methodologies such as Hegel's dialectics: "Even in the dialectical reversal, what is nonetheless lost is the possibility of another figure of human praxis, in which enjoyment and labor (which is restrained desire) are in the last analysis unassignable" (Agamben 2016: 37). In other words Agamben wants "to render inoperative the dialectic between master and slave" (Agamben

---

[1] "If we propose to translate *conor* with 'to demand' and *conatus* with 'demand' ('The demand by means of which each thing demands to persevere in its being'), it is on the condition of not forgetting the medial nature of the process that is here in question: the being that desires and demands, in demanding, modifies, desires, and constitutes itself" Agamben 2016: 171.

2016: 37). Much of Agamben's work revolves around the notion of the inoperative. Without referring to the figure of contaminations, Agamben (apart from his notion of use and contemplation) abstains from elaborating on how we can achieve such work that renders defunct the hierarchical and prioritizing structures of dialectical oppositions such as the one between master and slave, or native and foreigner, citizen and stranger. One of the main aims of this book is to analyze how we can arrive at such methodology of the inoperative via the figure and the theory of contamination.

Mourning the Loss of Contaminating Negativity in D. H. Lawrence's *Women in Love*

Agamben speaks of a loss. In this way, supreme knowledge is always already lost for Agamben: "the supreme knowledge is that which comes too late, when we no longer have any use for it" (Agamben 2011: 9). According to Agamben, true modernity and contemporaneity revolves around the experience of loss and that to the point that we lose our modern selves in the prehistoric past: "the key to the modern is hidden in the immemorial and the prehistoric" (Agamben 2011: 17). In order to come into its own, the avant-garde seeks to be contaminated by what it apparently has lost: "The avant-garde, which has lost itself over time, also pursues the primitive and the archaic" (Agamben 2011: 170). As will be explored in this section, a so far ignored aspect of modernist literature mourns the loss of contamination.

The loss of contamination is almost a tautological expression, because what is contaminated is exactly what is lost, what is to be forgone as negative. Modernism mourns the loss of negativity, of losing. It thus counters dialectical attempts to disavow disappointment that have shaped popular ideologies of ethnic and class struggles in the twentieth century and that have returned to the political arena with the contemporary rise of populism. As Jonathan Flatly has argued, mourning and melancholy instantiates a form of activity rather than being solely passive: "Instead, melancholizing is something one *does*: longing for lost loves, brooding over absent objects and changed environments, reflecting on unmet desires, and lingering on events from the past" (Flatly 2008: 2). The melancholic mourning of a loss is one of modernity's prime activities. This activity contaminates the past with the present, the ancient with the modern, old age with youth.

According to Flatly, "Freud is not so much correcting or improving (as he supposed) our view of melancholia as giving us in his theory of melancholia an allegory for the experience of modernity, an experience [. . .] that is constitutively linked to loss" (Flatly 2008: 2). Building on Flatly's work, Sanja Bahun has recently argued that we should abandon the standard opposition between mourning and melancholia, that the melancholy of modernist literature instantiates the work of mourning. She makes clear that, far from opposing one to the other, Freud interconnects the terms "mourning" and "melancholia." Both are focused on a loss:

> According to Freud's 1917 essay, mourning and melancholia have the same cause (loss of a cherished person, object, or concept) and they entail similar symptoms (dejection, inhibition of the capacity to love, cessation of interest in the outer world, and others), but the two responses to loss differ in the structure of the relationship established between the subject and the lost other: while melancholia "pathologically" preserves the lost object in the mourner's ego, mourning a "normative" grief experience, dispels it. In a discourse strongly reminiscent of contemporary anthropology, Freud describes mourning-work (*Trauerarbeit*) as a slow, painful process of detaching oneself from the lost object through hyper-cathected reality testing. (Bahun 2014: 24)

Whereas in mourning we eventually control and attenuate our sense of loss, melancholia precludes such alleviation of symptoms. The melancholic cannot get over the experience of a loss. Freud famously connects individual case studies with an analysis of a larger group—he interlinks onto—with phyllo-genesis (as he famously does in the Oedipus complex). Loss here is both individual and generic: "from Freud's circumvention, loss emerges as at once individual and group, physical and abstract, factual and fictive, past and present, as its meaning and status are constantly renegotiated" (Bahun 2014: 26). Although writing in different geographies (and not knowing each other's work), both Kafka and Lawrence connect the individual experience of having lost a contaminated life world with that of history at large. Mourning shares with melancholy the experience of disappointment that accompanies the recognition of a loss. That the subject matter of melancholia and mourning are forms of contamination which render—via the avowal of disappointment—inoperative binary, dialectical oppositions such as master and slave, comes clearly to the fore in D. H. Lawrence's *Women in Love* as well as in Kafka's *Das Schloss*.

Compared with Kafka's last novel, D. H. Lawrence's *Women in Love* is much more historically grounded. For this reason, it is a text wherein we can contextualize close readings of key passages focused on a sense of disappointment. These passages question dialectical oppositions and mourn a loss of contaminations within modernity. In the first chapter of *Women in Love* we encounter a discussion about foreigners and natives, race and economics. This takes place against the background of the First World War during which Lawrence wrote the novel. Birkin, one of the main characters (and one whom some critics identify as being close to acting as a mouthpiece for the author),[2] summarizes this discussion as follows: "A race must have its commercial aspect. In fact it must. It is like a family. You *must* make provision. And to make provision you have to strive against other families, other nations" (Lawrence 1989: 77). Here we encounter the promise of borders and dialectical oppositions.

In order to improve, we need to have opposites, "others" which borders function to separate from us, thus establishing symbols of distinction and hierarchy (such as the one between Mexico and the United States in the TV series *The Bridge*). Vanquishing and transmuting these others—personifications of dialectical negatives—will eventually enrich and aggrandize our self-defined "positive" identity and entity. Birkin works in the educational sector. He is an intellectual. Gerald Crich is a new type of entrepreneur who abandons the paternalistic, traditionalist type of capitalism of his father for a more advanced, competitive one. He concurs with Birkin's analysis of the parallels between nationalistic antagonism and an economist paradigm of competition, countering Birkin's friend Hermione Roddice's "Yes, I think it is always wrong to provoke a spirit of rivalry. It makes bad blood. And bad blood accumulates" (Lawrence 1989: 77) with "But you can't do away with the spirit of emulation altogether" (Lawrence 1989: 77). Gerald argues for the necessity of antagonism claiming that it "is one of the necessary incentives for production and improvement" (Lawrence 1989: 77). Production and progress paradoxically depends upon destruction and strife. At this point Birkin retreats from his previous justification of nationalistic and economist rivalry: "'I must say,' said Birkin, 'I detest the spirit of emulation'" (Lawrence 1989: 77). Emulation describes the struggle for recognition where one entity strives to outdo the other. This is exactly what is going on in the dialectical struggle between master and slave where the very sign system prioritizes one (master) over the other (slave). It is not simply a matter of provision, as Birkin first claims; it is one of emulation, involving the struggle of recognition.

Much of *Women in Love* revolves around how to render inoperative the workings of emulation: the struggle for priority of two mutually opposed nations, families, companies, and so forth. Within this context, the novel probes what may appear to be benign, traditional, or positive capacities such

---

[2] Charles L Ross argues that the "the voices of Birkin and Lawrence seem identical" (Ross 1989: 23).

as volition and sight, which (as Judith Butler shows in the quote earlier) help establish the clear demarcation of oppositions. Some critics like Keith M. May have arrived at such critical perspective on volition through an investigation of the influence of Nietzsche's fragmented notion of a non-unified self on Lawrence. According to this interpretation, however, Lawrence would not be adumbrating a new concept of the negative and disappointing (part of a conception of contamination) but rather a more traditional organicist notion of wholeness founded in multiplicities:

> In this way Lawrence, like Nietzsche, in effect taught that all one's conscious psychic activities should be avowed and none arbitrarily suppressed. The activities would then compose themselves organically and grow through contact with the environment, as natural organisms grow. (May 1988: 143)

However, it is not so much the organic but an affirmation of that which we experience as negative and disappointment, as an impediment, such as a lack of clarity or the unpredictability of the unsystematic, which Lawrence celebrates in his writings.

Sight and will give way to the obscurity of feeling and touch: "Oh—one would *feel* things instead of merely looking at them. I should feel the air move against me, and feel the things I touched, instead of having to look at them. I am sure life is all wrong because it has become too visual—we can neither listen to nor feel nor understand, we can only see" (Lawrence 1989: 132). As described here, feeling and touch render borders porous. Emotion and the sensual allow for a contamination between self and air, the environment and one's sense of understanding. Sight, by contrast, establishes distance, where we cannot hear or feel or comprehend the other and instead only observe what we are not. Abbie Garrington has argued "that Lawrence extrapolates a contemporary mode of vision that reinserts the hand—to see darkly and fumblingly is, however counter-intuitively, to see *clearly*" (Garrington 2013: 157). The counter-intuitive is indeed what the term "contamination" highlights: the coincidence of apparent opposites which surprises us, which we would have thought to be impossible. Lawrence contaminates the visual with the tactile.[3]

Lawrence takes issue with an ideal of vision that is uncontaminated by touch. Through isolated, purified vision (that goes without the contaminations of the tactile) we are in control because, unlike feeling and

---

[3] Lawrence's work has been associated with more narrow, biological/clinical terms such as "contagion" or "disease." As Paul Eggert has shown, contemporary reviews of Lawrence's novels denounce them as "a form of disease, and with the some of the infective qualities a disease possesses" (Eggert 2009: 188).

touch, it establishes physical distance between self and Other. Gerald Crich's actions to control his horse's aversion to an oncoming train, epitomizes the volition of the modern self that has lost an appreciation of the forces of contamination (such as touch or feeling). Gerald defends his own priority over the horse by what he calls the "natural order" (Lawrence 1989: 200). The order of nature seems to establish a hierarchical relationship between humanity and its environment where the former has always already gained a position of priority over the latter (Mack 2016: 77–106).

Nowadays we use the term "Anthropocene" for such a prioritization of the human: "It is more natural for a man to take a horse and use it as he likes, than for him to go down on his knees to it, begging it to do as it wishes, and to fulfil its own marvellous nature" (Lawrence 1989: 200). Instead of a contaminating relationship between human and animal we are stuck in a rivalry whose winner is preestablished by a certain structure (as in Hegel's master-slave dialectics): that of the natural order that validates the priority of the human; the Anthropocene. Lawrence questions what we now call the Anthropocene in terms of Nietzsche's concept of the will to power. Negativity and disappointment avoids various promises of power and success as epitomized in the teleology of volition.

The novel theorizes modernity's emphasis on action and volition in what Nietzsche has famously called the *Wille zur Macht*. Birkin's lover Ursula identifies Gerald's control over the horse in order to force an accommodation with the noise of the train, with Nietzsche's will to power: "It is just like Gerald Crich with his horse—a lust for bullying—a real *Wille zur Macht*—so base, so petty" (Lawrence 1989: 213). Gudrun, Ursula, and Birkin detest this prioritization of the will and the active principle. Will and action crystallize in the mechanical: the machine of which the train partakes, to whose operations Gerald attempts to subdue his horse.

Lawrence affiliates the human with the machine, trains, and other mechanical operations that are indeed the products of humanity's labor. He radicalizes what Judith Butler calls obscurity and, as we have seen at the end of the previous section, she refers to the opaque in order to counterbalance the clear demarcation of Hegel's dialectical oppositions. Lawrence evokes the darkness of death that turns inoperative human emulation and the will power: "But the great, dark, illimitable kingdom of death, there humanity was put to scorn. So much they could do upon earth, the multifarious little gods that they were. But the kingdom of death put them all to scorn, they dwindled into their true vulgar silliness in the face of it" (Lawrence 1989: 263). Lawrence's posthumanism is one that sets out to outdo the working of volition and its mechanical products. This farewell to the will partakes of a paradoxical affirmation of disappointment and of what we would consciously castigate as the failed, the unpredictable, and the contaminated multiplicity of unsystematic life. In Lawrence, disappointment does justice to the uncontrollable and unpredictable diversity of nature. Nature's multiplicity disappoints the one-dimensional will and scheme of human volition. It renders absurd and questionable human promises and presumptions—the "multifarious little gods"—based, as they are, on the achievements of the will and its various activities.

The human will and its products—that is, technology—is, however, the symptom of a modern loss of an affirmative sense of disappointment implicit in the concept of contamination that Lawrence's novel mourns. It becomes apparent that this loss occurred a long time ago. To be precise in a period of prehistory before the split into opposed gender binaries took place: "Why should we consider ourselves, men and women, as broken fragments of one whole. It is not true. We are not broken fragments of one whole. Rather we are the singling away into purity and clear being, of things that were mixed, the unresolved" (Lawrence 1989: 271). This important quotation unmasks illusions of purity. Such illusions are not the product of darkness but, paradoxically, of too much light and clarity. Clear, rather than obscure, beings resemble the state of purity which is an illusion, a fiction which nevertheless shapes the structure of our sociopolitical lives.

Critics have not sufficiently appreciated the ways in which alleged transgender or homosexual tendencies in Lawrence's work participate in his modernist mourning of a loss of contamination whose inception *Women in Love* locates in the sphere of gender specification and purification. Lawrence's contamination of gender roles is radical and has caused offence, most famously resulting in the censure of the gender-crossdressing episode of *Sons and Lovers* (where Paul Morell puts on the stockings of his girlfriend).

Transgender identities address the loss of contaminations of which purified gender roles are the modern offspring. Against such modernity of gender oppositions, Lawrence evokes the now lost prehistory of gender contaminations: "In the old age, before sex was, we were mixed, each one a mixture. The process of singling into individuality resulted in the great polarity of sex" (Lawrence 1989: 271). The contemporary and the modern describe further separations and oppositions of what has once been not a unity but a contamination of opposites. After prehistory and well into modernity and contemporaneity, male and female become gradually more separated from each other reaching a state of isolated purity:

> The womanly drew to one side, the manly to the other. But the separation was imperfect even then. And so our world-cycle passes. There is now to come the new day, when we are beings of each of us, fulfilled

in difference. The man is pure man, the woman pure woman, they are perfectly polarized. (Lawrence 1989: 271)

Modernity introduces the world of the purified, isolated individual where "we are beings of each of us, fulfilled in difference." However, this constitutes uncontaminated difference that seeks not the other but a state of priority and autarchy where we do not need the other: "But there is no longer any of the horrible merging, mingling self-abnegation of love. There is only the pure duality of polarization, each one free from any contamination of the other" (Lawrence 1989: 271). What has been lost is the experience of contamination. This is an obscure encounter wherein clear identities contaminate each other. As a result of such contaminating obscurity (or, negativity) clear demarcations and oppositions cannot be established and counted. As a negative but nonetheless liberating force, the figure of contamination escapes the grasp of identification and enumeration: it is beyond biopolitics.

Against this background, it is important to make clear that Lawrence does not idealize unity. He indeed disappoints promises of organicist wholeness as he questions hopes for systemic completeness or mechanical slickness. What he has in mind is a diversity of opposites that are not dialectically separated from and opposed to each other but rather live in a state of cohabitation where they contaminate each other, cross-dressing each other's clothes and identities as Paul Morell does in *Sons and Lovers*.

Lawrence indeed casts the promise of unity into a disappointing ambience wherein its reactionary tones come fully to the fore. Gerald's father personifies unity not as promise but as disappointment. He epitomizes the paternalistic capitalist whose world literally breaks asunder with the rise of mechanical capitalism and the technological warfare of the First World War: "The whole unifying idea of mankind seemed to be dying with his [i.e., Gerald's] father, the centralising force that had held the whole together seemed to collapse with his father, the parts were ready to go asunder in terrible disintegration" (Lawrence 1989: 293). Whereas his father tried to bring the working classes to his side in a quasi-state of unity, Gerald reduces his subordinates to separate entities, to numbers that can be used at his—the boss's—will: "What mattered was the pure instrumentality of the individual. As man as of a knife: does it cut well? Nothing else mattered" (Lawrence 1989: 295–6). Gerald reduces the workers to numbers, to objects, to instruments that implement the master's will: "The will of man was the determining factor. Man was the arch-god of earth. His mind was obedient to serve his will. Man's will was the absolute, the only absolute. And it was his will to subjugate matter to his own ends" (Lawrence 1989: 296). The master's will strives with those of his subordinates.

Mirroring the dialectical opposition of Hegel's master and slave, Lawrence's will to power of the Anthropocene endeavors to subdue and radically deform its environment: "He had to fight with Matter, with the earth and the coal enclosed. This was the sole idea, to return upon the inanimate matter of the underground, and to reduce it to his will" (Lawrence 1989: 301). The principle of the Anthropocene (Gerald) enforces the will to power through endless repetitions of its action: through "an activity of pure order, pure mechanical repetition, repetition ad infinitum, hence eternal and infinite" (Lawrence 1989: 301). Lawrence's bends language to bring home the repetitiveness of repetition, repeating the word and its infinity ("repetition, repetition ad infinitum, hence eternal and infinite").

Lawrence casts modernity's purification project into a quasi-liturgical, religious language. The immanent power of the machine-god of the Anthropocene becomes a new godhead, venerated by those whom it exploits (the workers):

> Gerald was their high priest, he represented the religion they really felt. His father was forgotten already. There was a new world, a new order, strict, terrible, inhuman, but satisfying in its very destructiveness. The men were satisfied to belong to the great and wonderful machine, even whilst it destroyed them. It was the highest that man had produced, the most wonderful and superhuman. They were exalted by belonging to this great and superhuman system which was beyond feeling or reason, something really godlike. (Lawrence 1989: 304)

Here the promise of overcoming the human through volition and teleology coincides with the destruction of diversity. Individuals delight in their self-destruction—annihilating their diverse peculiarities—in order to support and feed the smooth running of the machinery for which and within which they work. Is this not exactly what Kafka describes as the magical veneration of officialdom and its quasi-divine elevation in *Das Schloss*? In Kafka's last novel there are only a few historical points of orientation. *Women in Love*, as we have seen, establishes long historical horizons from prehistory to modernity to contemporaneity. Gerald Crich embodies the Anthropocene in terms of the machine age where all traces of contamination have been eliminated. Here we live in a world of purely demarcated opposites which is the realm of numbers, mathematical distinctness, and purity: "He [i.e., Gerald] was just ahead of them in giving them what they wanted, this participation in a great and perfect system that subjected life to pure mathematical principles" (Lawrence 1989: 304–5). Crucial here is not the meaning but the doing. Anticipating our digital age, where numbers (algorithms) are by and large in charge of initiating actions triggering either large sell or buy orders on the stock markets, here the principle of mathematics is not one of meaning but of action.

Activity elevates the new entrepreneur Gerald Crich into a deity of sorts: "It was so perfect that sometimes a strange fear came over him, and he did not know what to do. He went on from some years in a sort of trance of activity. What he was doing seemed supreme, he was almost like a divinity. He was a pure and exalted activity" (Lawrence 1989: 305). Divinity and activity become one, evoking what Eric Santner has recently called, Kafka's "*traumamtliches Schreiben*, a neologism that brings together the meanings: dream, trauma, and *Amt*, or office" (Santner 2016: 27). Santner's term *traumamtlich* derives from a reading of Kafka's texts and it illuminates the fusion of religion, economics, and politics in Lawrence's works. As we have seen earlier, Lawrence casts the modern entrepreneur Gerald Crich into a quasi-religious mold. Crucially, this is an immanent religion—what Benjamin, radicalizing Max Weber, has called "the religion of capitalism." It is a religion of doing and Crich's whole character is absorbed by activity. He even turns into a personification of the active principle, a "divinity." Immanence radically depleted of any transcendence produces its own supernatural aura; a specter-like quality which Marx has called value's and labor's *gespenstische Gegenständlichkeit*. Indeed, according to Santner:

> Marx's labor theory of value concerns precisely this dimension of the *traumamtlich* as the site at which a surplus of immanence—the royal remains left to the People—comes to be elaborated and managed as the real subject-matter of political economy. His theory concerns, that is, the flesh as a social substance *materially abstracted* from the busy body of labor, a substance that he will famously refer to as *gespenstische Gegenständlichkeit*, the spectral objectivity/materiality of Value. (Santner 2016: 27–8)

The political theology of the King's Two Bodies persists within modern political economy infusing what ostensibly is purely numerical and business-like with a quasi-magical aura that demands respect, veneration, and distance. Here we encounter the fusion of economic success through quantitative enumeration (this product has been sold so many times to create such an impressive profit margin) and the social distinction of belonging to a certain class or ethnicity (being a native). This co-symbolization of one's ethnic, economic, and social standing is precisely the subject matter of Kafka's *Das Schloss*. By abundantly depicting the debility as well as depravity of the castle society, Kafka's last novel makes the reader undergo various disappointing experiences with one of the most aspired to symbols of hierarchical elevation (the castle itself). In so doing, Kafka exhausts the binary structure of dialectical operations that spend all their energies on distinguishing the social recognition of success from the lowly sphere of those who are failures, who are included only to be excluded, like Kafka's stranger K. However, Kafka empties the immanence of matter of its materiality, leaving us with the bare signs and structures of an ever-active life whose heart has paradoxically stopped beating; and it is after the last beat, as it were, that it continues turning, endowing almost dead life with glimpses of zeal and busyness.

Kafka's Stranger K. and the Contamination of Economic and Nationalist Rivalries Whose Historical Coordinates Have Been Rendered Inoperative

As has been explored in the preceding section, in Lawrence's novel *Women in Love*, the immanent and repetitive activity of the modern entrepreneur Crich turns into a deity of sorts. In Kafka's *Das Schloss* the main protagonist K. describes himself as a land surveyor, but from the start the new environment that classifies him as foreign, as immigrant, denies him any form of employment. As Schwarzer puts it, "land surveyor?—nothing of the sort, a common, lying vagrant, probably worse" (*"wahrscheinlich aber Ärgeres"*) (Kafka 1926: 7; Kafka 1997: 5–60). From the opening, the stranger K. has been narratologically cast into symbols of negativity, of trouble (*Ärger*). Is it appropriate to refer to narratology in a discussion of Kafka's way or writing?

As J. Hillis Miller has recently argued,

> the strategy of narratology and structuralism might even be defined as a form of defense against the threatening irrationality of modernist and postmodernist fiction or of human cultures generally as recent anthropologists have found them to be, and as modern history has shown them to be, for example (it is more than an example), in the perpetration of the Holocaust. (Miller 2011: 105)

Not only does its main protagonist provoke negative and rather disappointing reactions within the confines of Kafka's narration, but this sense of trouble also seems to spill over and outside the confines of the text, spelling trouble for those who are its recipients (i.e., its audience). Kafka's novel keeps disappointing the reader's quest for both reliable information and signification. Rather than experiencing a fulfilling sense of orientation and coordination, the audience undergoes various frustrations and disappointments of narratological sense or meaning. We do not even know for sure whether K. has truly been invited to come to work in the region of the castle as land surveyor:

> The narrative voice's silence on the question whether K. is lying is evidence of its lack of omniscience or at any rate its inexplicable reserve about important points. The reader might hypothesize that Kafka the author wanted to keep an impenetrable secrecy about whether or not K. is telling the truth about his appointment as land surveyor. The reader's uncertainty about this might be taken as the generative kernel of the entire fragmented narrative. (Miller 2011: 116)

Although K. intends to conduct an active life and gain employment as land surveyor, he never attains what he expects, and what he claims had been promised to him before he left his native country for the strange region that consists of the castle and its neighboring village.

Being classified as a stranger, K. is an object. Indeed, the case of K. describes the meeting point of objectification and disappointment. Being objectified here clearly means that K.'s hopes for an active and socially valid life keep encountering disappointments of various sorts. Social classifications preprogram such disappointing experiences. Being by definition a stranger and outcast, K. fills the role and the sign of the slave in all his social encounters. He always signifies and enacts the negativity of what is lacking, what is thus strange, deriving from an absent origin.

K.'s lack of social status and agency comes across more powerfully through the way in which the narrative voice of the novel gives access to his inner life of disappointment. As Hillis Miller has shown, Kafka's novel provides almost exclusive access to the main protagonist's sense of frustration and thwarted expectations:

> What is possible for Kafka is a disembodied narrative voice that is almost completely limited to entering just one mind, K.'s. The narrator is restricted to ironically miming in free indirect discourse what goes on in that mind or to naming objectively what that mind saw, heard, and felt. Kafka himself, in an often-quoted statement in the diaries, expressed this constitutive narratological doubling as follows: "What will be my fate as a writer is very simple. My talent for portraying my dreamlike inner life has thrust all matters into the background." The dreamlike inner life is, in *The Castle*, Kafka's imagination of K.'s adventures after he enters the village on that snowy night. Kafka's "talent for portraying" that dreamlike inner life is manifested in his genius as a storyteller and

inventor of unsettling dialogue, behaviour, and settings, as well as in the change from *Ich* to *er* that generates the doubling of protagonist by the detached, slightly ironic, narrative voice. (Miller 2011: 143)

Dreamlike in Kafka's context has nightmarish connotations. Miller's excellent analysis of Kafka's narrative voice requires further exploration for what it implies for the larger structure of the novel. The narrative voice's exclusive concern with just one mind contrasts with the absence of social recognition that greets that mind in the social arena of *The Castle*. The reader experiences the mental world of K. who occupies the position of a victim, the excluded and thwarted slave; whose actions (like his arrival in the novel's castle vicinity) keeps being out of place, futile, and nugatory.

However, the oneiric aspect of Kafka's novel does not mean that it is a-historical. In terms of intellectual history, K.'s position of being invited only to be cast out plays on Hegel's master-slave dialectics. By focusing the attention of the narrative on K.'s inner life, the reader experiences this master-slave dialectics, from the perspective of negativity, of disappointment. Reading the novel the audience lives through what it means to be included only to be excluded. Inclusion here is K.'s mere life, his bare presence near the castle. The ban on him actually accessing the symbol of hierarchic accomplishment (i.e., the castle) epitomizes his exclusion from the society that, he claims, invited him in the first place. Various thwarted attempts at an employed and active life reinforce this sense of exclusion and the accompanying mental forms of disappointment in the mind of both the main protagonist and that of the reader.

To read the novel only in terms of its form and idiosyncratic narratology is to focus the attention on the narrative voice, which appears to reside in the mind of K. This preoccupation with the main protagonist would be solipsistic. Miller seems to read Kafka's last novel as being concerned with K.'s closure on to himself. He interprets the title of Kafka's *Das Schloss* as a word play on both castle and the device, which closes a door, that is, a lock (the German word *Schloss* has a double meaning: next to a castle, it also denotes a lock for closing a door). Pointing out "what is implied by the German word for Castle, *Schloss*, a sealed enclosure" Miller draws the general conclusion that the "characters of *Das Schloss* are sealed off from one another" (Miller 2011: 125). Miller extends this generalization further when he argues toward the end of his interpretation, that Kafka's novel pivots around our solipsistic inability to read the mind of others: "The genius of *Das Schloss* is to have shown that the sad situation of his hero, is, in part at least, the result of not having direct access to other people's mind and feelings" (Miller 2011: 144).

Far from being exclusively concerned with the mind of K., Kafka's last novel, however, provides ample evidence of its main protagonist's societal marginalization. Isolation and marginalization are not merely a result of a misunderstanding or K.'s inability to read the mind of those with whom he interacts. His position in society is clearly that of someone who is at the mercy of others. He occupies the role of Hegel's slave, because he lacks social recognition. Society deprives him of meaningful action and social integration. His employment is worse than menial. It is insignificant and futile, depriving him of social recognition. He may act and work but the outcome of his endeavors keeps turning out pointless und socially unrecognized. The castle and its vicinity outdoes whatever K. attempts to do.

K.'s isolation and inactivity contrasts with the busyness and social recognition of the castle and its surrounding village. Indeed, only those who have been granted individual agency by belonging to the castle and its vicinity are socially recognized. Those who partake of the highest echelons of society (who are close to or favored by the officials of the castle) have proportionally the biggest arena for the realization and social recognition of their desires: in Hegel's terms, they are the masters, whereas K., who lacks social recognition, occupies the role of the slave.

Thus meaningful action accompanies social recognition. As the figure of the industrial chieftain Gerald Crich in *Women in Love* intimates, action in *Das Schloss* is a synonym for power. By contaminating action with power, both Kafka and Lawrence introduce the disappointing moment of objectification into their respective social setting. The industrial Crich objectivizes his horse and his workers in his actions, which manifest his will to power. Objectification deprives subjects of their status and independence and thus renders them slaves within Hegel's dialectics of social recognition. In both Lawrence's and Kafka's contaminating perspectives on disappointment, the objectifying divide between hierarchical and thereby dialectical distinctions—such as the famous one of master and slave—makes social recognition possible with reference to society's structure in its entirety.

The power of action resides in what motivates the teleological and volitional actor: the promise of the fruits of activity or the hoped-for product (which the machinery of labor produces, as in Lawrence's *Women in Love*) or the longed-for and once promised entrance into the castle. K. remains excluded from the sphere of action and stability, because he is an immigrant and a stranger, and as such both categorically and socially lacks power. Power in terms of social distinction (measured in closeness or distance to the castle) seems to be the only criterion that establishes the leeway for action and narration in *Das Schloss*. K. learns this political lesson right after his arrival in the village, when the intricacies of hierarchical social gradations in all their mysterious complexities and intricacies open up to his daunted and disappointed state of mind:

> "Schwarzer was exaggerating yesterday, his father is only an under-governor, and one of the lowest at that." [*und sogar einer der letzten.* Kafka 1926: 12] Just then, for a moment, the landlord looked at K like a child. "The rascal!" K. said with a laugh, but the landlord did not join in the laughter, saying only: "Even *his* father is powerful" [*Auch sein Vater ist mächtig*] (Kafka 1926: 12) "Go on!" said K, "you think everyone's powerful. Me too, I suppose?" [*"Geh," sagte K., "du hälst jeden für mächtig. Mich etwa auch?"* Kafka 1926: 12] "You," he said shyly but in earnest, "I do not consider powerful." [*"Dich," sagter er schüchtern, aber ernsthaft, "halte ich nicht für mächtig"* Kafka 1926: 12] "In that case you are an observant man," said K., "because powerful, between you and me, is something I really am not. And I probably, as a result, have no less respect for the powerful than you do, only I'm not as honest as you and won't always admit it." (Kafka 1997: 8)

K. here plays with the promise of a nonhierarchical and non-objectifying society, which does not distinguish between different levels of social status and recognition and thus avoids the disappointment of being defined as negative, as slave in Hegel's dialectics. Should K. be considered powerful, everyone (*jeder*) would be. K. admits that like everyone he has taken to heart the dialectics of social recognition. Like everyone he lives in a society that distributes power and recognition unequally, dividing the world into either slave or master, in Hegel's dialectical terms.

What causes this all-encompassing veneration of power and the all-pervasive fear of masters (the officials of the castle)? Kafka's novel here strikes at the imaginative core not so much of literature as of the apparatus that keeps functional the hierarchical structure of different and often contrasting societies. As I have shown elsewhere, rather than being merely illusory or phantasmal, literature has the capacity to illuminate the numerous fictions into which we ordinarily and regularly buy into as part of our actual societal interactions (Mack 2012: 90–9). Recently, the philosopher Jeffrey Andrew Barash has highlighted the role of the imagination in the establishment of social cohesion:

> Certainly fantasy and myth play a central role at all levels of social existence, but, as I interpret it, the social bond is not simply based on imaginary creations, for it must be traced to a more fundamental

function of imagination in the communal sphere, which interweaves the very fabric of social cohesion. Imagination in this sense is a precondition for social existence per se and, as such, configures the basis for all that is communally significant. This primordial role of imagination, as I interpret it, while distinguishing it from all other connotations of the term, renders what is collectively significant communicable by embodying it in *symbols*. (Barash 2016: 46)

Symbols communicate via their embodied forms societal hierarchies of inclusion and exclusion, societal recognition, and societal demotion—in short, they visibly, tangibly, and audibly perform Hegel's dialectic of master and slave in society at large. Repeated performance establishes the collective memory of such symbolic markers of the societally accepted (positive) and societally denigrated or tabooed (negative): "imagination patterns a fund of remembered significations in the form of collective symbols" (Barash 2016: 46).

More than informing works of fiction, the imagination in often harmful ways shapes how societies perform their communal arrangements: "And here matters suddenly become more complex, for imagination, through this work of embodying communicable symbols, lies at the source both of group fantasy and fiction and of what is accepted to be communally significant reality" (Barash 2016: 46). The symbol of the castle as the publicly communicated experience of superiority and power (Hegel's master) exerts its stronghold of signification not only over K. but also over the whole of the community. Everyone who does not belong to the castle itself but lives in its vicinity automatically has their lives confined to inferiority and subservience (as we will see, they are literally the slave-like possessions and objects at the beck and call of castle officialdom).

The mere connection, however, to someone who appears to be powerful is enough to infuse respect, rather than any achievements or worthy deeds: "*His father is powerful.*" Families are ranked according to their supposed standing in relation to the mysterious castle that endows characters with the aura of power. The surface theme of Kafka's novel is the respect for power rather than its hidden kernel, which is the disappointment of power. The pervading tone of contamination in Lawrence's *Women in Love*, by contrast, articulates a disappointment in power that renders uncomfortable and disturbing the Anthropocene (as in Gerald beating his horse). The promise of power is what the term "castle" signifies in this context: in Kafka's novel, the castle does not seem to be so much a locality as an immanent symbolic formation that grants power, beauty, youth, and activity.

However, the actual sight of the castle is everything else but awe-inspiring. K. is disappointed when he first looks at the location of the castle:

> His eyes fixed on the castle, K. walked on, nothing else concerned him. [*Die Augen auf das Schloss gerichtet, ging K. weiter, nichts sonst kümmerte ihn.* Kafka 1926: 14] As he came closer, however, the castle disappointed him, [*Aber im Näherkommen enttäuschte ihn das Schloss* Kafka 1926: 14] it was really just a wretched-looking small town [*nur ein recht elendes Städtchen* Kafka 1926: 14], a collection of rustic hovels, its only distinction being that, possibly everything was built of stone, though the paint had peeled off long since and the stone looked as if it was crumbling away. K. had a fleeting memory of his own home town [*Heimatstädtchen* Kafka 1926: 14], it was scarcely inferior to this castle, if K. had been interested only in sightseeing [*Besichtigung* Kafka 1926: 14] it would have been a waste of all the travelling [*schade um die lange Wanderschaft*], he would have done better [*vernünftiger* Kafka 1926: 14] to revisit his old home, where he had not been for so long. (Kafka 1997: 9)

This passage shows how Kafka's Joseph K. is a new type of protagonist in the genre of the "disappointment novel." In contrast to Conrad's Lord Jim and Fitzgerald's Gatsby, K. does not disavow his sense of disappointment. Crucially, K.'s sense of disappointment grows out of the recognized discrepancy between symbolic promise and the actual experience, the actual sight of the castle.

Most striking here is the role of reason [*Vernunft*] in K.'s realization of how disappointing his life captivated and captured by the symbolic promise of the castle in an empirical sense turns out to be. This recognition of disappointment may rationally make K. realize the comedy of his quest for a defunct and debilitated castle. Teleology, however, gains the upper hand over a comic sense of understanding the absurdity of the goal that drives K.'s hopes. As we shall see soon, one of K.'s assistants identifies a serious approach toward the castle with irrationality toward the end of Kafka's last novel. Whereas the tone of Lawrence's *Women in Love* casts Gerald Crich's hope-inspired and quasi-religious fascination with mechanical efficiency and capitalist profitability into the trope of disappointment that effects a repetitive mood of monotony, in Kafka's *Das Schloss* we are mentally (i.e., internally) experiencing K.'s disillusionment and his regret of ever having been hopeful about his journey to the castle. This avowal of disappointment with the real existence of the searched for end point (i.e., the castle) is, however, short-lived and short-circuits back to the full investment of hopes that stirred K.'s delusionary quest in the first place. Teleology drives K.'s journey to and his obsession with the castle. The image of eyes fixed on a certain destination describes teleology's future-oriented goal. Hence, teleology is a promise and a hope. Disappointment thwarts such hope and makes us flinch from our intended journey or goal.

Maurice Blanchot's thought about death as the retreat of power and teleology is pertinent here. He argues that death outdoes all purposes. Our death is without teleology (in a non-Christian and secular context at least): "Dying to no end: thus (through this movement of immobility) would thought fall outside all teleology and perhaps outside its site" (Blanchot 1995: 39). The passage quoted earlier traces how K.'s actual sight of the castle makes him fall outside of its (and teleology's) site. The disappointed sight causes the eye to balk at what it previously held in a fixed state of promise and expectation. Reason as the realization of the discrepancy between mental or symbolic promise and actual, empirical reality introduces and stirs disappointing experiences in Kafka's K. The onset of disappointment has a rational and enlightening function here, not least by diminishing what Lawrence unmasks as the violence of Nietzsche's will to power. Blanchot, who grounds his writing and thought in a reading of Kafka, identifies disaster and death with the retreat of both power and teleology: "To think the way one dies: without purpose, without power, without unity, and precisely, without 'the way.'" (Blanchot 1995: 39). The sight of the site of teleology (i.e., the castle) switches K.'s mood from being hopeful and purposeful to one of disappointment.

From now on, he has lost his way but like the K. of *The Trial*, he disastrously clings to the hope of attaining power and a purpose within the feudal machinery of the castle. Rather than being "evil" or "impatient," as Blanchot has argued,[4] Kafka's K. is not to be discouraged from his fixed attention to attain any goal (and which precisely is irrelevant—be it "the trial" or "the castle"). Spurred by Spinoza's philosophical destruction of anthropocentricism, anthropomorphism, and associated forms of teleology and volition, Lawrence's narrative engagement with the trope of disappointment as well as Kafka's comic-tragic narrative paradigm of thwarted human expectations humiliates traditional notions of humanity's quasi-divine, central, and controlling position in the universe. Both Lawrence and Kafka call into doubt the validity of the Anthropocene—the presumption that human volition and the products of it should dominate our planet.

---

[4] "It is the palpable form of the error through which, before the impatient gaze, the inexorable force of the evil infinite is ceaselessly substituted for the absolute. K. always wants to reach the goal before having reached it" (Blanchot 1989: 79).

Kafka renders ridiculous, absurd, and shameful such presumptions. *The Trial* closes with the infinity of shame that attaches to K. and the Anthropocene beyond the purposeless end of death itself, when K. dies like a dog: "In *The Trial*, one might think that the death scene constitutes the pardon, the end of the interminable; but there is no end, since Kafka specifies that shame survives, which is to say, the infinite itself, a mockery of life as life's beyond" (Blanchot 1995: 53). Kafka's stance is, however, not that of a traditional moralist. He is concerned with epistemological limits (with *Vernunft*) and delusory, hopeful as well as ignorant attempts to transcend these limits in both comic and tragic ways. Promises of knowledge and power keep turning out disappointing in their actual manifestations as experienced by those who have invested an infinity of hope in them and yet Kafka's protagonists endlessly set out to make another start at getting to their non-existing end destination. The quotation earlier traces a radical switch from high expectations and a sense of obsession with the promise of the castle to an acknowledgment of disappointment with the actual sight of and experience with a rather derelict building that is not at all worth searching out and least of all travelling for. This switch in both thought and mood includes the mixed emotion of humor and sadness. In circular movement, sadness then reintroduces the seriousness of the renewed quest for the castle in its ideal, promissory symbolization and that now albeit having gained full sight of its rather pathetic actual manifestation.

Toward the end of the novel, his assistant Jeremias accuses K. of a lack of both reason and humor. He points out that Frieda acted against reason, when she agreed to become K.'s wife (*es lag für sie (i.e., Frieda) keine Vernunft darin, deine Frau zu warden*) (Kafka 1926: 452). Frieda lowers herself by marrying K. who is as stranger, the lowest of the low. By marrying K. Frieda embraces negativity. From the particular rational perspective of Hegelian and societal dialectics Frieda is indeed irrational, because reason here demands not the embrace or alliance with the negative (the stranger K.) but its overcoming or transmutation. There is, however, a different form of reason that avoids the exclusions of negativity. Kafka's is a contaminating rationality that allows for the comic, the absurd, and the negative. By embracing the negative, K. would reconcile himself with himself, albeit in an absurd and comic way. He would be able to amuse himself about his quest for an actually pathetic castle. This comic recognition of absurdity would unbind him from his quest and would render inoperative the hold of various symbols of social hierarchies and distinctions. Were K. to reconcile himself with his actual experience of disappointment, he would distance himself from being beholden to the communal fascination with symbolic embodiments of power and hierarchy. By not actually referring to an actually existing entity Kafka's term "castle" describes the work of symbols and their embodiment as fantasized promises rather than actual manifestations.

As Barash has shown, symbols "may be understood in two principle ways: either in the broader sense, as fundamental organizing principles of experience, or, in a more narrow sense, as representatives or signs of something that cannot present itself before immediate perception" (Barash 2016: 50). Preceding our perceptive capacities, symbols communicate societal promises and hierarchies. Establishing a distance to the symbolic order partakes of the care of the self. Through this distance we may reconcile ourselves to what society demotes and demeans as negative or disappointing. Care of the self would free K. from the promises of the castle and its society and make him more rational (*vernünftiger*) (Kafka 1926: 452).

However, this step toward lasting rational insight into the absurdity of his quest never takes place in Kafka's novel. Disappointment with the actual in turn stirs new hopes for the potential promises of an imaginary castle. Fiction here confronts us with the illusionary power that binds us via hopes and promises to awe-inspiring goals in real, ordinary life (similar to the ordinary expectations of K. to be employed and recognized in his humble profession of surveying land).

The irony is that K. is a sightseer of sorts. As powerless immigrant, no one allows him to stay permanently. He is a land surveyor in name only. Who could grant him employment and residence? The source of all power paradoxically is the symbolic spectacle of the castle. It is, however, a pathetic sight: it disappoints and seems to be only nominally a castle. It has connotations of obscenity. The village teacher warns K. not to mention the mere word of the castle in the presence of children: "'Remember these are innocent children.' ['*Nehmen Sie Rücksicht auf die Anwesenheit unschuldiger Kinder.*' Kafka 1926: 17]" (Kafka 1997: 10) However, there appears to be a deceptive or promissory leveling side to the castle in some of its characterization, such as when the schoolmaster informs K. that "'there is no difference between the peasants and castle.' ['*Zwischen den Bauern und dem Schloss ist kein Unterschied*' Kafka 1926: 17]" (Kafka 1997: 10). No difference here means power's indifference to those whom it rules. It is a unity of control as becomes apparent when the peasants can be commandeered in the name of officials from the castle. The mere naming of such officials yields powerful results when Frieda, while still being Klamm's mistress shouts at the peasants "'In the name of Klamm [*Im Namen Klamms,* Kafka 1926: 76], into the barn, all of you into the barn'" (Kafka 1997: 37). The invocation of the name evokes quasi-religious connotations (in Judaism the name of God is so powerful that there is an interdiction to invoke it). The banning of the peasants into the barn clearly partakes of an agricultural system of feudality where low social standing seems to be interchangeable with that of animals. The unity between castle and village may indeed be a feudal, paternalistic one wherein one commands the other, where one party is free to use the other. This feudal unity is the exploitative patriarchal form of governing with which we are familiar from Gerald Crich's father in *Women in Love*.

The party who is free to use the other at liberty as a possession of their feudal holdings is of course the elevated class of the castle's officialdom. References to traditions of rules (sovereignty) obfuscate the economic interests of exploitations. The castle takes great pain to show that they are not attentive to the economic ("value") contributions the immigrant K. could make to their possession. Instead, the ruling elite insist on clear distinctions and borders between belonging and not belonging. This denial of financial data only increases the hold on the real estate of officialdom's claim to power (the castle and its neighboring village): rather than allocating labor time to their underlings, they have an unlimited claim on the life of their possessions (lands, buildings, and the village population). By contaminating modern capitalism with archaic feudalism, Kafka's *Das Schloss ex negativo* charts a radical geography which:

> proposes a criticism that attends to the intrinsic difficulty of finding a possibility of establishing the literary as a form of capital—capital letters—that is not subsumed under the rather pessimistic spiral, in which we escape from feudal structures only to find that, through the various vagaries of a developing idea of capitalism itself, we end up back in the same place. (Docherty 2018: 34)

Kafka highlights the geography of such not only pessimistic but also comic spiral from the modern back to the archaic, from the presumed rationalism of capitalism to the irrational claims of patriarchal power and unlimited sovereignty in feudalism. In *Women in Love* Lawrence traces a development from the feudal and paternalistic Crich senior to the capitalist and mechanical Crich junior. Kafka's *Das Schloss* presents the simultaneity of the two: how the obscenity of the supposedly archaic is the kernel of the rationalism of the modern. The castle is the symbolic geography of disappointment: where high expectations of improvement meet the realistic sight of ever-increasing debilitation and exploitation.

While not resembling a location, the castle instantiates a symbol and its fictive embodiment: that of power—a power that divides life into important and unimportant, significant and insignificant, used and user, passive and active, bare life and meaningful life. As stranger K. both witnesses (as a sightseer, a tourist of sorts) and provokes the ceaseless symbolizations of power/the castle. As the landlady (Frieda's mother) explains to him life in this region of the world unfolds via structures of power that both include and exclude. As stranger he is a target of such dialectics that only includes by excluding; structures that humiliate and outdo what is considered negative or strange. K. like so many tries to be close or at least in contact with the supposedly positive power of the castle. The landlady makes clear to him that his inclusion is premised on the exclusion from Klamm, the castle official:

> Listen to me, sir. Mr. Klamm is a gentleman from the castle, that in itself, quite apart from his position otherwise, signifies very high rank [*das bedeutet schon an und für sich, ganz abgesehen von Klamms sonstiger Stellung, einen sehr hohen Rang.* Kafka 1926: 92]. But what are you, whose marriage permit we are so humbly applying for here. You're not from the castle, you're not from the village, you're nothing. [*Sie sind nicht aus dem Schloss, Sie sind nicht aus dem Dorfe, Sie sind nichts.* Kafka 1926: 92] Unfortunately there's one thing you are, though, namely a stranger, and outsider, someone who's superfluous to requirements and in everybody's way, [*ein Fremder, einer der überzählig und überall im Wege ist* Kafka 1926: 93] someone who's a constant source of trouble, on whose account the maids have to be moved out, someone whose intentions are unknown, someone who has seduced our dear little Frieda [*wegen dessen man die Mägde ausquartieren muss* Kafka 1926: 93] and to whom she must unfortunately be given in marriage. (Kafka 1997: 45)

As has been discussed in Chapter 4, Hannah Arendt would later, as a Jewish refugee from the Nazi-occupied European continent take up the notion of human beings whose life has been rendered superfluous in her analysis of the roots of modern anti-Semitism in the discourse and social practice of colonialism. The stranger as seducer of native women is a classic xenophobic and racist stereotype.

Kafka, however, is at pains not to refer to any specific historical and political context. His text focuses on the structure of power and reveals this structure to be dialectical and antagonistic: it opposes a good with an evil, importance (Klamn and the castle) with nothingness (K., the nobody, who is something being a stranger). Rank describes a struggle for recognition and power. It is a more abstract word for what promotes the economic strife between families and nations in Lawrence's *Women in Love*. As we have seen, Lawrence's novel narratively casts into the trope of disappointment the capitalist and industrialist paradigm of emulation between productive forces.

Within this modern conglomeration of industry, bodies are used at will by those who own the means of production (the Crich family and fellow chieftains of industry). The workers who are exposed to mechanical labor are nominally free agents but Lawrence's trope of disappointment reveals them to be mere tools of machinery. Kafka's *Das Schloss*, by contrast, conspicuously lacks forms of production. There is busyness but not business, activity but not any productive work. Here the economy is already depleted of matter. The castle itself is in decay but does not warrant any renovations because it is not a remarkable building anyway (resembling a rundown, ordinary town).

Lawrence depicts a materially manifest religion of immanence that constantly repeats mechanical procedures of production. In Kafka, this immanence has become gaunt and weary. It is an immanent fatigue that nevertheless clings to the illusion of rejuvenation and the sign "castle" seems to be able to resurrect those who are already dead while still alive. The power of this symbolic system resides in its capacity to encompass every aspect of life while ceaselessly separating forms of life according to various rubrics and categories such as that of rank. It is via such border-establishing symbols that the castle maintains its all-encompassing, feudal hold on those it claims as its possession.

The dominion over life is total and does not allow for any rest or sleep. The subjects of the castle are beholden to it at any time of the day or night. As the official Bürgel instructs K., the officialdom of the castle invades all aspects of life and does not allow for any form of rest or retrieve: "we see no difference between ordinary time and working time. Such distinction is alien to us" (Kafka 1997: 232). Other distinctions are all the more relevant. Indeed the lack of a difference between work and rest creates the restless zeal to be close to the castle and its officials. As K. desperately explains to Frieda:

> You know I want to reach Klamm, you also know you can't help me in this so I must manage it on my own, and you can see for yourself that I have not yet succeeded. Must I now, by recounting my futile attempts that already, in reality, amply humiliate me, humiliate myself twice over? Should I boast, for instance, of having spent a long afternoon waiting in vain, getting very cold, at the door of Klamm's sledge? [. . .] And Barnabas? Certainly I am expecting him. He's Klamm's messenger. (Kafka 1997: 143)

K. does not know yet that Barnabas, albeit Klamm's messenger, is included to be excluded too. This impossible closeness of the inferior (K.) to the superior (the castle) amounts to the tiredness and melancholia as well as the dark humor of high expectations and their dire disappointment that characterizes Kafka's novel.

Conclusion: Revising Agamben or the Negative, Disappointed, and Objectified as the Inoperative

As in the case of Barnabas and his family, a withdrawal of the official contacts with the castle leads to premature ageing, isolation, idleness, poverty, and social exclusion. In Lawrence's *Women in Love*, Gerald and his industrial machinery and technology command the actions of his workers. As the artist Loerke will put it toward the end of the novel, the worker turns into a prosthesis of the machine (rather than the machine as prosthesis of the worker): "the machine works him, instead of he the machine. He enjoys the mechanical notion, in his own body" (Lawrence 1989: 519). Mechanical activity renders passive those who have to perform it. This passivity here gives rise to enjoyment.

Does this sense of enjoyment derive from the state of rest that seems to define the passivity of mechanical action? The mechanical renders passive what strikes us to be actions. Is this not a form of inoperativity? When Agamben tries to explain the methodology by way of which we might arrive at the inoperative, he employs the notions of use and contemplation. In Lawrence's novel, the machine uses the worker rather than the worker using the machine. Usage seems to induce a state of rest conducive to contemplation:

> Contemplation is the paradigm of use. Like use, contemplation does not have a subject, because in it the contemplator is completely lost and dissolved: like use contemplation does not have an object, because in the work it contemplates only its (own) potential. Life, which contemplates in the work its (own) potential of acting and making, is rendered inoperative in all its works and lives only in use-of-itself, lives only its livability. We write "own" and "its" in parentheses because only through the contemplation of potential, which renders inoperative every *energeia* and every work, does something like the experience of an "own" and a "self" become possible. The self—whose work the modern subject will usurp—is what is opened up as a central inoperativity in every operation, as the "livability" and "usability" in every work. [. . .] habitual use is a contemplation and contemplation is a form of life. (Agamben 2016: 63)

What Lawrence critiques as the mechanical, Agamben seems to appraise as the habitual. Mechanical usage turns our activities into forms of rest which we no longer need to perform "actively," in an active state of mind and body. In different but related ways, Hannah Arendt and George Lukács have both shown how work may put workers into a position of passivity: they too focus on the inoperative moment of modern operations. However, their word for Agamben's notion of the inoperative is the objectified. The inoperative reduces the potentially active subject into a passive one, into an object that can be used at will, like Hegel's slave or the villagers of Kafka's feudal castle society.

Agamben takes issue with "Western philosophy" which from Aristotle onward "has always put at the foundation of the political the concept of action" (Agamben 2016: 23). He goes on to offer an alternative to this tradition with his concept of use: "One of the hypotheses of the current study is, by calling into question the centrality of action and making for the political, that of attempting to think use as fundamental political category" (Agamben 2016: 33). Agamben cannot sustain his questioning of action in terms of creativity (Hannah Arendt's notion of natality). Rather than dismissing action as such, he seems to argue that mechanical and narrowly goal-oriented activity (as opposed to the mere idleness of blue sky research) enslaves those who expect to profit from it. Action here is what Marx, Lukács, and Arendt unmask as the passivity of objectified labor.

As the preceding discussion of the mechanical has shown, use is, however, part of what Lawrence analyzes as the immanent, capitalist religion of activity (the busyness of Kafka's feudal castle society). As we have seen in this chapter, activity splits into an active and passive moment. Active is the one who initiates the action (Crich and the machines), passive are the workers who are literally used by their master and the machines in his possession. Later on, Agamben confers with this analysis of use and contemplation, and he indeed argues that modern technology deprives workers of an active moments: "Slavery (as a juridical institution) and the machine represent in a certain sense the capture and parodic realization within social institutions of this 'use of the body'" (Agamben 2016: 78). As we have seen, Lawrence's novel highlights the passivity of work, the inoperability of modern operations.

Kafka goes a step further. Here work has become pointless, non-productive, and in *Das Schloss* it barely occurs that we find workers. Kafka's modernity is archaic and his narratives show that modern capitalist workers are feudal subjects, like the superfluous land surveyor K. of *The Castle*. The stranger K. has embarked on a quest to find work as a land surveyor. Without actually performing any work, he ends up objectified as the stranger. Without any material economic activity, Kafka's ruling class establishes distinctions of worthiness as measured in the all-pervasive hold the castle as symbol of power exerts over K. and the residents of the village or as manifested in the symbolic aura of a name (such as Klamm's). It is these symbolic distinctions that run the show of anthropomorphic hierarchies wherein the economics of numbers are mere symbols of the objectifying and thereby rather disappointing reach of the Anthropocene. Both Lawrence and Kafka depict the Anthropocene as modernity's paradoxical point at which capitalism returns as feudalism, and the violence of traditional tribal and religious oppositions haunts and renders inoperative modern and postmodern business as busyness. Here, human gradations of desire and value have become the main geological force of our planet, overwhelming sea and land with its objectified and inoperative products.

8

Disappointing Expectations of Redemption

Modern Jewish Writing and Thought

Introduction: Bellow's Felix Davarr/Leo Strauss, Franz Rosenzweig, Emmanuel Levinas, Jacques Derrida, and Philip Roth's Literary Plea "to Let the Repellent In"

The preceding chapters have addressed our contemporary, postmodern, and modern sense of loss of, as well as disappointment with, traditional, transcendent meanings. As we have seen in Chapter 6, Bellow's *Ravelstein* sets the significance of modern Jewish thought into relief for understanding a disavowal of being disappointed with various promises of redemption (national, economic, ethnic, religious, and so forth). Bellow's last novel singles out the teaching of the modern Jewish thinker Leo Strauss (aka Felix Davarr) as key to understanding the history of anti-Semitism. According to Bellow's Davarr/Strauss, anti-Semitism evidences the absence of redemption. This book has further developed Strauss's insight and has argued that hatred of the Jews coincides with holding the Jews responsible for various failed promises of redemption or fulfillment. Throughout this book I have argued that it is the displacement of a sense of disappointment onto the Other (the Jew, the Muslim, the immigrant) that gives rise to various forms of racism and xenophobia. As we have seen in Chapter 7, in Kafka's *Das Schloss* Joseph K. performs the role of the Other, the stranger, the immigrant on whom the whole spectrum of the community—from the high-ranking castle officials to the ordinary residents of the village—offload their frustrations and their sense of thwarted expectations and failed promises of redemption.

Modern Jewish writing and thought tries to come to terms with the disappointment of signification. This and the following concluding chapters offer a new perspective on modern Jewish thought as a bridge between the modernist and contemporary, analyzing what Franz Rosenzweig calls his "dark drive, my Judaism" (Rosenzweig 1998: 96) and what Benjamin and Scholem discuss as a religious and modern void, thematizing current states of disappointment, which more idealist social theories of modernity (Weber's Protestant ethics) have marginalized. Addressing our contemporary, postmodern, and modern loss of traditional, transcendent coordinates, this chapter engages with the religious studies approach of modern Jewish thought. It will explore Rosenzweig's, Levinas's, Franz Baermann Steiner's, Philip Roth's, Paul Auster's, and Derrida's works on a social, epistemological, and religious void. In doing so this chapter prepares for the discussion in Chapter 9: it analyzes issues that have become all the more urgent social problems for contemporary communities. The multidisciplinary methodology employed thus renders porous not only disciplinary boundaries but also those of literary periodization.

As we have seen in Chapter 7, Kafka's new narratology renders unstable traditional expectations for certain knowledge of our world. His last novel keeps leaving the reader in doubt whether K. has indeed been invited to work for the castle as land surveyor. Pondering on the work of Kafka, Scholem and Benjamin focus on this loss of traditional hopes of knowledge and revelation. In his letter of August 11, 1934, to Scholem, Benjamin quotes his friend writing "Your premise is 'the nothingness of revelation' ('*Nichts der Offenbarung*')" (Benjamin 1978: 617). Both Scholem and Benjamin cling to a theological interpretation of Kafka's literary work, while reducing the notion of revelation to a zero degree of significance.

Revelation and redemption are still relevant but expectations of knowledge thereof keep being disappointed. Benjamin calls Kafka's revelation "disfigured" (*enstellt* Benjamin 1978: 618). Benjamin sees in Kafka's text his weak or disappointed sense of the messianic. He argues that "Kafka's messianic category is that of the turning back (*Umkehr*) which is that of study (*Studium*)" Benjamin 1978: 618). "Turning back" (*Umkehr*) is the traditional theological category of *t'shuvah* as awareness and renunciation of misdeeds performed in the preceding year during the Day of Atonement (*Yom Kippur*). The critical study of one's disappointment with oneself remains the only door open to a still possible sense of revelation.

The study in question here is, however, that of a disfigured text of revelation. This disfigurement of revelation, truth, and knowledge will inform Derrida's postmodern notion of literature and philosophy in terms of an ironic state of uncertainty, nonknowledge, and undecidability. As Sarah Hammerschlag has recently pointed out, Derrida shifts modern Jewish thought from Socratic "to 'metarhetorical' or 'Abrahamic' irony" (Hammerschlag 2016: 33). In doing so, "Derrida moved irony from a site of knowledge to nonknowledge" and in this "process he situates irony as the condition par excellence of the subject faced with undecidability" (Hammerschlag 2016: 33). Placing a premium on irony, Derrida implicitly goes back to Schlegel's and the romantics' espousal of the fragment and their critique of idealist totality. Derrida's most immediate interlocutor in such questioning of idealist forms of totality and autonomy is his fellow French Jewish thinker Emmanuel Levinas. In his *Adieu to Emmanuel Levinas*, Derrida has traced such romantic disappointment with expectations of totality, revelation, and the Hegelian dialectics of the ever-progressing modern state to the German Jewish thinker Franz Rosenzweig. Derrida characterizes Levinas as a post-disappointment philosopher whose thought hovers between the political and what the late Foucault has theorized as the care of the self's going beyond the political. Levinas thus develops

> propositions at once *for and against* the "state principle," against what [i.e., Levinas's] *Totality and Infinity* had already called the "tyranny of the State" (according to an anti-Hegelian move in the style, at least, of Rosenzweig) against the State of Caesar, which, "despite its participation in the pure essence of the State, is also the place of corruption *par excellence* and, perhaps the ultimate refuge of idolatry"; against the State and yet leaving what Levinas calls the "beyond the State" or the "going beyond the State" an opening toward the "culmination of the State of David" in the messianic State, a going beyond of the State toward a "world to come." (Derrida 1999: 73–4)

This going beyond the state is what Leo Strauss might have had in mind when he established a radical break between philosophy as the art of life (Socrates) and politics. According to Strauss, Athens put Socrates to death because his teaching indeed posed a substantial danger to the polis. In his farewell to his friend Levinas, Derrida conceives of philosophy's departure from the state in terms of the Hebrew term *kadosh*—a word that refuses translation and that, according to Derrida, the Greek notion of what we now understand by ethics only adumbrates:

> The meshes or links of this chain [i.e., of separation or holiness] bear all their force toward this point of rupture or translation: "ethics," the word "ethics" is only an approximate equivalent, a makeshift Greek word for the Hebraic discourse on the holiness of the separated (*kadosh*). Which is not to be confused—especially not—with sacredness. But in what language is this possible? The welcome of the separated, the movement of the one who becomes separated in welcoming when it becomes necessary to greet the infinite transcendence of separated holiness, to

say *yes* at the moment of separation, indeed of a departure that is not the contrary of an arrival—is it not this deference that inspires the breath of an *à-Dieu*? (Derrida 1999: 61)

Anticipating but diverging from the Greek derived term "ethics," the Hebrew term *kadosh* thinks together the antinomies of departure and arrival, of holiness and separateness, of safety and danger, of the native and the stranger.

Derrida's word play on *à-Dieu* and *Adieu* highlights this contamination of what the term *kadosh* separates. The anthropologist, poet, and modern Jewish thinker Franz Baermann Steiner describes this simultaneity of the close and separate, the safe and the risky as follows:

> God himself—this comes as shock to most superficial Bible readers—is never called holy, *qodesh*, unless and in so far as He is related to something else. He is holy in his capacity as Lord of Hosts, though he is not related to man. Very often the Bible says, The Holy One, blessed be He, or blessed be His name. The name is, in the framework of the doctrinal logic of the Pentateuch, always *qodesh* because it establishes a relationship. (Steiner 1967: 102)

Like Derrida, Steiner highlights the startling paradox of thinking together being related and separate, being holy and dangerous, being disappointing and promising, and being beneficial and destructive (Mack 2001: 178–203).

Indeed, Steiner draws out a similar simultaneity of opposites in the Hebrew term *hitborah*. Similar to Derrida's elaborations on the term *kadosh*, Steiner argues that there is a problem of translatability between Hebrew and English, and there is no European equivalent which could embrace the full range of meanings of the Hebrew word. Thus, the word *hitborah* has never had the same signification as the English term "blessing," by which it is frequently translated. Unlike *hitborah*, "blessing" does not have the connotations of contagion. Steiner's examination of *hitborah* shows that "blessing" involves contagions: "But however we look at it, contagion is the principle of transfer in blessing" (Steiner 1967: 64). The innocuous thus embraces the destructive, and the promising includes its presumed opposite, the disappointing (and vice versa). We cannot think holiness without evoking separateness and danger.

In his *Adieu to Emmanuel Levinas*, Derrida invokes the German Jewish thinker Franz Rosenzweig to highlight the simultaneity of what we take to be dialectical opposites such as positive and negative, native and stranger, home and dispossession: "For Rosenzweig emphasized this originary dispossession, this withdrawal by which the 'owner' is expropriated from what is most his own, the *ipse* from its ipseity, thus making of one's home a place or location one is simply passing through" (Derrida 1999: 42). This turning unhomely of one's home makes possible hospitality. In order to establish relationship with others, we have to let go of notions of autonomy and totality.

The home fragments into different rooms that make space for the arrival of strangers. For such hospitality, notions of purity become questionable. For Derrida, one's immunity as pure, uncontaminated entity turns autoimmune. Pure political endeavors feed what they set out to suppress: "For we know that repression in both its psychoanalytical sense and its political sense—whether it be through the police, the military, or the economy—ends up producing, reproducing, and regenerating the very thing it seeks to disarm" (Derrida in Borradori 2003: 99). To interrupt immunity's autoimmunity, pure forms have to let in their supposed opposite. As we will see in the following section, this is indeed what Rosenzweig and, following him, Levinas do when they undermine idealist notions of totality, supplementing the total with the romantic fragment, and the autonomy of the self with the heteronomy of the other.

To prevent falling prey to autoimmunity, the immune paradoxically has to let in the destructive, the autoimmune. Derrida makes clear that his notion of the autoimmune goes beyond Hegel's dialectics by thinking simultaneously what we have come to see as opposites:

> It is a question here, as with the coming of any event worthy of this name, of an unforeseeable coming of the other, of responsibility and decision of the other, of a heteronomy, of a law come from the other, of a responsibility and decision of the other—of the other in me, an other greater and older than I am. It is thus a question of separating democracy and autonomy. (Derrida 2005: 84)

Derrida here divests democracy of any form of totality or autonomy, thus countering the common conflation of the term with the will of the (total and autonomous) people: "Democracy is what it is only in the différance by which it defers itself and differs from itself" (Derrida 2005: 38). By deferring and differing from itself, true democracy lets in what is other, destructive, ugly, and repellent. According to Derrida, literature (and literary inflected religion) introduces this opening to what has otherwise been excluded and banned. By interrupting a form of politics grounded in the sovereignty and autonomy of the self, Derrida identifies literature with Conrad's destructive element. Literature turns the self's immunity autoimmune. However, this disappointing, autoimmune, destructive element frees the self from sovereign, political requests and commands of what it should be.

Being disappointed with the social and political order, the self takes care of itself by destroying its self-protecting operations which it has acquired as part of the inheritance of various ideologies premised on competition, hierarchy, and sovereignty. The destructive element of Derrida's autoimmunity is not a moral or ethical quality but a process of freeing the self from various protective mechanisms that it has acquired in a polis that renders selfhood, immune, defensive, and thereby sovereign and autonomous: "In this regard, autoimmunity is not an absolute ill or evil. It enables an exposure to the other, to *what* and to *who* comes—which means that it must remain incalculable" (Derrida 2005: 152). Strikingly Derrida here acknowledges the "ill or evil" within the implicit negativity of the destructive element that turns self-destructive with autoimmunity.

While avowing the purported disappointing aspect of negativity, Derrida first dismantles its foundation as being absolute (i.e., absolutely negative) only then to let us see anew aspects of what we have previously taken to be the disappointment of destruction and autoimmunity: both the destructive and the autoimmune can remove layers of protection that prevent us from encountering unforeseen and incalculable forms of existence such as those of literature, that is, of being absorbed in the incalculable, other world of a literary narrative. Literature is life too, albeit other to and outside of the calculations of sovereignty and autonomy to which selfhood has been obliged to conform in political and social life.

Literature is a different, other life, a counter-life. As Philip Roth has put it: "Art is life too, you know. Solitude is life, meditation is life, pretending is life, supposition is life, contemplation is life, language is life. Is there less life in turning sentences around than in manufacturing automobiles? Is there less life in reading *To the Lighthouse* than in milking a cow or throwing a hand grenade?" (Roth 1985: 109–110) Without this other life within life, we would fall prey to a paralyzing, paradoxically self-destructive autonomy. The purported disappointment of a meditative, passively open life of literature actually instantiates the promise of a self that no longer conforms to the political demands of sovereignty, hierarchy, and competition. Conrad's destructive element and Derrida's notion of autoimmunity adumbrate a new, literary form of life that is open to the arrival of the incalculable and unforeseen: "Without autoimmunity, with absolute immunity nothing would ever happen or arrive; we would no longer wait, await, or expect, no longer expect one another or expect any event" (Derrida 2005: 152). As postmodern thinker of the autoimmune, Derrida takes up Conrad's modernism of the destructive element. In this move of a contaminating embrace of the negative (destructive or autoimmune), we come to see disappointment in the light of its purported opposite, of promise and hope.

As we will see in the following section, it is this promise of what is presumed to be disappointing, which Rosenzweig idiosyncratically called my "dark drive, my Judaism" (Rosenzweig 1998: 96). Let me here briefly establish a way of thought that modern Jewish writing after the actual political disappointments of Spinoza's promise of a nonhierarchical, diverse, and open (non-teleological) modernity shares with the literary modernism of Conrad's destructive element. The earlier discussion of the literary as the democracy of the autoimmune in Derrida's work has shown that this counterintuitive embrace of negativity dismantles potentially violent forms of a predominant form of politics that is premised on sovereignty. Derrida's autoimmunity disintegrates the repression of autonomy as well as the defense and offence mechanism of various formations of totality which then oppose themselves to their supposed negative contrary (good versus evil, the negative becoming dialectically subsumed under the positive, and so forth).

Commenting on Conrad's "in the destructive element immerse yourself," Philip Roth has interpreted this phrase as the letting in of the unpalatable, saying that "literature begins with the unpalatable" (Roth 2013). As in Derrida's theory of the autoimmune, the literary embrace of the negative—however one chooses to call it, the unpalatable, the ugly, the repellent, the abject, and so forth—is a political act that avoids the self-defining, autonomous confinements of sovereign power. Claudia Piepont Roth has recently illuminated the political ramifications of Roth's literary hospitality toward what societal and political norms ban as the negative, the repellent as follows:

> But the idea of the repellent is also, for Roth, associated with a train of political thought. The repellent gets into the way of "ideal plans," he wrote in the notes for several classes that he taught about his own books, at Bard College, in the late nineties. "If only we could get rid of the repellent Jews, or the repellent rich," the notes continue—and we are back in the historical catastrophes of the twentieth century: "If we can just slay the repellent, we will be pure." There is probably not another category that Roth holds up to such suspicious scrutiny as "the pure." (Piepont Roth 2014: 199)

In the long history of anti-Semitism, the Jews have been identified with the contaminated and the impure. Because of such identification with what is negative and outcast, they could easily be cast as scapegoats for all kinds of disappointing experience in the public at large. Anti-Semites blamed the Jews for things not going according to what Roth calls the teleology of "ideal plans." Having been the unfair target of so many representations of the negative, the disappointing and autoimmune, modern Jewish writing and thought from Rosenzweig to Roth attempted to shed light on the promise in what has ordinarily been dismissed as repellent and disappointing

Rosenzweig's Dark Drive and Levinas's Critique of Totality in Terms of Letting Us See the Promise in Disappointment

Franz Rosenzweig, one of the most important modern Jewish thinkers, further develops romanticism's Spinozist critique of idealism's disavowal of worldly, embodied forms of disappointment. Rosenzweig takes issue with an ethical (Kant's moral philosophy) and political (Hegel's philosophy of history) attempt to turn the contingent into the material for its own overcoming, in a modern world that has lost its worldliness. According to Rosenzweig, this disavowal of disappointment with the contingencies and frailties of embodied, worldly life partakes of a Christian theological agenda which idealism modernizes and to some extend secularizes.

Rosenzweig made this point clear in his famous *Star of Redemption* when discussing what he theorizes as idealist production that he differentiates from God's creation. Here, he speaks of the "monumental error of idealism [*der ungeheure Irrtum des Idealismus*]" which "consists in thinking that the All was really wholly contained in its production [*Erzeugung*] of the All" (Rosenzweig 1990: 209). The autonomous, humanly produced modern world endeavors to overcome disappointments that accompany our embodied constitution. Indeed, the Kantian idealist notion of freedom denotes indifference to disappointing experiences within our merely natural and contingent existence. Out of this Anthropocene independence from the environmental limitations of nature, idealist freedom consists in the construction of an immanent world that the autonomous human mind builds along the lines of theological conceptions of the "otherworldly," which is purged of any bodily and therefore contingent imperfections that could give rise to a sense of disappointment.

However, what Rosenzweig critiques as "idealist production" (Rosenzweig 1990: 209) nevertheless requires the empirical as material with which to construct an otherworldly, that is to say, a non-contingent modern world that goes without disappointment (wherein Jay Gatsby could reclaim his past and Jim could live up to his ideal of duty). In this context Rosenzweig employs Marxist analysis of capitalist economics in order to analyze the disavowal of disappointment at the heart of idealism's rationality. Idealism obfuscates the means of production, that is to say, it hides the chaos of disappointing reifications, which turns workers into mere objects, that preconditions its idealist production: "But idealism does not cherish this allusion to an underlying chaos of the distinctive [*dunkles Chaos des Besonderen*], and it quickly seeks to get away from it" (Rosenzweig 1990: 141). Rosenzweig here refers to the material foundation of the divine, as delineated in Schelling's *Ages of the Divine*.[1] Schelling's idealism differed from that of German transcendental philosophy in that he argued for the chaos and materiality that constitute not only God's creation but also God's very character.

Most strikingly, Rosenzweig associates the particular (*das Besondere*), which resists an idealist transformation of the body into the body politic, with Judaism. In writing of "the dark chaos of the particular" (Rosenzweig 1990: 141), he recalls "the dark drive," which he characterizes as "my Judaism" (Rosenzweig 1998: 96), and of which he became aware in the year 1920, when, with reference to this darkness, he rejected the position of a university lecturer (offered to him by his academic mentor, Friederich Meinecke). Rosenzweig's "dark drive" denotes a sense of disappointment that partakes of the promise of both revelation and redemption. Disappointing is the frailty of our embodied life subject to illness, aging, and mortality. Rosenzweig (here following the German idealists) associates the Otherness of the worldly with Jewishness.

Whereas Rosenzweig's Jewish thought remains cognizant of its particularity, German idealism belies its own particularity and material foundations while attempting to erase what Schelling charmingly calls "the modesty of matter" (Schelling 2000: 150), by the production of a world that is "universal" owing to its indifference to the "worldly," that is to say, material and particular determinations. Rosenzweig points out that such production nevertheless works with matter. Matter provides the nourishment for the apparatus of "otherworldly" production, thus feeding—similar to the workers in D. H. Lawrence's *Women in Love* (see Chapter 7)—reason's autonomous machinery with energy. Rosenzweig interprets this immanent production of transcendence not a movement away from the theological but in terms of an anti-creaturely theology, as a rational theology that wants to do away with its disappointing, contingent, bodily foundations: "For us, Idealism had proven to be in competition not with theology in general, but only with the theology of creation. From creation we had sought the way to revelation" (*Von der Schöpfung hatten wir den Weg zur Offenbarung gesucht*) (Rosenzweig 1990:

---

[1] For a discussion of Rosenzweig's reading of Schelling, see Else Rahel-Freund (1979) and Ernest Rubinstein (1999).

209). Thus, the separation between world and God does not result in a radical divide between immanence and transcendence. Such a divide would indeed require the overcoming of the immanent by immanent means (reason's autonomy, which frees the human from any dependence on matter), or, otherwise, a miraculous destruction of immanence by transcendence. In Spinozist manner, Rosenzweig, however, affirms the independence of God, world, and humanity, only to prepare the ground for their correlation, in which, thanks to the distance between these three entities, love of the one for the Other becomes possible.

Strikingly, German idealism's production of the worldly as the otherworldly deprives matter of its Otherness. That is to say, it erases the promise of transcendence that dwells in the immanent and that comes to the fore in moments of revelation, which occur when one individual helps preserve the life of another. Thus, creation reveals redemption: "Both revelation and redemption are creation" (*Auch Offenbarung, auch Erlösung sind Schöpfung*) (Rosenzweig 1990: 114). In the course of *The Star of Redemption*, Rosenzweig indeed "links creation and redemption through revelation, the latter understood as *love*" (Cohen 1994: 95). Love, however, grows out of an awareness of an individual's promise of Otherness and distinctiveness, despite the disappointing and general attributes of contingency and mortality.

By equating the general with the particular (Rosenzweig's formula A = B), idealism reduces the individual to the generality of death, from which he or she can only escape by willingly forsaking his or her empirical existence for the sake of a greater entity. As we have seen throughout this book this risking of one's life in the struggle for recognition is the underlying motive of Hegel's master-slave dialectics. It is this immanent struggle for recognition which Rosenzweig critiques when he argues that Hegel's philosophy of disavowed disappointment "had closed its view off from every Beyond" (*Den Blick in jedes Jenseits verschlossen*) (Rosenzweig 1990: 8). He clarified this point by arguing that the worldly has become the other of reason's autonomy: "So the world is a beyond for the intrinsically logical and total" [(*So ist die Welt dem eigentlich Logischen, der Einheit gegenüber ein Jenseits*) (Rosenzweig 1990: 15). Rosenzweig had Hegel's dialectical reduction of being to nothingness in mind, when he wrote that the worldly has become the transcendent.

To this extent, philosophy "has to expel the particular from the world and this expulsion of matter is why it has to be idealistic" (Rosenzweig 1990: 4) What Rosenzweig criticizes here in German idealism, Levinas depicts as violence *qua* totality, and he contrasts it with ethics *qua* infinity. Indeed, Levinas opposes the idealist (and Heideggerian) notion of freedom to that of justice. Levinas's *Totality and Infinity* in fact radicalizes the philosophical *qua* ethical, critique of German idealism as first and most clearly spelled out in *The*

Star of Redemption, a work to which Levinas refers only once to emphasize that it "is too often present in this book to be cited" (Levinas 1969: 28). Critiquing Hegel's master-slave dialectics of the struggle for recognition, Levinas defines "moral consciousness" as "an access to external being," maintaining that "external being is, *par excellence*, the Other" (Levinas 1990: 293). Rather than being opposed to the disappointment of the material, embodied world, Levinas's and Rosenzweig's metaphysics resides in the ethical care for mortal existence. According to Levinas, a metaphysics that correlates transcendence (or, for that matter, freedom) and heteronomy perceives the promise within disappointment. It does so by seeing in mundane, material life an opening toward the spiritual. The Other, or the flesh-and-blood neighbor with whom we interact in everyday life, embodies the revelation of promise: "The absolute other, whose alterity is overcome in the philosophy of immanence on the allegedly common plane of history [i.e., in Hegel's immanent philosophy of history], maintains his transcendence in the midst of history" (Levinas 1969: 40). What Levinas describes as a "philosophy of immanence" delineates his as well as Rosenzweig's understanding of Hegel's dialectical idealism.

As we have seen in this section, Rosenzweig's *The Star of Redemption* analyzes idealism via an examination of idealist attempts to erase from the face of the earth the potential disappointment of the frail embodied, particular Other, subject as he or she is to aging and mortality. In Rosenzweig's, and later in Levinas's, view this constitutes a theoretical wish for the reconfiguration of the empirical as pure spirit. Rosenzweig and Levinas take issue with the ethical consequences of such philosophical displacement of disappointment, for, on a sociopolitical plane, the theoretical manifestation of immanence that has fully turned into transcendence results in the expulsion of those who are perceived to remain immutably bound to the limitations of what Hegel calls the slave (attached to his or her life that is not to be thrown into the struggle for recognition). From a theological perspective, these philosophical abolitions of distance anticipate redemption, for they turn the world into the otherworldly, the outcome being that the immanent has now—at least within the parameters of idealist discourse—fully become the transcendent by its own (namely rational) means. When Rosenzweig and Levinas characterize "history" as idealism's collaborator, they clearly refer to Hegel's dialectics. As we have seen throughout this book, Hegel theorized his master-slave dialectics as a struggle for social recognition in which the members of a specific community become acquainted with their "master," death—as realization of the idealist insight into the "nothingness" of the disappointment which here is empirical, embodied life.

Counterposing this totalitarian reduction of the embodied and particular, in short, the Other, to the sameness of mortality, Levinas developed his philosophy of the face by means of which he illustrated the Mosaic commandment "Thou shalt not kill." Thus the human face embodies two aspects of the promise in disappointment: that of the neighbor as I interact with him or her in the external, mortal world and that of the divine whose correlated image I perceive in the face through which, as through a burning bush, God speaks with me. Thus Levinas's philosophy of the other both affirms the separateness between immanence and transcendence and theorizes the disappointing (in the sense of frail and mortal) body as the site of revelation, as broken embodiment of the spiritual.

Spinoza, Modern Jewish Writing and Thought or Why We Need to Contaminate Aging with Youth

From its inception modern Jewish thought has abstained from attempts at overcoming our potentially disappointing, embodied condition. Rather than seeking redemption in a world that, in Rosenzweig's terms, has idealistically and immanently been reproduced as otherworldly, modern Jewish thought has held open the possibility of experiencing promise in disappointment. As we have seen in the preceding section, thinkers such as Levinas and Rosenzweig have perceived the promise in what is supposed to be disappointing.

Moreover, modern Jewish writing and thought pays attention to dark topics which traditional humanist and Christian philosophies tend to marginalize or neglect. Facing one such difficult topic of our embodied life—aging—this and the following two sections keep returning to Spinoza. Why bring into the discussion of aging a thinker who does not explicitly address this topic? Although Spinoza wrote next to nothing about aging, his thought nevertheless prepared the ground for a discussion of the traditional, humanist neglect of the frailty of the body, with which the seventeenth-century thinker took issue, thereby offering an alternative to traditional philosophical approaches ranging from Plato to Descartes and beyond. Spinoza's work on how the mind cannot control or escape from the frailty of the body prepares for a new understanding of aging. Spinoza's concern with the fallacies and frailties of our embodied existence sheds light on the neglect of these issues in the more established works of the Christian, and, in a more secular context, humanist tradition.

Developing the preceding discussion of Rosenzweig, Levinas, and Derrida, the following sections explore how modern Jewish writing and thought pays attention to the more uncomfortable or darker aspects of our life which tend to get ignored in the redemptive narratives with which we are familiar from Christian and, in its secular form, humanist and idealist philosophies. Perfection here gives way to frailty, progress to the potential of regression—or in Freud's famous psychoanalytical case studies, repression— and light to darkness. As we have seen in the preceding section, Rosenzweig famously understood his Jewishness, as his "dark drive" (Rosenzweig 1998: 96). Aging is a dark topic, because it involves a deterioration of our health and our capacities. Modern Jewish writing and thought pays attention to dark topics which traditional humanist and Christian philosophies tend to marginalize or neglect.

In this way, this and the following two sections of this chapter explore how the symbolic presentation of age plays a crucial but often unacknowledged role in debates about idealism, humanism, and posthumanism. It will do so by discussing how post-traditional modern Jewish writing and thought approach topics of social exclusion, marginalization, and aging. As we have seen in the first two chapters of this book, the seventeenth-century philosopher Baruch Spinoza was the first modern or post-traditional Jew. As a rationalist Spinoza was aware of the inaccuracy of the body and how it might mislead—via passions and affects—our mind. Yet Spinoza discovered in the disappointment of our embodied constitution the promise of a better rational, life that accepts rather than dismisses limitations. In what is relevant for Philip Roth's critique of notions of purity, Spinoza's discerned an identity of mind and body that confounds idealist notions of a pure intellect or spirit.

Indeed, Spinoza denied that the purported purity of binary oppositions is natural or scientifically accurate. As has been discussed in Chapters 1 and 2, he argued that they are socially constructed, and that they are the product of anthropomorphic conceptions of nature or god. Humans "judge that what is most important in each thing is what is most useful to them, and rate as most excellent all those things by which they were most pleased" (Spinoza 1996: 29). From this non-anthropomorphic perspective, Spinoza argues that the whole array of philosophical and ethical values is nothing more than an expression or representation of appetites: "Hence, they [i.e., humans] had to form these notions, by which they explained natural things: *good, evil, order, confusion, warm, cold, beauty, ugliness*. And because they think themselves free, those notions have arisen: *praise* and *blame, sin* and *merit*" (Spinoza 1996: 29). Spinoza here analyzes mind-based concepts such as good and evil, sin and merit within a corporeal-material context. He does not, however, call into question the validity and significance of ideas, notions of good and evil, or the life of the mind. Indeed, the very title of his book *Ethics* highlights its concern to provide an accurate account of how to embark philosophically on a good life.

What is crucial for the discussion of Philip Roth's contamination of aging with youth in the concluding section of this chapter, the good in question here is, however, no longer a pure entity. Rather than being purely cerebral or purely corporeal, the good life here emerges as always already contaminated: involving a mind that is simultaneously embodied and a body that is at once mindful. This contaminated rather than dialectical approach to the sciences of human knowledge shapes much of the literary and also cinematic work on aging in the twenty-first century (such as Michael Haneke's 2012 film *L'Amour*).

As we have seen throughout this book, while acknowledging the existence of different characteristics, dialectics separates and opposes these within temporal as well as spatial frameworks. Dialectics works first by the positing of oppositions which then exchange places. Contamination, however, operates on the embodied model of symbiosis (Mack 2016: 2–22), wherein the promising is simultaneously the disappointing and the disappointing is filled with promise.

The term "contamination" has a negative denotation that accompanies disappointing experiences. It evokes uncomfortable or dark topics such as the deterioration of the body which can occur during aging. Aging has become associated with the negativity which the term "contamination" highlights. Aging contaminates health with illness, the mind's autonomy with the pathologies of the body, hence the importance of how Spinoza contaminates the mind with embodied states of deterioration for the larger discussion of aging. In the concluding part, this chapter briefly analyzes how some of Philip Roth's late novels contaminate constructions of age and aging with their purported opposite. He does so most scandalously by presenting the reader with forms of embodiment shared by both the young and the old. Roth is not alone in his contaminating approach to aging. In his *Winter Journal*, Paul Auster highlights the body of the writer when he interconnects birth with aging: "The soles of your feet anchored to the ground, but all the rest of you exposed to the air, and that is where the story begins, in your body, and everything will end in the body as well" (Auster 2012: 12). The body itself is not a pure entity. It is contaminated: simultaneously grounded to the earth and suspended in mid-air (a *Luftmensch*, as it were). The body makes us discover aspects of our life which our cerebral, societal values and educational training have done their best to suppress: our frailty, our proneness to failure, aging, and mortality.

Auster's *Winter Journal* struggles to bring across how the body is more mentally alert a propos disappointments and their promise than what has traditionally been understood as the purely cerebral:

Whenever you come to a fork in the road, your body breaks down, for your body has always known what your mind doesn't know, and however it chooses to break down, whether with mononucleosis or gastritis or panic attacks, your body has always borne the brunt of your fears and inner battles, taking the blows your mind cannot or will not stand up to. (Auster 2012: 68)

The body absorbs disappointing experiences which the mind has been societally or culturally trained to repress, ignore, or marginalize. Mental forms of repression or ignorance are the subject of critical reflection in the work that has recently been summarized under the name "posthumanism." The term "posthumanism" is rather misleading, because the "post" could imply some form of triumphal movement of progression. At its best, posthumanism does not proclaim the epoch of the *Übermensch* (something better than the human). Rather it denotes the spirit of a critical form of humanism that endeavors to include what the humanistic tradition excluded as negative, scandalous, or contaminated.

The concept of contamination highlights the copresence or simultaneity of humanistic values and what they traditionally marginalize, repress, or banish as the negative or the scandalous. To include the excluded means to bridge the gulf between the world and the word. The word often attempts to cover up the frailty of the world. The world is that of the body that is at once the mind. The word separated from the world gives rise to illusions of youth, invincibility, and immortality. From the different but related perspectives of Auster's and Roth's writings, we can grasp literature's work at bridging various divides between world and word. As Auster has put it, the writer falls through "the rift between world and word, the chasm that divides human life from our capacity to understand or express the truth of human life" (Auster 2012: 223). The incapacity for understanding the truth of human life results from traditional, uncritical humanist and idealist constructions of pure entities such as mind and body, wherein the former is autonomous and the latter frail and heteronomous, subject to decay and aging. Literature makes us experience the discovery of the often repressed contamination of mind and body. Here the body writes the mind: "Writing begins in the body, it is the music of the body, and even if words have meaning, can sometimes have meaning, the music of the words is where meanings begin" (Auster 2012: 224–5). From Spinoza's rationalist perspective, bodily impressions partake of mental life. They are often misleading us.

Embodied sensations may stimulate us to represent "the sun to us as two hundred paces distant, but we discover that this perception is false, because reason explains to us that the sun is not a big round ball that shines at our horizon but a star that we are very far away from and that is found at the center of a system of stars, of which we occupy only a part" (Macherey 2011: 68). The crucial point here, however, is that, as Macherey has shown, Spinoza does not dismiss such appearances prompted by corporeal sensations, as being unworthy of philosophical reflection:

> The sage is not the one who decides voluntarily to reform his intellect for once and for all, to eliminate, once and for all, all the false ideas that can be found there, and in this way to suppress from his existence all the effects of the imaginary mode of knowledge. It is the half-wit who believes himself to be delivered from all his passions, as they do not truly belong to him and do not depend on him; on the contrary, the free man knows how to reckon with them, because he grasped adequately the manner in which they are necessary. *Verum index sui et falsi*: the true takes into account the false as well in its objectivity, exactly to the point where it ceases to appear false in order to demonstrate its own truth. (Macherey 2011: 69)

The imagination reveals a bodily perception that may not be adequate in an objective or universal way but reflects our limited condition as being a small, subjective part of the universe. In this way, the "false image of the sun is a true idea if we relate it to our corporeal existence" (Macherey 2011: 70). The false partakes of the true, and there is disappointment in promise and promise in disappointment. Pure entities dissolve in Spinoza's philosophy of the identity of that which is separate for us.

Spinoza and the Inclusion of the Excluded— Aging—in Modern Jewish Writing and Thought

What makes possible such contaminating simultaneity rather than a dialectical spacing out and opposition, between promise and disappointment, between the true and the false? It is the absence of any sense of hierarchical subordination of the corporeal under the cerebral, the false under the true. In eliminating a mentalist and idealist hierarchy of the true, Spinoza confronts us with a dialectic that has abandoned the one-dimensional line of teleology. Without the teleological movement toward a hierarchically prioritized goal, dialectics, however, ceases to be dialectics and gives way to what I would call the concept of contamination where oppositions coexist with each other in a state of at one- and once-ness. Spinoza has thus first conceptualized this simultaneity of what has traditionally been categorized as mutually opposed entities.

As has been discussed in Chapters 1 and 2, Spinoza argued that the mind is the idea of the body. This means that, as in Auster, the corporeal is at once the core of the cerebral. As I have shown elsewhere (Mack 2010), Spinoza proposed an ethics of diversity as alternative to judgmental and profoundly hierarchical conceptions of nature which have shaped Western philosophical as well as theological traditions. This nonhierarchical divergence from the philosophical tradition results from Spinoza's identity (rather than prioritization of one over the other) between body and mind, between disappointment and promise, between the false and the true, and between narrative and scientific discourse. Narratives of various sorts shape our socioeconomic life. These narratives may be false, but they are nevertheless a true aspect of our historical existence. Literature is of course concerned with narratives and fictions. However, it would be misleading to relegate literature to the fictitious. Rather, it often critiques various fictions which shape our real, social, and embodied life. As Auster has put it in an exchange with his fellow writer J. M. Coetzee about the recent financial crisis:

> What we are talking about here, I think, is the power of fiction to affect reality, and the supreme fiction of our world is money. What is money but worthless pieces of paper? If that paper has acquired value, it is only large numbers of people who have chosen to give it value. The system runs on faith. Not truth or reality, but collective belief. (Auster and Coetzee 2013: 22)

Spinoza takes seriously the often neglected power of fiction to affect reality. He might be more radical than Auster, when he argues that the falsity of fiction nevertheless contributes to the diverse and multifaceted reality or truth of our social and embodied life. We exchange intrinsically worthless pieces of paper under the name "money" and in doing so, the unreal or false morphs into a real and important entity.

By highlighting how what we sometimes take to be naturally real is in actual fact a socially constructed fiction, based on convention, literature may be able to work toward a change in our approach to such socially constructed fictions. There are fictions of chronometric time that distort the meaning of both youth and aging. Beyond such chronometric distortions, our bodies are, however, subject to various breakdowns in both youth and age. We are in the philosophical habit of neglecting or marginalizing such collapses and relegating them to a delayed time horizon of age. A diverse and more comprehensive perspective strives to include what philosophy has been in the habit of excluding. Here modern Jewish writing and thought may be salient, because from Spinoza onward it explores topics of diversity and plurality.

Apropos of German Jewish writing and thought, Paul Mendes-Flohr has coined the notion of a dual identity, writing "that Jewry's articulate struggle to live with a plurality of identities and cultures—which is increasingly recognized to be a salient feature of Western modernity—is a mirror of a larger phenomenon beyond the specifics of Jewish existence" (Mendes-Flohr 1999: 3–4). This preoccupation with issues of diversity in modern Jewish writing and thought helps us see aging in a different light where it is no longer a marginalized, tabooed, or silenced topic.

Aging has been associated with the vulnerability and mortality of our embodied existence. As we have seen, Spinoza subjected Plato's and the Cartesian assumption of the mind's control over the body to ironic treatment, arguing that there is an identity rather than a hierarchical relationship between the two. While the body is subject to the disappointment of decay and death, the mind here promises the prospect of timeless mastery. Jan Baars has analyzed the relevance of this Cartesian model of the mind's controlling role for the exclusion from philosophical discussion of mortality and aging:

> This is basically Descartes' idea of a rational being that sets out to become the master of the "outside reality." Sometimes we get the impression that this rational individual could create itself or, like a Baron Münchhausen, pull himself from the mire of irrational nature by his own hair and take on a rational essence. This type of rationalist pretension is especially problematic when the time perspective moves from fairly clear actions to complicated and essentially unpredictable developments within the span of human lives. (Baars 2012: 29)

As Robert Pippin has abundantly shown, the idealist promise of overcoming the disappointments associated with embodiment had a huge impact on society at large from the work of Kant and Hegel onward. Hegel's post-Kantian dialectics promises freedom from disappointing experiences through "an insistence on a radical self-determination by subjects of their own activity" (Pippin 1999: 165). Philosophical notions of the mind's control over the body, and the self's autonomy in regard to merely embodied, material circumstances have interacted with larger sociopolitical and economic developments that have helped to increase our sense of independence from corporeal and material conditions.

Baars writes that in late modernity, "the market cultivates the illusion that everything can be bought and that choices would be unlimited for those who can afford them" (Baars 2012: 235). Disappointments and risks, which accompany our embodied life—prone as it is to various deteriorations which we have come to associate with aging—cannot, however, be overcome through the positing of notions (such as those of freedom or autonomy):

> there is often a lack of the most needed information, influence, or power to make adequate decisions and realize life plans accordingly. Moreover, the fundamental uncertainty of the future limits the ability to plan ahead. Choices are inevitable but also limited, as we can learn from the fate of the many fascinating but inadequate attempts at a prognosis of the future. In other words, you have to choose, but you cannot determine the outcomes. (Baars 2012: 235)

There is a pronounced sense of disappointment, the uncertain, the unexpected, and the absence of teleology (the aimless or goalless) in literature. As we have seen, Spinoza may well have been the first thinker to include in his account of truth the false reality of the fictitious in which we sometimes put our trust (as in money, for example). Hannah Arendt and Walter Benjamin are two Jewish thinkers of the twentieth century whose works have been informed by a literary sensibility which allows for disappointment and promise, for uncertainty, contingency, transformation, and new beginnings.

Benjamin's entire oeuvre focuses on time in a way that significantly deviates from Heidegger's conception of being as thrown-ness toward death. Michael Löwy has clearly shown that "Benjamin made crystal clear his feelings of hostility towards the author of *Sein und Zeit* long before Heidegger revealed his allegiance to the Third Reich" (Löwy 2005: 3). Benjamin contaminates paradise and progress with their traditional opposites: hell and regression. The storm from paradise (or, in other words, progress) prevents Benjamin's angel from resuscitating history's old age. The progressive force of this storm turns out to be not only deadly but also violent. Benjamin wrote his theses on the concept of history in 1940, a year in which the Nazis categorized Jews and Judaism as old, ill, infectious, and contaminating: no longer fit for life or mere survival but ready for extermination as enacted a few years later in the death camps of the Nazi genocide (only fit to be preserved as dead objects in a museum such as the one the Nazis planned to build in Prague).

Benjamin's angel of history is highly relevant for a non-chronometric understanding of aging. The angel pays attention to those who are left behind by progress. Those whom she or he wants to rescue from the onslaught of time are the ill, the aged, and the dead. Benjamin's angel cares for the embodied frailties which we associate with aging. Significantly, Benjamin based his conceptual, philosophical work on concrete, embodied works of art and literature. His angel of history was inspired by living with Paul Klee's painting *Angelus Novus* (Benjamin owned the painting and literally lived with it). Benjamin combines literature with philosophy. He started out in the academic German literary school of philology and subsequently wrote most of his oeuvre as a freelance literary critic. This does not mean that he fits into a traditional literature department. Even though much of his writing reflects on literature (Goethe), literary tropes (allegory), and its translation (Proust and Baudelaire), it departs from the traditional tenets of either the German tradition of philology or the English strand of practical criticism. Benjamin gives literary studies a highly theoretical bent.

What does this mean? Benjamin relates the literary to larger sociopolitical and economic topics, albeit insisting on the distinct and unique contribution works of literature make to transforming how we approach and perceive these topics. By doing so, he alienated the traditional academic establishment, and not surprisingly his habilitation thesis on the German Mourning Play was failed by the philological German literature department of Frankfurt University.

Having studied under Karl Jaspers and Martin Heidegger, Hannah Arendt was more professionally attached to the discipline of philosophy than Benjamin. She nevertheless attempts to undermine philosophical hostility to the plurality or diversity of embodied life. She also took issue with the determinism implicit in Heidegger's notion of thrown-ness (*Geworfenheit*), developing her counter-concept of natality. As Baars has argued, natality "is not only something that happens at birth, but it qualifies human lives from birth to death, inspiring hope, creativity, critique, rebirth, and the emergence of new horizon" (Baars 2012: 241). Baars refers to Arendt's notion of natality in order to undermine chronometric perspectives on aging. Arendt's idea of natality indeed partakes of the conceptual framework of contamination: it contaminates birth with its traditional, dialectical opposite—age and aging.

Aging may actually be contaminated with its apparent opposite: birth and youth. This would be an unexpected emergence of promise within disappointment, and Arendt's notion of natality highlights the reality of the diverse, the non-determined, and the unpredictable newness of beginnings where we would not have hoped to encounter them. As Miguel Vatter has recently shown, Arendt developed her understanding of natality not on the basis of Augustine's writing but on that of her friend and collaborator Benjamin. Admittedly, Arendt credited Augustine with the philosophical discovery of a new beginning. Augustine was, however, part of a larger philosophical tradition which Arendt took issue with for its hostility toward plurality. Vatter has argued that in "his discussion of the reasons for God's creation of Man, Augustine claims that God created human beings as 'Adam,' that is, as a singular 'man,' in contrast to the creation of animals, which is always plural" (Vatter 2014: 143). Arendt critiqued the single-mindedness of Augustine's traditional, humanist perspective when she tries to "protect men in their being-animal, that is to say, in their plurality" (Arendt 2002: 70–1). The diversity of humanity needs protecting, precisely because it does not fit into the straight line of dialectical logic and thus raises the suspicion of disappointing promises of one exclusive positive itinerary in history, politics, and society at large. As Vatter has maintained: "Natality, then is a concept that Arendt employs to deconstruct the "humanist" opposition between animality and humanity based on the neo-Aristotelean distinction between *zoe* and *bios*" (Vatter 2014: 145). Arendt and Benjamin in different but related ways attempt to undermine various theological as well as philosophical traditions that oppose the human with the animal, thereby playing off the promises of the mind (conceived as properly human) against the disappointing frailty of the body, the presumed territory of the animalistic.

Like Spinoza, Arendt and Benjamin try to establish identities, simultaneities, and contaminations between different entities, rather than oppositions. In doing so, they theoretically delineate what Philip Roth describes in his late novels about aging. Similar to Auster (in the quotations earlier), they try to bridge the gulf between world and word, by highlighting both the body's cognitive faculties and the embodiment of apparently abstract, signifying structures. By undermining the philosophical traditions of teleology, anthropocentricism, and unicity, Spinoza's, Benjamin's, and Arendt's works fall outside the parameters of mainstream philosophy. It is neither philosophy nor literature and perhaps its deviance and defiance of theological and philosophical creeds may go under the term "theory."

It is in this theoretical ambience that literature describes and reflects upon age and aging more extensively than philosophy. Aging has traditionally been marginalized in philosophical discussions. Instead, philosophy has emphasized the significance of death in order to establish the quasi-immortality of cerebral entities such as Plato's ideas that supposedly endure in a free realm that is autonomous in its radical independence from material conditions which are exposed to aging, decay, and death. As Baars has emphasized

> throughout history death has been a subject of intense debate and reflection, while discussions about aging have been scarce. One important reason for this lopsided attention is that throughout history death was much more part of everyday life and would strike at all ages, while mortality has over the last century gradually been concentrated in later life. (Baars 2012: 235)

Aging has been subsumed under the topic of death, and as such it has been contrasted with birth. This chapter attempts to contaminate these traditionally binary oppositions. While this and the preceding sections have focused on how a philosophical approach that takes the embodied disappointment of frailties seriously (as discussed in modern Jewish thought from Spinoza to Benjamin and Arendt) contributes to a non-chronometric understanding of aging, the concluding part attempts to illustrate this theoretical discussion with a close reading of Philip Roth's literary work.

Before proceeding to this concluding part, let me briefly address the question of how a contamination of aging and birth (as discussed earlier) relates to recent debates about humanism and posthumanism. By relegating aging to the domain of death, the Western philosophical tradition has treated it as an unsavory topic which associates the human with mortality and vulnerability and the presumed disappointing prospect of animal life. As Alasdair MacIntyre has pointed out, throughout the history of philosophy ("from Plato to Moore"), "there are 'only' passing remarks to human vulnerability and affliction and to the connections between them and our dependence on others" (MacIntyre 1999: 1). While further developing MacIntyre's ethics of human vulnerability, the following discussion of Roth's literary work on aging contributes to comprehending the reason for philosophy's neglect of the human animal in its embodied dependency. The *rationale d'être* for such neglect resides in the assumption of the mind's promising, controlling position over the disappointingly fickle and frail body which characterizes both the Platonic and the Cartesian conceptions of humanity.

Philip Roth and the Promise in Disappointment

The following renders mutually contaminated the traditionally opposed terms of disappointment and promise, of aging and birth. As we have seen in the preceding section mainly through an analysis of Hannah Arendt's and Spinoza's thought, we have come to contrast and oppose birth with aging. Rather than being natural, this opposition between birth and aging accompanies the constructed or fictional character that governs aspects of our societal system of categorization. As Hannah Arendt has shown in her analysis of both anti-Semitism and totalitarianism (as discussed in Chapter 4), prejudicial fictions may be appealing and may thus win over large groups of people if not entire societies, due to their neat and coherent appearance:

> Before they seize power and establish a world according to their doctrines, totalitarian movements conjure up a lying world of consistency which is

more adequate to the needs of the human mind than reality itself; in which, through sheer imagination, uprooted masses can feel at home and are spared the never-ending shocks which real life and real experiences deal to human beings and their expectations. (Arendt 2004: 464–5)

In this important quote, Arendt analyzes the public attraction of totalitarian and racist doctrines. They beguile popular opinion with the appearance of consistency and thus promise to overcome the messy, contradictory, and disappointing reality of actual socioeconomic circumstances. They "neatly" displace real existent experiences of disappointment onto the other. In the process of such displacement politics turns reality into a fiction. This pressure to displace what is presumed to be negative and disappointing is most pronounced in totalitarianism: here we encounter in the most striking form the demand to conform to norms prescribing the appearance of health and youth as an all-encompassing political necessity. The population which has become totalitarian sees in this beautification (or aestheticization) of politics—as Benjamin has put it in his treatise on the "Work of Art in the Age of Mechanical Reproduction"—a device that guards against the chaos of our diverse human condition:

Before the alternative of facing the anarchic growth and total arbitrariness of decay or bowing down before the most rigid, fantastically fictitious consistency of an ideology, the masses probably will always choose the latter and be ready to pay for it with individual sacrifices—and this not because they are stupid or wicked, but because in the general disaster this escape grants them a minimum of self-respect. (Arendt 2004: 464)

In terms of political appeal, cerebrally constructed fictions are much more attractive than our organic reality of decay, aging, and death. Fictions of the real tend to rule our politics, and this no more so than in totalitarianism. Here, the coherence and consistency of a constructed world safeguards against disappointments that occur in our embodied existence. The escape from this embodied existence is an avoidance of "anarchic growth" and aging ("total arbitrariness of decay").

Throughout his writing, Philip Roth has described various versions of society's hostility to the messiness of our organic unpredictability that confounds the seemingly well-defined categories of birth, youth, and aging. This is one reason why his novels critique the way fictions of predictability, coherence, and consistency hold sway over our sense of reality. In some way or another, Roth's novels are concerned with the disappointments and promises that accompany our limited, human condition. Related to the a-moral horizon of Greek tragedy, Roth abstains from allocating praise or blame:

> Roth's heroes have not committed any crimes. They are punished because punishment is the human lot. Roth says today that a reasonable overarching title for his previous series of books would be *Blindsided: An American Trilogy*. We are helpless before history, aging, other people, our endless getting of everything wrong: the unknowable future. (Pierpont Roth: 312)

Here literature takes issue not so much with the fictions we construct in order to make life simple and easy. More radically still, we see life through blinding or distortive lenses: "The *Nemeses* quartet, and its last books, above all, demonstrates that our blindness is real, even if we are blind to that, too" (Pierpont Roth: 312). Our lopsided perspective is all the more reason to avoid rigid distinctions and opposition between disappointment and promise.

In this context, Roth has spoken of his "continuing preoccupation with the relationship between the written and the unwritten world" (Roth 1961: xiii). He explores this relationship in his novels. This means that the novel becomes a ground on which to test the unwritten world's (let's call this "reality") entanglement and entrapment with the written world of fiction. Roth's Zuckerman novels are a case in point and so is his early novel *Portnoy's Complaint*. Portnoy cannot get over the fact that the real sometimes gets caught in fictive nets of narratives promising redemption and/or superiority. It is this sense of unruliness that pervades Roth's novels from his early works on adolescent revolt to his more recent literary approach toward aging and decay. As Patrick Hayes has recently put it:

> Against the Kantian safety-net that Sontag throws around the work of art, the way Roth's novels transgress the distinction between art and pornography enables it also to transgress onto the terrain of ethics, and pollute a form of discourse that, to borrow from Sontag's terms, tends to emphasize the primacy of the "intellect" and the "self-evident value... of self-consciousness" over the desiring body. More rigorously opposed to "the Platonic devaluation of the world," *Portnoy's Complaint* is a playfully serious experiment in exactly what is at stake in liberating what Helen Kepesh called "the stuff itself." (Hayes 2014: 108)

Here, literature is a disruptive force that changes the way we think by interrupting our ways of seeing and doing things. Literature runs counter to our accustomed lives. It is a counterforce. Roth calls it "counterlife" (the title of one of his Zuckerman novels). "Counterliving," as Ross Posnock has put it, is "a way of understanding the capacity—propensity—of individuals and history for defying the plausible and predicable" (Posnock 2006: 274). The unpredictability of the diverse and the disappointment of the unforeseen or implausible is literature's subject matter.

According to Roth, this is exactly what characterizes life. Life is the democracy of the nonhomogeneous and unpredictable; it is the ongoing flow of organisms that diverge, split up, and forever renew themselves, confounding categories of youth and aging: "Life *is* and: the accidental and the immutable, the elusive and the graspable, the bizarre and the predictable, the actual and the potential, all the multiplying realities, entangled, overlapping, conjoined—plus the multiplying illusions!" (Roth 1988a: 310). To be stuck in one perspective is to be caught in a delusion and yet this is our human condition: "Is an intelligent human being likely to be much more than a large-scale manufacturer of misunderstanding? I do not think so" (Roth 1988a: 310). What we take to be a disappointment turns out to be promising.

By allowing for contradictions and various contaminations, literature not so much imitates as sustains life, giving succor to its exuberance of both growth and decay—two entities that are not separate, and we should thus be careful not to oppose them. As Roth has put it in one of his late novels about aging, *The Dying Animal*: "But being old also means that despite, in addition to, and in excess of your beenness, you still are. Your beenness is very much alive. You still are, and one is as haunted by the still-being and its fullness as by the having-already-been, the pastness" (Roth 2001: 36). The narrator of *The Dying Animal* attempts to intervene in public health discourse which equates aging with chronometric time: "The only thing you understand about the old when you're not old is that they have been stamped by their time. But understanding only that freezes them in their time, and so amounts to no understanding at all" (Roth 2001: 36). The chronometric approach toward aging which is part of medicine (i.e., of medicine as defined in terms of positivism) misunderstands aging as being a question of near-death. Roth's literary work intervenes and confronts us with the life of those we have come to define as almost dead.

This is not to say that Roth reduces literature to a form of medical practice. In his *Anatomy Lesson*, he warns against a confusion of literature with medicine. Literature's distinction from medicine does not invalidate its potential for interventions in our embodied social world. This potential is, however, not a calm or didactic one, but that of the unquiet, the contaminated. In *Ghost Writer*, the young Zuckerman encounters via his literary idol, the imagined, fictive writer E. I. Lonoff, Henry James's conception of literature's dark drive. The elderly Lonoff requests to have three sentences from James's story "The Middle Years" "hanging over his head while beneath them he sat turning his own sentences: 'We work in the dark—we give what we have. Our doubt is our passion and our passion is our task. The rest is the madness of art'" (Roth 1988b: 77). The young Zuckerman is taken aback: "I would have thought the madness of everything but art. The art was what was sane, no? Or was I something missing?" (Roth 1988b: 77). What Zuckerman is missing here is the disruptive and unsettling force of literature and art. In *Zuckerman Unbound*, he has become acquainted with the uncontained and with what made Plato ban artists from his city.

Literature and art's passion is that of the unpalatable, destructive, and disappointing. What Henry James in the quotation from Roth *Ghost Writer* describes as the passion of doubt and its disappointment is part of literature's paradoxical promise. A sense of disappointment drives the constant revision of artistic work on a formal level. The rest which is the madness of art manifests itself in its craziness, in its disruptive effect on its audience. It makes the audience doubtful of what it has become accustomed to believe to be true, good, beautiful, and representative of our human condition. From early on, Roth's novels have focused on sex as being akin to art's disruptive aspects.

In his late novels, Roth couples sex with aging. This combination of the sexual energy with the aging process calls into doubt traditional representations of the elderly. By depicting age within the context of sex, Roth questions the opposition between birth or youth and aging. The hero of *Sabbath's Theatre* is an elderly man who refuses to live up to representations of what it means to be old. He rebels against death and thrives in his sexual as well as obscenely artistic life: "Oh Sabbath wanted to live! He thrived on this stuff! Why die?"(Roth 1996: 172) There is no denying the facts of death and disease. The flat representation of these facts does, however, a disservice to art's and literature's so far untapped resources that not so much represent what we are as offer alternatives to the status quo by showing us our unrealized or unacknowledged lives. In this innovative form of representation, the arts help us imagine what we could be as well as confront us with what societal norms dismiss and exclude as being disappointing. This nonrepresentational—in the sense of nonrepresentative or nonnormative—show of art is disruptive.

The shows Sabbath put on public display are obscene and call into doubts norms and regulations. This is part of their hilarity. The sexual disruptions of an elderly man are what the art of this novel is:

> There was a kind of art in his providing an illicit adventure not with a boy of their age but with someone three times their age—the very repugnance that his aging body inspired in them had to make their

adventure with him feel a little like a crime and thereby give free play to their budding perversity and to the confused exhilaration that comes of flirting with disgrace. (Roth 1996: 213)

Sex is no longer merely sex here: it has become a form of art that disrupts our relationship to standard forms of representation which depict aging in terms of pain and therefore a shrinking or closed-in world—a limited world that does no longer allow for the uncontainable and excessively expansive urges of libidinal energy. Elaine Scarry has provided the following account of representations of aging, which Roth's *Shabbath's Theatre* counteracts and violates:

> As the body breaks down, it becomes increasingly an object of attention, usurping the place of all other objects, so that finally, in the very old and sick people, the world may exist only in a circle of two feet out from themselves; the exclusive content of perception and speech may become what is eaten, the problems of excreting, the progress of pains, the comfort or discomfort of a particular chair of bed. Stravinsky once described aging as: "the ever-shrinking perimeter of pleasure." This constantly diminishing world ground is almost a given in representations of old age. (Scarry 1985: 32–3)

Sabbath's Theatre renders unpalatable and obscene socially acceptable representations of old age. The novel disappoints expectations of the aging process that have renounced the promises of a sexual relationship. Roth's late novels contend with representative description of the aging process's "exclusive content": a content that is filled with the absence of youth and birth. Literature here renders inclusive what we have come to think and perceive as excluded or exclusive.

This disruption of what we are used to see as representations of old age is partly achieved through the evocation of madness. One housewife Mickey Sabbath tries to seduce, accuses him of being a "maniac," and she goes on to substantiate her charge through an account of his intergenerational abnormality: "You have the body of an old man, the life of an old man, the past of an old man, and the instinctive force of a two-year old" (Roth 1996: 335). Sabbath, however, turns the tables on the accuser, calling the moral idea of fidelity madness: "The *madness*. There is no punishment too extreme for the crazy bastard who came up with the idea of fidelity. To demand of the human flesh fidelity. The cruelty of it, the mockery of it, simply unspeakable" (Roth 1996: 336). Within this context, the novel compares its hero with that of another protagonist of aging.

Sabbath's Theatre in all its profanity evokes the cruelty meted out on King Lear by his two daughters Regan and Goneril. The novel establishes parallels between Mickey Sabbath, the elderly but virile man whom society mocks and casts out of its halls of residence, and the outcast Lear who is "mightily abused" (Roth 1996: 297). Mickey quotes Lear's "Pray, do not mock me. / I am a very foolish, fond, old man," and elaborates on what it means not to be in "perfect mind" (Roth 1996: 296): "The mind is the perpetual motion machine. You're not ever free of anything. Your mind's in the hand of *everything*" (Roth 1996: 296). The madness of the old Lear turns into the sexual excess of Mickey Sabbath whose craziness is his breaking of the norms associated with aging: his mind will not let go of the world, and his world refuses to diminish—it manifests the opposite of a shrinking perimeter of pleasure cited earlier.

Sabbath Theatre's quotations from *King Lear* are quite significant. As Helen Small has shown, Shakespeare's play counters Aristotle's account of aging: "At this moment [i.e., Lear's soliloquy in Act 3 Scene 4. 28-36] such a reading would say, Lear is not—as Aristotle's rhetorical portrait of old men had it— made 'small minded' by age. He is not reduced to chilliness, cowardice, or a desire for 'nothing more exalted or unusual than what will keep him alive'" (Small 2007: 84). Even though he may be mad, Lear's intelligence is quite active and perceptive (rather than nonfunctional or "senile"). He "is capable of smelling out the bad faith that speaks in injunctions to be patient, when what is intended is that one surrender meekly to injustice. 'Being weak, seem so,' as Regan says (2.4.190)" (Small 2007: 84). Regan and Goneril's physical assault on Lear transmutes into the social and psychological cruelty which Roth's novel makes us cognize as a certain moral code which we are expected to live up to. To disappoint such societal expectations is to find promise in what has been excluded and interdicted. We have to live up to society's representation of "human purity" (Roth 1996: 274). Roth's novel most preoccupied with the theme of purity is *The Human Stain*. This novel focuses on the intricacies involved in violating socially and hereditary assigned roles of an aging self. Impure is precisely the targeted disappointment of societal expectations for one's role: "Yet to give up playing any but the role socially assigned [...], that is what is unacceptable" (Roth 2000: 155). Seen from this perspective, we violate societal purity rules when we step out of the role we have been assigned to impersonate (that of an aging self). This ideology of purity mocks and denies the reality of youth within age by stigmatizing the coupling of sex with aging. The outrage of Mickey Sabbath is precisely that he is both erotic and old.

The associations of sex include what it may on occasion result in: procreation or birth. As a sexually driven elderly man, Mickey commingles what society represents as binary opposites. Rather than opposing age and birth/youth with each other, he reconciles them, rendering compatible what is supposed to be incompatible. In doing so, he unmasks the representative morality of aging as cruel mockery against which he protests in Lear-like fashion: "That is what it comes down to: caricaturing us, insulting us, abhorring in us what is nothing more than the delightful Dionysian underlayer of life" (Roth 1996: 237). As modern Lear, Mickey Sabbath vents his anger at the segregation of the procreative and the youthful from what is represented and considered to be old: "'No, too old for that. Finished with that.' He waves his hand almost angrily, 'That's *done*. That's *out*. Good-bye, girl-friends'" (Roth 1996: 395). It is as though the aged need to live up to their representations. In order not to disappoint their assigned roles of impersonation, the elderly have to be old and sexless and noncreative. Otherwise, they become objects of insult and mockery.

The elderly have to find their way into the nomenclatural box where they are cut off from youth or birth: "All the existence, born, and unborn, possible and impossible, in drawers. But empty drawers looked at long enough can probably drive you mad" (Roth 1996: 395). Mickey leaves the representative drawers open and does not fill them with his age. This drives society mad. So mad that Mickey, again a modern version of Lear in this respect, is "waiting to be murdered" (Roth 1996: 450) by those who cannot endure what represents to them his madness. Roth's late novels from *Dying Animal* to *Nemesis* (2010) interrupt channels that connect representations of aging to accustomed forms of our thinking about age, youth, and birth.

In this context, we could read his *Everyman* (2007) as an attempt to change our perception of what is our common biological itinerary. Literature disrupts the monolithic path of the trajectory traversing birth and death. It highlights within the supposedly shrinking world of aging "that sharp sense of individuation, of sublime singularity, that marks a fresh sexual encounter or love affair and that is the opposite of the deadening depersonalization of serious illness" (Roth 2007: 134). Roth's everyman diverges from what we have come to cognize and recognize as aging, decay, and death. The ending of this short novel is striking. Even though, it, as we all do, ends in death, the moment preceding anesthetization (for what proves to be a fatal surgery) is not that of a closing but expanding world: "He went under feeling far from felled, anything but doomed, eager yet again to be fulfilled, but nonetheless he never woke up" (Roth 2007: 182). There is of course no denying: death is our common fate, and aging is the life experience of every man and every woman. This experience is, however, not restricted to those whom we commonly represent as elderly or aged.

Aging starts with birth. Literature questions fictions, and the fictitious opposition between birth and aging is one of them. The moment before death might indeed be the feeling of the "eager yet to be fulfilled." It is this contaminating reconfiguration of what we previously thought to be separate and incompatible that is part of literature's interruption of the fictitious prejudices, stigmas, norms, and segregations that render not only the world of the aged an ever-shrinking perimeter of pleasure. As we have seen throughout this book, Spinoza's identity of mind and body prepares the ground for what I call the "figure of contamination" (Mack 2016). "Contamination" discovers promise in disappointment and experiences disappointment in promise. It does so by allowing for the simultaneous interdependence of what has previously been conceived as opposed or separate (as in traditional mind-body divisions). Spinoza contaminates dialectically opposed entities (such as the body and the mind, the intellect and the appetites, and so forth).

From a Spinozist perspective, literature expands our world and opens it up to what is there but so far has been neglected or marginalized. It counteracts pain not as quasi-medical antidote to suffering we have already incurred but by cogitatively expanding society's sense of our truly open world, freeing it from fictions that diminish it to one where suffering turns out to be—but does not need to be—our common lot. Literature is thus the truthful—but not empirically real—cosmos where we encounter admonishments of the fulfilled and wide open even in moments that precede oblivion. By allowing for possible worlds of non-diminishing reality in the here and now, literature changes human knowledge, reconfiguring both disappointment as part of life's promise and disappointment as already partaking of what inspires our sense of promise.

9

Conclusion

Expecting Disappointment, or, from Pynchon's, Roth's, Strauss's, and Vonnegut's Postmodernism to Anna Burns's *Milkman* and D. F. Wallace's *The Pale King*

Introduction: Our Contemporary Setting of Expecting Disappointment

Our contemporary situation brings to the fore a striking reversal of promise as disappointment and of disappointment as promise. With a hard Brexit on the horizon in the UK, with the political and economic uncertainties of the present, the ideological certainties of the past have come home to roost. This is perhaps no more so than in Anna Burns's novel *Milkman* (2018). Crucially, Burns goes back to Kafka's suspension of any historical or political points of reference (as has been discussed in Chapter 7). The metaphorically sounding "Milkman" of the title is actually the surname of a top-ranking paramilitary man. We do not know where the narrative takes place and the only indication of history is the term "border": on our side or on their side, which means this side of the border or the other way round.

This lack of specificity has the Kafkaesque effect of rendering the question of where one belongs arbitrary and interchangeable, similar to the ways in which hope and disappointment change places to the point that the two opposed terms might actually be contaminated or entangled with each other.

Mr. Milkman rather obtrusively introduces himself into the life of the adolescent female narrator, stalking her. The narrator lives in what she calls a "totalitarian enclave" where paramilitaries command absolute power and where the self is always at the beck and call of sectarian forces. This becomes clear with the real milkman (not Mr. Milkman) who delivers bottles of milk from his van to houses within the community. This man goes under the label of lacking any empathy or love, because he turned various weapon arsenals which the paramilitaries have stored in his house (while he was away) out onto the street, shouting that he does not want to support violence. Refusing to support bloodshed thus becomes communally categorized as rejecting love. In a linguistic order of promise and its accompanying communal life wherein violence and love thus become synonymous, it might not be surprising that a paramilitary leader has sexual harassment (of the narrator) go under the label of love or courtship. Where terms such as "violence" and "love" have troubling reaches of certainty, we might long for the leeway of the uncertain where it is actually promising to expect disappointment.

Along with its title, this book has challenged schematic historical boundaries, separating the romantic from the modern or the modern from the postmodern. The breakdown of rigid historical periodization comes all the more to the fore in our contemporary moment, and it is with this contemporaneity in mind that this concluding chapter refers to Roth together with Pynchon and the Austrian contemporary writer Elfriede Jelinek as rather dubious "postmodernist" writers. The discussion of postmodernism is positioned in between Strauss's provocative philosophical critique of a reductive, instrumentalist, and consumerist postindustrial modernity and the new sincerity of David Foster Wallace that turns not so much ironic as, sometimes, sadly humorous in Anna Burns's recent novel *Milkman*. Mutations of periodization in philosophy and literary history indicate the fluidity and contamination of what historical terms often too rigidly set out to purify as distinct and separate. Hence this study's attempt to shift the perspective from compartmentalized categories (tied to movements and periods) to a more inclusive vantage point from which to see modernity under the tragic, ironic, and often melodramatic experience of various disappointments with ideas and their crude Anthropocene historical manifestations.

Philip Roth and the Destructive Element: Leo Strauss, Postmodernism, and Sincerity

The Devil of the Little Place—the gossip, the jealousy, the acrimony, the boredom, the lies. No, the provincial poisons do not help. People are bored here, they are envious, their life is as it is and as it will be, and so, without seriously questioning the story, they repeat it—on the phone, in the street, in the cafeteria, in the classroom. (Roth 2000: 290)

A reversal of roles in which disappointment emerges as promise and promise simultaneously announces disappointment (as discussed in the concluding section of Chapter 8) has shaped the intellectual form of this book. As we have seen, to reverse such moods and capacities often disturbs societal conceptions of propriety and purity. The preceding quotation from Roth's *Human Stain* describes how fantasized or, indeed, fictional impersonations become distributed via gossip and other lies—generated out of jealousy, acrimony, boredom—throughout a given community setting, allotting each individual its societal role, which is the outcome of communal imagination. The fictional thus turns real *qua* impersonation (as construct of social stereotyping, gossip, or rumor).

What has been the product of communal imagination (i.e., gossip) then becomes a reality through habit, through repetition. This is precisely the way how gender turns from a socially constructed entity into the illusion of a "natural" characteristic: through repetition, which causes expectations for the realization of what has been anticipated from remembered or habituated actions. These endless loops of habit that become anticipated expectations which are then reconfirmed characterizes what Butler calls the performativity of gender:

> In the first instance, then, the performativity of gender resolves around this metalepsis, the way in which the anticipation of a gendered essence produces that which it posits outside itself. Secondly, performativity is not a single act, but a repetition and a ritual, which achieves its effects though its naturalization in the context of a body, understood, in part, as culturally sustained temporal duration. (Butler 2007: xv)

In this way gender roles partake of larger societal impersonations which paradoxically shape our communal sense of reality. This decoding of the "natural" as the constructed and hence impersonated (rather than genuine) highlights the simultaneity of promise and disappointment which has been the underlying theme of this book. Unmasking the social construction of gender roles promises the liberation of those who have been oppressed by patriarchy. Traditional assignations of female and male capacities are not the product of nature but that of unfair and unequal distributions of power.

This study has analyzed various male-centered novels of disavowed disappointment. Here the narrator observes how the main male protagonists fails to live up to societal gender expectations (of duty as in Conrad's Lord Jim, romance as in Fitzgerald's Gatsby or intellectual and political influence as in Bellow's Ravelstein and of societal inclusion as in Kafka's K.). Being modernist works of fictions, these novels highlight not so much failed actions but their internal repercussions. That is to say, the narrator dwells on how the main character of his narration disavows experiences of disappointment.

By foregrounding the potentially disastrous consequences that accompany various disavowals of disappointment, the novels simultaneously holds out the promise of liberating its readers from their own societally assigned roles (of gender, of class, of ethnicity, and so forth). In doing so the novel disrupts its genre specific boundaries and institutionalized classification. An active awareness of how fictions encroach into our everyday life is all the more urgent in a media-saturated world such as ours and that of Roth's twentieth-century America. Indeed, Roth makes clear that this cognizance of the fabricated and fictional aspect of societal interactions partakes of the critical link that connects the separate spheres of the word and the world.

Literature may prepare its readers to resist various fictitious projections in ordinary, empirical life: "Defying a multitude of bizarre projections, or submitting to them, would seem to me at the heart of everyday living in America, with its ongoing demand to be something palpable and identifiable" (Roth 1985: 86). The palpable and identifiable constitutes one part of Roth's work: it is what Debra Shostak has called "the power of realism—which insists on the materiality and historicity of the real—as mode of knowing and telling" (Shostak 2011: 11). Strikingly Roth contaminates the palpable materiality of what is identifiable (appearing to be real) with the disturbing or destructive element of the unpalatable. This has been identified as Roth's "generic experiments in postmodernism" (Shostak 2011: 14), but as we have seen in the discussion of Conrad destructive element, it is part of a Spinozist romantic and then modernist (Conrad's destructive element) and also postmodernist openness to the incomplete, the fragmentary that outdoes various notions of order and teleology. In the words of Debra Shostak, the "uncontrollability of real things matters most because the real cannot be foreseen" (Shostak 2011: 14). The unforeseen disrupts our habituation to what we take to be purity, normality, and order.

Crucially, this is not only a specialized issue for literary studies and their historicist periodization. Roth makes clear that exposing the palpability of the real to the destructive element of the unpalatable should have extra-literary repercussions. Fiction makes us question the purported realism of the identifiable, and in doing so it might sensitize its audience to resist various realist strategies to adopt co-opted voices and appearances in everyday life. The disappointment of the unpalatable, destructive element in modernist, postmodernist, and contemporary literature holds out the promise of impeding various pressures to impersonate preassigned roles. Roth describes such role assignments in real, ordinary life as follows: "Everyone is invited to imitate in conduct and appearance the grossest simplifications of self that are mercilessly projected upon them by the mass media and advertising, while they must, of course, also contend with the myriad expectations that they arouse in those with whom they have personal and intimate associations" (Roth 1985: 86-7). In the extra-literary, real world we have to live up to various expectations (whether generated by the reified workings of commodification in mass media and the advertisement industry or by the more intimate sphere of romance). Literature confronts us with the impersonation of disappointment, of the unpalatable, the destructive element. What I call literature's extra-literary aspect is this unsettling of our sense of promise and disappointment. Here we come to see that the hidden, shameful disappointment of social expectations might actually hold out the promise of life freed from various pressures to live up to prearranged, extraneous norms.

Roth approaches literature in terms of impersonation. Fiction is to make the audience momentarily believe what is not real: "The idea is to perceive your invention as a reality that can be understood as a dream. The idea is to turn flesh and blood into literary characters and literary characters into flesh and blood" (Roth 1985: 122). Strikingly, much of our reality paradoxically consists of such impersonations of the untrue: "Millions of people do this [i.e., impersonations or make believe] all the time, of course, and not with the justification of making literature. They *mean* it. It is amazing what lies people can sustain behind the mask of their real faces" (Roth 1985: 124). Conrad's modernist and Roth's postmodernist destructive element disrupts such fallacious meaning of the act of deception in real life. How does it manage to do so? In an extended way, it renders unpalatable the appearance of redemption or beauty.

In contrast to real impersonators who mean to deceive with the illusion of innocence or promise, Roth's literary impersonations do not suppress but let in the unpalatable, the ugly, the disappointing (Conrad's destructive element): "The impersonator can't afford to indulge the ordinary human instincts which direct people in what they want to present and what they want to hide" (Roth 1985: 126). Developing further Conrad's destructive element, Roth's texts depict characters who "act counter to what" they and society assume them to be "or would like" (Roth 1985: 196) them to be. Going beyond the enclosure of their literary genre, literary fiction alerts us in an extra-literary way to how we can disappoint various pressures to live up to expectations:

> The world of fiction, in fact, frees us from circumscriptions that society places upon feeling; one of the greatness of the art is that it allows both the writer and the reader to respond to experience in ways not available in day-to-day conduct; or, if they are available, they are not possible, or manageable, or legal, or advisable, or even necessary for the business of living. (Roth 1985: 195)

According to Roth, literature expands our consciousness and in doing so also enhances our interaction with the world.

Our consciousness is itself factually real and active, because (as neuroscientific findings of mirror neurons have proven to be the case) the traditional opposition between the contemplative and the active is false and while observing an act our brain undergoes the same experience as if we had done it ourselves. Due to historical disappointment with various ideologies, by the mid-twentieth century—and not necessarily as late as 1989 as Michaels proclaims explicitly endorsing Huntington's and Fukuyama's thesis that history ended with the collapse of the Soviet Union (Michaels 2004: 78)—literature may have abandoned revolutionary missions of changing the world. However, the frustration with purely political ideas and their disappointing if not lethal realization highlight for Roth literature's hospitality that offers readers a space in which they can live without societal pressures, assignations, and demands. In the nonliterary world governed by politics, economics, and organized religion we are exposed to societal interactions where "everybody else is working to change, persuade, tempt, and control" (Roth 1985: 147) us.

Roth envisions a reader who wants a different way of life, similar to what Foucault has theorized in terms of the self's care for oneself as a form of unmooring from societal constrains: "The best readers come to fiction to be free of all that noise, to set loose in them the consciousness that's otherwise conditioned and hemmed in by all that isn't fiction" (Roth 1985: 147–8). Literature opens up the mental sphere of different kinds of consciousness and interaction wherein we cease "for a while to be upright citizens" (Roth 1985: 195). There are, however, different kinds of fiction, literary and nonliterary ones.

The fictitious in a nonliterary, real, or factual way shapes the way we constitute ourselves, changing ourselves to please or to disappoint others and society at large: "We are writing fictitious versions of our lives *all* the time, contradictory but mutually entangling stories that, however subtly or grossly falsified, constitute our hold on reality and are the closest thing we have to truth" (Roth 1985: 161). Roth highlights the radical, all-comprehensive hold of the fictitious and the fabricated onto our sense of reality and of truth. Paradoxically, the fictitious is the kernel of the real and falsehood is the flipside of truth.

As we have seen in Chapters 1 and 2, Spinoza explained this simultaneity of the real and the fictitious, of the true and the false with the limitations of our human condition, that is to say, with the identity of mind and body. Our mind fabricates stories or fictions about the world, which are sometimes accurate and sometimes false, depending on the restrictions of our frail and mortal embodied existence. Like the novel, life takes unforeseen and unpredictable turns where what we have imagined to be true turns out to be false: "Life, like the novelist, has a powerful transforming urge" (Roth 1985: 162). By being free of societal constrains, literature may care for the self by allowing for the disappointing, the promising, the true, and the false in a sphere that is open to transformation.

The notion of the unforeseen is closely related to Roth's literary critique of purity in his major novels (in *American Pastoral, Sabbath's Theatre*, and *The Human Stain*). The destructive element is the impure, the unpalatable that occurs unforeseen. Roth's engagement with American history and culture runs counter to a puritan tradition and develops a "deconstruction of the Utopian dreams and rituals of purification" (Brauner 2007: 8). However, beyond the immediate American, there is a larger context for Roth's taking issue not only with traditional, puritanical, and other religious notions of purity but also with so-called progressive, Kantian, and Hegelian notions of pure forms of modern political order and autonomy. The unforeseen has been banished from the history of Western thought, because it runs counter to the idealist, theological, and moralist foundation of order, of a purposeful, prime mover or deity who created an ordered cosmos with a redemptive or fulfilling aim (telos).

As we have seen throughout this book, Spinoza's radical critique of teleology destroyed such a traditional view of a personal God and a purpose-driven (i.e., teleological) world and nature. In the words of Leo Strauss, up to Spinoza "philosophy was understood as the most comprehensive knowledge, and as such the knowledge concerned with what is always and eternal" (Strauss 2017: 224). In a recent study Patrick Hayes relates Roth's oeuvre to the thought of perhaps Spinoza's most significant philosophical descendent, Nietzsche, in particular to "Nietzsche's attempt to position aesthetics as a rival to both ethics and the theory of knowledge" (Hayes 2014: 3). Without doubt Roth's work either implicitly or explicitly reflects upon both fiction and power. As the earlier discussion has shown, for Roth the power of the fictitious (be it in literature or in real life) is highly ambiguous.

I would argue that Joseph Conrad and his notion of the destructive element is an illuminating point of reference for a better understanding of Roth's writing and thought. Nietzsche is a notoriously multivalent thinker whose "writings contain such a mass of provocative, wilfully extreme, and often downright contradictory remarks assembled with such scant regard for all the normal (to his way of thinking, inertly conformist) protocols of rational discourse" (Norris 2011: 17). Moreover, as we have seen in Chapter 7, a heavily Nietzsche-influenced writer such as D. H. Lawrence does not abstain from subjecting Nietzsche's central concept of "the will to power" to a most sustained literary critique in his novel

Women in Love. Lawrence identifies Nietzsche's "will to power" with the Anthropocene, with the oppression of nature—animal and human nature (that of the workers). Here the will to power is far from being subversive or aesthetic. On the contrary, from Lawrence's perspective Nietzsche affirms rather than undermines capitalist, bourgeois forms of oppression.

An admirer of Nietzsche such as Strauss was nevertheless aware of the "will to power's" easy manipulation into a fascist or Nazi "triumph of the will." Strauss warned his students not to lose sight of Nietzsche's amenability to have his writing distorted in the service of extreme right-wing ideologies: "Nietzsche created on the right a political radicalism and let it be opposed to the radicalism of the extreme left, especially the communists; and one cannot for one moment overlook the fact, or minimize it, that Nietzsche's doctrine was with a kind of inevitability corrupted into fascism" (Strauss 2017: 246). Strauss presented a number of seminars on Nietzsche at the University of Chicago in the 1950s, roughly at the time when Roth was a graduate student and instructor there.

Roth shares with Strauss an avowed sense of disappointment with political ideologies. In related ways, Roth and Strauss identify ideology with its post–Second World War American manifestation, as a scientifically or technologically enhanced consumerist society where there is increased pressure to "perfect conformity" (Strauss 2017: 129). Strauss makes clear that the significance of Nietzsche's writing and thought consists in potentially undermining such societal homogeneity. This is what he calls the return to nature as well as to the Socratic tradition of the care of the self.

In this context Strauss reads Nietzsche's multivalent concept of the eternal return as the self's creative and contemplative relationship to nature and the world that diminishes the pressure upon him or her to conform to societal expectations. As I have shown throughout this book, Strauss's Spinozist return to nature implicitly takes issue with the Anthropocene which here partakes of consumer society's total conformity which does not respect nature's limits:

> So nature becomes radically problematic because the conquest of nature means, in the words of Marx, pushing back nature. At no point can you legitimately refer anymore to natural limits, because theoretically it is possible that these limits may be overcome. What is the limit of human power? Nature in the old sense was meant to be such a limit. (Strauss 2017: 191)

Strauss focuses on the nature-centered Spinozist element in Nietzsche's work. In doing so Strauss turns upside down Nietzsche's overtly hostile position on Socrates whom he famously attacks as arch-scientist and rationalist (as an ancient precursor of Hegel, as it were). However by grappling with the conformist reduction of philosophy to usefulness (what Nietzsche identifies as rationalism's philistine tradition), according to Strauss, Nietzsche paradoxically returns to the spiritual core of Socrates, which is indeed philosophy's independence of societal and political pressures (what Foucault, as we have seen throughout this book has theorized as the care of the self).

For Strauss Nietzsche "tries to uproot Socrates and everything built on a Socratic foundation, but by going to the root—to the root of the whole tradition of rational philosophy, of rationalism in any sense of the word, he meets Socrates again, because he goes so far. That is the secret, I think, of the fact of this strange fascination which Socrates had for Nietzsche" (Strauss 2017: 209). Nietzsche's paradoxical return to the Socratic tradition of the care for the self fully crystalizes for Strauss in the concept of the eternal return. Here, the contemplation of nature simultaneously enacts the creativity that unbinds us from a conformist and homogenous politics: "the peak of creation is contemplation or, differently stated, true contemplation is creation. And if the theme of contemplation is nature, nature is only, at least in its fullness, by virtue of contemplative creation. That is the paradoxical teaching of Nietzsche" (Strauss 2017: 211). What Strauss discerns as paradox emerges from the contamination of two purportedly opposed entities: contemplation and creation (or on a different level nature and humanity).

In a fascinating way, Roth characterizes the workings of literature by a similar simultaneity of allegedly mutually opposed terms. As Hayes has found out studying Roth's unpublished notes and papers, there is in his work a well-thought through contamination of literature's contemplative aspect with the purportedly opposed sphere of action (allegedly the prerogative of non-bookish activities such as sports or politics): "As 'equation with action' the literary text is a performance that establishes value through aesthetic heightening, but as 'symbolic action' it sustains a mode of ironic reflection on the nature and consequences of such heightening, rather than aiming simply to enrapture the reader in the becoming itself" (Hayes 2014: 24). The symbolic does the work of irony which is a crucial Socratic (from David Foster Wallace's vantage point, postmodern) element in Roth's writing (which he admired in the work of Thomas Mann). This reflexive and ironic aspect complicates literature conceived as form of action. This presupposes, however, that the contemplative, sedentary work of reading and writing is highly active and creative.

In different ways, Roth and Strauss theorize art and contemplation not in terms of what Leo Bersani has analyzed as yet another redemptive, Hegelian narrative—as "culture of redemption" (Bersani 1990)—but in terms of resistance to the ever-increasing demands of conformity in the consumerist culture of mid-twentieth-century America. Strikingly, Strauss as well as Roth relied for their respective positions on David Riesman's 1950 sociological study *The Lonely Crowd* which analyzed the mid-twentieth-century shift from D. H. Lawrence's industrial culture of production to a postindustrial or postmodern culture of consumption. Crucial for both Roth's and Strauss's critique of "perfect conformity" (Strauss 2017: 129) is Riesman's term "other-directeds" (Riesman 1950: 22). Riesman's neologism exactly describes conformists for whom "their contemporaries are the source of direction for the individual—either those known to him or those with whom he is directly acquainted, through friends and through the mass media" (Riesman 1950: 22). For Roth, literature's uneasy provocations render visible what, in close relation to Ellison's *Invisible Man*, anti-Semitism has rendered invisible, thus disturbing the perfect conformity that governs consumerist and racist WASP American society:

> Going wild in public is the last thing in the world that a Jew is expected to do—by himself, by his family, by his fellow Jews, and by the larger community of Christians whose tolerance for him is often tenuous to begin with, and whose code of respectability he flaunts or violates at his own risk, and perhaps at the risk of his fellow Jews' physical and social well-being. (Roth 1985: 258)

In this way, Roth counters anti-Semitism "not by pretending that Jews have existences less in need of, and less deserving of, honest attention than the lives of their neighbors, not by making Jews invisible" (Roth 1985: 207). As will be explored further, Roth follows Henry James (and his brother, the psychologist William James) when he identifies the contemplation of literature with its supposed opposite, that of action.

There is action in contemplation and contemplation in action. Through this copresence of the active and the contemplative, the act of writing or reading grants us different spheres of life outside the conformist pressures of society and politics (where in Foucault's terms the self can take care of itself): "For this distinctively post-Nietzschean kind of intellectual literature is valued less for this capacity to explore human situations, [. . .] than for its capacity to act as what Michel Foucault called a 'technique of the self': a way of modelling forms of heightened becoming with which the reader can experiment" (Hayes 2014: 21). Forms of troubled and engaged contemplation nourish forms of resistance to the ever-increasing pressure to conform in a consumerist, postindustrial society governed by the public image of mass media and its advertising.

Part of this conformity is the reduction of experience to what is useful. Strauss differentiates philosophy (as quest for wisdom) from its practically applied applications in politics. As political philosopher, he provocatively opposes philosophy (wisdom, or Socratic care of the self) to the conformist pressures and utopian expectations for redemption that partake of politics, science, culture, and society. In the *Künstlerroman I Married a Communist* which traces the intellectual itinerary of the adolescent writer Nathan Zuckerman, Roth depicts a Strauss-like professor at the University of Chicago in the 1950s. Professor Leo Glucksman in that novel maintains a firm distinction between literature and politics that recalls Strauss's famously radical separation between the political and the philosophical. Like Strauss, Glucksman tries to persuade his students (Nathan Zuckerman, in this case) of the severely "*antagonistic* [in italics in Roth's text to underline the severity of this point] relationship" (Roth 1999: 223) between literature and politics. However, neither in Roth's Glucksman nor in Strauss's writing and thought is this antagonism a moral, dialectical or ethical, but a provocative one.

As we have seen in Chapter 6, Strauss makes clear that Socrates indeed poses a danger to the city and that Athens may in fact have been justified in sentencing him to capital punishment. This justification, however, only applies if seen from the perspective of the political which does not allow for non-conformism or anything that contradicts its creeds. Politics here is not that of Hannah Arendt's or Walter Benjamin's mold where it avoids being closely related to the one-way street of ideology and easily consumable, social usefulness but instead partakes of the plural and diverse space of the aesthetic that allows for the quirky, dangerous, and contradictory.

Roth's Glucksman conceptualizes art in a way that resists social application or usefulness (not to be imbibed as ethically or morally meaningful or utopian, redemptive truth) and in this way resembles Strauss's position of Socratic philosophy, namely, as a danger to the polis. According to Roth's Glucksman, art and literature are as dangerous and disturbing to society at large as is Socratic wisdom and its care for the self. Glucksman advises young Nathan Zuckerman to let in Conrad's destructive element, to let in what is, unpalatable, ugly, dangerous, startling, quirky, and contradictory:

> To allow for the chaos, let it in. You *must* let it in. Otherwise you produce propaganda, if not for a political party, a political movement, then stupid propaganda for life itself—for life as it might itself prefer to be publicized. During the first five, six years of the Russian Revolution the revolutionaries cried, "Free love, there will be free love!" But once they were in power, they couldn't permit it. Because what is free love? Chaos.

And they didn't want chaos. That isn't why they made their glorious revolution. They wanted something carefully disciplined, organized, contained, predictable, scientifically, if possible. Free love disturbs the organization, their social and political and cultural machine. Art also disturbs the organization. Literature disturbs the organization. Not because it is blatantly for or against, or even subtly for or against. It disturbs the organization because it is not general. The intrinsic nature of the particular is to be particular, and the intrinsic nature of particularity is to fail to conform. Generalizing suffering: there is Communism. Particularizing suffering: there is literature. In that polarity is the antagonism. Keeping the particular alive in a simplifying, generalizing world—that's where the battle is joined. (Roth 1999: 223)

Leo Glucksman—Roth's literary studies version of the modern Jewish thinker Leo Strauss—in this engaged and engaging quote explains to young Zuckerman that literature's chaos, its destructive element, is that of the particular. And what is the particular but another term for the self, failing to conform to generality? (The whole topic of the general and the particular is an important topic in modern Jewish writing and thought, in that of Franz Rosenzweig especially, as discussed in Mack [2003: 125–35].) This resistance to become part of the general flow of life, culture, science, and politics disappoints expectations of art and literature to fulfill hopes for redemption. Rather than being part of a general culture of redemption, the aesthetic here is dangerous in Strauss's Socratic sense of thwarting various promises.

Crucially, Strauss's and Roth's opposition between either the literary/aesthetic or the philosophical and the political is not a binary, dialectical one. It is not so much an absolute truth statement as a stumbling block, scandal and provocation for thought. Hayes illuminates how Nietzsche's Spinozist contamination of the joyful and the tragic informs Roth's writing and thought: "Tragic joy is a festive meaningfulness that challenges the most fundamental oppositions: the opposition between the transcendent realm of the mind that perceives truth and the fallen realm of the mutable body" (Hayes 2014: 87). As we have seen in Chapters 1 and 2, Spinoza first outdid these metaphysical oppositions and Nietzsche was the only philosopher before the current neuroscientific rediscovery of the Jewish Dutch thinker who took to heart the Spinozist insight into the identity (rather than opposition) of body and mind.

While Strauss admits to not understanding Spinoza's complicated argument about the mind as the idea of the body (as discussed in Chapter 2), Roth's literary work limns the limitations of idealist and rationalist notions of cerebral purity, showing in highly ironic and playful ways from his breakthrough novel *Portnoy's Complaint* onward how the cerebral cannot transcend its embodied and affective constitution.

Rather than being tragic or sublime, there is clearly a postmodern element of ironic inversion, in Portnoy's tongue-in-cheek grief about his mind's folly that consists exactly in desperate attempts to transcend the disappointing identity of lofty political thought with the libidinal: "My politics, descended entirely to my putz! JERK-OFF ARTISTS OF THE WORLD UNITE! YOU HAVE NOTHING TO LOSE BUT YOUR BRAINS!" (Roth 1995: 251). In a further irony, the term "brain" denotes precisely the mind's embodiment that it shares with the putz. As in so many other agitated and comically troubled passages of Roth's 1968 novel, Portnoy reveals his repressive, idealist self when he bewails the descent of elevated political hopes to the libidinal, disappointing objectified thingness of his member.

Irony is Roth's distinctive postmodern characteristic that sets his work apart from the philosophical seriousness of Strauss's modernism as well as the contemporary return to a "new sincerity" (Kelly 2010) that characterizes David Foster Wallace and our contemporary critically disillusioned moment of what I call "expecting disappointment." As we have seen in Chapters 3 and 4, Conrad's modernist literary style is profoundly ironic. There is nevertheless a remainder of idealism pertaining to modernism that is exactly irony's work to disappointedly uncover as the rude historical truth of a colonialist and exterminatory (Kurtz's quasi-totalitarian "Exterminate all the brutes") betrayal which, in an apocalyptic way, opens up "the idea's only" disturbingly horrific reality.

As we will see later in this chapter, Wallace defines his new sincerity in opposition to what he characterizes as postmodernism's defining characteristic: a non-committed, insincere ironic world that refuses to genuinely engage with the troubles of the world. Roth is wary of the more-than-sincere, quasi-religious culture of redemption, that he calls the "salvationist literary ethos in which I had been introduced to high art in the fifties" (Roth 1985: 67). From at least *Portnoy Complaint* onward Roth's novels in a self-conscious way foreground a sense of acting out a fictional persona. However, this does not mean that his work, or postmodernism more generally speaking, disavows cross-references between the word and the world.

Pertaining to the problematic element within categorizations of historical, philosophical, and literary-aesthetic periods is the exclusion of what does not fit into the elusively and illusorily certain grasp of a given nomenclature. Roth's apparent exclusion from postmodernism is a case in point. He has rarely been identified as a postmodernist and when he has been, as in Wayne Booth's criticism of "the merely theatrical roles that Philip Roth's Zuckerman seems to celebrate" (Booth 1988: 259), then the troubling issue resides in the complex notion of impersonation. However, the way in which literary characters and, indeed, the author's namesake, impersonate themselves, here does not undermine but, instead, enhances the appearance of literary realism *qua* make believe.

Grounds for denying that Roth's style of writing is postmodern have to do with his much noted realism and, relatedly, with his 1981 (while interviewed by the French philosopher Alain Finkielkraut) agreement with his fictional character David Kepesh's (in *The Professor of Desire*) rejection of purportedly deconstructionist characterizations of language as non-referential. To cast postmodernism and Derrida's deconstruction as non-referential (Nussbaum 1990: 21; Graff 1979: 215) would deny postmodernist works of literature and philosophy claims to ethical and political validity. As Derrida himself has made clear (Derrida 2005: 87), this is not the case.

While postmodernism does not exclude a referential or realist relationship to the world, it nevertheless has somewhat shifted the coordinates by which we register our environment in a more playful and messy, and, in Spinozist terms, contingent, non-teleological way that in France emerged from the anti-Hegelianism of Levinas, Macherey, Foucault, and Derrida (Habermas 1987: 34). In his most influential and comprehensive study *Postmodernism: Or, the Cultural Logic of Late Capitalism*, Frederic Jameson describes the mutation from Conrad's modernism to Pynchon's postmodernism referring to an increase of a sense of disorder as well as the emergence of a dispersed, fragmented selfhood that opens up to various impersonations (as of the author Philip Roth and his imposturous doppelgänger in *Operation Shylock*):

> if the great negative emotions of the modern moment were anxiety, terror, the being unto-death, and Kurtz's "horror," what characterizes the newer "intensities" of the postmodern, which have also been characterized in terms of the "bad trip" and of schizophrenic submersion, can just as well be formulated as in terms of the messiness, the perpetual temporal distraction of the post-sixties life. (Jameson 1992: 117)

On closer scrutiny, Jameson's notion of messiness is not a postmodern invention but Spinoza's seventeenth-century disordering of traditional ideas of order and teleology, grounded as we have seen (in the first two chapters of this book) in a Platonic, Cartesian and then Kantian and Hegelian hierarchical structure wherein the mind autonomously and idealistically controls the mere materiality of embodied life. In Pynchon's *Gravity Rainbow* I. P. Pavlov's discovery of nervous reflexes functions to dismantle the notion of the mind's autonomy from its environment. Roth's opening up of the notion of an ordered, contained self here has an explicit postmodern and Spinozist parallel in Pynchon's fascination with Pavlov's scientific demolition of traditional oppositions between mind and body as well as self and its environment:

> Pavlov was fascinated with "ideas of the opposite." Call it a cluster of cells, somewhere on the cortex of the brain. Hoping to distinguish pleasure from pain, light from dark, dominance from submission. . . . But when, somehow—starve them, traumatize, shock, castrate them, send them in over into one of the transmarginal phases, past borders of their waking selves, past "equivalent" and "paradoxical" phases—you weaken this idea of the opposite, and here all at once the paranoid patient would be master, yet now feels himself a slave. . . . who would be loved, but suffers from the world's indifference, and, "I think," Pavlov writing to Janet, "it is precisely the *ultraparadoxical phase* which is the base of the weakening of the opposite in our patients." Our madmen, our paranoid, maniac, schizoid, morally imbecile. (Pynchon 1975: 48–9)

What is "mad" is precisely the overturning of traditional conceptions of dialectical opposition and teleological order. Paranoia in Pynchon's postmodern and Spinozist literary oeuvre does not so much denote what it does in everyday usage.

Rather than perceiving the Other as threat, Pynchon's paranoid self outdoes all such oppositions and lets them dissolve. Here the self impersonates the Other, the Other thus becomes the self. Crucially, Pynchon's *Crying of Lot 49* deprives the term "paranoia" of its clinical, psychiatric meaning and situates it as part of empirical reality that is in Spinozist ways open to outside stimuli and unplanned and unforeseen inputs: "For there either was some Triestero beyond the appearance of the legacy of America, or there was just America, and if there was just America then its seemed the only way she could continue, manage to be relevant to it, was an alien, unfurrowed, assumed full circle into some paranoia" (Pynchon 1967: 126). Pynchon's Oedipa refuses to be contained in one self, unresponsive to the heteronomy of unpredictable environments.

In a similar way, Foucault's care of the self does not resurrect a normative conception of subjectivity which his 1969 essay "What Is an Author" has set to call into question. The care of the self goes back to a pre-Christian and pre-Cartesian understanding of selfhood that is "paranoid" in the postmodern sense of both Pynchon and Roth. This mad or paranoid self is open-ended and quasi-postmodern in the sense that it is radically exposed to the unpredictable, non-domesticated, and thereby contingent existence that the traditional, harmonious, or "sane" order of knowledge has deemed inadmissible and utterly off bounds to its teleological universe. In Pynchon's postmodern paranoia and in Roth's fluid, multiple senses of selfhood all characters are subject to the randomness of chance occurrences.

Pynchon's idiosyncratic usage of the term "paranoia" evokes a Spinozist identity between internal and external, body and mind that are part of a new paradigm shift developing toward the end of the twentieth century. Crucial to this shift are the new sciences of biophysical emergency and neuroscience (Atlan 2010) that diverge with their focus on the unpredictable and the contingent or random from deceptively ordered conceptions of nature that have characterized the public image of science as amenable to consumerist needs in the mid-twentieth century. As has been intimated earlier, Strauss vehemently rejected a positivist and instrumental reduction of philosophy to science. He took issue with increased societal pressures to narrow philosophy down to what was practically useful, and he identified what we now call "impact" with the public perception of science in terms of facilitating the shallow and consumerist culture of post–Second World War America.

There are striking parallels within postmodern literature to Strauss's philosophical critique of a reductive notion of modernity, premised on scientific instrumentality. In his 1963 novel *Cat's Cradle*, Kurt Vonnegut created the fictional school of Bakononists to question precisely this travesty of scientific knowledge as facilitator of conformism, consumerism, and wealth. The novel outdoes the modern opposition between science and superstition by having everyday admirers of the father of the atomic bomb, Dr. Felix Hoenikker, proclaim the expectation that "science was going to discover the basic secret of life some day" (Vonnegut 1965: 21). Researching the life and work of the fictional creator of the atomic bomb, Dr. Hoenikker, the narrator of *Cat's Cradle*, interviews a certain Dr. Breed and then cringes at the commodification of science with which Strauss takes issue. "New knowledge is the most valuable commodity on earth," Dr. Breed tells him: "The more truth we have to work with, the richer we become" (Vonnegut 1965: 31). During the course of the novel, the narrator discovers Bokonism, which turns such instrumentalist idealization of science in terms of social, or rather, antisocial usefulness (the destruction wreaked by nuclear bombs) upside down. Hence the narrator's belated distance from the narrative about science's societal progress: "Had I been a Bokonist then, that statement [i.e., of Dr. Breed in the preceding quotation] would have made me howl" (Vonnegut 1965: 31). The narrator metaphorically howls at the suggestion that the work of numbers, or, in other words, the quantification of truth and knowledge translates into an increase of wealth. This is further proof of the symbolic reach of numbers which serves not only to raise expectations of certain and all-comprehensive fulfillments (of health and wealth) but also, more radically still, to have overcome any forms of political, economic, and religious disappointment by the superstitious, magical wand of science.

Countering such promises of science turned magic, like Strauss, Roth is careful to steer clear of leaving one Hegelian utopia (that of dialectics' positive move toward a fully satisfied, homogenous world) for another where art or the aesthetic promises redemption. As Richard Velkley has shown, Strauss wants to rescue contemplative activity from a modern reduction of philosophy to what is narrowly and consumerist defined as impactful or useful. This is precisely at issue in his critique of modern philosophers: "Strauss ascribes to the modern philosophy the primacy of a practical end that is beneficial to all humans, although perhaps above all to the philosopher. The practical end surpasses, if it does not simply replace contemplative activity as the core of philosophy" (Velkley 2017: XII). Pynchon's postmodern appraisal of paranoia and madness relates to Strauss's and Foucault's respective attempts to question conceptions of knowledge that are not contemplatively transformative but rather applied to the solving of practical problems. For Strauss, Socrates poses a genuine danger to the polis and the public perception of madness (and paranoia, schizophrenia, and so forth) is precisely that of being dangerous.

This postmodern letting in of the dangerous, mad, paranoid, and destructive element is premised on an understanding of knowledge not so much as organized and ordered but as transformative. Foucault's care of the self is precisely its transformation that frees it from preordained societal conceptions or hierarchy, value, and order. Literature in its most claustrophobic and oppressive forms carries with it this counterforce toward transformation and change in the way we interact with the world. In historical terms Roth here refers to how Czech intellectuals turned to Kafka's work to support their resistance to a totalitarian government under Soviet rule: "Ways of knowing the world that he [i.e., Kafka] entitled *The Trial* and *The Castle*—which look to most people like no way of knowing anything—were exploited by these Czech intellectuals as means of organizing a perception of *their* world persuasive enough to augment a political movement already under way to loosen the bonds of Soviet totalitarianism" (Roth 1985: 155). As we have seen in Chapter 8, Kafka does not refer to any historical coordinates while presenting an oppressive society that marginalizes and excludes the stranger and immigrant Joseph K. in *Das Schloss*.

This sense of disappointment in Kafka's fiction renders fluid the distinction between the real and the imaginary, between the credible and the incredible and this especially in openly oppressive societies like that of Czechoslovakia under Soviet rule. This openness, however, also requires the freedom to play with the intra-literary rules of genre. "Genre," a specialized literary term, transgresses the boundaries that define it. The very term "genre" embraces the extra-literary, societal sphere of gender and genus. Derrida has explored the way how such transgression of borders is nevertheless what the very term "genre" interdicts: "The genre has always in all genres been able to play the role of order's principle: resemblance, analogy, identity and difference, taxonomic classification, organization and genealogical tree, order of reason, order of reasons, sense of sense, truth of truth, natural light and sense of history" (Derrida 1992: 152). However, "genre" disappoints the order it promises to uphold and this disappointment establishes the promise of potential liberations from ordered or assigned roles of propriety and assignation in society at large. Genre has thus "inundated *and* divided the borders between literature and its others" (Derrida 1992: 152).

The Extra-literary Disturbance of the Para-literary

Emre Merve has shown how such border crossing between the literary and the societal can be in the interests of upholding established roles of patriarchal power in a para-literary way. I call "extra-literary" literature's liberating potential where we become aware of the stifling and often gratuitous pressures that keep us attached to harmful habits. The extra-literary denotes the light literature sheds on what lies outside its boundaries. It is the word that makes us see our world in a new way. The para-literary, by contrast, has a utilitarian or instrumentalist approach (what, on a different level, Strauss criticizes as modern philosophy's positivism, that is to say, its attempt to be scientific in terms of being useful as quasi-technological facilitator of a comfortable, consumerist society): it merely attempts to copy superficially pleasant or pleasing aspects of art so as to enhance its commodification and political usefulness in society at large.

In this way, the para-literary clears "the communicative channels by which fiction would shape embodied practices of expression around the world" (Merve 2017: 24). According to Merve, Henry James's literary texts set the standards for para-literary impersonations of genre-characters in mid-twentieth-century America: "What mattered for James's readers, then, was a very particular logic of identification: a pragmatic investment in a fictional character's exoteric and seemingly imitable behaviour—her 'charming, diplomatic' visage, her 'face' modelled after a work of art—rather than an unobservable psychological melding of minds between reader and character" (Merve 2017: 27). Ironically, James instructs his readers to reject and object to such superficial reading of his texts and in the 1908 preface to *The Portrait of a Lady* he makes clear that Isabel Archer's internal workings of the mind are more fascinating, instructive, and captivating that any outward form of refinement or action (Mack 2016: 130–5).

Indeed, the stereotypical image of Henry James as upholder of established notions of propriety, beauty, and refinement is quite misleading. Ross Posnock has convincingly shown how James was in fact Roth's guide to introducing rude truths into literature. Rather than establishing the social validity of established gender roles of refinement, Posnock discerns "James's audacious turning against his own sanctification of Art, a turning that reveals the limits of formal shapeliness" (Posnock 2006: 121). In the para-literary context of the mid-twentieth century Roth discovers the truth of a disturbing, anti-genteel, James of what I call the extra-literary (to distinguish it from the para-literary):

> Roth's Gabe Wallache and James's Isabel Archer finally let go the relentless drive to fortify the self and subdue experience, a relaxing of defences that unfreezes adulthood and risks immaturity. From early on Roth seems to have been drawn to this risk and its latent power, and early on too he subtly discerned a similar preoccupation in James. I say subtly because Henry James in the 1950s was above all the forbidden master, the icon of impeccable seriousness. Yet, rather than simply and predictably regarding James as either a monument to worship or a target to shoot at, Roth looks past the canonical image of Henry James the quintessential "Paleface," as Philip Rahv has influentially dubbed him. (Posnock 2006: 118)

Immaturity in terms of nonsense or, more precisely, the nonsensical lack of connection between cause and effect is, however, a striking feature of postmodernism. This "funny" disconnect between an action and its effect radically subverts our sense of progression and teleology.

As we have seen in Chapters 1 and 2, Spinoza's critique of teleology informs romanticism's espousal of the incomplete and fragmentary. One of Spinoza's most influential intellectual inheritors within the French Radical Enlightenment, Denis Diderot, attempted his famous encyclopedic project out of a suspicion of totality and other forms of ordered, systematic knowledge. In an important recent study that analyzes the continuity of a sense of the fragmentary and nonsensical from Spinoza's seventeenth century to Diderot *Encyclopaedia* to the *Encyclopaedia Britannica* of 1910 and the modernism of Virginia Woolf, Ford Madox Ford, and James Joyce to the postmodernism of Thomas Pynchon's *Gravity's Rainbow*, Paul K. Saint-Amour has clearly shown how a "profound sense of arbitrariness and contingency" (Saint-Amour 2015: 9) has shaped our intellectual life since the inception of modernity.

As I have argued throughout this book, modernity may be rethought as a reflective encounter with disappointment that either becomes acknowledged or disavowed. As Saint-Amour has explored (without referring to Spinoza) a Spinozist critique of traditional, anthropocentric projections of sense *qua* teleology accompanies not only an open-minded approach to what has been negatively dismissed as "contingent," "immature," or "nonsensical" and therefore disappointing. This awareness of the disappointment of sense and order also explains the encyclopedic desire to warehouse "enlightenment knowledge against the possibility of its loss in war, revolution, or natural disaster" (Saint-Amour 2015: 9). As Edward Mendelson has noted, "the world's knowledge is larger than anyone can encompass" (Mendelson 1976: 1269) and a striking feature of the encyclopedic novel is its incompleteness.

The encyclopedic novel from *Moby Dick* to *Ulysses* to *Gravity's Rainbow* and to, more recently, David Foster Wallace's *The Pale King* combines this Spinozist and postmodern sense of the messy, non-teleological, and contingent with an apprehension of vulnerability and the precariousness of both human life and human knowledge: "*Gravity's Rainbow* may well have been the first post 1944 text of any kind to grasp the relationship between its interwar precursors' encyclopaedism and total war; we might even go so far as to say that Pynchon's novel *is*, among other things, a reading of encyclopaedic modernism from across the nuclear divide" (Saint-Amour 2015: 204). The nuclear divide roughly fell into the second-half of the twentieth century. It also shaped Strauss's critique of modern philosophy's reduction to what is technologically useful to the ideological prepositions of society at large. As Strauss kept emphasizing, science's touted freedom from values indicates its use-oriented existences. Being instrumental, it is a mere means and cannot articulate why it should exist in the first place. The question of the why, Strauss pointed out, becomes all the more urgent in the post-1945 world of the hydrogen bomb.

For Roth, the immediate post-1945 Eisenhower and then Truman era was first one of American national pride, having defeated Nazi Germany. As the young adolescent Nathan Zuckerman put it in *I Married a Communist*: "I was a Jewish child, no two ways about that, but I didn't care to partake of the Jewish character. [. . .] I wanted to partake of the national character. [. . .] the excited feelings of community that the war aroused" (Roth 1999: 39). Then the obvious collars of feelings for the community gradually collapsed first with McCarthy and then with Nixon and the Vietnam War in the 1960s. Roth's postmodernism articulates a general sense of disappointed expectations for national identity and community. This is perhaps most strikingly the case in his most celebrated novel, *American Pastoral*.

Conclusion

There have been attempts to read the novel as evidence for Roth's renunciation of *Portnoy's Complaint* and the extra-literary provocation that makes us see the repressions of conformist, patriarchal society in a new way (as Portnoy's agitated shock at finding his mind at the mercy of his contingent and imperious body, his *putz*). From neoconservative thinkers (Podhoretz 2004; Alexander 1999) to embarrassed or disappointed critics (Menand 1997; Parrish 2000; Gentry 2000; Posnock 2006) different scholarly positions agree that *American Pastoral* renounces Roth's earlier successful attempts at blurring the lines between the fictional and the real so as to provoke new, extra-literary (rather than para-literary) views on the life of his readership.

Almost anticipating such conservative or para-literary misreading of his work, toward the end of *The Counterlife* Roth implicitly refers to Pynchon's postmodern outdoing of binary opposites and this at the point of discussing what I call the extra-literary. Ironically the text refers to life but, and here is the irony, the life denoted here is of course literary (being enclosed in a novel). Literary life thus points to what is extra to it, to what is outside it, in a way similar to which "real life" refers to its outside, the ghostly dream life of the fictive: "Life *is* and: the accidental and the immutable, the elusive and the graspable, the bizarre and the predictable, the actual and the potential, all the multiplying realities, entangled, overlapping, colliding, conjoined—plus the multiplying illusions!" (Roth 1988a: 310) The "and" outdoes and contaminates binary oppositions of actuality and potentiality and, in a related way, of disappointment and promise.

Literary life here collides in a ghostly way with real life: in both separated spheres, story lines revolve around understanding and misunderstanding. Because our limited embodied perspective can never be that of omniscience or totality, in everyday life we are constantly at risk to take the fictive for the factual: "The treacherous imagination is everybody's maker—we all the invention of each other, everybody a conjuration conjuring up everybody else. We are all each other's authors" (Roth 1988a: 149). Roth's entire oeuvre has highlighted contaminations of truth and falsehood, of fiction and reality, of disappointment and promise and this perhaps nowhere as subtly as in his novel of a nation's misunderstanding of itself. This is *American Pastoral*, which narrates not Roth's (Podhoretz 2004; Alexander 1999; Menand 1997; Parrish 2000; Gentry 2000; Posnock 2006: 102–18) or his narrator's, Nathan Zuckerman's, respective disillusionment (Hayes 2014: 111–28) with the promise of the 1960s counterculture, but rather the narrative's own misperceptions of purity (America either as purely pastoral or as purely berserk).

It is time to shift the critical analysis from an emphasis on a historical period or from "history as an abstraction" (Brauner 2011: 20) and relatedly from "the problems of historiography" (Brauner 2011: 20) to the investigation of deception in fiction as revealing the larger extra-literary significance of a given community's or, in this case, nation's (i.e., America) illusion about itself. As regards historical periodization, the hidden center of history is here not the obvious focal point of narration (i.e., the 1960s) but the immediate post-1945 era, which is that of a deceptive communal sense of promise. Promise gives way to disappointment in what Roth characterizes as the demythologizing era of the 1960s. Rather than being merely concerned with the narrator's or author's perspective, the novel presents a nation's self-understanding being revealed as misunderstanding, as fiction or myth of itself: the American pastoral turns out to be a deception, opening up to yet another misunderstanding of America turned violent or berserk.

Neither disappointment in its pure form—separated from its purported opposition, hope—is true nor promise compartmentalized from its supposed counterpart (i.e., disappointment). The American pastoral here is an image of hope which in its pure form emerges as a myth or lie and, which, crucially Roth's novel reveals to provoke what his narrator, Zuckerman, misleadingly assumes to be genuinely American, because it is the pure other of the purity of the hopeful, promissory (i.e., the romanticism of the pastoral): "the violence, and the desperation of the counterpastoral, [. . .]—the American berserk" (Roth 1998: 86). Rather than espousing a position, Roth's novel complicates hopes for any form of pure understanding that is not liable to misunderstanding. *American Pastoral* does so by highlighting the emotional bias of its narrator.

Nathan Zuckerman is clearly upset with the main character of his narration. From its opening pages the novel draws attention to its chagrined narrative voice. Zuckerman's impetus seems to be some form of resentment. It is the anger of the narrator that explains the problematic usage of stereotypes (of Jew and Greek, of northern and Mediterranean). Clearly the narrator draws attention to his own issues when (on the opening pages of the novel) he ponders the "elevation of Swede Levov into the household Apollo of Weequahic Jews" (Roth 1998: 4). The Greek god Apollo as kitschy, idolatrous intrusion into the households of Weequahic Jews evokes notions of impurity. On an intertextual level, Apollo also refers to Nietzsche's counter-deity of Dionysus. Whereas the former turns into Nietzsche's principle of order and clarity—the American pastoral—the latter embodies the disorder and disappointment of the American berserk. If there is a reference to Nietzsche's thought in Roth's work, then it is here. The crucial and rather ironic point is that Nietzsche argued for a contamination of Apollo with Dionysus. The narrator of *American Pastoral* refuses to acknowledge precisely this entanglement of opposites clinging to the purity of the berserk as counter-pastoral.

The absent center of Roth's *American Pastoral* (as that of his last novella *Nemesis*) is the Nazi genocide. Zuckerman evokes the genocidal abyss of the twentieth century in terms of a fate-like, deterministic force, which "the Swede" attempted to ignore when he set out to build his American pastoral. Once the Swede's daughter—as a 1960s radical-turned-terrorist—bombs the local post office of the Swede's idyllic hamlet Old Rimrock, lines of communication unravel and understandings become revealed as misunderstandings, promises as disappointments.

In a highly problematic mode, the narrator Zuckerman imputes to Swede Levov, thoughts of absconding from responsibility by equating his daughter's violent actions with those of history: "Thinking [i.e., these are the thoughts that the narrator ascribes to the Swede]: She is not in my power and never was. She is in the power of something that does not give a shit. Something demented. We all are" (Roth 1998: 256). We all are, the narrator included as becomes clear in the following paragraph, when Zuckerman articulates his anger at the Swede for his hubris in trying to avoid the mythic force of history, here turned from promise to the disappointment of being utterly dark and demented. The totalitarian, all-encompassing force of this fate-like, inevitably teleological progression is that of history personified in the narrator's mind: "The something that's demented, honky is American history!" (Roth 1998: 257) The crucial issue here is the narrator's s own involvement in the fabrication of such myths of purity either of the pastoral or its fateful opposite, the berserk, which becomes mythologized as part of a dark, demented historical force which the Swede sets out to dodge:

> Yes, at the age of forty-six, in 1973, almost three quarters of the way through the century that with no regard for the niceties of burial had strewn the corpses of mutilated children and their mutilated parents everywhere, the Swede found out that we are all in the power of something demented. It's just a matter of time, honky. We all are! (Roth 1998: 256)

Critics have been blind to the problematic of the narrator who turns from one all-encompassing perspective of purity (that of the Swede's pastoral) to another, opposed one (that of the berserk).

Jelinek's Postmodern Satire of the Leader's Inflated Self

A more strikingly postmodern, in the sense of satirical, author, the Austrian writer Elfriede Jelinek does not refrain from putting front and center the highly fraught, totalitarian context of her narrator, the free indirect narrative of the piano teacher Erika Kohut. As I have shown elsewhere, Jelinek's postmodern satire radicalizes that of the German Jewish modernist writer Elias Canetti (Mack 2008).

Responding to the rise of fascism in Europe during the early 1930s, Canetti's only novel *Auto-Da-Fé* (1935) implicitly outdoes the binary opposition between selfhood and the crowd as well as the one between low and high culture. It does so while depicting the lonely scholar Peter Kien as a totalitarian ruler within the precinct of his private library. Here Kien rules over the masses of his books (Mack 2001: 32–46).

During and after the Second World War Canetti dedicated his work to a hybrid social-anthropological cum literary study entitled *Masse und Macht* (*Crowds and Power*). In close intellectual exchange with his friend and fellow exiled Prague Jewish poet and Oxford anthropologist Franz Baermann Steiner (Mack 2001: 46–179), Canetti tried to come to terms with the unprecedented horrors of the Nazi genocide—the hidden core of Roth's questioning of purity in his 1998 novel *American Pastoral* (as discussed in the preceding section).

Jelinek's 1983 novel *The Pianist* (*Die Klavierspielerin*) pivots around Canetti's thematic of selfhood and the power of crowds. On which conceptual issue does Jelinek focus her satirical and highly postmodern ironic approach? Like Canetti and the Frankfurt School, Jelinek unmasks rationality as the appetite for self-preservation. Going back to Spinoza and the Socratic question of self and society, Jelinek, Canetti, Strauss, and the Adorno/Horkheimer of *The Dialectics of Enlightenment* question rationality in terms of an inflated self which coincides with an imagined political community's appetite for self-preservation. These writers and thinkers see in politics the danger of a paradoxical aggrandizement of selfhood which has here turned crowd-like and totalitarian. In an important conversation with Canetti, T. W. Adorno has drawn attention to Spinoza's thought within the context of a self that has turned into the crowd-like phenomenon of twentieth-century totalitarian politics:

> In *Dialectics of Enlightenment* Horkheimer and I [i.e., Adorno] have indeed analysed the problem of self-preservation, that of a self-preserving rationality (*das Problem der Selbsterhaltung, der sich selbsterhaltenden Vernunft*) and in doing so we discovered that this principle of self-preservation, as it has classically, one could say, been formulated for the first time by Spinoza (*das dieses Prinzip der Selbsterhaltung, wie es also zum ersten Mal klassisch, könnte man sagen, in der Philosophie von Spinoza formuliert worden ist*) which you call the moment of survival (*das Moment des Überlebens*), namely the situation of survival in the

exact sense (*die Situation des Überlebens im prägnanten Sinn*), that this motive of survival (*dieses Motiv der Selbsterhaltung*), if it turns "wild," as it were (*wenn es "wild" wird gewissermaßen*), if, in so doing, it loses its connection to the others who stand diametrically opposed to it (*wenn es also die Beziehung zu den ihnen gegenüberstehenden anderen verliert*), that it turns in a destructive force, in a destructive and at the same time self-destructive force (*in ein Zerstörendes und immer auch gleichzeitig in ein Sebstzerstörendes*. Canetti 2005: 141)

Adorno highlights Spinoza's conception of self-preservation (*conatus*) for a better understanding of post-Shoah writing and thought. As we have seen in the first two chapters of this book, Spinoza diverges from the rationalism of both Descartes and Hobbes, by making the very notion of selfhood inclusive of that of the Other.

There is a chiasmus of self and Other that is the kernel of Spinoza's term *conatus*: "The self that endeavors to preserve its own being is not always a singular being for Spinoza, and neither does it necessarily succeed in augmenting or enhancing its life if it does not at once enhance the life of others" (Butler 2015: 63). Spinoza makes us question various oppositions which have shaped the predominant form of Western rationalism: from the mind-body opposition to various dialectical antagonisms of which the one between promise/hope and disappointment has been the central one throughout this book's discussion. It is due to this dialectical kind of thinking that the "self" emerges in opposition to the Other. Rather than being opposed to others, the self only comes into being through others. As Judith Butler has put it:

> The "I" never quite overcomes that primary impressionability, even though it might be said to be its occasional undoing. Oddly but importantly, if the thesis is right, then the "I" comes into sentient being, even thinking and acting, precisely by being acted on in ways that, from the start, presume that nonvoluntary, though volatile field of impressionability. Already undone, or undone from the start, we are formed, and as formed, we come to be always partially undone by what we come to sense and know. (Butler 2015: 11)

The self is the Other. Spinoza sheds light on how Foucault's Socratic technique of the care for the self always engages selfhood as an attempted liberation from society's self-harming oppression. To free the self from societal oppression contributes to diminishing the totalitarian hold of political restrictions on society as a whole.

Literature has a special role to play in this new insight into selfhood not in opposition to but as illumination of the Other, of society, of politics. This is why Adorno refers to Spinoza's *conatus* for a better understanding of Canetti's exclusive focus on a "wild," extremely narcissistic self-preservation. As I have shown elsewhere (Mack 2001: 46–78), the self as political leader is a key moment for an analysis of fascist and Nazi totalitarian forms of politics. Crowd theory from Le Bon to Freud linked modern forms of power to that of the increase in human crowd formation. Canetti radically differs from such approach toward the analysis of power and totalitarianism. He does not take issue with crowds as such. Rather, Canetti detects the principle of power within the triumph of the individual over the "masses." In what is important for a more nuanced comprehension of not only Jelinek's postmodern but also Wallace's approach to an early-twentieth-century conceptualization of selfhood, Canetti shifts the parameters for perceiving modernity when he does away with the dialectical opposition between rational and promissory leaders and irrational, disappointing crowds (which is foundational to both Le Bon's and Freud's respective and highly influential theories of the crowd).

Canetti's paradigm shift responds to the historical context of the Nazi genocide, where masses of human beings were systematically killed as part of an organized, rationalized, and highly administered process of annihilation, that from the start sets out to deprive its victims of a sense of selfhood and humanity. Like Adorno, Canetti implicitly returns to Spinoza's *conatus* by outdoing the opposition between self and Other, between the leader and the crowd. The destructive self does not only destroy the Other but in doing so it destroys itself. Conversely, to understand societal or political forms of totalitarian destruction we have to understand the individuals in charge of such devastation.

This is precisely what Jelinek does in her 1983 novel *The Pianist*: her focus is on a self that harms itself and others—what her antiheroine Erika Kohut dismissively calls "the masses." Jelinek's pianist is a high school piano teacher. The novel disappoints the artistic ambitions of its free indirect narration: "Erika Kohut to no avail put her arms forward, towards destiny but destiny does not make a pianist out of her"(*Vergebens streckt Erika ihre Arme dem Schicksal entgegen, doch das Schicksal macht keine Pianistin aus ihr*) (Jelinek 1997: 28). Art functions as instrumentalist part of societal and economic ideals that glorify success and punish failure. When Erika fails at an important finalist competition, her mother, who "spent her last savings on her daughter's concert dress" (*die ihr letztes Geld für Erikas Konzerttoilette ausgegeben hat*) (Jelinek 1997: 28) beats her.

In disappointing expectations of artistic fulfillment and societal success Jelinek's *The Pianist* has colorful melodramatic aspects and radicalizes

Canetti's satire on the populist leader and the crowd within the context of artistic petite bourgeois aspirations and their symbolic-societal value for our commercialized culture. Satire partakes of what Allyson Fiddler has called Jelinek's "aesthetics of exaggeration and simplified black-and-white representation" (Fiddler 1994: 126). Critics have noticed the gender politics that shapes the piano teacher's sadistic-masochistic relationship to her female identity. As Marlies Janz has shown Erika Kohut "only experiences femininity as lack and absence of power (*nur als Mangel und Ohnmacht*), against which she defends herself as master (*Herrin*)" (Janz 1995: 78). Her narrative is melodramatic, because there is a pervasive abyss between Erika's and her mother's artistic ambitions and the disappointment of their actualization. Indeed, Erika Kohut is a mediocre artist who assumes the role of a quasi-mad genius. It is this stereotypical and highly ironic image of the mentally ill genius which functions as a rather troubled excuse for torturing her pupils, thus repeating her own and her father's experience at the hands of her mother.

Jelinek's postmodern trope of irony highlights the gulf that divides social pretention from genuine action and speech. Here the self attempts to attain as well as to gain from symbolic-societal standing through ostentatious artistic accomplishments. There is a striking sense of the cruelty within ironic detachment emerging from Erika Kohut's free indirect narrative about her father's mental illness which she first employs to impress her student and lover Herr Klemmer: "Erika says [i.e., to Klemmer] that her father died completely mad (*vollständig umnachtet*) in Steinhof. This is why one should show consideration with Erika, because she went through heavy times (*Schweres habe sie schon durchgemacht*)" (Jelinek 1997: 73). However, when Erika is alone and speaks her free indirect narration to herself, as it were, the mentally ill father appears in the light of neither empathy and consideration nor artistic genius (of manic depressive composers such as Schumann and Schubert) but in a cold, discriminatory light, as trouble-maker (*Störenfried* Jelinek 1997: 97) who disrupts the bourgeois comfort of herself and her mother's life, and his move to the asylum Steinhof is a wider political one to exclude the mentally ill from everyday conformity and mediocrity: "By-By, it was so lovely. Everything must end sometime. Father shall wave goodbye to his two ladies, propped by his compulsory caretaker, in his white coat" (*Aufwiedersehen, es war so schön. Doch einmal endet alles. Der Vater soll, als sie abfahren, seinen zwei Damen, von einem unfreiwilligen Helfer in weißen Kitteln gestützt Winkewinke machen*) (Jelinek 1997: 97). This quotation is strikingly postmodern in its ironic self-consciousness. It is cold and detached and satirically imitates the would-be-happiness and fulfillment of commercial culture and the advertisement industry, while cruelly describing a Kafkaesque exclusion of a family member, partner, and parent, never to be seen again ("By-By *Auf Wiedersehen*").

This key quotation from Jelinek's *The Pianist* foregrounds the critical awareness which modernist and more radically still, postmodernist irony can provoke during the process of reading. By citing the diction and the clichéd images of the advertisement industry (By-by, it was so lovely but everything nice comes to an end at some time *Aufwiedersehen, es war so schön. Doch einmal endet alles*) Jelinek anticipates David Foster Wallace's critique of postmodern self-consciousness and irony as having been co-opted by the new media and advertisement industry. The passage seems to co-opt commercialist co-option by performing in terms of its form and its content the corruption of art to instrumentalist social conformity and cruelty.

As Marshall Boswell has shown, Wallace questions precisely the idealist element within postmodern irony. From this perspective, dialectical expectations of progress drive postmodernist detachment. According to Wallace, postmodernists (being idealists) assume that intellectual insight results in social and political improvements. Indeed, post 1960s demythologizations held out the expectation of a better world:

> Postmodern writers called attention to their fictional devices and undermined our faith in the truth-value of various interested conventions because these writers were, in Wallace's term, "frankly idealistic; it was assumed that etiology and diagnosis pointed toward cure, that revelation of imprisonment led to freedom." The prison we were in was the prison of naïve belief; the freedom they were offering was the intellectual and spiritual freedom of the cynic to see hypocrisy wherever it was at work. Unfortunately, by 1990 the once subversive strategies of postmodernism—self-reflexivity and irony—had been co-opted by television, even by television advertising, to such an extent that these same strategies had been sapped of their revolutionary power. (Boswell 2003: 13–14)

Brian McHale has argued that postmodernism extends modernism by shifting irony from an epistemological to an ontological plane (McHale 1987: 8–11). Jelinek's free indirect narration indeed calls into doubt the trustworthiness of being and significantly, Erika's father becomes insane dealing with the world: "Erika only came into being after twenty years of marriage (*Erika ist erst nach zwanzigjähriger Ehe in die Welt gestiegen*) (Jelinek 1997: 15); a world from which her father became mad (*von der ihr Vater irr wurde*) (Jelinek 1997: 15); locked up in an institution so that he could not pose a danger for the world" (*in einer Anstalt verwahrt, damit er keine Gefahr für die Welt würde*) (Jelinek

1997: 15). In stark contrast to Pynchon's idiosyncratic usage of the word "mad"—as a way of outdoing and doing away with dialectical opposition—here madness denotes the irredeemable viciousness not only of the petite bourgeoisie but also of the world as such.

It is a world wherein we can expect nothing but disappointment, and paradoxically this is precisely because everything has to partake of a teleology of success, hope, and fulfillment. The bleakness of Jelinek's *The Pianist* consists in its radical satire of perhaps the only remaining hopes of avoiding brutality and its instrumental use for the exertion of power: the novel depicts women (Erika and her mother) and art (music) in terms of petite bourgeois longings for mastery, possessiveness, and success. Erika's mother builds an icy construction of glory and fame (*Eisfabrik des Ruhmes*) for her daughter and demands her offspring to reach if not the historical hopes of Hegel's absolute spirit/intellect, then the "absolute world height" (*absolute Weltspitze* Jelinek 1997: 26) of success (artistic and of course financial too).

Indeed, Jelinek's *The Pianist* demythologizes art as totalitarian disappointment, almost as if parts of the novel had been taken out of Canetti's *Masse und Macht* (*Crowds and Power*). Erika turns into Canetti's lonely leader surrounded by "rotten crowds" (*miese Menschemassen* Jelinek 1997: 22) who are there to be used and abused like her pupils. Jelinek satirizes Thomas Mann's modernist contrast between the ill artist and the healthy populace, turning, as we have seen earlier, illness, into an excuse to tyrannize the Other: "This dimming away of Schubert and Schumann's light of life is exactly the stark opposite of what the healthy crowds intends, if it calls the tradition healthy. Health: do not touch it and let it be the devil's possession (*Gesundheit pfui Teufel*) (Jelinek 1997: 72). Health is the transfiguration of what is"(*Gesundheit ist die Verklärung dessen, was ist*) (Jelinek 1997: 72). The allusion to the devil in the context of art, the crowds, health, and illness is a direct allusion to Mann's *Doktor Faustus* whose irony here morphs into the meta-ironic, by disappointing modernist hopes for art. Art here turns into the bleak context of power and masochistic as well as sadistic abuses of the self and the Other. In this way Erika's self-harm replicates the suffering her mother has inflicted on her and which she inflicts on the crowds of her pupils in the music school of Vienna.

In a converse Spinozist way, Jelinek thus makes us see the self as Other. Erika insists on her individuality and in doing so replicates the brutal individualism of society and politics as a whole. The novel shows individualism to be part of the idealism by and through which the self reproduces societal expectations for success. The idealist mark of successful distinction is precisely a complete indifference to nature and our embodiment: "because everything depends on the spirit/intellect (*Geist*), on the inner attitude towards nature, not on nature in itself" (*auf die Einstellung zur Natur komme es an! Nicht auf die Natur selber*) (Jelinek 1997: 33). In a meta-ironic move, Erika's free indirect narrative establishes a radical opposition between self and society in which the two opposites actually collapse into each other. She has learned from her mother that the crowd's opinions are wrong and that in art, in Schubert's music, there is the rule of peace within the forest—the clichéd advertisement of forest landscapes as regions of peace—and not in the forest itself (*Die Mutter erwiedert messersharf, daß in Schuberts Sonaten mehr Friede des Waldes herrsche als im Frieden des Waldes selber*) (Jelinek 1997: 39). In Jelinek's novel art ironizes itself and thus delineates its co-option by commercialist endeavors of the advertisement industry that help to establish societal conformism within the self.

A. O. Scott has singled out a similar meta-ironic rendering problematic of art's irony as Wallace's distinct difference to both modernism and postmodernism (Scott 2000: 40). As the various discussions of this book have shown, critical meta-uses of irony have long before Wallace's "new sincerity" (Kelly 2010: 131) been part of romantic, modernist and postmodernist's ways to disturb dialectical oppositions between hope and disappointment. Instead of attempting yet another raising of public expectations for the work of art or subscribing to a new version of literature's "redemptive ambitions" (Hayes-Brady 2016: 196), Wallace's last, posthumously published work *The Pale King* attempts to dismantle what the critical consensus takes his work to formulate: that is, conceptions of literature in terms of redemption or utopia (albeit in insubstantial, or, illusory, non-embodied form). As David Hering has shown through detailed archival work, *The Pale King* found its form through the announced renunciation of its fictional form "within a putatively non-fiction essay" (which Hering argues "is *itself* fictional"; Hering 2016: 145): "Author here. Meaning real author, the living human holding the pencil, not some abstract narrative persona" (Wallace 2011: 68). Wallace throughout his literary career raises literary expectations of redemption only to disappoint his audience. There is a so far under-theorized semantics of disappointment at work in his writing that from his early collection of short stories in *Girl with Curious Hair* onward promises new, redemptive meanings in the formulation of neologism such as "vameesed" (Wallace 2012: 134) only to disappoint them. The "author here" intervention interrupts our desire for myths and fiction, deflating expectations of a disembodied overcoming of the abject and the frail and mortal. This, however, is the topic of a book of its own—focusing on Wallace and our contemporary situation wherein disappointment has come full circle as a form of expectation—for which the current one provides an historical-intellectual framework.

Bibliography

Achebe, Chinua (2006) "An Image of Africa: Racism in Conrad's *Heart of Darkness*." In Joseph Conrad, *Hear of Darkness*, edited by Paul B. Armstrong. New York: Norton, 336–49.
Agamben, Giorgio (2016) *The Use of Bodies: Homo Sacer IV, 2*. Translated by Adam Kotsko. Paolo Alto, CA: Stanford University Press.
Agamben, Giorgio (2011) *Nudities*. Translated by David Kishik and Stefan Pedatella. Paolo Alto, CA: Stanford University Press.
Agamben, Giorgio (2002) *Remnants of Auschwitz: The Witness and the Archive*. Translated by Daniel Heller-Roazen. New York: Zone Books.
Ahmed, Sara (2010) *The Promise of Happiness*. Durham, NC: Duke University Press.
Alexander, Edward (1999) "Philip Roth at Century's End." *New England Review* 20 (Spring): 183–90.
Ankersmith, Frank (2005) *Sublime Historical Experience*. Stanford, CA: Stanford University Press.
Arendt, Hannah (2004) *The Origins of Totalitarianism*. With an introduction by Samantha Power. New York: Schocken.
Arendt, Hannah (2002). *Denktagebuch 1950–1973*. Vol. 1. Edited by Ursula Ludz and Ingeborg Nordmann. Munich: Piper.
Arendt, Hannah (1990) *On Revolution*. London: Penguin.
Arendt, Hannah (1977) *Between Past and Future: Eight Exercises in Political Thought*. London: Penguin.
Atlan, Henri (2010) *The Sparks of Randomness: Volume 1: Spermatic Knowledge*. Translated by Jenn L Schramm. Stanford: Stanford University Press.
Auster, Paul and Coetzee, J.M. (2013) *Here and Now: Letters 2008–2011*. London: Faber and Faber.
Auster, Paul (2012) *Winter Journal*. London: Faber and Faber.
Baars, Jan (2012) *Ageing and the Art of Living*. Baltimore: Johns Hopkins University Press.
Bahun, Sanja (2014) *Modernism and Melancholia: Writing as Countermourning*. Oxford: Oxford University Press.
Barash, Jeffrey Andrew (2016) *Collective Memory and the Historical Past*. Chicago: University of Chicago Press.
Beer, Gillian (2018) *George Eliot and the Woman Question*. Second Enlarged Edition. London: Edward Everett.
Beiser, Frederick (2003) *The Romantic Imperative: The Concept of Early German Romanticism*. Cambridge, MA: Harvard University Press.
Bellow, Saul (2000) *Ravelstein*. London: Penguin.
Benjamin, Walter (2002) *The Arcades Project*. Translated by Howard Eiland and Kevin McLaughlin Prepared on the basis of the German Volume edited by

Rolf Tiedemann. Cambridge, MA: The Belknap Press of Harvard University Press.

Benjamin, Walter (1999a) *Illuminations*. Edited and with an Introduction by Hannah Arendt. Translated by Harry Zorn. New York: Schocken Books.

Benjamin, Walter (1999b) *Selected Writings. Volume 2: 1927–1934*. Cambridge, MA: Belknap Press of Harvard University Press.

Benjamin, Walter (1978) *Briefe*. Edited by Gershom Scholem and Theodor W. Adorno. Frankfurt a. M.: Suhrkamp.

Bennett, J. (1984) *A Study of Spinoza's Ethics*. Indianapolis, IN: Hackett Publishing Company.

Berlin, Isaiah (2000) *The Roots of Romanticism. The A. W. Mellon Lectures in the Fine Arts, 1965 The National Gallery of Art, Washington, D C*. Edited by Henry Hardy. London: Pimlico.

Bersani, Leo (1990) *The Culture of Redemption*. Cambridge, MA: Harvard University Press.

Blanchot, Maurice (1995) *The Writing of the Disaster*. Translated by Ann Smock. London: University of Nebraska Press.

Blanchot, Maurice (1989) *The Space of Literature*. Translated with an introduction by Ann Smock. London: University of Nebraska Press.

Bloom, Allan (1987) *The Closing of the American Mind*. New York: Simon Schuster.

Booth, Wayne C. (1988) *The Company We Keep: An Ethics of Fiction*. Berkeley: University of California Press.

Borradori, Giovanna (2003) *Philosophy in a Time of Terror: Dialogues with Jürgen Habermas and Jacques Derrida*. Chicago: University of Chicago Press.

Boswell, Mashall (2003) *Understanding David Foster Wallace*. Columbia, South Carolina: University of South Carolina Press.

Bourdieu, Pierre (2010) *Distinction: A Social Critique of the Judgement of Taste*. Translated by Richard Nice, with a new introduction by Tony Bennett. London: Routledge.

Bowie, Andrew. (1996) "John McDowell's Mind and World, and Early Romantic Epistemology." *Revue Internationale de Philosophie* 50, No. 197: 515–54.

Brauner, David (2011) "'What Was Not Supposed to Happen Had Happened and What Was Supposed to Happen Had Not Happened': Subverting History in American Pastoral." In Debra Shostak (ed.), *Philip Roth: American Pastoral; The Human Stain; Plot against America*. London: Bloomsbury, 19–32.

Brauner, David (2007) *Philip Roth*. Manchester: Manchester University Press.

Brown, Bill (2003) *A Sense of Things: The Object Matter of American Literature*. Chicago: University of Chicago Press.

Burns, Anna (2018) *Milkman*. London: Faber and Faber.

Butler, Judith (2015) *Senses of the Subject*. New York: Fordham University Press.

Butler, Judith (2007) *Gender Trouble: Feminism and the Subversion of Identity*. London: Routledge.

Butler, Judith (2005) *Giving an Account of Oneself*. New York: Fordham University Press.
Byron, Lord (George Gordon). (1975) *The Poetical Works of Byron*. Cambridge Edition. Revised and with a new introduction by Robert F. Gleckner. Boston, MA: Houghton Mifflin Company.
Canetti, Elias (2005) "Gespraech mit Theodor W Adorno." In *Canetti, Aufsaetze, Reden, Gespraeche*. Munich: Hander, 140–63.
Churchwell, Sarah (2013) *Careless People: Murder, Mayhem and the Invention of the Great Gatsby*. London: Virago Press.
Cohen, Richard A. (1994) *Elevations: The Height of the Good in Rosenzweig and Levinas*. Chicago: University of Chicago Press.
Coleridge, Samuel Taylor (1991a) *Poems*. Edited by John Beer. London: Dent/Everyman.
Coleridge, Samuel Taylor (1991b) *Biographia Literaria: Or Biographical Sketches of my Literary Life and Opinions*. Edited, with an introduction, by George Watson. London: Dent/Everyman.
Conrad, Joseph (1986) *Lord Jim*. Edited by Cedric Watts and Robert Hampson. London: Penguin.
Conrad, Joseph (1973) *Heart of Darkness*. Edited with an Introduction by Paul O'Prey. London: Penguin.
Dahlbeck de Lucia, Moa (2019) *Spinoza, Ecology and International Law: Radical Naturalism in the Face of the Anthropocene*. London: Routledge.
Damasio, Antonio (2003) *Looking for Spinoza: Joy, Sorrow, and the Feeling Brain*. Orlando, FL: Harcourt, Inc.
Davidson, Arnold I (1995) "Introduction: Pierre Hadot and the Spiritual Phenomenon of Ancient Philosophy" in Pierre Hadot, *Philosophy as a Way of Life: Spiritual Exercises from Socrates to Foucault*. Edited with an Introduction by Arnold I Davidson. Translated by Michael Chase. Oxford: Blackwell.
Della Rocca, M. (2008) *Spinoza*. London: Routledge.
Derrida, Jacques (2005) *Rogues: Two Essays on Reason*. Translated by Pascale-Anne Brault and Michael Naas. Stanford, CA: Stanford University Press.
Derrida, Jacques (1999) *Adieu to Emmanuel Levinas*. Translated by Pascale-Anne Brault and Michael Naas. Stanford, CA: Stanford University Press.
Derrida, Jacques (1994) *Specters of Marx: The State of the Debt, the Work of Mourning, and the New International*. Translated from the French Peggy Kamuf. Introduction by Bernd Magnus and Stephen Cullenberg. London: Routledge.
Derrida, Jacques (1992) "The Law of Genre." Translated by Avital Ronell. In *Acts of Literature*, edited by Derek Attridge. London: Routledge, 222–53.
Dickstein, Morris (2005) *A Mirror in the Roadway: Literature and the Real World*. Princeton, NJ: Princeton University Press.
Docherty, Thomas (2018) *Literature and Capital*. London: Bloomsbury.

Dollimore, Jonathan (2012) "Civilization and Its Darkness." In Nidesh Lawtoo (ed.), *Conrad's Heart of Darkness and Contemporary Thought*. London: Bloomsbury, 67–86.
Eagleton, Terry (2015) *Hope Without Optimism*. New Haven: Yale University Press.
Eagleton, Terry (2005) *The English Novel: An Introduction*. Oxford: Blackwell.
Eagleton, Terry (2003) *Sweet Violence: The Idea of the Tragic*. Oxford: Blackwell.
Eggert, Paul (2009) *Securing the Past: Conversation in Art, Architecture and Literature*. Cambridge: Cambridge University Press.
Eliot, T. S. (1969) *The Complete Poems and Plays*. London: Faber & Faber.
Fiddler, Allyson (1994) *Rewriting Reality*. Oxford: Berg.
Fitzgerald, Scott F. (2006) *The Great Gatsby*. London: Penguin.
Flatly, Jonathan (2008) *Affective Mapping: Melancholia and the Politics of Modernism*. Cambridge, MA: Harvard University Press.
Foucault, Michel (2011) *The Courage of Truth: The Government of Self and Others*. Lectures at the College de France 1983–1984. Translated by Graham Burchell. Foreword by Francois Ewald. Edited by Arnold I. Davidson and Frederic Gross. London: Palgrave Macmillan.
Foucault, Michel (2005) *The Hermeneutics of the Subject*. Lectures at the College de France 1981–1982. Translated by Graham Burchell. Edited by Arnold Davidson. London: Palgrave Macmillan.
Foucault, Michel (2000) "What Is an Author." In James Faubion (ed.), *Essential Works of Foucault. Vol. II. Aesthetics, Method and Epistemology*. Translated by Robert Hurley et al. London: Penguin, 205–22.
Franco, Paul (2019) "Introduction to the Transcript of Leo Strauss's 1965 Course on Hegel's *Philosophy of History*." In Paul Franco (ed.), *Leo Strauss on Hegel*. Chicago: University of Chicago Press, 1–19.
Frank, Manfred (2004) *The Philosophical Foundations of Early German Romanticism*. Translated by Elizabeth Millán-Zaibert. Albany: State University of New York Press.
Frank, Manfred (1996) "*Alle Wahrheit ist relative: alles Wissen symbolisch*—Motive der Grundsatz-Skepsis in der frühen Jenarer Romantik (1796)." *Revue Internationale de Philosophie* 50.197: 403–36.
Fukuyama, Francis (1992) *The End of History and the Last Man*. London: Penguin.
Fukuyama, Francis (2018) *Identity: Contemporary Identity Politics and the Struggle for Recognition*. London: Profile Books.
Garrington, Abbie (2013) *Haptic Modernism: Touch and the Tactile in Modernist Writing*. Edinburgh: Edinburgh University Press.
Gellner, Ernest (1988) "Zero of Cracow or Revolution of Nemi or the Polish Revenge in Three Acts." In Roy F. Ellen (ed.), *Malinowski between Two Worlds: The Polish Roots of an Anthropological Tradition*. Cambridge: Cambridge University Press, 164–94.
Gentry, Bruce Marshall (2000) "Newark Maid Feminism in Philip Roth's *American Pastoral*." *Shofar* 19: 74–83.

Gillespie, Michael Allen (1995) *Nihilism before Nietzsche*. Chicago: University of Chicago Press.
Glaser, Jennifer (2008) "The Jew in the Canon: Reading Race and Literary History in Philip Roth's *The Human Stain*." *PMLA* 123.5: 1465–78.
Goldstein, Rebecca (2009) *Betraying Spinoza: The Renegade Jew Who Gave Us Modernity*. New York: Schocken Books.
Graff, Gerlad (1979) *Literature Against Itself: Literary Ideas in Modern Society*. Chicago: University of Chicago Press.
Gray, John (2011) *The Immortalization Commission: Science and the Strange Quest to Cheat Death*. London: Allen Lane/Penguin.
Gray, John (2007a) *Enlightenment's Wake: Politics and Culture at the Close of the Modern Age*. London: Routledge.
Gray, John (2007b) *Black Mass: Apocalyptic Religion and the Death of Utopia*. New York: Farrar, Straus and Giroux.
Habermas, Jürgen (1987) *The Philosophical Discourse of Modernity: Twelve Lecture*. Translated by Frederick Lawrence. Cambridge, MA: MIT Press.
Hadot, Pierre (1995) *Philosophy as a Way of Life: Spiritual Exercises from Socrates to Foucault*. Edited with an introduction by Arnold I Davidson. Oxford: Blackwell.
Halmi, Nicholas (2012) "Coleridge's Ecumenical Spinoza." In Beth Lord (ed.), *Spinoza Beyond Philosophy*. Edinburgh: Edinburgh University Press.
Hammerschlag, Sarah (2016) *Broken Tablets: Levinas, Derrida and the Literary Afterlife of Religion*. New York: Columbia University Press.
Hampshire, Stuart (2005) *Spinoza and Spinozism*. Oxford: Clarendon Press.
Hayes, Patrick (2014) *Philip Roth: Fiction and Power*. Oxford: Oxford University Press.
Hayes-Brady, Clare (2016) *The Unspeakable Failures of David Foster Wallace: Language, Identity, and Resistance*. London: Bloomsbury.
Hegel, Georg Wilhelm Friedrich (1997) *On Art, Religion, and the History of Philosophy: Introductory Lectures*. Translated by E. S. Haldane. Edited by J. Glenn Gray. Introduction by Tom Rockmore. Indianapolis: Hackett Publishing Company.
Hegel, Georg Wilhelm Friedrich (1973) *Phenomenologie des Geistes*. Edited by Eva Moldenhauer and Karl Markus Michel. Frankfurt a. M.: Suhrkamp.
Heine, Heinrich (1968) *Werke*. Vol. 4 Schriften ueber Deutschland. Edited by Helmut Schanze. Frankfurt am Main: Insel.
Hering, David (2016) *David Foster Wallace: Fiction and Form*. London: Bloomsbury.
Hering, David (ed.). (2010) *Consider David Forster Wallace: Critical Essays*. Los Angeles, CA: Sideshow Media Press.
Hitchens, Christopher (2000) "The Egg-Head's Egger-On: Review of Saul Bellow's *Ravelstein*" *London Review of Books* 22.9 (27 April).
Hutchinson, Anthony (2007) *Writing the Republic: Liberalism and Modernity in American Fiction*. New York: Columbia University Press.

Israel, Jonathan I. (2001) *Radical Enlightenment: Philosophy and the Making of Modernity 1650–1750*. Oxford: Oxford University Press.

Jacobi, Friedrich Heinrich (1785) *Über die Lehre des Spinoza in Briefen an den Herrn Moses Mendelssohn*. Breslau: Gottlieb Löwe.

Jacobus, Mary (1984) "The Law of/and Gender: Genre Theory and *The Prelude*." *Diacritics* 14 (Winter/4): 47–57.

Jameson, Fredric (2002) *The Political Unconsciousness: Narrative as a Socially Symbolic Act*. London: Routledge.

Jameson, Fredric (1992) *Postmodernism: Or, the Cultural Logic of Late Capitalism*. London: Verson.

Jamison, Redfield Kay (1995) *An Unquiet Mind: A Memoir of Moods and Madness*. London: Macmillan.

Janz, Marlies (1995) *Elfriede Jelinek*. Stuttgart: Metzler.

Jayasena, Nalin (2007) *Contested Masculinities: Crises in Colonial Male Identity from Joseph Conrad to Satyajit Ray*. London: Routledge.

Jelinek, Elfriede (2004) *Bambiland*. With a foreword by C. Schlingensief and an essay by B. Lücke. Reinbek bei Hamburg: Rowohlt.

Jelinek, Elfriede (1998) *Ein Sportsück*. Reinbek bei Hamburg: Rowohlt.

Jelinek, Elfriede (1997) *Die Klavierspielerin*. Reinbek bei Hamburg: Rowohlt.

Jerischna, Jan (1988) "Polish Modernism and Malinowski." In Roy F. Ellen (ed.), *Malinowski between Two Worlds: The Polish Roots of an Anthropological Tradition*. Cambridge: Cambridge University Press, 128–48.

De Jonge, Eccy (2004) *Spinoza and Deep Ecology: Challenging Traditional Approaches to Environmentalism*. Aldershot, UK: Ashgate Publishing.

Josephson-Storm, Jason (2017) *The Myth of Disenchantment: Magic, Modernity, and the Birth of the Human Sciences*. Chicago: University of Chicago Press.

Kafka, Franz (1997) *The Castle*. A new translation by J. A. Underwood; with an introduction by Idris Parry. London: Penguin.

Kafka, Franz (1926) *Das Schloss*. Munich: Kurt Wolff.

Kant, Immanuel (1964) *Schriften zur Ethik und Religionsphilosophie. Volume 2*. Edited by Wilhelm Weischedel. Frankfurt a. Main: Suhrkamp.

Keats, John (1970) *The Complete Poems*. Edited by Miriam Allott. Harlow, Essex, UK: Longman.

Kelly, Adam (2013) *American Fiction in Transition: Observer-Hero Narrative, the 1990s, and Postmodernism*. London: Bloomsbury.

Kelly, Adam (2010) "David Forster Wallace and the New Sincerity in American Fiction." In David Hering (ed.), *Consider David Forster Wallace: Critical Essays*. Los Angeles, CA: Sideshow Media Press, 131–46.

Kojève, Alexandre (1969) *Introduction to the Reading of Hegel: Lectures on The Phenomenology of Spirit*. Assembled by Raymond Queneau, edited by Allan Bloom and translated by James H Nichols. Ithaca: Cornell University Press.

Lacoue-Labarthe, Philippe (2012) "The Horror of the West." In Nidesh Lawtoo (ed.), *Conrad's Heart of Darkness and Contemporary Thought*. London: Bloomsbury, 111–22.

Lawrence, D. H. (1989) *Women in Love*. Edited with an introduction and notes by C. L. Ross. London: Penguin

Levinas, Emmanuel (1990) *Difficult Freedom: Essays on Judaism*. Translated by Seàn Hand. Baltimore: Johns Hopkins University Press.
Levinas, Emmanuel (1969) *Totality and Infinity: An Essay on Exteriority*. Translated by Alphonso Lingis. Pittsburgh: Duquesne University Press.
Long, Robert Emmet 1966 "The Great Gatsby and the Tradition of Joseph Conrad." *Texas Studies in Literature and Language* 8.3 (Autumn): 407–22.
Löwy, Michael (2005) *Fire Alarm: Reading Walter Benjamin's "on the concept of history"*. London: Verso.
Löwy, Michael (1979) *Georg Lukács—From Romanticism to Bolshevism*. Translated by Patrick Camiller. London: NLB.
Lukács, George (1968) *Geschichte und Klassenbewußtsein: Studien über marxistische Dialektik*. Darmstadt: Luchterhand.
Macherey, Pierre (2011) *Hegel or Spinoza*. Translated by Susan M. Ruddick. Minneapolis: University of Minnesota Press.
Machiavelli, Niccolo (1961) *The Prince*. Translated by George Bull. London: Penguin.
MacIntyre, Alasdair (1999). *Dependent Rational Animals: Why Humans Need the Virtues*. Chicago, IL: Open Court.
Mack, Michael (2016) *Contaminations: Beyond Dialectics in Modern Literature, Science and Film*. Edinburgh: Edinburgh University Press.
Mack, Michael (2014a) "Two Different Approaches to the Relationship between Poetry, History and Philosophy: Walter Benjamin and Martin Heidegger." *New Readings* 14: 1–30.
Mack, Michael (2014b) *Philosophy and Literature in Times of Crisis: Challenging Our Infatuation with Numbers*. London: Bloomsbury.
Mack, Michael (2012) *How Literature Changes the Way We Think*. London: Bloomsbury.
Mack, Michael (2010) *Spinoza and the Specters of Modernity: The Hidden Enlightenment of Diversity from Spinoza to Freud*. London: Bloomsbury.
Mack, Michael (2009) "The Holocaust and Hannah Arendt's Philosophical Critique of Philosophy: *Eichmann in Jerusalem*." *New German Critique* 106 (Winter): 35–60.
Mack, Michael (2008) "On the Contemporary Relevance of Elias Canetti's Theory of Power." *Orbis Litterarum* 63: 487–509.
Mack, Michael (2003) *German Idealism and the Jew: The Inner Antisemitism of Philosophy and German Jewish Responses*. Chicago: University of Chicago Press.
Mack, Michael (2001) *Anthropology as Memory: Elias Canetti and Franz Baermann Steiner's Responses to the Shoah*. Tübingen: Niemeyer.
May, Keith M. (1988) *Nietzsche and Modern Literature: Themes in Yeats, Rilke, Mann and Lawrence*. London: Macmillan.
McClure, John (1981) *Kipling & Conrad: The Colonial Fiction*. Cambridge, MA: Harvard University Press.
McGann, Jerome (1983) *The Romantic Ideology: A Critical Investigation*. Chicago: University of Chicago Press.

McGurl, Mark (2009) *Writing in the Program Era: Postwar Fiction and the Rise of Creative Writing*. Cambridge, Mass: Harvard University Press.

McHale, Brian (2011) "Period, Break, Interregnum." *Twentieth Century Literature* 57.3-4 (Fall/Winter): 328-40.

McHale, Brian (1987) *Postmodernist Fiction*. New York: Methuen.

Menand, Louis (1997) "The Irony of Ecstacy: Philip Roth and the Jewish Atlantis." *The New Yorker*: May 19.

Mendes-Flohr, Paul (1999). *German Jews: A Dual Identity*. New Haven: Yale University Press.

Mendelson, Edward (1976) "Gravity's Encyclopaedia." In George Levine and David Leverenz (eds.), *Mindful Pleasures: Essays on Thomas Pynchon*. Boston: Little, Brown and Company.

Merve, Emre (2017) *Paraliterary: The Making of Bad Readers in Postwar America*. Chicago: University of Chicago Press.

Michaels, Benn Walter (2004) *The Shape of the Signifier: 1967 to the End of History*. Princeton, NJ: Princeton University Press.

Millán-Zaibert, Elizabeth (2007) *Friedrich Schlegel and Emergence of Romantic Philosophy*. Albany: State University of New York Press.

Miller, Hillis (2012) "Heart of Darkness Revisited." In Nidesh Lawtoo (ed.), *Conrad's Heart of Darkness and Contemporary Thought*. London: Bloomsbury, 39-54.

Miller, Hillis J. (2011) *The Conflagration of Community: Fiction Before and After Auschwitz*. Chicago: University of Chicago Press.

Miller, J. Hillis (1982) *Fiction and Repetition: Seven English Novels*. Oxford: Blackwell.

Miller, J. Hillis (1963) *The Disappearance of God: Five Nineteenth-Century Writers*. Cambridge, MA: The Belknap Press of Harvard University Press.

Moi, Toril (2017) *Revolution of the Ordinary: Literary Studies after Wittgenstein, Austin and Cavell*. Chicago: University of Chicago Press.

Mongia, Padmini (1992) "Narrative Strategy and Imperialism in Conrad's *Lord Jim*." *Studies in the Novel* 24.2 (Spring): 173-86.

Morton, Timothy (2013) *Hyperobjects: Philosophy and Ecology at the End of the World*. Minneapolis: University of Minnesota Press.

Nadler, Steven (2011) *A Book Forged in Hell: Spinoza's Scandalous Treatise and the Birth of the Secular Age*. Princeton: Princeton University Press.

Nadler, Steven (2006) *Spinoza's Ethics: An Introduction*. Cambridge: Cambridge University Press.

Nehamas, Alexander (1998) *The Art of Living: Socratic Reflections from Plato to Foucault*. Berkeley: University of California Press.

Norris, Christopher (2011) "Spinoza and the Conflict of Interpretation." In Dimitris Vardoulkis (ed.), *Spinoza Now*. Minneapolis: University of Minnesota Press, 3-37

Novalis (1999) *Friedrich von Hardenbergs Werke, Tagebücher und Briefe*. Edited by Hans-Joachim Mähl und Richard Samuel. Darmstadt: Wissenschaftliche Buchgesellschaft.

Nussbaum, Martha (1990) *Love's Knowledge: Essays on Philosophy and Literature*. Oxford: Oxford University Press.
Parrish, Timothy (2000) "The End of Identity: Philip Roth's *American Pastoral*." *Shofar* 19: 84–99.
Pickelhain, Lothar (1999) "The Importance of I. P. Pavlov for the Development of Neuroscience." *Integrative Physiology and Behavioural Science* 34 (April): 85–9.
Pippin, Robert B. (2010) *Nietzsche, Psychology & First Philosophy*. Chicago: University of Chicago Press.
Pippin, Robert (2000) *Henry James and Modern Moral Life*. Cambridge: Cambridge university press.
Pippin, Robert B. (1999) *Modernism as a Philosophical Problem: On the Dissatisfaction of European High Culture*. Second Edition. Oxford: Blackwell.
Podhoretz, Norman (2004) "Philip Roth, Then and Now." In Thomas L. Jeffers (ed.), *The Norman Podhoretz Reader*. New York: Free Press.
Posnock, Ross (2006). *Philip Roth's Truth: The Art of Immaturity*. Princeton: Princeton University Press.
Pozorski, Aimee (2011) *Roth and Trauma: The Problem of History in the Later Works*. London: Bloomsbury.
Pynchon, Thomas (1975) *Gravity's Rainbow*. London: Ban Books/Picador.
Pynchon, Thomas (1967) *The Crying of Lot 49*. London: Jonathan Cape.
Quinney, Laura (1999) *The Poetics of Disappointment: Wordsworth to Ashbery*. Charlottesville: University of Virginia Press.
Rachel-Freund, Else (1979) *Franz Rosenzweig's Philosophy of Existence: An Analysis of The Star of Redemption*. Translated by Stephen L. Weinstein and Robert Israel. Edited by Paul Mendes-Flohr. Dordrecht: Kluwer.
Richards, Robert J. (2002) *The Romantic Conception of Life: Science and Philosophy in the Age of Goethe*. Chicago: University of Chicago Press.
Riesman, David (1950) *The Lonely Crowd: A Study in Changing American Character*. New Haven, CN: Yale University Press.
Robbins, Bruce (1999) *Feeling Global: Internationalism in Distress*. New York: New York University Press.
Rosenzweig, Franz (1998) *Franz Rosenzweig: His Life and Thought*. Compiled by Nathum N. Glatzer. Cambridge, MA: Hackett.
Rosenzweig, Franz (1990) *Der Stern der Erlösung*. Frankfurt a. M.: Suhrkamp.
Ross, Charles L. (1989) "Introduction." In D. H. Lawrence, *Women in Love*. Edited with an introduction and notes by C. L. Ross. London: Penguin: 13–48.
Roth, Philip (2013) "In the Destructive Element, Immerse Yourself." Web of Stories https://www.webofstories.com/play/philip.roth/126.
Roth, Philip (2010) *Nemesis*. London: Jonathan Cape.
Roth, Philip (2007. *Everyman*. London: Vintage.
Roth, Philip (2001) *The Dying Animal*. London: Vintage.
Roth, Philip (2000) *The Human Stain*. London: Jonathan Cape.
Roth, Philip (1999) *I Married a Communist*. London: Vintage.

Roth, Philip (1998) *American Pastoral*. London: Vintage.
Roth, Philip (1996) *Sabbath's Theatre*. London: Vintage.
Roth, Philip (1995) *Portnoy's Complaint*. London: Vintage.
Roth, Philip (1988a) *The Counterlife*. London: Penguin.
Roth, Philip (1988b) *The Ghost Writer*. London: Vintage.
Roth, Philip (1985) *Reading Myself and Others*. New York: Vintage.
Roth Pierpont, Claudia (2014) *Roth Unbound: A Writer and his Books*. London: Jonathan Cape.
Rubinstein, Ernest (1999) *An Episode of Jewish Romanticism: Franz Rosenzweig's The Star of Redemption*. Albany: SUNY.
Safer, Elaine (2006) *Mocking the Age: The Later Novels of Philip Roth*. Albany, NY: State University of New York Press.
Said, Edward (1994) *Culture and Imperialism*. New York: Knopf.
Saint-Amour, Paul K. (2015) *Tense Future: Modernism, Total War, Encyclopaedic Form*. Oxford: Oxford University Press.
Sandy, Mark (2013) *Romanticism, Memory, and Mourning*. Farnham, Surrey, UK: Ashgate.
Santner, Eric L. (2016) *The Weight of All Flesh: On the Subject-Matter of Political Economy*. With commentaries by Bonnie Honig, Peter E. Gordon and Hent de Vries. Edited and introduced by Kevis Goodman. Oxford: Oxford University Press.
Scarry, Elaine (1985) *The Body in Pain: The Making and Unmaking of the World*. Oxford: Oxford University Press.
Schelling, F. W. (2000) *The Abyss of Freedom: Ages of the World*. Translated by Judith Norman. Ann Arbor: University of Michigan Press.
Schlegel, Friedrich (1971) *Philosophie der Geschichte: In achtzehn Vorlesungen gehalten zu Wien im Jahre 1828*. Edited and introduced by Jean-Jacques Anstett. Kritische Friedrich Schlegel-Ausgabe. Volume 9. Paderborn: Ferdinand Schöningh.
Scott, A. O. (2000) "The Panic of Influence." *The New York Review of Books* 49.2 (February): 39–42.
Sharp, Hasana (2016) "Endangered Life: Feminist Posthumanism in the Anthropocene?" In H. Sharp and C. Taylor (eds.), *Feminist Philosophies of Life*. Quebect/Kingston: McGill-Queen's University Press, 272–81.
Sharp, Hasana (2011) *Spinoza and the Politics of Renaturalization*. Chicago: University of Chicago Press.
Sherry, Norman (1966) *Conrad's Eastern World*. Cambridge: Cambridge University Press.
Sherry, Vincent (2015) *Modernism and the Reinvention of Decadence*. Cambridge: Cambridge University Press.
Shostak, Debra (2011) *Philip Roth: American Pastoral; The Human Stain; Plot against America*. London: Bloomsbury.
Small, Helen (2007) *The Long Life*. Oxford: Oxford University Press.
Smith, Steven B. (2006) *Reading Leo Strauss: Politics, Philosophy, Judaism*. Chicago: University of Chicago Press.

Snyder, Katherine (1999) *Bachelors, Manhood, and the Novel 1850–1925*. Cambridge: Cambridge University Press.
Spender, Stephen (1935) *The Destructive Element: A Study of Modern Writer and Beliefs*. London: Jonathan Cape.
Spinoza, Baruch (1996) *Ethics*. Edited and translated by Edwin Curley with an introduction by Stuart Hampshire. Harmondsworth: Penguin.
Spinoza, Baruch (1925) *Opera*, vol. II. Edited by Carl Gebhardt. Heidelberg: Carl Winter.
Stallman, Robert Wooster (1955) "Conrad and The Great Gatsby." *Twentieth Century Literature* 1.1 (April): 5–12.
Steiner, Franz (1967) *Taboo*. With a Preface by E. E. Evans-Pritchard. Harmondsworth: Penguin (Pelican Anthropology Library).
Strauss, Leo (2019) *Leo Strauss on Hegel*. Edited by Paul Franco. Chicago: University of Chicago Press.
Strauss, Leo (2017) *Leo Strauss on Nietzsche's Thus Spoke Zarathustra*. Edited with an Introduction by Richard L. Velkley. Chicago: University of Chicago Press.
Strauss, Leo (2000) *On Tyranny. Revised and Expanded Edition Including the Strauss-Kojève Correspondence*. Edited by Victor Gourevitch and Michael S. Roth. Chicago: University of Chicago Press.
Strauss, Leo (1997a) *Spinoza's Critique of Religion*. Translated by E. M. Sinclair. Chicago: University of Chicago Press.
Strauss, Leo (1997b) *Gesammelte Schriften. Vol2 Philosophie und Gesetz: Frühe Schriften*. Edited by Wiebke and Heinrich Meier. Stuttgart: J. B. Metzler.
Strauss, Leo (1997c) "Why We Remain Jews: Can Jewish Faith and History Still Speak to Us?" (1962). In L. Strauss (ed.), *Jewish Philosophy and the Crisis of Modernity: Essays and Lectures in Modern Jewish Thought*. Edited with an Introduction by Kenneth Hart Green. Albany: State University of New Press.
Strauss, Leo (1989) "Progress or Return? The Contemporary Crisis in Western Civilization." In Leo Strauss (ed.), *An Introduction to Political Philosophy: Ten Essays*. Edited with an Introduction by Hilail Gildon. Detroit: Wayne State University Press.
Strauss, Leo (1963) *The Political Philosophy of Hobbes: Its Basis and Genesis*. Translated from the German Manuscript by Elsa M. Sinclair. Chicago: University of Chicago Press.
Strenski, Ivan (2006) *Thinking about Religion*. Oxford: Blackwell.
Tanguay, Daniel (2007) *Leo Strauss: An Intellectual Biography*. New Haven: Yale University Press.
Vardoulkis, Dimitri (ed.). (2011) *Spinoza Now*. Minneapolis: University of Minnesota Press.
Vatter, Miguel (2014) *The Republic of the Living: Biopolitics and the Critique of Civil Society*. New York: Fordham University Press.

Velkley, Richard L. (2017) "Editor's Introduction." In Leo Strauss (ed.), *Leo Strauss on Nietzsche's Thus Spoke Zarathustra*. Edited with an Introduction by Richard L. Velkley. Chicago: University of Chicago Press, XI–XX.

Velkley, Richard L. (2011) *Heidegger, Strauss, and the Premises of Philosophy. On Original Forgetting*. Chicago: University of Chicago Press.

Vonnegut, Kurt (1965) *Cat's Cradle*. London: Penguin.

Wallace, Foster David (2012) *Girl with Curious Hair*. London: Abacus.

Wallace, Foster David (2011) *The Pale King: An Unfinished Novel*. London: Penguin.

Watt, Ian (1979) *Conrad in the Nineteenth Century*. Berkeley: University of California Press.

Watts, Cedric (1986) "Introduction." In Joseph Conrad (ed.), *Lord Jim*. Edited by Cedric Watts and Robert Hampson. London: Penguin, 11–30.

Weber, Samuel (2008) *Benjamin's-abilities*. Cambridge, MA: Harvard University Press.

Williams, Raymond (1993) *Keywords: A Vocabulary of Culture and Society*. London: Fontana.

Žižek, Slavoj (2010) *Less than Nothing: Hegel and the Shadow of Dialectical Materialism*. London: Verso.

Index

Achebe, Chinua   90
Agamben, Giogio   101–2, 182–3, 205–6
Ahmed, Sarah   124
Alexander, Edward   259
Anthropocene   6, 16, 18, 22–5, 27, 29, 36–7, 39, 42–3, 48–9, 65, 72, 77, 92, 105–6, 146–7, 152–3, 187, 190, 197, 199–200, 207, 216, 229, 240, 246, 258
aprioristic   34–5, 51, 59, 152
Arendt, Hannah   93–104, 114, 203, 205–6, 227–31
   colonialism   93–4, 96, 104
   dialectics   94, 96, 98, 100, 102–3
   ghosts   94–5
   totalitarianism   94, 96, 100, 230–1
atheism   20, 24, 33–4, 37
Atlan, Henri   36, 46, 51, 56–7, 254
Auster, Paul   222–3, 225

Baars, Jan   226–9
Bahun, Sanja   184
Barash, Jeffrey Andrew   196–7, 201
Bayle, Pierre   20, 50, 52
Beer, Gillian   132
Beiser, Frederick   38–40
Bellow, Saul   124–34, 141, 146–51, 153, 155–6, 158, 163–72, 209
   Ravelstein   125–34, 141, –51, 153, 155–6, 158, 163–72
Benjamin, Walter   32, 97, 99, 112–15, 123, 143–4, 153, 160, 191, 210, 227–31
Bennett, J.   42
Berlin, Isaiah   38
Bersani, Leo   247
Blanchot, Maurice   199–200
Bloom, Allan   125, 127, 146, 149–51, 158, 164, 166–7, 170–2

Booth, Wayne   251–2
Borradori, Giovanna   213
Boswell, Marshall   266
Bourdieu, Pierre   175
Bowie, Andrew   38
Brauner, David   245, 259
Brown, Bill   112
Burns, Anna   3, 239–40
Butler, Judith   14, 68–9, 80, 141, 181–2, 187, 241, 263
Byron, George Gordon   18, 63
   Childe Harold's Pilgrimage   18

Canetti, Elias   262–5, 267
care of the self   53, 58, 145, 147, 154, 160, 211, 246–7, 249, 253, 255, 263
Carlyle, Thomas   81
Churchwell, Sarah   138
climate change   7, 147
Coetzee, J. M.   225
Cohen, Richard A.   218
Coleridge, Samuel Taylor   44, 49, 58–9, 61
   Christabel   44, 49, 61
colonialism   76–8, 80, 82–4, 90–1, 93–4, 96, 100–4, 107–11, 117–19, 143–4, 157
Conrad, Joseph   69–94, 97–104, 107–11, 113–19, 121, 128, 132–3, 136–8, 143–5, 213–15, 242–3, 245, 249, 251–2
   destructive element   70–4, 84, 113–16, 121, 145, 213–15, 242–3, 245, 249
   Heart of Darkness   89–93, 97–104, 107, 110, 132–3, 136, 138, 143
   Lord Jim   69–71, 75–81, 84–6, 89, 108–9, 116–19, 132–3, 143

Index

Dahlbeck de Lucia, Moa 37, 42
Damasio, Antonio 2, 26
Davidson, Arnold I. 85–6
decadence 67, 69–70, 86–7
deconstruction 4, 8
De Jonge, Eccy 42
Derrida, Jacques 41–2, 210–15, 252, 256
  autoimmunity 213–15
Descartes, René 26–7, 35–7, 40, 46–7, 49–50, 55, 57, 59, 226, 230
the destructive element 70–5, 84–7, 240, 242–3, 245, 249–50, 255
Dickstein, Morris 134–5
Diderot, Denis 257
disappointment 1, 3, 5, 9–10, 14, 17, 19–22, 24–5, 27, 29–30, 33, 41–3, 45, 55, 63, 66, 69, 71, 73–4, 76–8, 81–3, 85–7, 89–90, 92, 96, 98–100, 102–4, 108–9, 111–14, 116–19, 121, 124–5, 127–32, 134–6, 138–41, 143, 145–8, 150–1, 155–6, 158, 166–7, 170–1, 174, 177–8, 181, 183–4, 187–9, 192–201, 204, 217–32, 234–46, 251, 255–6, 258–65, 267–8
  avowed 41, 55, 66, 71, 73–4, 85–6, 113, 117–18, 121, 132, 143, 184, 198, 246
  disavowed 3, 9–10, 20–2, 33, 42–3, 63, 66, 76–8, 81–3, 85–6, 92, 98, 102, 104, 108–9, 111, 114, 117–19, 130–2, 138, 146, 148, 166–7, 171, 174, 183, 218, 241–2, 258
Docherty, Thomas 202
Dollimore, Jonathan 91

Eagleton, Terry 123–4, 131–2, 147
Eggbert, Paul 186
Eliot. T. S. 136–8
end of history 6, 8, 17, 42–3, 64–5, 97, 104, 111, 114, 121, 128, 157–8, 163–4, 166–7, 169, 171–2
Enlightenment 16, 21, 24–5, 34, 46, 91, 150, 164, 166–7, 172

fatalism 33–5, 37–8
Fichte, Johann Gottlieb 28, 35–7, 57–8
  Ich 35–6
Flatly, Jonathan 183–4
Foucault, Michel 53–5, 58, 60, 102, 115, 119–21, 145, 147, 160, 211, 248, 253, 255, 263
  Care of the Self 53, 58, 145, 147, 160, 211, 248, 253, 255, 263
Franco, Paul 160
Frank, Manfred 22–4, 38
Frazer, James 99, 107
French Revolution 3, 17, 19, 21–2, 67–9, 124, 166, 176–7
Fukuyama, Francis 5–9, 167, 171–2
  The end of history and the Last Man 6, 8, 171

Garrington, Abbie 186
Gellner, Ernest 107
gender 80–1, 83, 131–2, 140, 241–2, 256–7, 265
generality 4–5
Gentry, Bruce Marshall 259
Gillespie, Michael 21, 72
Goethe, Johann Wolfgang 40, 48
Goldstein, Rebecca 41
Graff, Gerlad 252
Gray, John 92, 166–7, 171–2

Habermas, Jürgen 252
Hadot, Pierre 68, 85, 117
Halmi, Nicholas 59, 61
Hammerschlag, Sarah 210–11
Hampshire, Stuart 39–40
Hayes, Patrick 232, 245, 247–8, 250, 259
Hayes-Brady, Claire 268
Hegel, Georg Wilhelm 6–7, 9–10, 17, 20, 27–30, 32, 34, 36, 40,

42, 49–52, 57, 64–7, 75, 78, 81,
83–4, 94, 97, 99–100, 105, 107,
111, 123, 125, 128, 135, 145,
147, 149–51, 160–7, 170–2,
174–5, 179, 181–2, 185, 187,
190, 194–7, 206, 211, 218–19,
226, 255, 267
   dialectics   10, 28, 32, 49–50, 57,
64–7, 94, 97, 99–100, 107, 111,
123, 125, 135, 147, 160–2, 170,
174–5, 179, 181–2, 185, 187,
190, 194–7, 206, 211, 218–19,
226, 255
   Phenomenology of Spirit   40, 51,
64–5, 83, 125, 151, 171, 267
   struggle for recognition   6, 75,
78, 81, 84, 145, 160, 162, 185,
219
Heidegger, Martin   154
Heine, Heinrich   48, 105–6
Herder, Johann Gottfried   31, 48
Hering, David   268
Hillis Miller, J.   72–3, 90, 108, 117,
192–4
Hitchens, Christopher   149
Hobbes, Thomas   146–7, 156, 160

idealism   17, 23–4, 26, 28–30, 32–5,
37–8, 40, 50, 52, 57–9, 63–7,
71, 77, 81–6, 89–91, 94, 96,
105, 111, 114, 116–17, 123,
125, 133, 138, 141, 147, 152,
166, 169, 170–1, 210–11, 213,
216–21, 250–2, 254, 266–7
   German idealism   35, 37–8, 40,
50–1, 63, 138, 146, 217–18
identity politics   5, 7–9, 20
   in Franz Kafka   7
irony   23, 90, 98, 102, 109, 117, 247,
251, 265–8
Israel, Jonathan   2, 15–16

Jacobi, F. H.   19–22, 24–5, 31–5, 38,
40, 41, 43, 50, 71, 73
   leap of Faith (Salto Mortale)   21,
24–5, 31, 33–5, 41

nihilism   21–2
On the Doctrine of Spinoza   22,
24, 40, 43, 50, 59
pantheism controversy   19, 21,
38, 59, 71–3
the specter of Spinoza   21–2, 25,
41–3, 71, 73
and Strauss   19–20
Jameson, Frederic   76, 78, 83,
108–14, 116, 252
Janz, Marlies   265
Jayasena, Nalin   81, 83–4
Jelinek, Elfriede   240, 261–2, 264–8
Jerischna, Jan   107
Josephson-Storm, Jason   20–2, 92

Kafka, Franz   5, 7, 143–5, 153,
173–4, 177, 184, 190–204,
206–7, 210, 255, 266
   Das Schloss   173–4, 177, 184,
190–204, 206–7
Kant, Immanuel   33–4, 36, 138
Keats, John   66, 70–1, 73–9, 84,
86–7, 89, 91, 111, 112, 114–17,
119, 135, 139
   destructive element   71, 84, 89,
91, 111–12, 114–17, 119
   'To J H Reynolds Esquire'   71, 73,
75–7, 79, 86–7, 117
Kelly, Adam   251, 268
Kenner, Hugh   67
Kermode, Frank   67, 70
Kohut, Erika   262, 264–5
Kojève, Alexandre   64–6, 112, 114,
121, 125, 128, 149, 151–2,
154–5, 158, 160–5, 171–2

Lacoue-Labarthe, Philippe   90
Lawrence, D. H.   173, 177, 184–90,
196–9, 202–7, 245–6, 248
   Women in Love   173, 177,
184–90, 196–9, 202–7
Levinas, Emmanuel   68, 211, 213,
218–20
Long, Robert Emmet   136–8
Löwy, Michael   227

Lukács, George 96, 112–16, 118, 123, 205, 206
  Proletarian Consciousness 112–13, 115–16, 118

Macherey, Pierre 34, 46–51, 224
Machiavelli, Niccolò 146–7, 155–9
MacIntyre, Alasdair 230
Mack, Michael 3, 7, 13, 23, 31, 33–4, 38, 41, 45, 48, 51, 59, 68, 83, 98, 103, 107, 154, 161, 187, 196, 212, 222, 225, 238, 250, 257, 262, 264
Marx, Karl 42–4, 60, 105, 111–12, 115–16
May, Keith M. 186
McClure, John 83–4
McGann, Jerome 27–30, 63–4, 66–7, 73, 105
McHale, Brian 47, 266
Menand, Louis 259
Mendelson, Edward 47, 258
Mendes-Flohr, Paul 226
Merve, Emre 256
Michaels, Walter Benn 4, 8–9, 244
Millàn-Zaibert, Elizabeth (Millàn-Brusslan) 23–4, 31, 35–6, 38, 40, 50
mind and body 1–2, 13–15, 17, 26–8, 30–1, 34–7, 47, 49, 53, 55–6, 58–9, 63, 69, 84, 220–6, 229–31, 236, 238, 244, 250–4, 259, 263–4
modernity 13, 17, 21–5, 27, 32, 92–6, 99–100, 103, 106, 111–13, 115, 117, 123–5, 137–9, 141, 143, 145–9, 151–7, 160, 163–4, 166–8, 176–7, 183–4, 187–90, 192, 206–7, 242–3, 251, 254–8, 266–8
Moi, Toril 4, 5
Mongia, Padmini 83–4
Morton, Timothy 37

Nadler, Steven 42, 44
Nehamas, Alexander 43, 45, 52–5, 58, 65, 90, 115, 119–20
neoconservativism 125, 128, 141, 146, 148–51, 158, 164, 166–7, 169, 171, 259
Nietzsche, Friedrich 53, 86, 107, 153, 177–80, 186–7, 199, 245–8, 250, 260
nihilism 71–2, 150–1, 153, 178–80
Nordau, Max 91–2
Norris, Christopher 245
Novalis 28, 57–8
Nussbaum, Martha 252

orientalism 34, 40–1, 50
the Other 10, 20, 90–2, 94, 103, 105–7, 169, 173, 181, 185–9, 209, 213–14, 217–20, 253, 263–4, 267

pantheism 34, 38–9, 59, 61
Parrish, Timothy 259
Piepont Roth, Claudia 215
Pippin, Robert 176–9, 226
Podhoretz, Norman 259
populism 3, 10, 92–4, 96, 166, 171, 173–9, 183
Posnock, Ross 233, 257, 259
postmodernism 1, 4, 240, 242–3, 248, 251–5, 257–9, 261–2, 264–6, 268
Putnam, Hilary 51
Pynchon, Thomas 47–8, 252–5, 257–9, 267
  Gravity's Rainbow 47–8, 252, 257–8

Quinney, Laura 73

Rahel-Freund, Else 217
Realism 57, 59
Richards, Robert J. 48
Riesman, David 248
Rocca, Della 42

romanticism 17–18, 22–5, 27–30,
    32–3, 35–8, 40, 44, 52, 57–9,
    63–4, 66–7, 69–71, 73–4, 86,
    105, 114–18, 135, 139, 211,
    216
  German Romanticism 23–4
  and Spinoza's legacy 18, 22–4, 30
Rosenzweig, Franz 209–13, 215–21
Ross, Charles L. 185
Roth, Philip 143, 214–16, 221–3,
    229–35, 237–8, 240–55,
    257–62
Rubinstein, Ernest 217

Said, Edward 90
Saint-Armour, Paul K. 257–8
Santner, Eric 191
Scarry, Elaine 235
Schelling, Friedrich Wilhelm
    Joseph 217
Schlegel, Karl Wilhelm Friedrich
    23, 27, 30, 32, 36, 52–3, 211
Schmitt, Carl 147, 156
Scholem, Gerschom 210
Scott, A. O. 268
Scott Fitzgerald, F. 63, 126–41,
    146–9, 155, 164–5, 168, 172
the self 38, 48, 53–4, 60, 68–9,
    75, 77–9, 83–7, 96, 115–16,
    119–21, 145, 160–1, 163,
    213–15, 226, 236, 239, 244–55,
    257, 262–5, 267–8
Sharp, Hasana 42–3
Sherry, Vincent 67, 69–70, 86–7
Shostak, Debra 242
the sign 3–5
Small, Helen 236
Smith, Steven B. 16
Snyder, Katherine 82
Socrates 43–4, 52–5, 58, 60, 64, 68,
    85–6, 115, 119–21, 142, 145,
    147, 154–60, 162–3, 210–11,
    246–7, 249–50, 255, 262–3
spectral 89–90, 94–6, 100–2,
    106–11, 114–15, 118

Spender, Stephen 70–3
Spinoza, Baruch 1–3, 6, 10–11, 13,
    14–31, 33–59, 61, 68–9, 71,
    73, 92, 94, 106, 116, 124–5,
    129, 162, 171, 177–8, 182, 215,
    220–7, 229, 238, 244–6, 250,
    252, 254, 257–8, 262–3, 264
  conatus 48–49, 51, 54, 68, 116,
    182, 263, 264
  critique of anthropocene 16, 18,
    22–5, 29
  critique of teleology 245, 257–8
  critique of theology 14, 16, 19,
    24–8, 36, 39–40, 45, 178
  Ethics 2, 14, 22, 39, 45, 55
  notion of nature 16, 18, 31,
    38–9, 48
  parallelism of mind and
    body 1–2, 13–15, 17, 26–8,
    30–1, 34–7, 47, 49, 53, 55–6,
    58–9, 220–6, 238, 244, 250,
    254, 263–4
  and science 26, 28, 31, 39, 49, 92
  the self 14, 68
  the specter of spinoza 21–2, 25,
    41–4, 52, 60, 71, 73, 92, 94,
    106
  and strauss 13, 15–18
  romantic legacy 18, 22–4, 30,
    38, 44, 48, 59–60
  *A Theological-Political
    Treatise* 14, 19
Stallman, Robert 133, 138
Steiner, Franz Baermann 212
Strauss, Leo 11, 13–20, 25, 129–31,
    145–7, 151–66, 168, 170, 172,
    209, 211, 240, 245–51, 254–6,
    258
  and Jacobi 19–20
  and Spinoza 13, 15–18
Strenski, Ivan 99

Tanguay, Daniel 25, 170
teleology 18, 22–3, 35–6, 39–2,
    44–5, 48, 51–2, 59, 64–5, 67–9,

92, 97, 103, 105, 113, 121,
187, 190, 195, 198–9, 242,
245, 252–4, 257–8, 261,
267
telos 6, 7, 39
totalitarianism 93–6, 100, 102,
104, 239, 255, 261–4, 267

unbelief 72, 77

Vatter, Miguel 228–9
Velkley, Richard 154, 157, 255
Vonnegut, Kurt 254

Wallace, David Foster 9, 240, 251,
258, 264, 266, 268
Watts, Cedric 108
Weber, Max 110, 111, 153
Weber, Samuel 32
Williams, Raymond 63
Wilson, Edmund 67, 70
Woolf, Virginia 157
Wordsworth, William 69

Xenophon 153–9, 163

Žižek, Slavoj 38, 40–1, 57

In Memory of Michael Mack

Michael Mack was born in Germany on 23 August 1969 and grew up in Römerberg. Michael was educated at the University of Cambridge, where he completed his undergraduate and doctoral studies. Michael's first book, *Anthropology as Memory: Elias Canetti and Franz Baerman Steiner's Responses to the Shoah* (Niemeyer, 2001), developed out of his doctoral thesis. The concern of this book with the interstices of anthropology, philosophy, theology, history, and literature frame—as does the question Michael posed at the start of this book, "Can a literary depiction be more truthful than a historical account?"—the intellectual ambit of much of his subsequent thinking and writing. Michael was a specialist in the relationship between literature and philosophy, he wrote illuminatingly about Arendt, Benjamin, Freud, Heidegger, and Spinoza, often in tandem with penetrating analyses of literary works, for example by Saul Bellow, George Eliot, Henry James, Sylvia Plath, and Thomas Pynchon. His interests ranged across comparative literature, cinema (including the films of Pasolini and Hitchcock), and Jewish thought (in particular the legacies of Spinoza's philosophy) and culture, returning to the central preoccupations that his work sought to address, namely the constraints individuals face, and the possibilities for art, in modernity.

Michael did not settle for any easy sense that the arts restore our sense of well-being, but instead that they have the power to call into question the fallacies by which we live and so bring us closer, for better or worse, to the precise nature of the modern human condition. These concerns are at the fore of two previous and important books that Michael published both with Bloomsbury, *Philosophy and Literature in Times of Crisis: Challenging Our Infatuation with Numbers* (2014) and *How Literature Changes the Way We Think* (2012). These interests in the instructive role that literary and filmic representations play in providing a critique of long-held assumptions in Western Philosophy culminated in Michael's study of *Contaminations: Beyond Dialectics in Modern Literature, Science, and Film* (Edinburgh University Press, 2016).

Prior to these three major book-length studies, Michael explored what he understood as the "hidden Enlightenment" of the legacies of Spinoza's thought in the writings of Herder, Goethe, Rosenzweig, and Freud to reject, what he saw, as the divisive and destructive dominance of traditional Enlightenment values of autonomy, reason, and telos. Alternatively, Michael advocated, in *Spinoza and the Specters of Modernity: The Hidden Enlightenment of Diversity from Spinoza to Freud* (Bloomsbury, 2010), Spinoza's bequest of a principle of interconnection within (and between) the human and natural spheres. Michael's fascination with Jewish thought, culture, and history had culminated in an earlier study of *German Idealism and the Jew: The Inner Anti-Semitism of Philosophy and German Jewish Responses* (University of Chicago Press, 2003), which was shortlisted for the Koret Jewish Book Award in 2004.

The vast scope, subtlety, and ambition of Michael's intellectual achievements were justifiably acknowledged by the many international awards he won. Michael was a Visiting Professor at Syracuse University, a Fellow at the University of Sydney, and Lecturer and Research Fellow at the University of Chicago, and the recipient of two Leverhulme Research Fellowships. Having held a lectureship in the Department of Theology at Nottingham University, Michael was appointed as an Associate Professor (Reader) in the Department of English Studies at Durham University, where he worked for ten years from 2010 until his death.

www.ingramcontent.com/pod-product-compliance
Lightning Source LLC
Chambersburg PA
CBHW060945230426
43665CB00015B/2065